Lecture Notes in Computer Science 10647

Commenced Publication in 1973
Founding and Former Series Editors:
Gerhard Goos, Juris Hartmanis, and Jan van Leeuwen

Editorial Board

More information about this series at http://www.springer.com/series/7409

Songphan Choemprayong · Fabio Crestani
Sally Jo Cunningham (Eds.)

Digital Libraries:
Data, Information, and Knowledge
for Digital Lives

19th International Conference
on Asia-Pacific Digital Libraries, ICADL 2017
Bangkok, Thailand, November 13–15, 2017
Proceedings

 Springer

Editors
Songphan Choemprayong (iD)
Chulalongkorn University
Bangkok
Thailand

Sally Jo Cunningham (iD)
University of Waikato
Hamilton
New Zealand

Fabio Crestani (iD)
University of Lugano
Lugano
Switzerland

ISSN 0302-9743   ISSN 1611-3349   (electronic)
Lecture Notes in Computer Science
ISBN 978-3-319-70231-5   ISBN 978-3-319-70232-2   (eBook)
https://doi.org/10.1007/978-3-319-70232-2

Library of Congress Control Number: 2017957857

LNCS Sublibrary: SL3 – Information Systems and Applications, incl. Internet/Web, and HCI

Printed on acid-free paper

This Springer imprint is published by Springer Nature
The registered company is Springer International Publishing AG
The registered company address is: Gewerbestrasse 11, 6330 Cham, Switzerland

Preface

While the number of digital collections have been increased constantly and in diverse practices, there are some concerns regarding the relevancy and value of the efforts to expand, enhance, and sustain these collections to society at large. These concerns call for discussions and exemplifications of how research efforts and practices in digital libraries improve the quality of human life in all dimensions, such as education, business, socialization, public administration, culture, and humanities. In addition, these questions initiate a quest to discover novel methods in producing, managing, analyzing, and storing digital collections as well as to deliver state-of-the-art services in a complex, connected, and ever-changing environment that matter to our daily lives.

The annual International Conference on Asia-Pacific Digital Libraries (ICADL) series is a significant forum that provides opportunities for researchers, educators, and practitioners to exchange their research results, innovative ideas, service experiences, and state-of-the-art developments in the field of digital libraries. The theme of ICADL 2017 was "Data, Information, and Knowledge for Digital Lives" open to all opportunities that illustrate how digital libraries, digital collections, and corresponding methods would lead to better lives.

Since the first ICADL in 1998, the conference has grown to become one of the premier forums in the digital library community. Based on the success of the first 18 ICADL conferences, the 19th ICADL conference was hosted by the Department of Library Science, Faculty of Arts, Chulalongkorn University, Bangkok, Thailand. This year the conference was co-located with the 8th Asia-Pacific Conference on Library and Information Education and Practice (A-LIEP) under the collective title "International Forum on Data, Information, and Knowledge for Digital Lives." Hosting these conferences together in the heart of Bangkok brought together a diverse group of academic and professional community members from all parts of the world to exchange their cutting-edge knowledge, experience, and practices in various relevant issues in digital libraries and other related fields.

The submissions to ICADL 2017 covered a wide spectrum of topics from various areas, including information visualization, data mining/extraction, cultural heritage preservation, personalized service and user modeling, novel library content and use environments, electronic publishing, preservation systems and algorithms, social networking and information systems, Internet of Things, cloud computing and applications, mobile services, interoperability issues, open source tools and systems, security and privacy, multi-language support, metadata and cataloguing, search, retrieval, and browsing interfaces to all forms of digital content, e-Science/e-Research data and knowledge management, and cooperative service and community service.

The keynote speakers of ICADL 2017, as part of the International Forum, included Prof. Chayodom Sabhasri from Chulalongkorn University (Thailand), Prof. Makiko Miwa from the Open University of Japan, and Prof. Jane Greenberg from Drexel University (USA).

ICADL 2017 received 51 submissions from 21 countries. Each paper was carefully reviewed by the Program Committee members. Finally, 21 full papers and six short papers were selected. On behalf of the Organizing and Program Committees of ICADL 2017, we would like to express our appreciation to all the authors and attendees for participating in the conference. We also thank the sponsors, Program Committee members, external reviewers, supporting organizations, and volunteers for making the conference a success. Without their efforts, the conference would not have been possible.

September 2017   Songphan Choemprayong
                                                      Fabio Crestani
                                                  Sally Jo Cunningham

Organization

ICADL 2017 was organized by the Department of Library Science, Faculty of Arts, Chulalongkorn University.

ICADL Steering Committee Chair

Shigeo Sugimoto   University of Tsukuba, Japan

Local Advisory Board

Boonchai Stitmannaithum   Chulalongkorn University, Thailand
Kingkarn Thepkanjana   Chulalongkorn University, Thailand
Amorn Petsom   Chulalongkorn University, Thailand

General Conference Chair

Pimrumpai Premsmit   Chulalongkorn University, Thailand

Program Committee Co-chairs

Songphan Choemprayong   Chulalongkorn University, Thailand
Fabio Crestani   University of Lugano, Switzerland
Sally Jo Cunningham   University of Waikato, New Zealand

Workshop Chair

Marut Buranarach   National Electronics and Computer Technology Center,
                            Thailand

Organizing Committee

Pimrumpai Premsmit   Chulalongkorn University, Thailand
Somsak Sriborisutsakul   Chulalongkorn University, Thailand
Oranuch Sawetrattanasatian Chulalongkorn University, Thailand
Chindarat Berphan   Chulalongkorn University, Thailand
Songphan Choemprayong   Chulalongkorn University, Thailand
Sorakom Dissamana   Chulalongkorn University, Thailand
Duangnate Vongpradhip   Chulalongkorn University, Thailand
Nenuphar Supavej   Chulalongkorn University, Thailand
Wachiraporn   Chulalongkorn University, Thailand
  Klungthanaboon

Saowapha Limwichitr   Chulalongkorn University, Thailand
Naya Sucha-xaya   Chulalongkorn University, Thailand
Papatsara Arsa   Chulalongkorn University, Thailand

Conference Publication Committee Co-chairs

Chindarat Berphan   Chulalongkorn University, Thailand
Malivan Praditteera   Rangsit University, Thailand

Registration Committee Chair

Nenuphar Supavej   Chulalongkorn University, Thailand

Sponsorship and Exhibition Committee Co-chairs

Songphan Choemprayong   Chulalongkorn University, Thailand
Saifon Taokaew   Chulalongkorn University, Thailand

Venue and Facility Committee Chair

Duangnate Vongpradhip   Chulalongkorn University, Thailand

Hospitality Committee Chair

Chindarat Berphan   Chulalongkorn University, Thailand

Volunteer Management Committee Chair

Sorakom Dissamana   Chulalongkorn University, Thailand

Program Committee

Maristella Agosti   University of Padua, Italy
Hugo Alatrista-Salas   Universidad del Pacífico, Peru
Marut Buranarach   National Electronics and Computer Technology Center,
                             Thailand
Nisachol Chamnongsri   Suranaree University of Technology, Thailand
Youngok Choi   Catholic University of America, USA
Gobinda Chowdhury   Northumbria University, UK
Milena Dobreva   UCL Qatar, Qatar
Supol Durongwatana   Chulalongkorn University, Thailand
Nicola Ferro   University of Padua, Italy
Schubert Foo   Nanyang Technological University, Singapore
Edward Fox   Virginia Polytechnic Institute and State University,
                             USA
Dion Hoe-Lian Goh   Nanyang Technological University, Singapore

Jesús Vegas Hernández	Universidad de Valladolid, Spain
Annika Hinze	University of Waikato, New Zealand
Adam Jatowt	Kyoto University, Japan
Unmil Karadkar	University of Texas at Austin, USA
Hao Ren Ke	National Taiwan Normal University, Taiwan
Christopher Soo-Guan Khoo	Nanyang Technological University, Singapore
Monica Landoni	University of Lugano, Switzerland
Chern Li Liew	Victoria University of Wellington, New Zealand
Xia Lin	Drexel University, USA
Juan Antonio Lossio Ventura	University of Florida, USA
Akira Maeda	Ritsumeikan University, Japan
Stephane Marchand-Maillet	University of Geneva, Switzerland
Gary Marchionini	University of North Carolina at Chapel Hill, USA
Ida Mele	Università della Svizzera Italiana, Switzerland
Atsuyuki Morishima	University of Tsukuba, Japan
Eva Méndez	University Carlos III of Madrid, Spain
David Nichols	University of Waikato, New Zealand
Douglas Oard	University of Maryland, USA
Sanghee Oh	Chungnam National University, South Korea
Nicola Orio	University of Padova, Italy
Suporn Pongnumkul	National Electronics and Computer Technology Center, Thailand
Edie Rasmussen	University of British Columbia, Canada
Andreas Rauber	Vienna University of Technology, Austria
Seamus Ross	University of Toronto, Canada
Shigeo Sugimoto	University of Tsukuba, Japan
Hussein Suleman	University of Cape Town, South Africa
Claire Timpany	University of Waikato, New Zealand
Pucktada Treeratpituk	Bank of Thailand, Thailand
Feili Tu-Keefner	University of South Carolina, USA
Kulthida Tuamsuk	Khon Kaen University, Thailand
Pertti Vakkari	University of Tampere, Finland
Nicholas Vanderschantz	University of Waikato, New Zealand
Kasturi Dewi Varathan	National University of Malaysia, Malaysia
Marcia Zeng	Kent State University, USA
Yan Zhang	University of Texas at Austin, USA
Maja Žumer	University of Ljubljana, Slovenia

Additional Reviewers

Vichita Jienjitlert
Yufeng Ma
Panuakdet Suwannatat
Chih-Jau Wang

Contents

Social Media

User Behaviors

Automatic Classification
and Recommendation

Offering Answers for Claim-Based Queries: A New Challenge for Digital Libraries

José María González Pinto[(✉)] and Wolf-Tilo Balke

Institut für Informationssysteme, Technische Universität Braunschweig,
Braunschweig, Germany
{pinto,balke}@ifis.cs.tu-bs.de

Abstract. This paper introduces the novel problem of 'claim-based queries' and how digital libraries can be enabled to solve it. Claim-based queries need the identification of a key aspect of research papers: claims. Today, claims are hidden in its unstructured, free text representation within research documents. In this work, a claim is a sentence that constitutes the main contribution of a paper and expresses an association between entities of particular interest in a given domain. In the following, we investigate how to identify claims for subsequent extraction in an unsupervised fashion by a novel integration of neural word embedding representations of claims with a graph based algorithm. For evaluation purposes, we focus on the medical domain: all experiments are based on a real-world corpus from PubMed, where both, limitations and success of our solution can realistically be assessed.

Keywords: Claim-based queries · Word embeddings · Claim extraction

1 Introduction

The world is becoming an increasingly complex place, where information needs are not always simple to satisfy – even by sophisticated information retrieval algorithms over large digital libraries with carefully curated content. In this work, we introduce the novel problem of '*claim-based queries*' and show how to use focused indexing in digital libraries to reliably capture claims and subsequently answer respective queries.

So, what are claim-based queries? To get an intuition, consider the following example: a user interested in medical research may raise the general question of "which medication should be taken to alleviate a headache?" At first, the question may strike one as a bit naïve, since the answer will obviously be quite complex: there exist several medications with different pros and cons depending on the specific problem setting. Indeed, the main challenge of this example is that any 'good' answer has to deal with knowledge that is open to discussion and is highly dependent on some context missing in the question. In any case, users will need at least three steps to satisfy their query:

1. Find out what medications to alleviate a headache actually do exist (the *entity space* for possible answers),
2. Find documents, e.g. research papers, where each medication has been applied in particular problem settings (the *contextual space* for the above entities), and

© Springer International Publishing AG 2017
S. Choemprayong et al. (Eds.): ICADL 2017, LNCS 10647, pp. 3–13, 2017.
https://doi.org/10.1007/978-3-319-70232-2_1

3. Given all these documents, analyze them to decide which medicament fits the own particular context best (a *selection* or *ranking method*).

We see two basic requirements for any retrieval system to solve the problem. First, it needs to operationalize the notion of a claim-based query, and second, it needs high quality content as input. While the first part is indeed quite problematic, the second part may be solved by digital libraries offering high quality content, often curated by peer-review. However, a key semantic metadata element for such a system, the central claim(s) of each paper is usually not available. And this crucial step is the focus of this paper.

Previous work in the field of argumentation mining has shown the potential of algorithms to automatically identify argumentative structures such as claims from clearly structured online debate forums and from persuasive essays on various topics [1]. How-ever, is it possible to find a solution for scientific collections, too? In this paper, we focus on the proper identification of claims in research papers. We concentrate our efforts to answer the following questions: How difficult is the task? Is the claim of a research paper usually in a single sentence or can it stretch over several sentences? Can extractors reliably identify claims?

Addressing this challenge, this work focuses on the automatic identification of claims in research papers in an unsupervised fashion. Previously, we have shown the key role that *claims* can play for Digital Libraries [2]. In particular, how they can assist peer-review to support high quality content. In this work, we introduce a novel inte-gration of neural embedding representations of words within a technique that identifies claims in scientific articles. We test our approach on a representative corpus of PubMed articles with more than 1,000 different journals that have claims annotated.

The paper is organized as follows: Sect. 2 provides definitions and the problem statement that we aim to solve. Section 3 reviews related work. In Sect. 4, we first provide an analysis of the corpus used to assess the difficulty of the task. In particular, we perform an explorative analysis to answer whether the number of sentences in a claim varies, and whether specific vocabulary patterns at the beginning and ending of claims exist. Section 5 provides details on our experimental setup and discusses our findings. Finally, we draw conclusions in Sect. 6 and point to future work.

2 Model and Problem Definition

In this section, we introduce the idea behind claim-based queries. We provide defini-tions and the problem statement that we aim at solving in this paper. In general, a claim-based query is a query that represents a specific and complex type of information need: a question whose answer is subject to discussion. In particular, this type of questions follows a problem-solution pair-pattern. Moreover, more than one solution exists. For example, "which medication should I take to alleviate a headache?" In this case, 'medication' is the *solution*, and 'headache' is the *problem*. Moreover, specific instances of *medication* could solve this particular problem. Each sentence where an association between a specific instance of the solution and the problem appears, is what we have called a *claim*. In this work, we argue that to answer claim-based queries, the proper identification of claims is a fundamental first step.

We will focus in the medical domain; thus, more specifically, the relationship part of the claim will be relationships in which the consumption of a product, a drug, a substance, etc., carries an effect for a given disease. We recognize that health information is a complicated process and thus, as our first attempt, we assume that the claims can be found by identifying the sentences that correspond to the main contributions of a paper. Therefore, the challenge to identify automatically this type of sentences is the focus of this paper. More formally, we are given a collection of m documents (research papers) from a digital library $D = \{d_1, \ldots, d_m\}$, where each document is represented as a sequence of sentences. Our task is then:

Problem Statement. (Claim detection in research papers). Given a collection of documents D, and a pair of entities e_1, e_2, we intend to identify automatically from each document in D, the sentence(s) $\{s_1, \ldots s_n\}$ where e_1, e_2 are related with the constraint that the sentence(s) belong to the set of the main contribution(s) of the paper. We approach the claim detection problem by breaking it down into two tasks:

1. Identification of the sentence(s) that represent the main contribution of a paper.
2. Identification of the sentence(s) of 1 where the entities e_1, e_2 are found.

To address task 1, for a given s_i in d, and for each $d \in D$, we determine whether the given sentences should be considered as the claim of d. To generate such a binary decision, we perform a claim detection process $claim(d) \forall d \in D$ formalized in the following expression:

$$ClaimDetection\ task : \ <s, d> \ \rightarrow \{0, 1\} \forall s \in claim(d) \wedge d \in D \qquad (1)$$

Task 2 is trivial once task 1 has been solved: it is only a pruning process to consider the sentence(s) where entities e_1, e_2 appear. For completeness, we summarize in Algorithm 1 how to solve the claim detection problem. However, in the following section, we describe the main contribution of this paper: step 4. In particular, we aim at performing this step in an unsupervised fashion.

Algorithm 1. Claim Detection Method.

1. **Input:** Document d, entities e_1, e_2
2. **Output:** claims(s) where e_1 and e_2 occur
3. Given d, split it in all its sentences $< s >$
4. Decide for each sentence in $< s >$ whether the sentence is a claim $< s' >$
5. For each sentence that is a claim $s \in s'$, consider only the sentences where e_1 and e_2 occur $< Claims_{e_1,e_2} >$.
6. Return $< Claims_{e_1,e_2} >$

2.1   The TextRank Algorithm

In this section, we introduce the algorithm used in this work to find claims from scientific papers in an unsupervised fashion. Readers already familiar with the TextRank algorithm can skip this section. The algorithm called TextRank has its roots in the Natural Language Processing community [3]. TextRank is a graph-based ranking algorithm successfully used to extract keywords and sentences for the task of summarization. Recently, in [1] it has been shown to also have a positive effect on tasks related to argument mining. In particular, it was applied on online debating forum and persuasive essays corpora. The algorithm works as follows [3]:

1. Identify text units that best define the task at hand, and add them as vertices in the graph.
2. Identify relations that connect such text units, and use these relations to draw edges between vertices in the graph. Edges can be directed or undirected, weighted or un-weighted.
3. Iterate the graph-based ranking algorithm until convergence.
4. Sort vertices based on the final score. Use the values attached to each vertex for ranking/selection decisions.

For our task, the text units are sentences. TextRank used with sentences reduces the problem to select a 'similarity' metric between sentences that can lead to a good extraction. The original notion of similarity in TextRank is defined as the overlap between two sentences, which can be determined as the number of common words between the two sentences. Formally, given two sentences s_i and s_j, with a sentence being represented by the set of N_i words that appear in the sentence: $s_i = w_1^i, w_2^i, \ldots, w_N^i$, the similarity of s_i and s_j is defined in [3] as:

$$Similarity(s_i, s_j) = \frac{|\{w_k | w_k \in s_i \,\&\, w_k \in s_j\}|}{\log(|s_i| + \log(|s_j|)} \quad (2)$$

In this work, we investigate the impact of a modified similarity measure, which in-corporates neural representation of words. In particular, we use word embeddings created by word2vec from [4, 5]. Indeed, neural network based approaches [4–6] require only a large amount of unlabeled text data. The motivation of the use of this semantic embedding of words in vector spaces is twofold: it has been demonstrated that words with similar meanings are embedded nearby and also that natural word arithmetic of the vectors can be conveniently applied [5, 7]. Thus, to represent each sentence we sum the word2vec vectors of each of its words. We use this representation to compute different similarity metrics to plug into the TextRank algorithm.

3   Related Work

Our work builds on the Argumentation Mining field where researchers study the identification of argumentative structures in some given text. For instance, in [8] rhetorical roles of sentences were investigated to classify academic citations with respect to the citation effect. In particular, the idea of how a citation fits the argumentative structure. As features, they investigated the type of subject of the sentence, the citation type, the semantic class of main verb, and a list of indicator phrases that were manually evaluated. Work in [9, 10] studied persuasive essays from the discourse structure perspective. They introduced an approach to identify argumentative discourse structures. In their work, components such as claims and premises, and how they are connected with argumentative relations were studied. The researchers classified a pair of argument components as either support or non-support to identify the structure of argumentative discourse. After evaluating several classifiers, novel feature sets were proposed including structural, lexical, syntactic, and contextual features. In [11] a classification of argumentative sentences was introduced, namely four categories: none, major claim, claim, and premise. They used a supervised machine learning approach to learn these categories automatically, achieving a 0.72 macro-F1-score. In the work of [12] the idea of claim detection given a particular context was introduced. In particular, the work used annotated data from Wikipedia to assess a supervised machine learning approach. Another interesting approach was proposed by [13] where a method that used structured parsing information, detected claims without requiring contextual information. In [14] a relation based approach was introduced for Argumentation Mining. In particular, the extraction of argumentative relations. The researchers introduced a detailed use case where pairs of sentences were annotated to focus on identifying argumentative relations.

Particularly related to our work, in [1] the TextRank algorithm was used to detect argumentative components in an online debating forum and persuasive essays. What makes different our approach is that we incorporate two key components to the algorithm: firstly, different similarity metrics and embedding representation of sentences based on word2vec. In [15], researchers elaborated on the appropriate annotation scheme for argumentation mining. In particular, they studied the educational domain using German newspaper editorials from the Web and English documents from forums, comments, and blogs. They found that the choice of the argument components depends on several different factors and structures used for expressing argumentation, thus no argumentation scheme fits all the possible applications where Argumentation Mining may play an important role. In [16], the IBM Haifa Research Group collected context-dependent claims and evidence (facts) relevant to a given topic from Wikipedia pages. The researchers classified evidence into three types: study, expert and anecdotal using manually curated data from Wikipedia.

4 Dataset

The primary focus of our experiments is to determine to which degree of success the TextRank algorithm, an unsupervised approach, can perform the task of claim detection in scientific articles. In particular, in the medical domain. To do so, we perform experiments on a PubMed corpus extracted using the following query pattern in PubMed "(help AND prevent) OR (lower AND risk) OR (increase OR increment AND risk) OR (decrease OR diminish AND risk) OR (factor AND risk) OR (associated AND risk)" as in [17]. Out of more than 1M articles retrieved, we used a sample of 10,000

that featured abstract and conclusion as metadata elements. We did so because the
sentences in the conclusion metadata are considered as our ground truth. In this work,
we hypothesized that the sentences in the conclusion metadata are a good indicator of
the main contribution of the paper. Unfortunately, we cannot use as ground truth the
Mesh terms of the documents because they are not sentences expressing the main
contribution of the papers. Thus, the sentences of the abstract section and of the
conclusions section constitute the set of sentences that the TextRank algorithm uses as
input. Moreover, we will refer to the conclusions as the claims of the papers hereafter.

In this section, we report results of an exploratory analysis of our corpus. One
particular problem that we wanted to understand is the complexity of the diversity in
the content of the metadata available. Particularly, we shed light on the following
questions: (1) what is the distribution of the number of sentences of a claim considering
different journals? (2) What is the specific vocabulary at the beginning and ending of
claims?

Let us start with our first question: whether the number of sentences containing
claims differs considering different journals. Among the 1,000 different journals from
our query pattern, we found that 3% of the journals use on average between 3 and 5
sentences to represent the claim of the research papers. In other words, the number of
sentences used by the majority of the journals is between 1 and 3.

In Fig. 1 we see a box plot with the mass of the mean number of sentences falling
between 1 and 3 sentences. Concretely, each dot represents a different journal and the
x-axis features the average number of sentences that we found in the metadata that
corresponds to the claims of the papers.

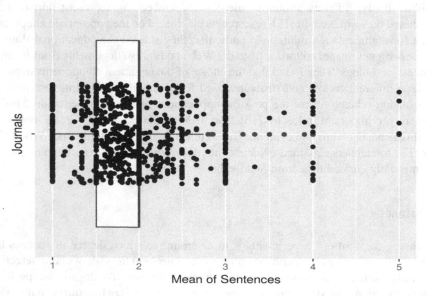

Fig. 1. Distribution of the mean number of sentences of 1K journals in PubMed

Let us continue with our second question: What is the specific vocabulary at the beginning and ending of claim(s)? To answer this question, we investigated the bigrams most frequently used at the beginning and ending of the claims sections. In particular, we used the median position of the bigrams within the claims sections. In Fig. 2, we plot bigrams used at least 50 times at the beginning and at the end of the claims section. It seems that there exist some text patterns than can help in the implementation of an algorithm for automatically detecting claims in medical research papers.

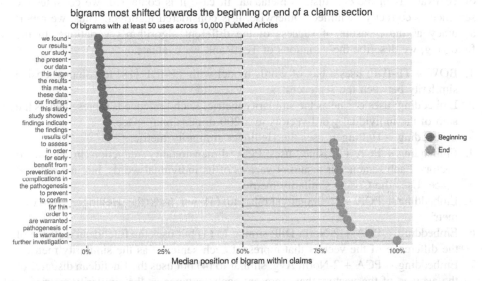

Fig. 2. Bigrams use at the beginning (left side of the graph) or end (right side of the graph) of the claim(s) section.

In Fig. 2, the x-axis represents the median position of bigrams within claims. Basically, the plot divides in two main groups the bigrams of the claims sections of the papers. The first position those whose median's position are less than 50% (beginning) and the second those that are whose median's position are more than 50% (end). For instance, the bigram "is warrant" appears at the end of the claims sections, corresponding to a median position of 91.1%. Building on these insights, in the next section we proceed to provide details of the actual implementation of our approach.

5   Experiments

In this section, we report the results of our experiments. Because the number of sentences in the conclusions shows diversity (see Sect. 4), we also vary the number of sentences in our experiments to evaluate the performance of the implementations of TextRank. We choose for each particular experiment different number of sentences to return considering the coverage of most of the cases we found in our exploratory analysis. Moreover, for each number of sentences we run eight different implementations of TextRank. The implementations differ in two fundamental aspects: the similarity metric used by the algorithm, and whether the implementation performs dimensionality reduction of the embedding space or not. For dimensionality reduction, we use principal component analysis (PCA) [18].

Furthermore, one of the implementations uses a Bag of Word model (BOW) with the cosine similarity as the similarity metric. We use that simple implementation to determine if the use of the word embedding for this particular task makes a difference. To compare the variations of the algorithm, we evaluate whether the returned sentence of TextRank is in the conclusions metadata. In case it is contained, we consider the sentence as correctly identified. Otherwise, it is considered incorrect. Thus, we report accuracy as the measure of success of the different algorithm's variations. In the following, we describe the variations of TextRank we evaluate.

1. BOW + TF-IDF: uses a bag of words model with TF-IDF [18] to compute cosine similarity between the sentences.
2. Embedding: uses cosine as the similarity metric. Each sentence is represented as the sum of the individual word vectors in a 200-dimensional space.
3. Embedding + Hellinger: uses the Hellinger similarity metric.
4. Embedding + PCA + Cosine: uses PCA dimensionality reduction in the word vectors. Each sentence is a sum of vectors of its individual words, but in a reduced space. Uses the Cosine similarity metric.
5. Embedding + PCA + Hellinger: similar to (4) but uses the Hellinger similarity metric.
6. Embedding + PCA + 2-Norm Diff: similar to (4) but uses the Euclidean distance of the difference of the vectors that represent each sentence as the similarity metric.
7. Embedding + PCA + 2-Norm Avg: similar to (4) but uses the Euclidean distance of the average of the vectors that represent each sentence as the similarity metric.
8. Embedding + PCA + 2-Norm Diff & Avg: similar to (4) but using the concatenation of the vectors that represent the differences and the average word2vec vectors of the sentences.

For the PCA variations, to determine the number of components to use, we use a measure known as 'explained variance', which can be calculated from the respective eigenvalues. Concretely, the explained variance tells us how much information can be attributed to each of the principal components. We experiment with different variances to empirically select the number of components and report the best results in this work.

To clarify our findings, we first provide an analysis of cases where the ground truth consists of two sentences and second, all cases where the ground truth has three sentences.

Let us start with the first case. We can observe from Table 1 that all the variations of TextRank using an embedding representation of the sentences outperform the Bag of Words model representation. This was expected, because word embedding capture semantics and syntactic features non-existent in the Bag of Words model. What is interesting to notice is that a sum over the word vectors of a sentence preserves these properties.

Table 1. Accuracy of the different variations of TextRank to identify claims. The value of k represents the number of sentences used to compute the accuracy

TextRank variation	$k = 2$	$k = 3$	$k = 4$
BOW + TFIDF	0.338	0.466	0.582
Embedding	0.418	0.566	0.662
Embedding + Hellinger	0.433	0.562	0.659
Embedding + PCA + Cosine	0.463	0.609	0.701
Embedding + PCA + Hellinger	0.383	0.510	0.613
Embedding + PCA + 2-Norm Diff	0.339	0.500	0.638
Embedding + PCA + 2-Norm Avg	0.393	0.550	0.679
Embedding + PCA + 2-Norm Diff & Avg	0.378	0.535	0.662

With respect to the similarity metric in the embedding space when PCA was not applied, the cosine similarity outperforms the Hellinger similarity with a very low margin when the top number of sentences returned by TextRank is k = 3 and k = 4 but the Hellinger similarity is a better choice when k = 2. Thus, for our particular task of retrieving claims in an unsupervised fashion, we consider both similarity metrics equally valuable. However, when using PCA the cosine similarity has no competition. In fact, this particular implementation of the TextRank algorithm delivers the overall best results. Moreover, the Hellinger distance was consistently outperformed by the implementation that uses the norm between the average representations of the vectors as the similarity metric.

Our finding confirms the work of [7], where a similar representation of the sentences performed on par with more computationally expensive deep learning models of sentences in the task of document classification. As expected, all the implementations increase performance as we increase the number of sentences that the algorithm returns. Nevertheless, considering that the ground truth only consists of k = 2 sentences, we can observe that all the implementations performed poorly on the task.

Let us continue with the experiments that correspond to cases where the number of sentences in the ground truth is three. We present the results in Table 2. Similar to what we observe in Table 1, any embedding representation outperforms the Bag of Word model. With respect to the similarity metric when PCA was not used, we cannot see a clear winner between Hellinger and the Cosine similarity metrics. However, when we perform PCA on the word vectors, the Cosine similarity shines outperforming the Hellinger similarity metric. Nevertheless, a fundamental difference between Tables 1 and 2, is that the method with best results in Table 2 is not the Cosine similarity with PCA but rather the implementation of the 2-Norm distance using the average vector of the sentences.

Discussion. In summary, we found that using an embedding representation of the sentences had a positive impact for our particular task. Furthermore, when dimensionality reduction was applied to the word vectors, with PCA, we obtained better results. Moreover, we also observed that as the parameter k that represents the number of sentences to extract is increased, an embedding representation with dimensionality reduction delivered the best results. In practice, we will have to make a decision

Table 2. Accuracy of the different variations of TextRank for the second test case to identify claims. The value of k represents the number of sentences used to compute the accuracy

TextRank variation	$k = 2$	$k = 3$	$k = 4$
BOW + TFIDF	0.548	0.685	0.789
Embedding	0.652	0.775	0.858
Embedding + Hellinger	0.659	0.765	0.857
Embedding + PCA + Cosine	0.729	0.814	0.900
Embedding + PCA + Hellinger	0.631	0.723	0.821
Embedding + PCA + 2-Norm Diff	0.709	0.821	0.884
Embedding + PCA + 2-Norm Avg	0.746	0.844	0.904
Embedding + PCA + 2-Norm Diff & Avg	0.735	0.840	0.908

regarding the number of sentences the algorithm should return. This aspect of the algorithm remains as a parameter that practitioners have to set empirically. We observed that the approach shows potential to solve the claim detection problem in the medical domain. However, more work needs to be done to improve the quality of the results. In particular, for Digital Libraries where high quality is essential, we consider that the current accuracy should be improved. And one particular way to improve the approach that we are currently considering is the use of attention mechanisms such as the one in [19]. With such an approach, the model of the sentences could be more robust to different word orders and in turn might increase the quality of the results.

6   Conclusions

In this work, we have introduced the novel problem of claim-based queries and argued how digital libraries can be enabled to solve it. One of the key parts of our solution to the problem, the automatic identification of claims in an unsupervised fashion, was in detail investigated and evaluated in this paper. In particular, the use of TextRank, a graph based algorithm, for the novel task of extracting claims of medical scientific articles. We performed a series of experiments, where we incorporated representations of sentences based on word embedding using word2vec with different similarity metrics with and without dimensionality reduction, using PCA. The representation of sentences using PCA turned out to provide best results in our evaluation with accuracy rate of over 70%. We evaluated our approach on a crawled corpus from PubMed and used all available manually assigned metadata as ground truth.

Although our results look encouraging for focused indexing of the claims found in a digital collection, in future work we need to further improve the unsupervised detection of claims. In particular, we would like to incorporate word order in the model that represent the sentences. Moreover, towards our goal of enabling digital libraries to answer claim-based queries, we would like to study the impact of claim indexing to investigate the features that can help to rank documents given a claim-based query.

References

1. Petasis, G., Karkaletsis, V.: Identifying argument components through TextRank. In: ACL. pp. 94–102 (2016)
2. González Pinto, J.M., Balke, W.-T.: Can plausibility help to support high quality content in digital libraries? In: TPDL 2017 – 21st International Conference on Theory and Practice of Digital Libraries., Thessaloniki, Greece (2017)
3. Mihalcea, R., Tarau, P.: TextRank: bringing order into texts. In: Proc. EMNLP, vol. 85, pp. 404–411 (2004)
4. Mikolov, T., Chen, K., Corrado, G., Dean, J.: Distributed representations of words and phrases and their compositionality. In: NIPS, pp. 1–9 (2013)
5. Mikolov, T., Corrado, G., Chen, K., Dean, J.: Efficient estimation of word representations in vector space. In: Proceedings of International Conference Learn. Represent (ICLR 2013), pp. 1–12 (2013)
6. Collobert, R., Weston, J.: A unified architecture for natural language processing. In: Proceedings of the 25th International Conference on Machine Learning - ICML 2008, pp. 160–167 (2008)
7. Lev, G., Klein, B., Wolf, L.: In defense of word embedding for generic text representation. In: Biemann, C., Handschuh, S., Freitas, A., Meziane, F., Métais, E. (eds.) NLDB 2015. LNCS, vol. 9103, pp. 35–50. Springer, Cham (2015). doi:10.1007/978-3-319-19581-0_3
8. Teufel, S.: Argumentative Zoning: Information Extraction from Scientific Text (1999)
9. Stab, C., Gurevych, I.: Identifying argumentative discourse structures in persuasive essays. In: Proceedings of 2014 Conference on Empirical Methods on Natural Language Processing, pp. 46–56 (2014)
10. Stab, C., Kirschner, C., Eckle-Kohler, J., Gurevych, I.: Argumentation mining in persuasive essays and scientific articles from the discourse structure perspective. In: CEUR Workshop Proceedings (2014)
11. Stab, C., Gurevych, I.: Annotating argument components and relations in persuasive essays. In: Proceedings of COLING 2014, 25th International Conference on Computational Linguistics: Technical Papers, pp. 1501–1510 (2014)
12. Levy, R., Bilu, Y., Hershcovich, D., Aharoni, E., Slonim, N.: Context dependent claim detection. In: International Conference on Computational Linguistics, pp. 1489–1500 (2014)
13. Lippi, M., Torroni, P.: Context-independent claim detection for argument mining. In: IJCAI International Joint Conference on Artificial Intelligence, pp. 185–191 (2015)
14. Carstens, L., Toni, F.: Towards relation based argumentation mining. In: Proceedings of the 2nd Workshop on Argumentation Mining, pp. 29–34 (2015)
15. Habernal, I., Eckle-Kohler, J., Gurevych, I.: Argumentation mining on the web from information seeking perspective. In: Proceedings of the Workshop on Frontiers and Connections between Argumentation Theory and Natural Language Processing, pp. 26–39 (2014)
16. Rinott, R., Dankin, L., Alzate, C., Khapra, M.M., Aharoni, E., Slonim, N.: Show me your evidence – an automatic method for context dependent evidence detection. In: EMNLP, pp. 440–450 (2015)
17. Ciccarese, P., Wu, E., Wong, G., Ocana, M., Kinoshita, J., Ruttenberg, A., Clark, T.: The SWAN biomedical discourse ontology. J. Biomed. Inform. **41**, 739–751 (2008)
18. Leskovec, J., Rajaraman, A., Ullman, J.D.: Mining of Massive Datasets. Cambridge University Press, Cambridge (2014)
19. Li, J., Luong, M.-T., Jurafsky, D.: A Hierarchical Neural Autoencoder for Paragraphs and Documents, pp. 1106–1115 (2015)

Application of k-Step Random Walk Paths to Graph Kernel for Automatic Patent Classification

Budi Nugroho$^{(\boxtimes)}$ and Masayoshi Aritsugi$^{(\boxtimes)}$

Computer Science and Electrical Engineering, Graduate School of Science
and Technology, Kumamoto University, Kumamoto, Japan
budinugroho@dbms.cs.kumamoto-u.ac.jp,
aritsugi@cs.kumamoto-u.ac.jp

Abstract. In this study, we focus on utilizing the patent citation graph structure. We investigate the effect of using only one document feature which is patent class along citation graph for the classification task. We collect advantages of a kernel-based method and build kernel function to represent feature and citation associated information. We use k-step random walk paths algorithm to calculate kernel values of each patent pairwise and SVM classifier to do the classification task. We employ sub graph technique for a large patent graph to represent citation graph information. The method is based on the property of neighborhood in a graph. The evaluation of the k-step random walk paths kernel metrics on three datasets from the United States Patent and Trademark Office (USPTO) database shows that using patent citation graph structure with only one feature achieved better performance than previous studies.

Keywords: Patent citation graph · Graph kernels · k-step random walk paths · Subgraphs · Automatic patent classification

1 Introduction

Research and development activities undertaken by industries, research institutes and universities often produce patent application as an institutional performance measure. To have granted patents, patent applicants must follow a process named classification. A patent document must be classified into a particular category according to its field and content. This process is manually done by applicant and examiner. They examine and analyze which category is appropriate for each patent. The manual classification process is a big challenge because categorizing a vast quantity of granted and application patent documents in patent offices is time-consuming and labor-intensive. The automated classification of patent applications into a particular patent classification system is still a challenge for many practical applications [1].

Computing similarities between structured objects is interesting, and graphs offer a natural way to represent structured objects. Citation between patent

S. Choemprayong et al. (Eds.): ICADL 2017, LNCS 10647, pp. 14–29, 2017.
https://doi.org/10.1007/978-3-319-70232-2_2

documents refers to the link between the citing and the cited. A graph can represent patent citation network in which nodes correspond with patent number and edges correspond with citation. In patent citation network, we can classify a patent document into a classification scheme by comparing how likely they are in patent citation graphs and computing the similarities.

Patents are linked with other patents through citations. A graph of citations accommodates much information about the connections among patents. These links represent the relationship among patent document's content. A graph of patent citation can be extracted and used in the classification task. Citation data have been shown useful in other linked document classification research [2]. Most current research work investigated assigning a patent document to a unique class is a problem of text categorization [3–5]. These works exploited content features from whole patent document text. Several works used the kernel-based method to classify patent documents and utilized patent citation graph advantages [6,7]. These works introduced features-based and citation-based approaches to optimize citation link to increase patent classification task performance.

Citation-based features have not been fully explored in this problem. A few previous studies used kernel-based methods to capture the structures of patent citation networks [6,7] by using k-step random walk paths algorithm with single step. Most of the previous studies employed kernel-based method in specific topic of patent datasets, such as patent in nanotechnology [6]. Better results were obtained by combining several approaches and features [4,7,8].

In this paper, we apply k-step random walk paths algorithm to calculate kernel values of each patent pairwise and SVM classifier to do the classification task. We used four standard evaluation metrics, namely accuracy, precision, recall, and F-measure to evaluate the performance of the SVM classifiers. The idea using k-step random walk paths was inspired by patent citation network-patent classification [6,7]. The method is based on the property of neighborhood in a graph. The main contributions of our work are:

- providing a simple approach by exploiting patent citation network based method for automatic patent classification, and
- applying a technique of subgraphing large patent graph to represent citation graph information

The remainder of this paper is organized as follows. Section 2 describes related work required for the discussions of this paper. Section 3 explains experiments we did for investigating the k-step random walk paths in patent graph citation and reports how we obtain empirical results. Section 4 presents results and discussion and Sect. 5 concludes this paper.

2   Related Work

2.1   Automatic Patent Classification

Many studies of patent analysis reported by Abbas et al. [1], including automatic patent classification, used dataset issued from US Patent Office. For example,

Hall et al. [2] reported the database of patent citation on U.S. patents for widely accessible to research and development activities. The dataset consists of about 3 million patents and 32 million citations in the form of edgelist with weight data frame. We used this dataset for our experiment.

Zhang et al. [9] reported a technological direction patent mining. This study described a summary of investigation on multiple research questions related to patent documents, including patent retrieval, patent classification, and patent visualization. Most of the patent analysis tasks considered Patent Retrieval (PR) as the foundation. Shalaby and Zadrozny [10] presented an extensive overview of PR methods and approaches. The overview covered issue of transferring recent successes and maturity in information retrieval applications to PR. Performance in automatic PR is essential for interactive search tools which provide cognitive assistance to patent professionals with minimal effort. Some other related tasks to PR are patent valuation, litigation, licensing, and highlight potential opportunities and wide directions for computational scientists. Patent retrieval has recently been made to use text-mining (i.e., extracting keywords from patent documents) for patent analysis purposes. Noh et al. [11] exploited keyword selection strategies for applying text-mining to patent data. The strategies included four factors, i.e., the element of a patent document, selection method, number of keywords and data format transformation. The four factors were evaluated and compared to k-means clustering, and entropy values experiment based on an orthogonal array of the four factors.

Kumar et al. [3] reported a content classification using Probabilistic Latent Semantic Analysis (PLSA) technique for patent application. The PLSA built an indexer which marked documents and generated a fit model for automatic document indexing. For compacting the size of term-document matrix and co-occurrences matrix, they used a singular value decomposition model which has some hidden categories. For determining the hidden categories, they computed probabilities of extracted words appearing in particular patent document and hidden class, also a probability of patent document containing hidden class, and then applied expectation maximization algorithm to develop clusters. D'hondt et al. [12] investigated the improvement of patent classification using different representations of the patent documents. Based on the Linguistic Classification System (LCS), an extensive analysis of the class models created by the classifiers, to examine which types of phrases are most informative for patent classification. The LCS has been developed for comparing different text representations. Three classifier algorithms are usable, i.e., Naive Bayes, Balanced Winnow. In our paper, instead of using content (Abstract, Claims, and Description) based on text extraction in the patent document, we exploit one feature embedded to citation graph to do classification task.

Nguyen et al. [4] proposed a method for Graph-Embedded-Tree-based ontology construction. The method promoted domain knowledge from a codification in the patent classification process. The ontology consists of four types of concept, namely Class, Document, Phrase, and Term that define their semantic information to give the classifier better analysis capability whenever the semantic ambiguation exists. This work developed a method to construct ontology based on the United State Patent Classification (USPC) Scheme without relying on a rule-based method for concept extraction. It can negate intensive manual efforts in traditional ontology construction. They developed a prototype application on top of Rocchio classifier, called the GeTCo-enabled Rocchio classifier, to evaluate proposed ontology. In our paper, we use one feature, i.e., Class from USPC and citation between patents.

Automated categorization based on International Patent Classification (IPC) classes was reported by Fall et al. [13]. The study used a series of multi-classification ranking tasks to categorize patent documents into IPC scheme. The multi-classification ranking tasks involved a complex hierarchical taxonomy, based on implementation of Naive Bayes, k-NN and SVM algorithms and a sparse network of linear functions. Patent document has many fields, such as title, abstract, claims and full description. The work investigated which are the best patent document fields to index, and at IPC sub-class level, where automated categorization would be more useful as the categories are more closely focused on a single topic.

To address the hierarchical multi-label task problem in automatic patent classification, Stutzki and Schubert [8] used location information contained in the metadata of a patent application in combination with text-based patent classification. Each patent application was associated with several categories within the class hierarchy. For improving class prediction, it requires additional sources of information. A difference of this paper from the approach is to reduce the number of features used to predict the class of patent document to achieve a better classification accuracy.

Shih and Liu [5] used ontology-based patent network analysis. Various types of nodes represent different features extracted from patent documents. The patent network is constructed based on the relationship metrics derived from patent metadata. They investigated obtainable vertices in the patent ontology network to compute their importance to query patents. A modified k-nearest neighbor (k-NN) classifier is applied to classify query patents. In this paper, we construct relationship metrics from citation and Class field in patent dataset. Instead of using k-NN classifier, we employ SVM classifier to do classification task to increase patent classification accuracy.

2.2 Kernel Based Method

Li et al. [6] optimized patent citation networks as a classification tool using graph kernels. The kernel functions were constructed based on the document features and citations. Kernel matrices of citation information were intended to capture the citation information effectively with two conditions: (1) the scope of the cited documents, and (2) mentioned document features. By considering these two conditions, four different kernels were introduced to capture patent citation information, i.e. bibliographic coupling kernel, labeled co-reference kernel, graph overlap kernel and labeled citation graph kernel. They also introduced a linear text kernel matrix that used text from patent abstract to represent the entire patent content and captured that information.

In the citation network-classification approach, each patent document has a citation network with cited vertex designated by its class. Calculating similarities between citation networks and those of other patents already classified into USPC categories leads to identifying a patent's class. The similarity of two patent citation graphs is calculated by comparing their random walk paths. This approach employs a three-stage, kernel-based technique for patent classification: data acquisition and parsing, kernel construction, and classifier training. SVM was used as the kernel machine. The kernel value is calculated in the following equation:

$$K(G_1, G_2) = \sum_h \sum_{h'} k(h, h') P(h \mid G_1) P(h' \mid G_2)$$

where G_1 and G_2 symbolize the patent citation graphs associated with two patents, h and h' are the random walk paths in the respective graphs and $P(h \mid G_1)$ and $P(h' \mid G_2)$ denote the probabilities of random walk paths that exist in the citation networks. If h and h' are identical, $k(h, h') = 1$; otherwise, $k(h, h') = 0$.

Kernel matrix is used for SVM classifier to generate a classification model. The kernel matrix is an enhanced matrix of patent similarity vectors of all patents in the training set and their class labels. The name is denoted as 1 assuming that the patent belongs to the unique class; differently, it is denoted as -1. This denotation is an alleged one-against-rest model for the SVM. To handle multiclass classification with m classes ($m > 2$), in which $m(m - 1)/2$ binary classifiers are trained; the chosen class is defined by a voting scheme. For each particular class, a well-trained SVM model is used to predict if a query patent belongs to the class. The final predicted class is then determined by applying a "winner-takes-all" strategy to the SVM models of all the classes. In our study, we use same strategy to predict patent classes.

The hybrid patent classification approach proposed by Liu and Shih [7] for combining patent network based classification method with three conventional classification methods. The approach aimed to analyze query patents and predict their classes. The occurrence of patent documents relationship metrics extracted from the patent metadata established the patent graphs. The classification method with a modified k-nearest neighbor classifier analyzed all reachable verteices in the patent graph and calculated their relevance to the query patent to predict a query patent's class. The approach merges content-based, citation-based, and metadata-based classification methods to develop a hybrid-classification method. In this paper, we limit our method in exploiting citation network based patent classification.

3   Application to Study

We did experiments to investigate the application of k-step random walk paths algorithm to classify patent documents by exploiting patent citation graphs.

The idea using k-step random walk paths was inspired by patent citation network-based approaches to automatic patent classification [6,7]. We trained classifier using the kernel matrix of the data instances in the training dataset. In this study, we used SVM as classifier because of its proven performance in previous studies [6,7,14,15].

We employed subgraph technique based on the property of neighborhood in a graph. The neighborhood of a given order n of a vertex v includes all vertices which are closer to v than the order. For example, order 0 is always v itself, order 1 is v plus its immediate neighbors, order 2 is order 1 plus the immediate neighbors of the vertices in order 1, etc. [16].

For our purposes, a similarity measure is a function that associates a numeric value with a pairwise of patent citation graphs with the concept that a higher value shows closer likeness between the graphs. There is a positive relation between a kernel matrix and a distance-based similarity matrix. We use a general framework of algorithms adapted from [17] as described below.

Training Algorithm

1. Let $\{K_1, K_2, ..., K_M\}$ be a set of normalized input similarity matrices calculated from the training data points $\{x_1, ..., x_l\}$ drawn from possibly unknown statistical distribution X.
2. Build a single symmetric similarity matrix $K^* - h(K_1, K_2, ..., K_M)$, in which h is a possibly non-linear function of the input matrices and the labels $\{y_1, ..., y_l\}$ of the training dataset.
3. If necessary, transform K^* into a kernel matrix K^*_{psd} (a symmetric positive semi-definite matrix).
4. Use K^*_{psd} to train an SVM for the computation of the vector of weights α that will be used to build the discrimination rule at the testing time.

Testing Algorithm

1. Consider an unlabeled point x
2. Calculate $f_{nclass}(x) = \sum_{i=1}^{l} \alpha_i y_i K^*_{nclass}(x, x_i)$, where $K^*_{nclass}(x, x_i)$ corresponds to $K^*_{psd}(x, x_i)$ assuming x belongs to class $nclass$, and α is the vector of weights.
3. Calculate $f(x) = sign(f_{nclass}(x))$.

Environment. Our machine environment is as follows: OS Windows 10 Pro, Processor Intel(R) Core(TM)i7-3770K CPU @3.50 GHz, Installed RAM 16.0 GB.

Datasets. We conducted experiments on the collection of patent documents obtained from the USPTO [2]. We used USPC to denote patent's class which provided in dataset. In pre-processing step, we generated total citation graph and selected three subgraphs of patent citation graph, denoted as $g1$, $g5$ and $g7$ to distinguish the classification effect, and randomly selected patent documents from each selected class. Some selected patent documents have no edge and thus were deleted from the dataset. We created subgraphs based on the number of patent for each class.

The patent documents represented in kernel matices were divided into two sets with random sampling in each iteration: (a) a training set (80% of the collected dataset) containing the patent documents whose classes were known and (b) a test set (20% of the collected dataset) containing patent documents whose classes were to be determined. The summary of each dataset is described in Table 1.

Table 1. Dataset summary

Datasets	Vertices	Edges	Classes
$g1$	3604	7345	9
$g5$	5819	14789	7
$g7$	10134	23547	51

Kernels. We employed k-step random walk kernel with $k = 1$, or single step. We conducted computation in R programming with *igraph* library [16] to generate graph objects and *graphkernels* package [18] to calculate the kernel matrix values.

Experiment Steps

1. Load graph dataset ($g1$, $g5$, $g7$)
2. Delete vertex in which degree $= 0$
3. Create a list of igraph objects from graph ($g1$, $g5$, $g7$) by subgraphing (make ego graph) where each vertex using $n = 3$ order.
4. Generate index label for class from graph ($g1$, $g5$, $g7$) and convert it into matrix, y_l.
5. Calculate kernel value of each pairwise of vertices and convert into kernel matrix K.
6. Define training set and testing set from kernel matrix K by random sampling 80% ($trainK$), 20% ($testK$), respectively.
7. Train the SVM classifier using training instances $trainK$ Kernel matrix with k-fold cross validation (cross $= 10$) to obtain the model m.
8. Transform $testK$ kernel matrix from the remaining 20% test kernel matrix K by indexing (using SVindex) to the model m.
9. Apply the model m to classify the $testK$ kernel matrix.
10. Evaluate the model performance by calculating accuracy, precision, recall, and F measure.

Performance Metrics

We used four standard evaluation metrics, i.e., accuracy, precision, recall, and F-measure to evaluate the performance of the classifiers. The metrics have been widely used in information retrieval and machine learning studies. The evaluation metrics equations are as follows:

$$accuracy = \frac{\sum diag}{N}$$

$$precision = \frac{diag}{colsums}$$

$$recall = \frac{diag}{rowsums}$$

$$F1 = 2 \times \frac{(precision \times recall)}{(precision + recall)}$$

where N is the number of instances, $diag$ is the number of correctly classified instances per class, $rowsums$ is the number of instances per class, and $colsums$ is the number of predictions per class.

4   Results and Discussion

Firstly, we conducted pre-processing steps of our dataset and analized some citation graph properties. Then, we applied the k-step random walk kernel to three datasets in patent citation graph classification and compared the results. 10-fold cross validation examined the evaluation metrics of each graph dataset with multiclass C-support vector classification (using *ksvm* in *kernlab* [19]), in which internal 10-fold cross validation chose the parameter C for C-svc and a parameter (if one exists) of each graph dataset only on the training dataset. We repeated the whole experiment 10 times and reported the averaged evaluation metrics with their standard deviation.

4.1   Graph Analysis

Table 2 shows overview of our citation graphs. From these statistics we can observe that the maximum steps required to cross the graph are eight for $g1$, nine for $g5$ and ten for $g7$ respectively, which would seem to indicate graphs without a lot of clustering. The values of Avg. Path Length indicate a fairly low value relative to the total number of nodes. It takes nodes close to two steps (2.136 for $g1$, 2.399 for $g5$ and 2.348 for $g7$) on average to reach any other node in the graphs. We would then anticipate a lower average path length, as a higher proportion of members would have first degree connections.

Avg. Clustering Coefficient is a measure that determines the percentage of available triplets that are fully closed. From Table 2, we observe that the measures are 0.936 for $g1$, 0.902 for $g5$ and 0.923 for $g7$. In the case of our patent

Table 2. Graph overview of $g1$, $g5$, $g7$

Statistic	$g1$	$g5$	$g7$
Average Degree	20.63	2.542	2.324
Network Diameter	8	9	10
Modularity	0.936	0.902	0.923
Connected Component	124	129	431
Avg. Clustering Coefficient	0.093	0.08	0.092
Avg. Path Length	2.136	2.399	2.348

citation graph, the total graph number is almost exactly 90% closed, with the remaining 10% still open (two of three edges are connected), but the third edge is missing. The modularity statistics split these graphs into ten distinct clusters. This might be satisfactory for our purpose, or if we need further splits, we can employ one of the dedicated clustering algorithms. A quick way to determine if this number of nodes for each cluster is adequate is to color the graph using the modularity class. Figure 1 below illustrates the complete graph of $g7$.

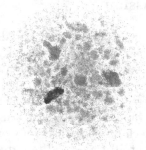

Fig. 1. Complete graph of $g7$

For calculating the kernel value, we added name class (USPC) of each patent as an attribute of a vertex. We generated a list of *igraph* objects by subgraphing the graph into each vertex subgraph by $n = 3$ order, as shown in Figs. 2 and 3.

From Fig. 2, we can observe that the $g1$ dataset is clustered into nine clusters. The clusters indicate the number of patent classes in this dataset. As confirmed in Table 1, we have nine classes in $g1$ with described USPC codes[1]. Although a few nodes are clustered into different color of clusters, patent citation graph is significant for the basis of classification task.

---

[1] http://www.ibiblio.org/patents/classes.html.

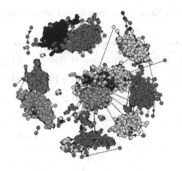

USPC codes: ● 109 ● 201 ● 191 ● 26 ● 86 ● 296 ● 12 ● 150 ● 213

Fig. 2. Complete graph of $g1$

Figure 3 illustrates an example of $g1$ subgraph generated from patent citation graph $g1$ by subgraphing (making ego graph) for each vertex using $n = 3$ order. Each node has a label which represents the patent document ID. For example, node 6877623 with USPC code ● 213 is a patent entitled "*Elastomeric spring assembly for a railcar and method of making same*"[2]. An edge between node 6877623 and node 5351844 represents citation between them. This edge is labeled by its weight which is 6. We used the weight value for calculating the kernel value. After we obtained the subgraphs of each vertex, based on the k-step random walk paths algorithm, we calculated the kernel value and resulted in the kernel matrix that reflected similarity probability of each pairwise of vertices.

Fig. 3. Example of $g1$ subgraph, $n = 3$

4.2 Classification Results Overview

Table 3 reports the performance metrics achieved by the SVM classifier trained on different datasets. We can observe that $g1$ is highly accurate (97.71%) which is significantly higher than $g5$ and $g7$, respectively 89.49% and 88.26%.

---

[2] https://goo.gl/aMX8pm.

Table 3. Classification performance evaluation

Datasets	Accuracy	Precision	Recall	F-measure
$g1$	97.71 ± 0.029	97.61 ± 0.109	98.20 ± 0.055	98.33 ± 0.037
$g5$	89.49 ± 0.103	89.82 ± 0.249	94.00 ± 0.142	88.39 ± 0.229
$g7$	88.26 ± 0.041	89.17 ± 0.256	91.77 ± 0.177	89.65 ± 0.194
Li, et al. [6]	86.67	89.09	87.97	88.04
Liu and Shih [7]	69.5	71.4	73.5	72.4

We created $g1$ dataset consisting of 300 to 500 patent documents for each class. For $g1$ dataset which has 3604 vertices and 7345 edges, the vertices were classified into nine classes. Using SVM classifier and pre-computed kernel matrix, from the patent citation graph we obtained the results 97.71% accuracy, 97.61% precision, 98.20% recall and 98.33% F-Measure. The result outperformed previous studies, which were 86.67% of accuracy (in [6]) and 69.5% of accuracy (in [7]). By defining n order of subgraph, and obtaining pre-computing of the kernel matrix value for SVM classifier, we achieved better classification performance. Applying model to the $g1$ test set yielded results as shown in Fig. 4.

```
preds \orig   109  12  150  191  201  213  26  298  86
      109    84   0   0    0    0    0   0   0   0
       12     0  68   0    0    0    0   1   0   0
      150     0   0 101    0    0    0   0   0   0
      191     0   0   0   79    0    1   0   0   0
      201     0   0   0    0   84    0   0   0   0
      213     0   0   0    0    0   78   0   0   0
       26     0   0   0    0    0    0  75   0   0
      298     0   0   0    0    0    0   0  85   0
       86     6   0   0    0    0    0   0   0  58
```

Fig. 4. Classification results for $g1$

In this experiment which produced best accuracy (97.71 ± 0.029) for $g1$ dataset, we used a technique for pre-computing the kernel value by generating subgraph based on n number of order. This technique handed the better result of pre-computed kernel matrix because we were able obtain the similarity value of each pairwise of each subgraph. By comparing the random walk paths of class labeled vertex, we were able to predict the class of each patent.

In order to assess the performance with respect to every class in the dataset, we computed common per-class metrics such as precision, recall, and the F-Measure scores. As shown in Fig. 5, the precision-recall curve for $g1$ indicates the model can achieve a relatively high precision and recall for each class.

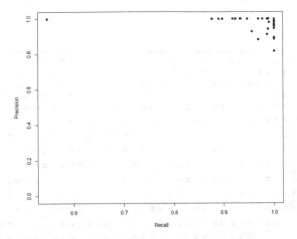

Fig. 5. Precision-recall curve for $g1$

We examined second patent citation dataset with the smaller number of patents for each class. We created $g5$ dataset consisting of 900 to 1000 patent documents for each class. We obtained $g5$ dataset with 5819 vertices and 14789 edges. We applied the same algorithm with $g1$ dataset. The results we obtained are as follow 89.49% accuracy, 89.82% precision, 94.00% recall and 88.39% F-Measure. The accuracy decreased from 97.71% to 89.49% comparing with the $g1$ results. Figure 6 shows the results of $g5$ dataset patent classification.

preds \orig	125	14	140	225	281	329	63
125	164	0	0	0	0	0	2
14	0	181	140	1	1	0	0
140	0	0	1	0	0	0	0
225	14	0	0	165	0	0	0
281	0	0	0	0	155	0	0
329	0	0	0	0	0	163	0
63	0	0	0	0	0	0	173

Fig. 6. Classification results for $g5$

We also conducted other experiment using the $g7$ dataset which consisted of 10134 vertices, 23547 edges and 51 classes. We created $g7$ dataset consisting of 1 to 600 patent documents for each class. By using the same algorithm, we obtained results of 88.26% accuracy, 89.17% precision, 91.77% recall and 89.65% F-Measure. These results are better than previous study [7] that used more than one feature to do patent classification task. [7] used a combination of [content, citation, metadata, and patent network]-based methods. The best accuracy achieved by this combination is 84.1%. Figure 7 shows the results of $g7$ dataset patent classification.

preds \ orig	109	12	142	147	150	157	159	163	168	171	185	186	191	193	196	201	213	217	23	231	234	245	26	260	27	289	291	295	298	300	334	412	413	449	453	462	470	476	527	54	69	79	86	87
109	93	0	0	0	0	0	0	0	0	0	0	0	0	0	0	0	0	0	0	0	0	0	0	0	0	0	0	0	0	0	0	0	0	0	0	0	0	0	0	0	0	0	0	0
12	0	81	0	0	0	0	0	0	0	0	0	0	0	0	0	0	0	0	0	0	0	0	0	0	0	0	0	0	0	0	0	0	0	0	0	0	0	0	0	0	0	0	0	0
142	0	0	11	0	0	0	0	0	0	0	0	0	0	0	0	0	0	0	0	0	0	0	0	0	0	0	0	0	0	0	0	0	0	0	0	0	0	0	0	0	0	0	0	0
147	0	0	1	0	0	0	0	0	0	0	0	0	0	0	0	0	0	0	0	0	0	0	0	0	0	0	0	0	0	0	0	0	0	0	0	0	0	0	0	0	0	0	0	0
150	0	0	0	0	85	0	0	0	0	0	0	0	0	0	0	0	0	0	0	0	0	0	0	0	0	0	0	0	0	0	0	0	0	0	0	0	0	0	0	0	0	0	0	0
157	0	0	0	0	0	77	0	0	0	0	0	0	0	0	0	0	0	0	0	0	0	0	0	0	0	0	0	0	0	0	0	0	0	0	0	0	0	0	0	0	0	0	0	0
159	0	0	0	0	0	0	67	0	0	0	0	0	0	0	0	0	0	0	0	0	0	0	0	0	0	0	0	0	0	0	0	0	0	0	0	0	0	0	0	0	0	0	0	0
163	0	0	0	0	0	0	0	3	0	0	0	0	0	0	0	0	0	0	0	0	0	0	0	0	0	0	0	0	0	0	0	0	0	0	0	0	0	0	0	0	0	0	0	0
168	0	0	0	0	0	0	0	0	42	0	0	0	0	0	0	0	0	0	0	0	0	0	0	0	0	0	0	0	0	0	0	0	0	0	0	0	0	0	0	0	0	0	0	0
171	0	0	0	0	0	0	0	0	0	42	0	0	0	0	0	0	0	0	0	0	0	0	0	0	0	0	0	0	0	0	0	0	0	0	0	0	0	0	0	0	0	0	0	0
185	0	0	0	0	0	0	0	0	0	0	11	0	0	0	0	0	0	0	0	0	0	0	0	0	0	0	0	0	0	0	0	0	0	0	0	0	0	0	0	0	0	0	0	0
186	0	0	0	0	0	0	0	0	0	0	1	49	0	0	0	0	0	0	0	0	0	0	0	0	0	0	0	0	0	0	0	0	0	0	0	0	0	0	0	0	0	0	0	0
191	0	0	0	0	0	0	0	0	0	0	0	1	70	0	0	0	0	0	0	0	0	0	0	0	0	0	0	0	0	0	0	0	0	0	0	0	0	0	0	0	0	0	0	0
193	0	0	0	0	0	0	0	0	0	0	0	0	0	99	0	0	0	0	0	0	0	0	0	0	0	0	0	0	0	0	0	0	0	0	0	0	0	0	0	0	0	0	0	0
196	0	0	0	0	0	0	0	0	0	0	0	0	0	0	11	0	0	0	0	0	0	0	0	0	0	0	0	0	0	0	0	0	0	0	0	0	0	0	0	0	0	0	0	0
201	0	0	0	0	0	0	0	0	0	0	0	0	0	0	0	79	0	0	0	0	0	0	0	0	0	0	0	0	0	0	0	0	0	0	0	0	0	0	0	0	0	0	0	0
213	0	0	0	0	0	0	0	0	0	0	0	0	0	0	0	0	75	0	0	0	0	0	0	0	0	0	0	0	0	0	0	0	0	0	0	0	0	0	0	0	0	0	0	0
217	0	0	0	0	0	0	0	0	0	0	0	0	0	0	0	0	0	8	0	0	0	0	0	0	0	0	0	0	0	0	0	0	0	0	0	0	0	0	0	0	0	0	0	0
23	0	0	0	0	0	0	0	0	0	0	0	0	0	0	0	0	0	0	38	0	0	0	0	0	0	0	0	0	0	0	0	0	0	0	0	0	0	0	0	0	0	0	0	0
231	0	0	0	0	0	0	0	0	0	0	0	0	0	0	0	0	0	0	0	2	0	0	0	0	0	0	0	0	0	0	0	0	0	0	0	0	0	0	0	0	0	0	0	0
234	0	0	0	0	0	0	0	0	0	0	0	0	0	0	0	0	0	0	0	0	1	0	0	0	0	0	0	0	0	0	0	0	0	0	0	0	0	0	0	0	0	0	0	0
245	0	0	0	0	0	0	0	0	0	0	0	0	0	0	0	0	0	0	0	0	0	2	0	0	0	0	0	0	0	0	0	0	0	0	0	0	0	0	0	0	0	0	0	0
26	0	0	0	0	0	0	0	0	0	0	0	0	0	0	0	0	0	0	0	0	0	0	82	0	0	0	0	0	0	0	0	0	0	0	0	0	0	0	0	0	0	0	0	0
260	0	0	0	0	0	0	0	0	0	0	0	0	0	0	0	0	0	0	0	0	0	0	0	10	0	0	0	0	0	0	0	0	0	0	0	0	0	0	0	0	0	0	0	0
27	0	0	0	0	0	0	0	0	0	0	0	0	0	0	0	0	0	0	0	0	0	0	0	0	76	0	0	0	0	0	0	0	0	0	0	0	0	0	0	0	0	0	0	0
289	0	0	0	0	0	0	0	0	0	0	0	0	0	0	0	0	0	0	0	0	0	0	0	0	0	30	0	0	0	0	0	0	0	0	0	0	0	0	0	0	0	0	0	0
291	0	0	0	0	0	0	0	0	0	0	0	0	0	0	0	0	0	0	0	0	0	0	0	0	0	0	3	0	0	0	0	0	0	0	0	0	0	0	0	0	0	0	0	0
295	0	0	0	0	0	0	0	0	0	0	0	0	0	0	0	0	0	0	0	0	0	0	0	0	0	0	0	16	0	0	0	0	0	0	0	0	0	0	0	0	0	0	0	0
298	0	0	0	0	0	0	0	0	0	0	0	0	0	0	0	0	0	0	0	0	0	0	0	0	0	0	0	0	87	0	0	0	0	0	0	0	0	0	0	0	0	0	0	0
300	0	0	0	0	0	0	0	0	0	0	0	0	0	0	0	0	0	0	0	0	0	0	0	0	0	0	0	0	0	35	0	0	0	0	0	0	0	0	0	0	0	0	0	0
334	0	0	0	0	0	0	0	0	0	0	0	0	0	0	0	0	0	0	0	0	0	0	0	0	0	0	0	0	0	0	13	0	0	0	0	0	0	0	0	0	0	0	0	0
412	0	0	0	0	0	0	0	0	0	0	0	0	0	0	0	0	0	0	0	0	0	0	0	0	0	0	0	0	0	0	0	89	0	0	0	0	0	0	0	0	0	0	0	0
413	0	0	0	0	0	0	0	0	0	0	0	0	0	0	0	0	0	0	0	0	0	0	0	0	0	0	0	0	0	0	0	0	50	0	0	0	0	0	0	0	0	0	0	0
449	0	0	0	0	0	0	0	0	0	0	0	0	0	0	0	0	0	0	0	0	0	0	0	0	0	0	0	0	0	0	0	0	0	28	0	0	0	0	0	0	0	0	0	0
453	0	0	0	0	0	0	0	0	0	0	0	0	0	0	0	0	0	0	0	0	0	0	0	0	0	0	0	0	0	0	0	0	0	0	0	0	0	0	0	0	0	0	0	0
462	0	0	0	0	0	0	0	0	0	0	0	0	0	0	0	0	0	0	0	0	0	0	0	0	0	0	0	0	0	0	0	0	0	0	0	27	0	0	0	0	0	0	0	0
470	0	0	0	0	0	0	0	0	0	0	0	0	0	0	0	0	0	0	0	0	0	0	0	0	0	0	0	0	0	0	0	0	0	0	0	0	43	0	0	0	0	0	0	0
476	0	0	0	0	0	0	0	0	0	0	0	0	0	0	0	0	0	0	0	0	0	0	0	0	0	0	0	0	0	0	0	0	0	0	0	0	0	87	0	0	0	0	0	0
527	0	0	0	0	0	0	0	0	0	0	0	0	0	0	0	0	0	0	0	0	0	0	0	0	0	0	0	0	0	0	0	0	0	0	0	0	0	0	39	0	0	0	0	0
54	0	0	0	0	0	0	0	0	0	0	0	0	0	0	0	0	0	0	0	0	0	0	0	0	0	0	0	0	0	0	0	0	0	0	0	0	0	0	0	81	0	0	0	0
69	0	0	0	0	0	0	0	0	0	0	0	0	0	0	0	0	0	0	0	0	0	0	0	0	0	0	0	0	0	0	0	0	0	0	0	0	0	0	0	0	14	0	0	0
79	0	0	0	0	0	0	0	0	0	0	0	0	0	0	0	0	0	0	0	0	0	0	0	0	0	0	0	0	0	0	0	0	0	0	0	0	0	0	0	0	0	2	0	0
86	0	0	0	0	0	0	0	0	0	0	0	0	0	0	0	0	0	0	0	0	0	0	0	0	0	0	0	0	0	0	0	0	0	0	0	0	0	0	0	0	0	0	64	0
87	0	0	0	0	0	0	0	0	0	0	0	0	0	0	0	0	0	0	0	0	0	0	0	0	0	0	0	0	0	0	0	0	0	0	0	0	0	0	0	0	0	0	0	46

Fig. 7. Classification results for g7

We reported experiments to study the impact of only one feature on the performance of patent document classifier. Feature reduction by this experiment remarkably outperforms automatic patent classification based on many features. Overfitting is the problem of fitting parameters too tightly to the training data. Overfitting results in the model were discovering random noise in the finite training set instead of the wider relationship between the features and the output variable. Consequently, the model performs well on the training data (low training set error) but perform quite poorly on the test data (high predictive error). Using one feature combined with patent citation network may lead to the avoiding overfitting.

We evaluated the performance by calculating the average and standard deviation of accuracy, precision, recall and F-measure over ten runs of each technique. As shown in Table 3, for each evaluation metric, we acquired relatively small values of standard deviation. It indicates that the results were homogenous and confirmed that the model could produce a consistent prediction in the classification task.

5   Conclusions

Processing a large number of patent documents in big data repositories require automatic patent classification for several patent processing procedures. Different from prior automated patent classification approaches that exploited particular patent documents and utilized patent contents, we appointed the information in patent citation graph for classification. In our study, we focused on using the patent citation graph structure. We investigated the effect of using only one cited documents' feature, i.e., the name of patent classes along citation graph for the classification task. We collected advantages of a kernel-based method and built kernel function to represent features and citation associated information. We used k-step random walk paths algorithm to calculate kernel values of each patent pairwise and SVM classifier to do the classification task. We proposed a technique of subgraphing large patent graph to represent citation graph information. The method is based on the property of neighborhood in a graph. The investigation of the k-step random walk paths kernel metrics on three datasets from the USPTO database showed that using patent citation graph structure with only one feature achieved better classification performance.

The random walk paths algorithm consumed much computing resources and only fit for smaller size of datasets. We need to scale up the algorithm to our whole dataset which consists of $3,155,172$ vertices, $23,650,890$ edges, and 426 classes. For improving our work, we consider to conduct several modifications as follows:

1. Add the "International Patent Classification (IPC) System" as vertices attribute instead of USPC.
2. Apply parallel computing environment to scale up the algorithm to complete patent citation graph dataset.

3. Modify the k number of k-step random walk algorithm.
4. Modify the n order in subgraphing step.
5. Apply the vertex label histogram algorithm to address the limitation of the computing environment. This algorithm may perform well for large patent citation graph dataset.

References

1. Abbas, A., Zhang, L., Khan, S.U.: A literature review on the state-of-the-art in patent analysis. World Pat. Inf. **37**, 3–13 (2014)
2. Hall, B.H., Jaffe, A.B., Trajtenberg, M.: The NBER Patent Citations Data File: Lessons, Insight and Methodological Tools (2001)
3. Kumar, R., Math, S., Tripathi, R.C., Tiwari, M.D.: Patent classification of the new invention using PLSA. In: Proceedings of the First International Conference on Intelligent Interactive Technologies and Multimedia, pp. 222–225 (2010)
4. Nguyen, H.M., Phan, C.P., Nguyen, H.Q.: GeTCo: an ontology-based approach for patent classification search. In: iiWAS 2016 Proceedings of the 18th International Conference on Information Integration and Web-based Applications and Services, pp. 241–244 (2016)
5. Shih, M.J., Liu, D.R.: Patent classification using ontology-based patent network analysis. In: Proceedings Pacific Asia Conference on Information Systems PACIS 2010, Taipei, pp. 962–972 (2010)
6. Li, X., Chen, H., Zhang, Z., Li, J.: Automatic patent classification using citation network information: an experimental study in nanotechnology. In: Proceedings of the 7th ACM/IEEE Joint Conference on Digital Libraries - Building & Sustaining the Digital Environment, pp. 419–427 (2007)
7. Liu, D.R., Shih, M.J.: Hybrid-patent classification based on patent-network analysis. J. Am. Soc. Inform. Sci. Technol. **62**(2), 246–256 (2011)
8. Stutzki, J., Schubert, M.: Geodata supported classification of patent applications. In: GeoRich 2016 Proceedings of the Third International ACM SIGMOD Workshop on Managing and Mining Enriched Geo-Spatial Data, pp. 4:1–4:6 (2016)
9. Zhang, L., Li, L., Li, T.: Patent mining: a survey. ACM SIGKDD Explor. Newsl. **16**(2), 1–19 (2015)
10. Shalaby, W., Zadrozny, W.: Patent retrieval: a literature review. arXiv preprint, January 2017
11. Noh, H., Jo, Y., Lee, S.: Keyword selection and processing strategy for applying text mining to patent analysis. Expert Syst. Appl. **42**(9), 4348–4360 (2015)
12. D'hondt, E., Verberne, S., Koster, C., Boves, L.: Text representations for patent classification. Comput. Linguist. **39**(3), 755–775 (2013)
13. Fall, C.J., Torcsvari, A., Benzineb, K., Karetka, G.: Automated categorization in the international patent classification. ACM SIGIR Forum **37**(1), 10–25 (2003)
14. Li, Y., Bontcheva, K.: Adapting support vector machines for F-term-based classification of patents. ACM Trans. Asian Lang. Inf. Process. **7**(2), 1–19 (2008)
15. Wu, C.H., Ken, Y., Huang, T.: Patent classification system using a new hybrid genetic algorithm support vector machine. Appl. Soft Comput. **10**(4), 1164–1177 (2010)
16. Csardi, G., Nepusz, T.: The igraph software package for complex network research. InterJ. Complex Syst. **1695**, 1–9 (2006)

17. Diego, I.M.D., Muñoz, A., Moguerza, J.M.: Methods for the combination of kernel matrices within a support vector framework. Mach. Learn. **78**(1–2), 137–174 (2010)
18. Sugiyama, M.: graphkernels: Graph Kernels. R package version 1.2 (2017)
19. Karatzoglou, A., Smola, A., Hornik, K., Zeileis, A.: kernlab - an S4 package for kernel methods in R. J. Stat. Softw. **11**(9), 1–20 (2004)

Detecting Target Text Related to Algorithmic Efficiency in Scholarly Big Data Using Recurrent Convolutional Neural Network Model

Iqra Safder[1] ⓘ, Junaid Sarfraz[1] ⓘ, Saeed-Ul Hassan[1(✉)] ⓘ,
Mohsen Ali[1] ⓘ, and Suppawong Tuarob[2] ⓘ

[1] Information Technology University, Ferozepur Road, Lahore 54000, Pakistan
saeed-ul-hassan@itu.edu.pk
[2] Faculty of ICT, Mahidol University, Nakhon Pathom 73170, Thailand

Abstract. We are observing an exponential growth of scientific literature since the last few decades. Tapping on the advancement of web-enabled tools and technologies, millions of articles are stored and indexed in the digital libraries. Among this archived scientific literature, thousands of newly emerging algorithms, mostly illustrated with pseudo-codes, are published every year in the area of Computer Science and other related computational fields. Previously, an array of techniques has been deployed to retrieve information related to these algorithms by indexing their pseudo-codes and metadata from a vast pool of scholarly documents. Unfortunately, existing search engines are only limited to indexing a textual description of each pseudo-code and are unable to provide simple algorithm-specific information such as run-time complexity, performance evaluation (such as precision, recall, or f-measure), and the size of the dataset it can effectively process, etc. In this paper, we propose a set of algorithms that extract information pertaining to the performance of algorithm(s) presented and/or discussed in the research article. Specifically, sentences in the paper that convey information about the efficiency of the corresponding algorithm are identified and extracted, using the Recurrent Convolutional Neural Network (RCNN) model. To evaluate the performance of our algorithm, we have collected a dataset of 258 manually annotated scholarly documents by four experts, originally downloaded from CiteseerX. Our proposed RCNN based model achieves encouraging 77.65% f-measure and 76.35% accuracy.

Keywords: Algorithm effectiveness · Scholarly big data · Recurrent convolutional neural network (RCNN) · Digital libraries

1 Introduction

Literature pertaining to academic research is growing with exceptionally. There are millions of research articles on the web [1], many of which are stored and indexed by digital libraries. Apart from these libraries, hundreds of articles are published digital libraries. Apart from these libraries, hundreds of articles are published and/or added to

© Springer International Publishing AG 2017
S. Choemprayong et al. (Eds.): ICADL 2017, LNCS 10647, pp. 30–40, 2017.
https://doi.org/10.1007/978-3-319-70232-2_3

digital archives on monthly and yearly basis [2]. Bhatia et al. [3] estimated that approximately 900 algorithms have been published in major computer science conferences during the years 2005-2009. This clearly shows that researchers are working actively to propose new algorithmic solutions or to improve the existing ones. There is always a possibility that new algorithms may help to improve the existing deployed techniques. Therefore, it is understandable to assume that there is a need for the researchers generally and the computer scientists specifically to always keep themselves informed about new algorithms and solutions related to their technologies.

The exponential growth in the academic research community and resultant published literature has made it difficult for a human to be abreast to all the related research, proposed algorithms and their reported results on a specific dataset(s). Digital libraries, like Google Scholar, PloS One, CiteSeerX etc., have efficient search capabilities that help users to search relevant research literature. However, they have intrinsically searching limitations because of simple and traditional text matching techniques for user queries without complete understanding the context and semantics of the text. Recently, few research-studies have been carried out to investigate the possibility of building a management system and a search engine for the algorithms [4, 5]. However, such a searching mechanism is merely a matching algorithm on textual metadata, such as caption text, reference text etc., with the search queries. Generally, algorithmic solutions are evaluated on particular datasets and have various computational costs and evaluation results. Algorithmic technique with less computational cost and with better evaluation results is considered to be an efficient one.

In order to report the experimentation and evaluation results authors use plain text and sub-objects (like figures, tables, etc.). The text written related to the reported results contains more details about the effectiveness of the deployed algorithm and provides a context that helps to interpret the text. Following is an example of text pertaining to the performance of an algorithm discussed in one of the publication in our dataset: *"...We have evaluated the LDA-SVD multi-document summarization algorithm by considering both cases of removing stop-words and not removing stop-words from the computed and the model summaries. Table 2 tabulates the ROUGE-1 recall values and its 95% confidence interval..."*. Previously, proposed text matching techniques such as bag-of-words or bag-of-n-gram, latent Dirichlet allocation [6] and mutual-information, etc. completely fail to capture the semantic and word sequence of the text. These two features, text semantics and its word sequence, are essential in effective extraction of the portion of the text where performance of the related algorithm is discussed. While, other text matching techniques like high order n-gram (5-gram, 6-gram) and Tree kernels may also help to understand the text semantic and contextual information, but these techniques still fail to fully understand the sentence's context which may heavily affect the classification accuracy.

In this paper, we propose a novel model for automatic detection of text from scientific publications pertaining to the discussion of algorithms, in terms of their effectiveness like precision, recall or f-measure etc. We tap into the advancement in deep learning and create sentence representations using word embeddings. The representation is fed into the Recurrent Convolutional Neural Network (RCNN) [7] classification algorithm, allowing us to accurately find the 'evaluation results related text lines' in full text documents. Finally, we evaluate our proposed method using a dataset of 258 manually annotated scholarly documents from the CiteSeerX repository. After 100 training epochs, our model achieves 76% training accuracy, whereas we report 77.65% f-measure and 76.35% accuracy on testing data.

2 Literature Review

The literature review has been categorized into two subsections; the first one discusses the related work on information extraction in academic articles to enhance digital repositories and search engine capabilities for important sub-objects (tables, figures, algorithms) that are found in research articles. The second one is concerned with deep learning based techniques which gave us the inspiration to employ such algorithms for related target text extraction in research articles.

2.1   A Brief Review on Information Extraction from Full Text Publication

A significant amount of work has been done to extract sub-objects (tables, figures, algorithms) from research articles [5–8]. The browsing and searching of sub-objects from digital libraries have gained increasing popularity, especially in the era where a human is overloaded with information. Sub-objects such as algorithms, tables and figures are often used by authors to present proposed algorithms and pseudo-codes, experimentation results and their comparisons. In the literature [9, 10], optical character recognition based techniques have been designed for automatic extraction of sub-objects. Furthermore, this extracted information has been made available for searching by efficient indexing. A specialized results figure extractor *FigureSeer* [11] has been designed to automatically extract information from figures (taken as images), by deploying computer vision techniques. Furthermore, the extracted information is provided for searching, coupled with efficient indexing.

Recently, an improved table detection approach for multi-page pdf documents has been proposed [12]. The technique implements a visual separator approach that refers to not only graphic ruling, but also the white spaces to handle the tables with or without ruling lines. *TableSeer* [13] was proposed as a search engine designed for table searching in the digital articles. This search system proposes an algorithm for automatic extraction of tables along with table metadata. Finally, a vector space model based ranking algorithm is designed to rank the search results.

ChemxSeer [14], a specialized table search system has been designed for automatic extraction of tables & figures from full text articles in the field of Chemistry. Another well-known search engine, *AckSeer* [15], has been used for indexing and searching acknowledgements in the CiteSeerX digital library. While both PlosOne and CiteSeerX digital libraries support tables and figures search functionality, none of these systems supports the text summarization of the document elements. To fill this gap, Bhatia and Mitra [16] have proposed a method to automatically generate a summary or textual description for a document element, by utilizing machine learning techniques to extract and re-order relevant sentences of the paper in which the corresponding document element appears. Their summarization approach helps the end user to understand the relevance of a document element to his/her information needs.

Recently, *AlgorithmSeer* [4], an algorithm search engine, was deployed as a hybrid of rule and machine learning based approach for algorithm and pseudo-code detection. Furthermore, pseudo-code metadata was also used to generate a synopsis for efficient searching and indexing [4].

2.2 A Brief Review on Deep Neural Networks for Text Mining

Advancements in the Deep Neural Network models and deep representation learning have achieved remarkable improvements for data sparsity and word embeddings [17]. The word representations, word embeddings, are real valued vectors used to find semantic similarity by simply computing the distance between embedding vectors of different documents. Recently, Convolutional Neural networks [18], designed for text analysis, have also outperformed other approaches used for the sentence categorization. However, CNN performance has very strong dependency on the filter size and other hyper-parameter selection.

Meanwhile, the evolution in pre-trained embeddings and use of memory based deep neural networks, such as Recurrent convolutional neural network [19] (RNN), have shown promising results on the tasks like caption generation, text translation, chat-bot creation, etc. Nevertheless, RNN (and LSTM), when used for text representation, the final text representation has more influence of latter words than former words. This behavior is problematic when used for text context learning and text classification tasks since important words can be found anywhere in the text. The RCNN builds many local representations using the context (neighboring words) and previous local representation, and finally uses the max-pooling to automatically understand which word plays important role. Models based on RCNN have been previously used for text classification [7], paraphrase detection [20] and semantic role labeling [21]. They have also been used to find the semantic relatedness of phrases and sentences in the scholarly documents.

In this paper, we deploy RCNN to extract the lines where the algorithms have been discussed in terms of their effectiveness like precision, recall or f-measure etc. Our choice of using RCNN is based on its ability to automatically find which part of the sentence is important. Our extensive experiments indicate that the employed model comprehensively accomplishes the non-trivial task of identification of sentences in the text that convey information about the efficiency of the corresponding algorithm with very encouraging accuracy.

3 Data and Method

3.1 Data

The dataset consists of 258 scholarly articles, selected from the CiteSeerX repository [4]. Note that, of the total there are 37,000 text lines in our dataset. Further, the data was manually annotated by four human experts who identified 2,331 text line as target line, thus, only 6.3% contained target text that conveys information about the efficiency of the corresponding algorithm.

3.2   Approach

Figure 1 gives the high level architecture of our proposed system for Target-text extraction, named as evaluation metrics detection (EMD). Our proposed system inputs the scholarly documents in a Portable Document Format (PDF) since a huge digital search libraries are in the pdf format. In the first step, PDF document is converted into a plain text by using PDFbox library (https://pdfbox.apache.org/). The extracted text is passed to the documents-segmentation module for section extraction, inspired by Tuarob [22]. Further, we preprocess extracted sections for cleaning purpose. Finally, the text is input to the RCNN model based target-text-line classification system.

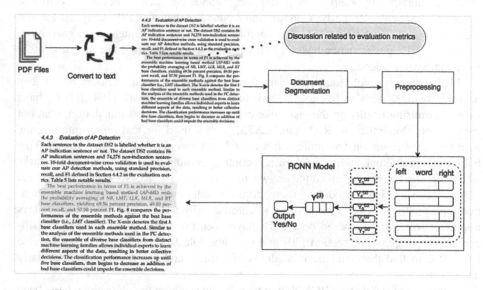

Fig. 1. The proposed evaluation metrics detection (EMD) system architecture

Our EMD method uses RCNN to capture the text semantics for target texts lines classification. It takes the input of preprocessed related sections text as sequence of words $w_1, w_2, w_3...w_n$ and outputs the class of the text. Afterwards, probability function $p(k|D, \theta)$ is used to find the probability of text line that belong to a class containing target lines or not. The following preprocessing steps are taken:

Standard Section Extraction. Generally, scholarly articles are organized into standard sections (i.e. Abstract, Introduction, Background and Related Work etc.). Sections such as Methodology, Results, Experiments, and Abstract etc. have very high probability to contain result related discussion. Therefore, section extraction is a very crucial task for our EMD method. We employ a rule based technique [22] for section extraction. The said section extraction technique eventually helps us to keep on related sections (i.e. Methodology, Results, Experiments, Abstract etc.) and slice up the non-important sections where chances of target lines are minimum or close to none (i.e. Introduction, Related work, References, Acknowledgement etc.). Further, text cleaning is performed to remove header/footers, paper title, and author affiliations etc. Lastly, the cleaned and related sections text is given as input to RCNN model.

$$c_l(w_i) = f((W^{(l)})c_l(w_{i-1}) + (W^{(sl)})e(w_{i-1}))$$ (1)

$$c_r(w_i) = f((W^{(r)})c_r(w_{i-1}) + (W^{(sr)})e(w_{i-1}))$$ (2)

The Recurrent Convolutional Neural Network Model. Figure 1 shows the detailed architecture of our RCNN [7] based approach. The word representation is the combination of word and its context. The bidirectional nature of RCNN generates the representation $y_i(w_i)$ of each word w_i, that captures the context and semantic meaning of words. For that it first calculates the vectors $c_r(w_i)$ and $c_l(w_i)$, Eqs. 1 and 2 *respectively*, containing the context of words that are left and right to word w_i.

Here, $W^{(l)}$ and $W^{(r)}$ are matrices used to transform context between the hidden layers. $W^{(sl)}$, $W^{(sr)}$ matrices are used to combine the left and right words context with the current word. Similarly, $e(w_{i-1})$ is a real valued word embedding vector of word w_{i-1}. The final word w_i represented in Eq. 3 is learned by combining left and right contexts. The c_l and c_r vectors are computed by the model in forward and backward passes. Afterwards, a linear transformation $(wx + b)$ with *tanh* activation function is applied to add nonlinearity (see Eq. 4).

$$x_i = [c_l(w_i); e(w_i); c_r(w_i)]$$ (3)

$$y_i^{(2)} = tanh(W^{(2)}x_i + b^{(2)})$$ (4)

The next layer in the network is the max pooling layer (see Fig. 1) which is applied on the $y_i^{(2)}$ vector that represents the most important and significant features for the text representations after evaluating each and every semantic factor. The pooling layer is used to convert the varying length text to a fixed length vector to only represent the most significant information from the full text. The Eq. 5 shows the max pooling layer representation which is applied on element level and only picks maximum element from $y_i^{(2)}$ against each position. Lastly, a single fully connected (FC) hidden layer as output layer with Softmax activation function is applied to compute the probability (Eqs. 6 and 7).

$$y^{(3)} = max_{i=2}^n y_{(i)}^{(2)}$$ (5)

$$y^{(4)} = W^{(4)}y^{(3)} + b^{(4)}$$ (6)

$$p_{(i)} = \frac{exp\left(y_k^{(4)}\right)}{\sum_{k=1}^n exp(y_k^{(4)})}$$ (7)

4   Experimentation and Results

The experiments are run to detect target text lines (that convey information about the efficiency of the corresponding algorithm) using RCNN. All experiments are performed on Nvidia Titan 750 GPU with 2 GB memory, running Ubuntu operating system. We use the Python Chainer Library (https://chainer.org/) to implement RCNN model.

4.1   Training Model

For training purposes, first we defined and initialized all the model parameters θ, shown in Eq. 8. The vectors $b^{(2)}$, $b^{(4)}$ are real valued vectors, E is a real valued word embedding and $c_l(w_1)$, $c_r(w_n)$ are initial left and right context vectors. During training we maximize the probability of positive class log-likelihood with respect to θ, as shown in Eq. 9, where D is the set of documents, and $class_c$ is the positive class.

$$\theta = \{E, b^{(2)}, b^{(4)}, c_l(w_1), c_r(w_n), W^{(2)}, W^{(4)}, W^{(l)}, W^{(r)}, W^{(sl)}, W^{(sr)}\} \qquad (8)$$

$$\theta \rightarrow \sum_{c \in D} log p(class_c | D, \theta) \qquad (9)$$

Our dataset suffers from the class imbalance problem, since target-text constitutes very small portion of the document. This imbalance can adversely affect the classification results. To deal with this problem, we incorporated following two balancing approaches: (a) *Random Over-sampling (ROver):* minority class instances are randomly replicated, until positive and negative class instances become equal. (b) *Random Under-sampling (RUnder):* majority class instances are randomly excluded until positive and negative class instances become equal.

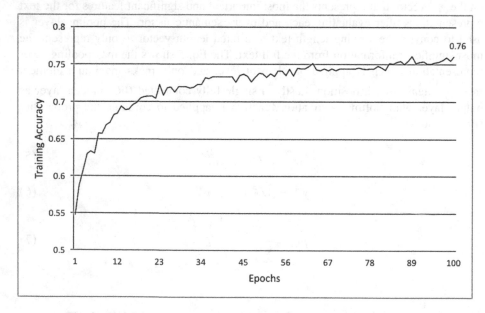

Fig. 2. Training accuracy of RCNN based EMD method with 100 epoch

After applying the balancing techniques, we get 4337 positive samples, i.e. the target lines, and 4770 negative instances, i.e. text lines without target text and with no discussion about the evaluation results of the algorithm. Data is split into 70% and 30% for training and testing respectively. Figure 2 shows training accuracy of our EMD method for 100 epochs to depict the behavior of our model during training. The y-axis shows the training accuracy along with epochs on x-axis.

Note that the network hyper parameters are assigned as follows: hidden layer size (H) to 1000, learning rate to 0.01, vocabulary size (V) to 3000 and training epochs set to 100.

4.2   Testing and Evaluation of Target Text Lines Detection

For the baseline results, a rule based approach is designed. First, we manually extracted evaluation metrics keywords (i.e. precision, recall, f1-score, f-measure etc.) from a subsample of our dataset. Afterwards, a conventional keywords matching approach is implemented to extract target text lines. The approach does not perform well because the text matching was only performed on the basis of keywords; no contextual or semantic information was considered. Note that the evaluation metrics are not necessarily always directly discussed in the text; at times the text contains indirect meanings which a human can understand due to its context, therefore, a rule based approach would lack to detect such target lines.

Table 1 compares the classification results of our RCNN method and the baseline (keyword detection), in terms of precision, recall and f-measure. The baseline yields reasonable precision (0.42), but suffers from very low recall (0.08). Such a phenomenon is expected from rule-based approaches, which do not generally work well when modeling multi-dimensional, semantic-characterizing data such as ours. Our RCNN based method outperforms the baseline in both precision and recall, by achieving very encouraging 0.79 precision and 0.77 recall.

Table 1. Precision, recall and F-measure scores for RCNN and baseline method.

Method	Model	Pr.	Re.	F1.	Acc.
EMD	Baseline	0.42	0.08	0.14	0.69
EMD	RCNN	0.79	0.77	0.77	0.76

The results clearly depict that contextual and semantic information help to our model performs well than traditional keywords matching approach. Table 2 shows some examples of correctly and incorrectly classified lines of results related text by our model. One of the limitation of our proposed technique is the use of same embedding vectors for English language text and numeric figures found in text lines e.g. *"...Implemented technique achieve precision 60.5 and recall 50.4...."*. Currently, the proposed model can only understand the contextual meaning by looking on English language text. However, the numeric text may also contain useful information regarding the performance of the respective algorithms. Table 2 shows some examples of correctly and incorrectly classified lines of results related text.

Table 2. Examples of extracted result-discussion sentences

Correctly classified examples	Incorrectly classified examples
"…Figure 1 shows the normalized RMS errors when using the linear and nonlinear regression methods, and the KNN impute procedure over 1 and 5% data missing. The nonlinear regression method performs best over the range of K, and the linear regression method performs slightly poorer…"	"…Our results indicate that CAEP has a competitive behavior with respect to the NSGA-II, which is representative of the state-of-the-art in evolutionary multi objective optimization…"
"…We have evaluated the LDA-SVD multi-document summarization algorithm by considering both cases of removing stop-words and not removing stop-words from the computed and the model summaries. Table 2 tabulates the ROUGE-1 recall values and its 95% confidence interval…"	"…Extensive simulation results using computer-generated signals, real-world speech and real-world biomedical signals have confirmed the high efficiency and usefulness of the proposed approach in comparison with the conventional counterparts. The proposed approach is very promising, especially in the analysis of EEG and MEG signals where the SNR is below 0.0 dB…"

5 Concluding Remarks

In this paper we have proposed the use of word embedding and recurrent convolutional neural network model to discover and retrieve sentences in the document that convey the information about the effectiveness (such as precision, recall, and f-measure) of the corresponding algorithm. This information could be used by the algorithm searchers to further drill down the desired algorithms using 'performance' as a criterion. In future, we plan to employ natural language processing and machine learning techniques to extract numeric representation of algorithm's performance. This information will enable direct comparison between algorithms. Furthermore, we plan to investigate the possibility of extracting other algorithm-specific metadata such as run-time complexity, input, output, and compatible data structures. Note that dataset and code to reproduce the results can be accessed at the following URL: https://github.com/slab-itu/rcnn_icadl_2017.

References

1. Khabsa, M., Giles, C.L.: The number of scholarly documents on the public web. PLoS ONE **9**(5), e93949 (2014)
2. ArXiv stats. https://arxiv.org/stats/monthly_submissions. Accessed 17 July 2017

3. Bhatia, S., Tuarob, S., Mitra, P., Giles, C.L.: An algorithm search engine for software developers. In: Proceedings of the 3rd International Workshop on Search-Driven Development: Users, Infrastructure, Tools, and Evaluation, pp. 13–16. ACM (2011)
4. Tuarob, S., Bhatia, S., Mitra, P., Giles, C.L.: AlgorithmSeer: a system for extracting and searching for algorithms in scholarly big data. IEEE Trans. Big Data 2(1), 3–17 (2016). IEEE
5. Tuarob, S., Bhatia, S., Mitra, P., Giles, C.L.: Automatic detection of pseudocodes in scholarly documents using machine learning. In: Document Analysis and Recognition (ICDAR), pp. 738–742 (2013)
6. Hingmire, S., Chougule, S., Palshikar, G.K., Chakraborti, S.: Document classification by topic labeling. In: Proceedings of the 36th International ACM SIGIR Conference on Research and Development in Information Retrieval, pp. 877–880. ACM (2013)
7. Lai, S., Xu, L., Liu, K., Zhao, J.: Recurrent convolutional neural networks for text classification. In: AAAI, vol. 333, pp. 2267–2273 (2015)
8. Coüasnon, B., Lemaitre, A.: Recognition of tables and forms. In: Doermann, D., Tombre, K. (eds.) Handbook of Document Image Processing and Recognition, pp. 647–677. Springer, London (2014). doi:10.1007/978-0-85729-859-1_20
9. Chen, S.Z., Cafarella, M.J., Adar, E.: Searching for statistical diagrams. Frontiers of Engineering, National Academy of Engineering, pp. 69–78 (2011)
10. Kataria, S., Browuer, W., Mitra, P., Giles. C.L.: Automatic extraction of data points and text blocks from 2-dimensional plots in digital documents. In: AAAI 2008, vol. 8, pp. 1169–1174 (2008)
11. Siegel, N., Horvitz, Z., Levin, R., Divvala, S., Farhadi, A.: FigureSeer: parsing result-figures in research papers. In: Leibe, B., Matas, J., Sebe, N., Welling, M. (eds.) ECCV 2016, LNCS, vol. 9911, pp. 664–680. Springer, Cham (2016). doi:10.1007/978-3-319-46478-7_41
12. Fang, J., Gao, L., Bai, K., Qiu, R., Tao, X., Tang, Z.: A table detection method for multipage Pdf documents via visual seperators and tabular structures. In: International Conference on Document Analysis and Recognition (ICDAR), pp. 779–783. IEEE (2011)
13. Liu, Y., Bai, K., Mitra, P., Giles, C.L.: TableSeer: automatic table metadata extraction and searching in digital libraries, In: Proceedings of the 7th ACM/IEEE-CS Joint Conference on Digital Libraries, pp. 91–100. ACM (2007)
14. Mitra, P., Giles, C.L., Sun, B., Liu, Y., Jaiswal, A.R.: Scientific data and document processing in chemxseer. In: AAAI Spring Symposium: Semantic Scientific Knowledge Integration, pp. 51–56 (2008)
15. Khabsa, M., Treeratpituk, P., Giles, C.L.: AckSeer: a repository and search engine for automatically extracted acknowledgments from digital libraries. In: Proceedings of the 12th ACM/IEEE-CS Joint Conference on Digital Libraries, pp. 185–194. ACM (2012)
16. Bhatia, S., Mitra, P.: Summarizing figures, tables, and algorithms in scientific publications to augment search results. ACM Trans. Inf. Syst. (TOIS) 30(1), 3 (2012)
17. Mikolov, T., Yih, W.T., Zweig, G.: Linguistic regularities in continuous space word representations. In: hlt-Naacl, vol. 13, pp. 746–751 (2013)
18. Kim, Y.: Convolutional neural networks for sentence classification. arXiv preprint arXiv: 1408.5882 (2014)
19. Tang, D., Qin, B., Liu, T.: Document modeling with gated recurrent neural network for sentiment classification. In: EMNLP, pp. 1422–1432 (2015)
20. Socher, R., Huang, E.H., Pennin, J., Manning, C.D., Ng, A.Y.: Dynamic pooling and unfolding recursive autoencoders for paraphrase detection. In: Advances in Neural Information Processing Systems, pp. 801–809 (2011)

21. Collobert, R., Weston, J., Bottou, L., Karlen, M., Kavukcuoglu, K., Kuksa, P.: Natural language processing (almost) from scratch. J. Mach. Learn. Res. **12**, 2493–2537 (2011)
22. Tuarob, S., Mitra, P., Giles, C.L.: A hybrid approach to discover semantic hierarchical sections in scholarly documents. In: Document Analysis and Recognition (ICDAR), pp. 1081–1085. IEEE (2015)

Semantic Facettation in Pharmaceutical Collections Using Deep Learning for Active Substance Contextualization

Janus Wawrzinek[✉] and Wolf-Tilo Balke

IFIS TU-Braunschweig, Mühlenpfordstrasse 23, 38106 Braunschweig, Germany
{wawrzinek,balke}@ifis.cs.tu-bs.de

Abstract. Alternative access paths to literature beyond mere keyword or bibliographic search are a major success factor in today's digital libraries. Especially in the sciences, users are in dire need of complex knowledge spaces and facettations where entities like e.g., chemical substances, genes, or mathematical formulae may play a central role. However, even for clear-cut entities the requirements in terms of contextualized similarities or rankings may strongly differ. In this paper, we show how deep learning techniques used on scientific corpora lead to a strongly contextualized description of entities. As application case we take pharmaceutical entities in the form of small molecules and demonstrate how their learned contexts and profiles reflect their actual use as well as possible new uses, e.g., for drug design or repurposing. As our evaluation shows, the results gained are quite comparable to expensive manually maintained classifications in the field. Since our techniques only rely on deep embeddings of textual documents, our methodology promises to be generalizable to other use cases, too.

Keywords: Digital libraries · Information extraction · Facettation · Deep learning

1 Introduction

In pharmaceutical digital libraries, (active) substance similarity forms the basis of various innovative services for information access such as structure search, grouping and facettation of drugs, suggestion lists and many others. However, what makes a similarity measure between entities semantically *meaningful* in a domain? While there usually is no single universally true answer, there are generally several accepted methods of determining similarity differing in their complexity, accuracy, and applicability given a task. Yet, from a digital library provider's perspective, there is another important distinction between these similarity measures: can the necessary features for their computation be extracted automatically in a scalable way or are they based on semantic features that still need expensive manual curation? Given the current promising developments in automatic information extraction and the indexing challenges posed by rapidly increasing publication numbers, this is indeed a central question.

© Springer International Publishing AG 2017
S. Choemprayong et al. (Eds.): ICADL 2017, LNCS 10647, pp. 41–53, 2017.
https://doi.org/10.1007/978-3-319-70232-2_4

Consider the example domain of pharmaceutical collections: Here, to compute active substance similarity two approaches are widely used: on one hand a (sub-) structural similarity (chemical or molecular similarity), and on the other hand a taxonomical similarity regarding therapeutic uses, etc. (usually curated manually by domain experts).

For efficiently deriving *(sub-)structural similarity* between substances, all molecular structures are usually encoded in bit-string fingerprints. To reduce dimensionality and ease comparison the bits are set with respect to molecular features such as atom sequences, ring compositions or atom pairs of each molecule. The exact composition of fingerprints may thus vary depending on the specific use case and research field [1]. However, this does not only result in numerous and different fingerprint types (e.g. Extended Fingerprint, MACCS, Estate, etc.), but also in different similarity measures between substances, such as Tanimoto, cosine, dice, etc. In brief, the combination of fingerprints and similarity measures leads to a wide variety of possible results, and it is interesting to note that their respectively induced rankings of most similar substances are usually only weakly, if at all correlated [2]. Moreover, while structural similarity is extremely useful for screening, it does not capture other important semantic features.

The *taxonomical similarity* approach to compute active ingredient similarity is based on mostly manually curated semantic classification systems. Drugs, chemicals, or in general active ingredients are grouped according to their chemical, therapeutic or anatomical features. Considering pharmacy, there are a couple of popular classification systems such as the Medical Subject Headings (MeSH) Trees,[1] the Anatomical Therapeutic Chemical (ATC) Classification System[2] or the American Hospital Formulary Service (AHFS) Pharmacologic-Therapeutic classification.[3] Of course, their applicability is limited by the actual number of substances indexed: querying Drug-Bank[4] as a relatively complete resource [3], most active ingredients are not classified by any of the above-mentioned classification systems.

Recently, many research efforts have considered a new way of generating semantically meaningful similarities for scientific entities: *facettation with categories dynamically created from large document corpora* (for a good overview see [4]). Indeed, the enrichment of entity metadata with information from different sources like external knowledge bases or focused document collections has been proven extremely successful in scientific search scenarios, see e.g., [5, 6]. The key to success can be seen in a *contextualization of entities* as expressed by their actual use in research, which is in turn reflected in respective publications. In this paper, we present a novel deep learning-based technique to contextualize entities. Following our pharmaceutical use case, we evaluate our method over the PubMed collection and show that the facets gained from embeddings in high-dimensional document spaces are semantically meaningful, while measuring similarity regarding different entity aspects. Thus, our method adds alternative facets statistically justified by a large body of existing research

---

[1] https://www.nlm.nih.gov/mesh/intro_trees.html.

[2] https://www.whocc.no/atc_ddd_index/.

[3] http://www.ahfsdruginformation.com/ahfs-pharmacologic-therapeutic-classification/.

[4] https://www.drugbank.ca/.

publications, giving users easy access to hidden entity semantics for digital library searches. Moreover, these facets can be automatically derived without expensive manual curation.

The paper is organized as follows: Sect. 2 revisits related work. Section 3 details our method for facettation of drugs, accompanied by an extensive evaluation against curated classification systems in Sect. 4. We close with conclusions in Sect. 5.

2 Related Work

Capturing semantically meaningful similarities for scientific entities has since long been an active field of research. Today, most recognized systems are to a large degree still *manually maintained* to guarantee usage experience and to provide a reliable foundation for value adding services and research planning. While the current explosion of scientific results clearly calls for automation, the quality of resources cannot be compromised, i.e. a high degree of precision has to be maintained. The most prominent classification systems (later used as ground truth) for pharmaceutical uses are:

- The *Anatomical Therapeutic Chemical (ATC) Classification System.* ATC subdivides drugs according to their therapeutic uses and chemical features. Maintained by the World Health Organization (WHO), it is currently the most used drug classification system and serves as an important source for tasks like e.g., drug repurposing and drug therapy composition [7].
- The *Medical Subject Headings (MeSH)* MeSH is a controlled vocabulary and serves as general classification system for biomedical documents in MEDLINE maintained by the National Library of Medicine (NLM). MeSH descriptors are organized in 16 main categories, e.g. category C for diseases and D for drugs, further divided in finer levels (subgroups) leading to a hierarchical structure.
- The *American Hospital Formulary Service (AHFS).* AHFS distinguishes drugs according to their pharmacologic and therapeutic effect with a focus on drug therapies. Like ATC and MeSH, AHFS shows a hierarchical structure.

Manual drug annotation may yield superior quality, but it is also related with high costs. Therefore, in recent years many approaches to *annotate drugs automatically* have been designed. In general, these approaches rely on a blend of machine learning, information retrieval, and information extraction techniques. To annotate properties in pharmaceutical texts reliably, a wide variety of methods has been devised. For instance, [7] employs support vector machines to predict ATC class labels for yet unclassified drugs and shows that given rich training sets, document-based classification can actually outperform classifications performed on chemical structures only. For the same task, [8] shows the power of text mining to create enriched drug fingerprints and after some manual curation their subsequent benefit for retrieval. In [9] an approach for the automatic annotation of biomedical documents with MeSH terms is presented. Different classification systems are compared to reproduce manual MeSH annotations.

With classification accuracies of already around 80%, all of the above document-based approaches show the benefits and general applicability of text mining for entity metadata enrichment. Thus, a domain-specific contextualization of entities in scientific digital libraries seems appealing. To find central topics in documents two major approaches have been used: latent semantic analysis (LSA [10]) performs singular value decompositions over term-document matrices to get topics as linear combinations of vocabulary terms. Latent Dirichlet Allocation (LDA [11]) sees documents as mixtures of different topics, where each term's generation is attributable to one of the document's topics. Since both models show problems in NLP tasks like polysemy detection or syntactic parsing, recently Word Embeddings [12] quantifying and categorizing semantic similarities between linguistic items based on their distributional properties in large samples of language data have been proposed as a powerful deep learning alternative. Therefore, in the following we will rely on word embeddings as the state of the art method for entity contextualization and in particular, will use the Word2vec Skip-Gram model implementation from the open source Deep-Learning-for-Java[5] library.

3   Building New Facets Based on Word Embeddings

The basic idea of our approach is to create a new contextualized facet for entity-based search in scientific digital libraries: in particular, a selection of closely related entities with respect to the search entity. For actually building contextualized facets every corpus of scientific documents can be used, but normally the selection of the document base for subsequent embedding strictly reflects the type of entities under scrutiny. For example in the case of pharmaceutical entities such as active ingredients, the National Library of Medicine's PubMed collection would be a good candidate.

After the initial crawling step the following process can be roughly divided into four sub-steps:

1. *Preprocessing of crawled documents.* After the relevant documents were crawled, classical IR-style text preprocessing is needed, i.e. stop-word removal and stemming. The preprocessing helps mainly to reduce vocabulary size, which leads to an improved performance, as well as improved accuracy. Due to their low discriminating power, all words occurring in more than 50% of the documents are removed. These are primarily often used words in general texts such as '*the*' or '*and*', as well as terms used frequently within a domain (as expressed by the document base), e.g., '*experiment*', '*molecule*', or '*cell*' in biology. Stemming further reduces the vocabulary size by unifying all flections of terms. A variety of stemmers for different applications is readily available.

2. *Creating word embeddings for entity contextualization.* Currently, word embeddings [12] are the state-of-the-art deep learning technique to map terms into a multi-dimensional space (usually about 200-400 dimensions are created), such that terms sharing the same context are grouped more closely. According to the distributional hypothesis, terms sharing the same context in larger samples of language data quite often, in general also share similar semantics (i.e. have similar meaning). In this sense, word embeddings group entities sharing the same context and thus

---

[5] https://deeplearning4j.org/.

collecting the nearest embeddings of some search entity leads to a group of entities sharing similar semantics.

3. *Filtering according to entity types.* The computed word embeddings comprise at this point a large portion of the corpus vocabulary. This means, for each vocabulary term there is exactly one word vector representation as output of the previous step. Each vector representation starts with the term followed by individual values for each dimension. In contrast, classical facets only display information of the same type, such as publication venues, (co-)authors, or related entities like genes or enzymes. Thus, for the actual building of facets, we only vector representations of the same entity type are needed. Here, dictionaries are needed to sort through the vocabulary for each type of entity separately. The dictionaries either can be directly gained from domain ontologies, like e.g. MeSH for illnesses, can be identified by named entity recognizers like e.g., the Open Source Chemistry Analysis Routines (OSCAR, see [13]) for chemical entities, or can be extracted from open collections in the domain, like the DrugBank for drugs.

4. *Clustering entity vector representations.* The last step is preparing the actual facettation of entities closely related to some search entity. To do this, we first consolidate the individual document spaces of the filtered entities by multidimensional scaling (reducing its dimensionality to about 100-150). This steep dimensionality reduction removes noise and enables a meaningful subsequent clustering. We then apply a k-means clustering technique on all representations and decide for good cluster sizes: in our approach optimal cluster sizes are not decided by a fixed threshold, but by an analysis of intra-cluster vs. inter-cluster similarity

While the basic algorithm promises to be applicable for a wide variety of domains, testing its effectiveness in creating high quality entity facets needs a domain specific focus. The following section evaluates our approach in a pharmaceutical use case.

4   Evaluation of Entity Contextualization

For the evaluation, we will first describe our pharmaceutical text corpus and basic experimental set-up decisions. Moreover, we perform a ground truth comparison and show the meaningfulness of the facets automatically derived by our facettation method: we compare results with the three established classification systems from Sect. 2.

4.1   Experimental Setup and Algorithm Implementation

Experimental Setup

Evaluation corpus. With more than 27 million document citations, *PubMed*[6] is the largest and most comprehensive digital library in the biomedical field. However, since many documents citations do not feature full texts, we relied solely on abstracts for learning purposes. As an intuition, the number of abstracts matching each

---

[6] https://www.ncbi.nlm.nih.gov/pubmed/.

pharmaceutical entity under consideration should be 'high enough' because with more training data, contexts that are more accurate can be learned, yet the computational complexity grows. Thus, we decided to use the 1000 most relevant abstracts for each entity according to the relevance weighting of PubMed's search engine.

Query Entities. As query entities for the evaluation, we randomly selected 275 drugs from the *DrugBank*[7] collection. We ensured that each selected drug featured at least one class label in ATC, MeSH, or AHFS, and occurred in at least 1000 abstracts on PubMed. Thus, our final document set for evaluation contained 275.000 abstracts. As ground truth, all class labels were crawled from both, *DrugBank* and the *MeSH thesaurus.*[8] For example, all retrieved classes for the drug '*Acyclovir*' are shown in Table 1. Since all classification systems show a too fine-grained hierarchical structure, we remove all finer levels before assigning the respective class label to each drug. For example, one of the ATC classes for the drug 'Acyclovir' is '*D06BB53*'. The first letter indicates the anatomical main group, where '*D*' stands for 'dermatologicals'. The next level consists of two digits '*06*' expressing the therapeutic subgroup 'antibiotics and chemotherapeutics for dermatological use'. Each further level classifies the object even more precisely, until the finest level usually uniquely identifies a drug.

Table 1. Classes in different classification systems for the drug 'Acyclovir'

Classification System	Assigned Classes
ATC	J05AB01, D06BB53, D06BB03, S01AD03
AHFS	08:18.32, 84:04.06
MeSH Trees	D03.633.100.759.758.399.454.250

Algorithm implementation and parameter settings

1. *Text Preprocessing:* Stemming and stop-word removal was performed using a *Lucene*[9] index. For stemming we used Lucene's *Porter Stemmer* implementation.
2. *Word Embeddings*: After preprocessing, word embeddings were created with DeepLearning4 J's *Word2Vec*[10] implementation. To train the neural network, we used a minimum word frequency of 5 occurrences. We set the word window size to 20 and the layer size to 200 features per word. Training iterations were set to 4. We tested several settings, but the above-mentioned turned out best for subsequent clustering.
3. *Entity filtering.* While Word2Vec generated a comprehensive list of word vector representations, we subsequently filtered out all vectors not related to any DrugBank entity (resulting in 275 entity-vectors). For corpus consolidation

---

[7] https://www.drugbank.ca/.

[8] https://meshb.nlm.nih.gov/search.

[9] https://lucene.apache.org/.

[10] https://deeplearning4j.org/word2vec.

(dimensionality reduction) after the filtering step, we used a *Multidimensional Scaling* (MDS[11]) technique: we scaled word vector representations from 200 down to 120 dimensions. The intention of the MDS step was to smooth out possible noise. Smoothing out noise in high-dimensional representations can have a positive impact on overall performance [15]. Whereby overall performance means in our case an improvement in F-score. Compared to unscaled entity-vectors, the MDS step resulted in an improvement of $\sim$ 10% in F1-score. In addition, we tested the MDS with different parameters, with respect to F1-score best results were achieved with a scaling to 120 dimensions. Surprisingly, an initial layer size setting of 120 features (for Word2Vec training) did not lead to a similar improvement. Instead the result was comparable to results achieved with a layer size setting of 200 features but without an additional MDS step. We conclude that the improvement in F1-score is the consequence of the MDS step.

For the MDS step, we also experimented with different similarity measures to calculate the dissimilarity matrix: best results were achieved using cosine similarity to calculate the matrix.

4. *Clustering vector representations.* In this step, we clustered the 275 entity vector representations obtained in the previous filtering step. For the clustering step we used Apache Commons' Multi-KMeans[12] ++ clusterer. For a fair comparison to our ground truth, our goal is to choose the class most suitable for a drug as well as for the entire cluster. Thus, for comparing class labels of entities within a cluster, we assign the majority class label to each cluster and regard all entities in that cluster sharing the majority label as true positives. To avoid double counting these true positives as false positives for additional labels they carry, we strip all remaining class labels. Entities in a class not sharing the majority class label are false positives and will be labeled with their respective label that is most frequent in that class. Again, to avoid double counting all other labels are removed.

4.2   Experimental Evaluation

For the experimental evaluation, we first have to determine what quality criteria a document-centric contextualization approach should meet to be useful for dynamically creating entity facets. Since the subsequent facettation will be based on the clusters generated by our approach (i.e. for each query entity all other entities sharing its cluster will be presented in the facet), each cluster has to exhibit certain criteria:

- *Semantic accuracy*: A facet should group entities under some *common theme* that seems most suitable with respect to the query entity. This is influenced by the semantic purity of clusters as well as a good trade-off between precision and recall. Since higher recall values might produce overly large facets, the emphasis should rather be on reaching higher precision values.
- *Semantic coverage*: For a good handling of the subsequent facets, the distribution of entities over the clusters should be *well balanced*. Clusterings exhibiting many large

---

[11] http://algo.uni-konstanz.de/software/mdsj/.

[12] http://commons.apache.org/proper/commons-math/.

and/or many small clusters will result in unsatisfactory usage experience in the respective faceted interface.

- *Semantic suitability*: The selected entities per facet should be *clearly justified* by the underlying document collection. Since there are different document-centered approaches, a quantitative comparison regarding a ground truth is needed.

Semantic Accuracy of the Facettation: In our first experiment, we test the semantic accuracy of our facettation, i.e. how well do entities in each cluster reflect a common topic. Since this is obviously dependent on cluster sizes (smaller clusters inherently show higher purity) and the respective granularity of the topic (in the sense of semantic distances), we will vary both, the *number of clusters* in the clustering procedure and the *granularity* of the topics (first level vs. second level accuracy). As ground truth, we use only the categories given by the largest three pharmaceutical classification systems ATC, MeSH, and AHFS (see Sect. 2). Please note that this ground truth restriction is overly strict on document-centered contextualization, since commonly understood contexts reflected in literature might not be reflected by any of the three systems. Thus, our experiments can be seen as a worst-case boundary for our approach.

First, we quantify the accuracy in terms of precision/recall and F-measures on the top categorization level only. We use the standard method for clustering accuracy described in [14]. Because facets should tend towards higher precision for improved user experience, we report both, F1- and F0.5-scores. We vary the number of clusters (k) in our k-means clustering between 10 and 80. Since the randomly chosen query entities might not be evenly distributed over the respective categories chosen as majority labels, we compare our approach against a base line of clusters, where items have been randomly exchanged between clusters. If there would be clearly dominant categories, such a random baseline would show high accuracies.

Figure 1 shows averaged results of 30 independent runs for each number of clusters. As could be expected, precision steeply increases for higher numbers of clusters (i.e. small cluster sizes), whereas recall decreases the more clusters are built. However, the F-scores show a clear optimum at 25 clusters (F1-score) and 35 clusters (F0.5-score). Hence, preferring smaller cluster sizes (on average of 8-10 entities per facet) in stark contrast to the random baseline that always prefers the smallest number of clusters possible. Moreover, our approach's F-scores constantly outperform the baselines with 0.55 (F1-score) and 0.65 (F0.5-score) reaching precisions beyond 80%. Thus, surprisingly our generalist approach is even comparable in overall accuracy to approaches specifically designed to predict ATC or MeSH classifications, as reported in Sect. 2.

We repeated the above experiments for the second layer of granularity in the classification systems and achieved quite similar results (graphs have been omitted for space reasons), again clearly outperforming the baseline. Of course, with finer granularity the relative size of clusters has to be expected to be much lower. However, again measuring the F0.5-score, we achieved best results with a moderate 97 clusters at an accuracy level of still 0.61. This is only 4% less, compared to the first level of granularity. For the F1-score, best results were achieved with 69 clusters at an accuracy level of 0.55.

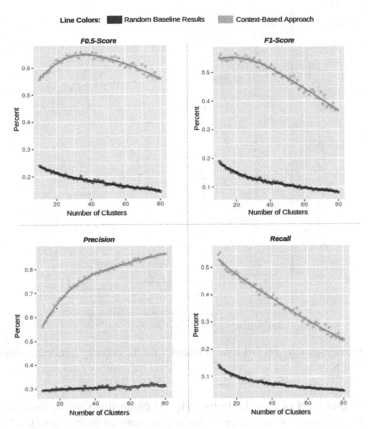

Fig. 1. Comparison of contextualized facettation (red) and random clustering (blue). (Color figure online)

Semantic coverage of the Facettation: To investigate how well the individual semantics of the different categorization systems are reflected by our contextualized facets, we show that our facettation is indeed balanced, i.e. it does not generate extreme distributions in either cluster sizes or majority label provenance. For instance, it would not be desirable, if our facettation created one single big facet, while the remaining facets only contain a single entity each. Moreover, the distribution of majority class label regarding their respective source classification system should be balanced.

Again, we performed experiments on two levels of granularity: top-level and second level. For the top-level granularity we calculated average cluster sizes for the sweet spot (i.e. at $k = 35$ clusters) of our last experiment and show the respective results as box plots in Fig. 2. As we can clearly see, there are only few larger clusters, while the majority of clusters features between 3 and 8 entities, with a median of 4.8. Clusters with sizes smaller than 3 are quite rare. Moreover, it is encouraging to note that the overall distribution of entities in clusters strongly resembles the distribution exhibited by the respective classification systems. That means, the cluster sizes decided by our deep learning-based contextualization are on the correct resolution level, which together with the high accuracy speaks for a good semantic coverage.

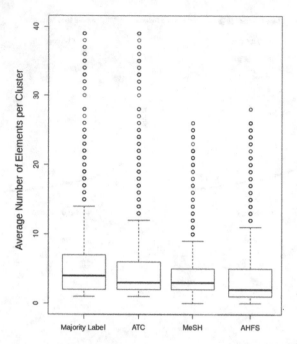

Fig. 2. Average cluster sizes on first level granularity for the majority label compared to ATC, MeSH, and AHFS.

On the second level of granularity (see Fig. 3) the medians of the distributions are noticeably lower, as was to be expected for higher number of clusters ($k = 97$). Still, our approach's distribution again closely resembles the distributions of the respective classification system. Moreover, in contrast to MeSh and AHFS our approach avoids empty clusters and shows fewer outliers with large cluster sizes, quite similar to the ATC classification system.

Looking at the provenance of majority cluster labels we find that on top-level granularity the majority labels chosen for each cluster on average reflect 60.3% from ATC classes, 34.3% from MeSh tree classes, and 5.4% from AHFS classes. For second level granularity, we get 51.8% from ATC, 36.8% from MeSh, and 11.4% from AHFS. Thus, our contextualization approach does indeed reflect different semantics as given by the individual, manually created classification systems.

Semantic suitability of the Facettation: In our last experiment, we compare the clustering accuracy of our approach with the accuracy achieved by classical IR techniques based on term frequencies. Hence, we computed a TF-IDF-weighted vector space model on all pharmaceutical texts in our selected document corpus for the 275 query entities, again followed by a k-means clustering step. We then compared the respective accuracies of the two methods with respect to the three manual classification systems as ground truth.

In the clustering step for the top-level granularity, also TF-IDF shows highest accuracy values for a number of 35 clusters and thus seems quite suitable for the task.

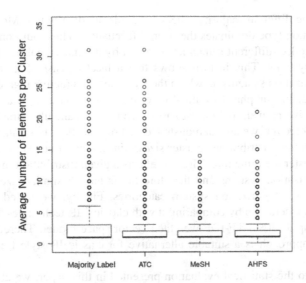

Fig. 3. Average cluster sizes on second level granularity for the majority label compared to ATC, MeSH, and AHFS.

However, in comparison with a TF-IDF-weighted vector space model, the contextualized facets achieved noticeable improvements with respect to accuracies: the F0.5-score was on average 30% higher, and the F1-score still 18% higher. In brief, our deep learning-based approach leads to a much higher precision as compared to classic IR-style frequency-based approaches.

5 Conclusions and Future Work

In this paper, we presented a novel deep learning-based technique to contextualize entities for building semantically meaningful facettations in pharmaceutical collections. In pharmaceutical digital libraries, substance similarity forms the basis for various innovative services for information access such as finding active ingredients or structure search. Today, substance similarity is based either on manually curated semantic classification systems, or on comparisons of the underlying chemical structures. Both methods are extremely useful, but on the one hand chemical structure approaches do not capture important semantic features, on the other hand most active ingredients are not classified by manually curated categorization systems.

We demonstrated in our experiments, that our proposed method for a new facettation of active ingredients, achieves a high semantic accuracy. Since, on both levels of granularity, our approach constantly outperforms the baselines as well as reaches high precisions (beyond 80%). Thus, our facettation method clusters active ingredients in a meaningful way and therefore elements, contained in the same facet, share with a high accuracy a similar semantic. Next, we proved the sematic coverage of the facettation by investigating how well the individual semantics of the different categorization systems are reflected by our contextualized facets. Here, on both levels of granularity the different majority labels are moderate distributed. Moderate means, none categorization type dominates the overall facettation. Thus, our contextualization approach does reflect different semantics as given by the individual, manually curated categorization systems. This in turn shows that a facet consist of a composition of different categorization systems, in which the facet elements (active ingredients) share a similar semantic. In our pharmaceutical case, the facettation can be a suitable alternative to expensive as well as in most cases incomplete manually curated categorization systems. Moreover, we also demonstrated that our facettation is balanced and does not generate extreme distributions cluster sizes. Since, small (cluster size < 3) as well as very large cluster are quite rare. Thus, it reflects a given distribution in respect to the different categorization systems and therefore facets have a similar size compared to manually curated categorization system categories. Finally, we tested the semantic suitability of the facettation by comparing it with classical IR techniques. Our approach outperformed (up to 30%) TF-IDF-weighted vector space model. Therefore, our deep learning-based approach is a suitable alternative for classic IR-style frequency-based approaches.

In addition to the statistical evaluation presented in this paper, we also questioned domain experts for a first interpretation of our facettation. Surprisingly, they found hidden semantics for some of the low-accuracy facets. This may indicate that our facettation technique is able to discover hidden active ingredient contexts. A better understanding of such hidden contexts would be interesting. Furthermore, labeling of facets was however not considered in this paper. Such a labeling would prove quite useful for an interpretation of the individual facets as well as it could lead to a better understanding with respect to our facettation.

References

1. Willett, P., Barnard, J.M., Downs, G.M.: Chemical similarity searching. J. Chem. Inf. Comput. Sci. **38**(6), 983–996 (1998)
2. Tönnies, S., Köhncke, B., Balke, W.T.: Taking chemistry to the task: personalized queries for chemical digital libraries. In: Proceedings of the ACM/IEEE Joint Conference on Digital Libraries (JCDL 2011), Ottawa, Canada (2011)
3. Wishart, D.S., Knox, C., Guo, A.C., Shrivastava, S., Hassanali, M., Stothard, P., Chang, Z., Woolsey, J.: DrugBank: a comprehensive resource for in silico drug discovery and exploration. Nucleic Acids Res. **34**(1), D668–D672 (2006). Database issue
4. Sacco, G.M., Tzitzikas, Y.: Dynamic Taxonomies and Faceted Search: Theory, Practice, and Experience. Springer, Heidelberg (2009). doi:10.1007/978-3-642-02359-0
5. Köhncke, B., Balke, W.-T.: Context-sensitive ranking using cross-domain knowledge for chemical digital libraries. In: Aalberg, T., Papatheodorou, C., Dobreva, M., Tsakonas, G., Farrugia, C.J. (eds.) TPDL 2013. LNCS, vol. 8092, pp. 285–296. Springer, Heidelberg (2013). doi:10.1007/978-3-642-40501-3_29
6. Gonzalez Pinto, J.M., Balke, W.T.: Demystifying the semantics of relevant objects in scholarly collections: a probabilistic approach. In: Proceedings of the ACM/IEEE Joint Conference on Digital Libraries (JCDL), Knoxville, TN, USA (2015)
7. Gurulingappa, H., Kolárik, C., Hofmann-Apitius, M., Fluck, J.: Concept-based semi-automatic classification of drugs. J. Chem. Inf. Model. **49**(8), 1986–1992 (2009)

8. Dunkel, M., Günther, S., Ahmed, J., Wittig, B., Preissner, R.: SuperPred: drug classification and target prediction. Nucleic Acids Res. **36**(suppl 2), W55–W59 (2008)
9. Trieschnigg, D., Pezik, P., Lee, V., De Jong, F., Kraaij, W., Rebholz-Schuhmann, D.: MeSH Up: effective MeSH text classification for improved document retrieval. Bioinformatics **25** (11), 1412–1418 (2009). Oxford University Press
10. Dumais, S.T.: Latent semantic analysis. In: Annual Review of Information Science and Technology (ARIST), Association for Information Science & Technology, vol. 38, no. 1 (2004)
11. Blei, D.M., Ng, A.Y., Jordan, M.I.: Latent dirichlet allocation. J. Mach. Learn. Res. **3**(Jan), 993–1022 (2003). MIT Press
12. Mikolov, T., Sutskever, I., Chen, K., Corrado, G.S., Dean, J.: Distributed representations of words and phrases and their compositionality. In: Proceedings of the Annual Conference on Neural Information Processing Systems (NIPS), Lake Tahoe, NV, USA (2013)
13. Jessop, D.M., Adams, S.E., Willighagen, E.L., Hawizy, L., Murray-Rust, P.: OSCAR4: a flexible architecture for chemical text-mining. J. Cheminform. **3**(1), 41 (2011). Springer
14. Manning, C.D., Raghavan, P., Schütze, H.: Introduction to Information Retrieval. Cambridge University Press, Cambridge (2008)
15. Borg, I., Groenen, P.J.: Modern Multidimensional Scaling: Theory and Applications. Springer, Heidelberg (2005). doi:10.1007/0-387-28981-X

Cultural Heritage and Indigenous Knowledge

A Foundry of Human Activities and Infrastructures

Robert B. Allen[✉], Eunsang Yang, and Tatsawan Timakum

Yonsei University, Seoul, South Korea
rballen@yonsei.ac.kr, esy220@nyu.edu,
tatsawan@gmail.com

Abstract. Direct representation knowledgebases can enhance and even provide an alternative to document-centered digital libraries. Here we consider realist semantic modeling of everyday activities and infrastructures in such knowledgebases. Because we want to integrate a wide variety of topics, a collection of ontologies (a foundry) and a range of other knowledge resources are needed. We first consider modeling the routine procedures that support human activities and technologies. Next, we examine the interactions of technologies with aspects of social organization. Then, we consider approaches and issues for developing and validating explanations of the relationships among various entities.

Keywords: Community models · Digital humanities · Direct representation · Faceted ontologies · Histories · Social science · Tangible and intangible culture heritage

1 Infrastructures, Human Activities, Community Models, and Cultures

In [1] and related studies we explored indexing digitized historical newspapers. It was difficult to index the articles for retrieval or, even, to unambiguously identify what text should be treated as an article. Thus, we proposed the development of knowledge-rich "community models" to improve retrieval. Many aspects of infrastructure associated with everyday activities and infrastructure generally can be described with such community models. Such models would cover both tangible and intangible cultural heritage such as pottery, clothing, dance, and religious traditions.

This work is parallel to a proposal we have made for direct representation of scientific research results [4]. However, there are additional challenges for descriptions of culture and history because of the lack of consensus about the definitions for social entities and because there are disagreements about the details of cultures and histories. Nonetheless, as information scientists, we believe that it is useful to develop frameworks for articulating and exploring the possibilities. Ultimately such frameworks should support tools both for the public and for scholars.

© Springer International Publishing AG 2017
S. Choemprayong et al. (Eds.): ICADL 2017, LNCS 10647, pp. 57–64, 2017.
https://doi.org/10.1007/978-3-319-70232-2_5

2 Ontologies and Models

2.1 Upper Ontologies and the Model Layer

The knowledge representation system for direct representation must go beyond simple linked data to incorporate structured knowledge from many domains. To provide a framework we use an upper or formal ontology, specifically, the Basic Formal Ontology (BFO) [7]. BFO is widely applied for biomedical ontologies. It is a carefully designed, realist ontology which follows Aristotle in distinguishing between Universals and Particulars. BFO also distinguishes between Continuants (those Entities which are constant across time) and Occurrents (those Entities which change across time).

We have proposed extending BFO with a Model Layer [5] that gives it aspects of object-oriented modeling.[1] The Model Layer considers Thick Entities, which are Independent Continuants, together with their associated Dependent Continuants, Parts, and Processes[2]. Such Thick Entities should allow for States and State Changes. Such States and State Changes would not be first-class ontology entities; rather, they can be defined as derived entities [5]. If they were formalized to include State Changes, Processes could be considered as analogous to "abstract methods" in object-oriented programming. The Model Layer would also include Mechanisms and Procedures[3]. The Model Layer should be able to show how Thick Entities interact with other Thick Entities much as the objects in an object-oriented program interact when the program is executed.

2.2 Foundries as Knowledgebases and Extended Foundries

The Open Biomedical Ontology (OBO) Foundry [22] is a large curated collection of domain ontologies and partonomies based on the BFO.[4] We propose the development of a similar foundry to cover human activities and infrastructures. Because "direct representation" follows BFO as a realist approach, our focus is first on describing

---

[1] In some cases, "object-oriented" simply means entity or object-based. We use "object-oriented" in the stronger, programming-language sense of objects that include specific processes and procedures.

[2] The descriptions of Thick Entities we envision are analogous to the descriptions of Model or Reference Organisms. The latter often includes anatomies (i.e., partonomies) and, less often, descriptions of related Procedures and Mechanisms.

[3] A Mechanism describes how a Process is implemented. A Procedure is like a workflow with flow control and decision points. There is no direct way for BFO to represent control statements such as loops and conditionals needed for Procedures, although it is possible to represent control statements with OWL on an ad hoc basis and to use those representations in combination with BFO. A pure BFO modeling language should be developed that, like the C programming language, is self-compiling.

The distinction in some object-oriented languages between "private methods" and "public methods" can also be applied to Thick Entities. Private methods are those which interact internally only with other Parts of a given Thick Entity whereas Public Methods support interaction with other Thick Entities.

[4] obofoundry.org, obofoundry.org/docs/OperationsCommittee.html.

infrastructure objects, their use and their interaction with other objects. The role of entities in collections and records are important but secondary [6].

3 Material Technologies and Infrastructure

The contents of historical newspapers and other historical records for small towns often describe entities and activities which are routine, even mundane. A partial list of such entities and activities includes roads, farming, fishing, blacksmithing, weaving, coin minting, pottery making, and bookbinding. Each of these is associated with specific types of objects and procedures.

There are many levels for representing and modeling everyday human activities. At a general level, we might describe infrastructures and technologies for supporting basic human needs such as food and shelter. Such models could be increasingly refined as they are applied to specific scenarios. While Aristotle focused on Universals as natural entities, BFO has included human artifacts related to scientific research such as flasks. We further extend the scope of Universals to include all types of human artifacts.

As noted above, we also propose using model oriented Thick Entities for these descriptions. Thick Entities would include Processes and Procedures. There is a complex web of interactions in Processes and Procedures. For instance, farming procedures are affected by the availability of different metals for plows. Similarly, the introduction of a train line may dramatically affect a community (cf., [1]).

The development of a large and internally consistent collection of infrastructure entities will require a major effort that is in its early stages. Ontologies and other controlled vocabularies have been developed for many entities and functions; for instance, FGDC (fgdc.gov) provides descriptions for highways. Similarly, standard descriptions for Mechanisms and Procedures such as from the *Handbook of Synthetic Organic Chemistry* could also be included. Some aspects of Human Activities and Infrastructures (such as farming or silkworm cultivation) could be linked in the OBO. Ultimately the foundries should be unified.

4 Structures and Activities Within a Given Social Framework

While the previous section focused on material technologies and infrastructures, ultimately, it will not be possible to separate the technologies and infrastructures from their interaction with social activities. Social structures may be considered as entities in a social ontology.[5]

---

[5] Smith (Social Objects, http://ontology.buffalo.edu/socobj.htm) claims that social entities are entirely consistent with the BFO framework. There has been significant work on social ontology by some of the designers of the BFO framework but there does not yet seem to have been a concerted effort to directly integrate that work into the BFO. Much of the discussion about social ontologies for BFO has focused on commitments and obligations [21]. Other specific proposals have focused on contracts, economics, and social aspects of medicine [14].

There are many examples of the interaction of material infrastructure with social entities. For example, textiles play an important role in traditional Thai society [8]; the fabrics are integral to courtship, marriage, death, and a variety of Buddhist rituals. A structured description of the materials and technologies would include aspects of fabrics and weaving tools and techniques as well as their role in society.

In addition to tangible cultural heritage such as Thai silks, some cultural heritage like dance and music can be both tangible and intangible. On one hand, musical instruments are Continuants but musical performances are Occurrents. Moreover, music also has a social dimension. For example, descriptions of Korean music (gugak) need to include social distinctions between different genres (e.g., folk music vs. court music) [16].

In many contexts, the models of the social framework would generally be from the perspective of the participants. For historical local newspapers [1], we would generally follow the presentation of the newspaper editors in developing models of schools, businesses, government, churches, and families. Of course, there are frequently alternative interpretations beyond the normative descriptions. Therefore, flexible frameworks would need to be developed to present and contrast differing viewpoints.

5 Explanations and Social Science

We have described how material infrastructures are interrelated and dependent on each other. Beyond those simple descriptions, we can explore claims about the relationships among components of the material and social infrastructures at the level of both Universals and Particulars. However, in many cases, the relationships are complex and not susceptible to proof. For instance, culture can be described as a web of relationships [11]. We need to develop a flexible framework for making claims and demonstrations about possible relationships and mechanisms (cf., [9, 10]) as well as showing the arguments and evidence for those claims.

To understand the relationships among Universal Entities in the physical world, we turned to natural science [4]. For social entities, we could turn to social science. This is reasonable since we accept the position that social entities are "real". Moreover, to the extent that social science makes causal predictions, we can use those predictions to confirm the validity of Entities. For physical phenomena, this type of confirmation of Entities is known as scientific warrant. Because there is more uncertainty about social science models, we may express our lower level of confidence for social entities by referring instead to consistency warrant.

In sociology, there are several grand theories, or major theoretical frameworks. Social ontology is a central aspect of each of these theories because they propose theoretical constructs and relationships among the constructs. Here, we focus on Parsons's AGIL [17] which asserts that there are four essential attributes a society must have to endure:

- **Adaptive:** This describes the need to adjust to the environment. Both shelter and farming would be considered as part of the Adaptive dimension. It covers many of the human needs identified by [16].

- **Goal Oriented:** This requires specification and accomplishment of social goals, and would include regulations, laws, and politics.
- **Integration:** This describes cohesion of the social group such as through family, religion, and language.
- **Latency:** A social group must renew its customs, knowledge, and values for the next generation through education.

Parsons's work is an application of Systems Theory to sociology (cf., [5]) and is often described as structure-functionalist[6]. Following our analysis of functionality, we propose that the Function of an Independent Continuant produces (or prevents) a State Change in a specific Independent Continuant-Process pair [5].[7] Thus, we might say:

- The Function of a ladle is to carry liquids.
- The Functions of Court music are to entertain and to impress guests. (Integration)
- The Function of certain types of physical structures (e.g. a house) is to shelter the inhabitants. (Adaptive)
- The Function of the education subsystem is to transmit knowledge. (Latency)

This description of Parsons's work just scratches the surface; for instance, he has an extensive discussion of the function of the family. It may be possible to develop a structured version of his entire framework. However, we should also note that among sociologists, there is disagreement about the value of the AGIL system.

Our emphasis on realism for social entities is also relevant to anthropology. We might first focus on the social science perspective to anthropology rather than the humanities perspective [18] (cf., [20]). Thus, we might emphasize archaeology and physical anthropology. Nonetheless, many entities and social activities such as rituals and icons that are the subject of anthropology clearly have deep symbolic, aesthetic, and emotional significance which we would need to account for.

6   Models of Particulars

One of the main goals of our direct representation approach is to provide highly-structured descriptions of specific cultures and histories. BFO defines Histories as a type of Occurrent [9]. Histories are said to be all the Processes associated with a given Continuant. This is an elegant definition but it tells us little about the relationships among those Processes.

Much of the discussion about the nature of historical explanations revolves around the notion from Hempel of a "covering law" which requires that any change should be justified (i.e., covered) by a law or reason for its occurrence. The expectation that there should be broad covering laws to account for events in history and culture has been

---

[6] A full Functionalist model could have a web of Functions that address Needs. Mechanisms which satisfy Needs may themselves generate new Needs. BFO seems to lean toward a Structuralist view but its inclusion of Procedures with an object-oriented flavor suggests it could become more Functionalist.

[7] For an internally consistent ontology/model, all terms in the definitions should also be included in the ontology.

widely criticized. Instead, Roberts [19] proposes that most major historical events (e.g., revolutions) do not have a single over-arching covering theory but are composed of smaller events each of which can be accounted for with covering theories. [12] makes a similar point, that claims about causal relationships among social phenomena need to be supported by models of mechanisms for how the entities interact.[8]

Because social situations are complex and because Thick Entities are generally composed of many parts it may be difficult to confirm causal processes. For instance, while it is easy to believe that the prosperity in the Roman Empire during the reign of the Antonine Emperors was due to their good policies [13], we cannot make that case with scientific rigor. After documenting the evidence, we may apply the generalization only while retaining some caution about it.

7 Repositories and Knowledgebases

Just as [4] proposed a variety of interrelated repositories for scientific research, similar interlocking repositories will be needed to complement the foundry of everyday activities and infrastructures. There would be several layers of knowledge resources:

- **Ontology and Model Foundry:** The everyday Human Activities and Infrastructures Foundry would include not only ontologies but also models of Thick Entities. The complete Foundry will require details of many different types of Procedures. In addition to the ontologies, the Foundry might include Reference Models such as of Bronze Age communities or Midwestern U.S. towns.

  We may not have full confidence in some of the Universals because there are competing theoretical frameworks. Thus, we may allow alternative representations using several of those frameworks. Related to this, we may apply a weaker consistency warrant rather than scientific warrant as a criterion for inclusion.

  Ontologies based on the BFO can be considered a type of classification system; after all, each BFO ontology is a taxonomy. A collection of BFO ontologies (i.e., a Foundry) can be viewed as an entity-based faceted classification.[9]

- **Models of Particulars:** See Sect. 6 above.

- **Primary Source Materials:** [3] called for cleaned and consistent repositories of historical source material. Moreover, these materials should have standard markup. In addition, databases of locations, climate, records, economic data, census reports, sports scores can also be coordinated with the Foundry ontologies and models.

---

[8] Much of what is termed systems analysis appears focused more on process re-engineering than on systematic analysis of existing systems. Case studies can support what might properly be considered as systems analysis. Specifically, convergent case studies can be useful to evaluate possible causal mechanisms [12].

[9] The links of other entities (such as Locations, Dependent Continuants, and Processes) to the Object forms a sort of faceting. Indeed, it is easy to see the similarity to Raganathan's PMEST and to FrameNet's Frame Elements [2]. However, such entity-based faceting should be distinguished from other faceted classification systems which are subject based.

- **Evidence, and Argumentation:** The evaluation of internal and external validity was a major factor in our discussion of scientific research reports [4]. We should have a similar focus here. For instance, [12] describes issues for the use of case studies in social science; we could develop an argumentation schema to organize and save evaluations of the validity of case studies.
- **Annotations, Secondary Materials, and Indexes:** Given that the foundry should be coordinated with other relevant repositories, we should allow annotations and include secondary materials. Potentially, structured direct representation would support many services such as supporting text and narrative generation for discourse functions such as explanation and argumentation.

8 Discussion

We have examined issues for collecting and coordinating applied ontologies and models for Everyday Human Activities and Infrastructures. These ontologies and models build on the rigorous semantics of the BFO and extend the constraints of BFO to everyday infrastructures and then to social and cultural descriptions. To do that, we relax some of the constraints but we expect that these will be flagged appropriately. This effort is as much about developing a useful information resource as about maintaining the purity of the ontological framework.

References

1. Allen, R.B.: Toward an Interactive Directory for Norfolk, Nebraska: 1899–1900. IFLA Newspaper and Genealogy Section Meeting, Singapore (2013). arXiv:1308.5395
2. Allen, R.B.: Frame-Based Models of Communities and Their History. In: Nadamoto, A., Jatowt, A., Wierzbicki, A., Leidner, J.L. (eds.) SocInfo 2013. LNCS, vol. 8359, pp. 110–119. Springer, Heidelberg (2014). Histoinformatics. doi:10.1007/978-3-642-55285-4_9
3. Allen, R.B.: Issues for direct representation of history. In: ICADL 2016, pp. 218–224. doi:10.1007/978-3-319-49304-6_26
4. Allen, R.B.: Rich semantic models and knowledgebases for highly-structured scientific communication (2017). arXiv:1708.08423
5. Allen, R.B.: Rich semantic modeling, in preparation
6. Allen, R.B., Song, H., Lee, B.E., Lee, J.Y.: Describing scholarly information resources with a unified temporal map. In: ICADL 2106, pp. 212–217. doi:10.1007/978-3-319-49304-6_25
7. Arp, R., Smith, B., Spear, A.D.: Building Ontologies with Basic Formal Ontology. MIT Press, Cambridge (2015). http://purl.obolibrary.org/obo/bfo/Reference
8. Conway, S.: Thai Textiles. British Museum Press, London (1992)
9. Chu, Y.M., Allen, R.B.: Formal representation of socio-legal roles and functions for the description of history. In: TPDL, pp. 379–385 (2016). doi:10.1007/978-3-319-43997-6_30
10. Diamond, J.: Guns, Germs, and Steel. Norton, New York (1997)
11. Gasser, L.: Information and collaboration from a social/organizational perspective. In: Nof, S.Y. (ed.) Information and Collaboration Models of Integration, pp. 237–261. Kluwer, the Netherlands (1994)

12. George, A.L., Bennett, A.: Case Studies and Theory Development in the Social Sciences. MIT Press, Cambridge (2004)
13. Gibbon, E.: The History of the Decline and Fall of the Roman Empire (1845). www.gutenberg.org/files/731/731-h/731-h.htm
14. Jansen, L.: Four rules for classifying social entities. In: Hagengruber, R., Riss, U. (eds.) Philosophy, Computing and Information Science, pp. 189–200. Pickering & Chatto, London (2014)
15. Lee, B.W., Lee, Y.S. (eds.): Music of Korea. National Center for Korean Traditional Performing Arts, Seoul (2007)
16. Maslow, A.H.: A theory of human motivation. Psychol. Rev. **50**, 370–396 (1943)
17. Parsons, T.: The Structure of Social Action. Free Press, Boston (1968)
18. Peregrine, P., Moses, Y.T., Goodman, A., Lamphere, L., Peacock, J.L.: What is science in anthropology? Am. Anthropol. **114**, 593–597 (2012). doi:10.1111/j.1548-1433.2012.01510.x
19. Roberts, C.: The Logic of Historical Explanation. Pennsylvania State University Press, State College (1995)
20. Schilbrack, K.: A realist social ontology of religion. J. Relig. **27**, 161–178 (2017). doi:10.1080/0048721X.2016.1203834
21. Smith, B.: Searle and de Soto: the new ontology of the social world. In: Smith, B., Mark, D., Ehrlich, I. (eds) The Mystery of Capital and the Construction of Social Reality, Open Court (2015). http://ontology.buffalo.edu/document_ontology/Searle&deSoto.pdf
22. Smith, B., Ashburner, M., Rosse, C., Bard, J., Bug, W., Ceusters, W., Goldberg, L.J., Eilbeck, K., Ireland, A., Mungall, C.J., Leontis, N., Rocca-Serra, P., Ruttenberg, A., Sansone, S.A., Scheuermann, R.H., Shah, N., Whetzel, P.L., Lewis, S.: The OBO foundry: coordinated evolution of ontologies to support biomedical data integration. Nat. Biotechnol. **25**, 1251–1255 (2007). doi:10.1038/nbt1346

Conceptualising the Digitisation and Preservation of Indigenous Knowledge: The Importance of Attitudes

Eric Boamah[1] and Chern Li Liew[2(✉)]

[1] School of Health and Social Science, Open Polytechnic,
Wellington, New Zealand
Eric.Boamah@openpolytechnic.ac.nz
[2] School of Information Management, Victoria University of Wellington,
Wellington, New Zealand
ChernLi.Liew@vuw.ac.nz

Abstract. In this paper, we discuss factors that influence the digitisation of cultural heritage resources and outline differences in the challenges faced by memory institutions in developed and developing countries.

Increasingly, memory institutions (galleries, libraries, archives and museum) are taking advantage of digital technologies, including social Web technologies to digitise, share and preserve heritage resources to create national repositories with the hope of eliminating gaps in future memory. They also seek opportunities to engage with and involve owners of cultural heritage resources and key stakeholders in the digitisation of their heritage collections. Nevertheless, memory institutions have faced various challenges in doing so.

In developed countries, memory institutions are mainly challenged by how to navigate the enormity of the collections that need to be digitised and preserved. In developing countries, different forms of negative attitudes towards digitisation hinder progress in digital preservation management. Owners of cultural heritage resources fear permanent loss of their heritage, key stakeholders lack interest in heritage digitisation, and information professionals have conflicting ideas on how to go about the digitisation process. Our analysis reveals attitudinal issues can have a significant impact on digital preservation. Even though attitudinal issues have been mentioned in previous studies, they are often treated more at an implicit level. We argue that in the context of cultural heritage digitising and preserving involving source communities and various stakeholders, the attitudinal dimension ought to be a key consideration and as such, should be made explicit in discussion of these.

Keywords: Cultural heritage · Digitisation · Memory institutions · Developed countries · Developing countries · Indigenous knowledge · Source communities · Policy · Strategy · Resources

© Springer International Publishing AG 2017
S. Choemprayong et al. (Eds.): ICADL 2017, LNCS 10647, pp. 65–80, 2017.
https://doi.org/10.1007/978-3-319-70232-2_6

1 Introduction

Digital technologies that are used for generating, collecting, managing and preserving heritage knowledge are developing so rapidly that both information professionals and the institutions involved the management of heritage resources are concerned about possible gaps that can occur in the development of memory for the future. Some custodians of heritage resources and owners of cultural knowledge also fear they may lose their heritage resources through digitisation. Consequently, memory institutions face various challenges in their attempt to collaborate with people from sources communities and other key stakeholders to digitise and preserve cultural knowledge.

Memory institutions, including libraries and museums have become keen on opportunities to engage with potential partners and collaborators to develop heritage digitisation and preservation programmes. Examples of memory institutions' involvement with source communities include the Europeana project where various memory institutions across Europe collaborated to facilitate an innovative cultural knowledge transfer. The national library, national archive and national museum of New Zealand provide examples with what they are doing to preserve the cultural heritage of New Zealand. Through the efforts of these cultural institutions, New Zealand has now established a National Digital Heritage Archive (NDHA). The American Memory and the Australian Digital Collections are other examples of national digital memory projects that have all been developed through collaborations with people from source communities and key stakeholders.

The achievements of these cultural institutions are nevertheless not without challenges, especially as the digital technologies landscape is evolving quickly and memory institutions need to keep abreast. For instance, many archives, libraries and museums are exploring and experimenting with the use of social media and Web 2.0 technologies to enable participatory digital cultural heritage and indigenous knowledge management and are battling a range of issues [1]. For such participatory construction of cultural knowledge to be successful and to ensure the effective involvement of multiple source cultural communities in heritage digitisation and preservation, the various challenges and underlying issues need to be identified and dealt with. Appropriate planning, policies and strategies need to be developed and sufficient resources allocated accordingly. Also, there is the need to create more awareness among key stakeholders of the benefits of digital preservation [2]. In this paper, we examine various factors that influence the digitisation of cultural heritage resources and the challenges faced by memory institutions. We also seek to outline and discuss the differences in the challenges and issues faced by memory institutions in developed and developing countries. The discussions in this paper is guided by the following research questions:

- What are the contemporary challenges faced by memory institutions in digitising cultural heritage knowledge for preservation purposes, in both developing countries and developed countries?
- Are there any differences in challenges faced in these different contexts?

For our discussions in this paper, we use cases from New Zealand and Australia as examples from developed countries, and cases from Ghana as examples from a developing country perspective.

2   Literature Review

Preservation is a very complex phenomenon. Krtalic and Hassenay [3] (2012) observe that some of the contradictory issues affecting preservation management arise from the material properties of heritage resources themselves, environmental changes, funding possibilities, legal documents, selection criteria, user needs, presentation possibilities, cultural and historical values, national and international context, just to mention a few. These issues present significant challenges to memory institutions in their quest to undertake digitisation and digital preservation programmes and projects. Krtalic and Hassenay categorised these issues into five main clusters: strategic and theoretical, economic and legal, educational, technical and operational, and cultural and social [3]. These clusters of factors, according to Krtlic and Hassenay [3] provide starting points for improving the organisation of systematic preservation and management of heritage resources in developing country contexts.

Issues and challenges faced by memory institutions, including libraries, archives and museums, in digitising cultural heritage knowledge for preservation purposes can be seen from the stage of setting up the institution. For instance, various researchers in the literature have discussed the challenges that affect the establishment of digital libraries, [4–7]. Others have also looked at issues affecting the setting-up of digital museums [8–10] and problems relating to digital archives and records management [11–13]. From the onset, there are concerns on how to effectively setup the technical infrastructure, how to build the digital collection, how to fund the digitisation, dealing with metadata concerns, naming, identifiers, copyright issues, intellectual property issues, just to mention a few. It is important to identify potential problems and to understand how to deal with the specific issues around those problems [14]. Hence, in this section, we will explore the challenges that have been discussed within the literature relating to how memory institutions engage with their stakeholders (including source communities) to digital heritage resources for preservation purposes so that those issues can be highlighted for further empirical study to understand them deeper.

All cultural heritage institutions, including galleries, libraries, archives and museums (GLAM) play a role in information management by handling specific aspects in the preservation of cultural heritage of society. The roles performed by each member of the GLAM work towards the management of a common heritage for preservation purposes. In view of this, Mallan [15] identifies that the term collective memory is increasingly being used in the last decade to help with the recognition of the roles played by the various institutions in the GLAM sector. Each of these institutions is also seriously taking advantage of the improvements in digital technologies to incorporating digitisation in their activities to ensure the effective preservation and provision of access to cultural heritage resources.

As Huvila [16] observes, there has been an increasing political interest in memory institutions and the roles they play in contemporary society in the last couple of decades. However, contemporary GLAM professionals have divergent views of their roles their institutions. While Huvila [16] sees the diverse opinions and a number of practiced visions as useful for shaping and reshaping the roles of memory institutions, he also acknowledges that there is a lack of theoretical depth to function as a common ground explaining the roles of GLAM in modern society. The lack of common grounds can pose a threat for the building of a common memory for the future society and it can be seen as one of the important challenges faced by memory institutions today. The different opinions can hinder effective collaborations among memory institutions when it comes to digitising heritage resource for the purpose of preservation and developing the common memory. Cathro [17] examined opportunities for the different collecting institutions in Australia and found improved collaboration as well as effective models the support collaboration is the way forward for the GLAM sector.

Development of the new digital technologies is advancing very fast in modern times [18, 19]. Advancement in digital technologies also present memory institutions with both opportunities to take responsibility for their digital collections, including digit heritage resources and also provide challenges for the handling of digital infor-mation and indigenous knowledge for preservation [20, 21]. About a decade ago, memory institutions were identified also face some less technical challenges that need to be explored and understood. These challenges, whether technical or general, can sometimes lead to what Barker [22] describes as partial successes or failures of projects relating to digitisation of heritage resources for preservation purposes. Recognising the opportunities and challenges presented by the new digital technologies for memory institutions, Mallan [15] examined the specific benefits and challenges that arise in the process of digitising cultural heritage materials. She identifies digitisation as a new cultural tool that provide many benefits to cultural institutions. Some of the usefulness of digitisation include the following:

- Digitisation improves access and enhances preservation
- Ensuring the integrity of digital information over time
- Creating digital surrogates can facilitate traditional efforts to preserve cultural heritage objects
- Once digitised fragile or unstable items may be placed in secure temperature-controlled storage, reducing or preventing further deterioration through handling and use [15]

Mallan, classifies the challenges faced by memory institutions in digitising heritage resource into three areas relating to technology, interface and language. In most developing countries, both the institutions and their users have very limited access to the necessary digital technologies. Another issue Mallan identified as affecting access and use is language. Each culture is expressed in a unique and specific language, which can fully be understood by people associated with the culture. When digitised, heritage resources are made available online, language can be pose a challenge for outsiders to fully appreciate the digital heritage resources and possibly, to interpret them accord-ingly (i.e. appropriate to the culture concerned). Auckland, New Zealand for instance, has been identified to have the fourth most cosmopolitan city in the world [23].The country has English, Māori and New Zealand Sign Language as its national languages.

The growing number of immigrants from other cultures may find it difficult to fully appreciate the digitised Māori collection within its Mātauranga Māori vision.

3 An Analysis of Challenges Faced by Memory Institutions in Developed Countries (Australia and New Zealand)

The challenges faced by Australian memory institutions when it comes to digitising heritage materials for preservation purposes are mainly around three elements: ownership, access and context. The GLAM sector in Australia are also facing pressure to either go digital or lose their relevance [24]. This presents a pressing issue for some memory institutions. As Sansom [25] puts it, going digital is a mammoth task for many GLAM institutions in Australia because of the massive scale of collections, the expense of digitisation and the head ache of wrestling with copyright and cultural law. Sansom details that the combine collections of Australia's GLAMs encompass more than 100 million objects, ranging from natural and human-crafted objects, records, books, artworks and records. Only 25% of this is digitised and only a few Australian GLAM organisations have made fundamental attempts to digitise some of this huge heritage. The main challenges facing the Australian GLAM sector regarding the digitisation of their heritage collection includes a mix of resistance, ignorance, piecemeal adoption of the digitisation process and in some cases wholes embracing of digital [25].

New Zealand memory institutions and the country as a whole started to achieve significant progress in digitisation of its heritage resources since the development of its first national digital strategy in 2005 [26] and digitisation strategy 2014-2017 to guide memory institutions in the digitisation activities [27]. In 2016, the National Library of New Zealand undertook an environmental scan of the current state of "born digital" archival and special collection materials across the country [28]. Their aim was to uncover data about how well prepared and positioned the GLAM sector was to collect and preserve born digital archival materials in memory institutions and to assess this progress against international benchmarks. Challenges uncovered included building staff expertise and developing institutional support. Other issues uncovered in the survey include the need for:

- adequate collaborative approach to knowledge sharing, planning and collection born materials between New Zealand collecting institutions working in digital spaces
- shifting perception among New Zealand memory institutions that born digital collections is credible content to collect
- more extensive policies to support institutional prioritisation and management of born digital materials
- support from national institutions for digital repositories, practice, training and financially viable solutions for born digital materials
- better control over physical collection to enable born digital content to be seen a priority and importance
- regional memory institutions (usually smaller) to benefit from the research/processes of larger, municipal institutions with greater resources in their areas.

Another recent study analysed the impacts of digitised te reo Māori archival collections on its users. Their main aim was to examine the use of the archive and to develop a methodology that can be used in impact assessment for digital collection providers [29]. This study shows that some members of source communities who donated their heritage resources to be digitised and included in the te reo collection required assurance that their taonga (cultural treasures) would not be violated, which called for culturally appropriate ways of involving sources communities in the digitisation of their cultural knowledge. It was also evident that some members of the source communities were distrustful of online information and they did not trust outsiders of their culture to getting full access to their cultural knowledge. Crookston et al. describe this lack of trust and its impact on cultural heritage digitisation:

> For indigenous communities, the stigma of being "the other" in research presents an obstacle to researchers looking to involve themselves in indigenous knowledge acquisition. Yet, through respectful means, and genuine collaboration, more dynamic and trusted research can eventuate [29].

This study also reveals a mixed reaction to digitising cultural knowledge. While some believed that digitisation enhances access to their cultural some others worried that digitisation degrades the original versions of the heritage resources and cause them lose some of the wairua (spirit) you could get from learning the same information from a kaumātua (elder). They believe that some of the cultural documents have voices and sounds of those who may have passed. Digitising them deprive them of this quality [29]. These beliefs present additional considerations that need to be addressed appropriately in the digitisation of indigenous knowledge for preservation.

4 An Analysis of Challenges Faced by Memory Institutions in Developing Countries (Ghana)

In the developing world, Africa is one of the most deprived areas while being highly rich in culture heritage. Memory institutions in Africa therefore have a huge task to protect the memories of their countries for the future society. Nevertheless, they face many challenges when it comes to digitising cultural heritage resources for preservation purpose. Many authors have written about some of these challenges in the region. For instance, Boamah and Tackie looked at the state of digital heritage resources management in Ghana and found that memory institutions in Ghana operated in poor conditions [30]. Asamoah, Akusah, and Mensah [31], argued that the poor state of memory institutions in Ghana were due to lack of funding from government, who is the main financier of memory institutions in the country. Also, Sigauke and Nengomasha [32] examined the challenges faced by National Archives of Zimbabwe and found that this important national memory institution did not even have any rigorous laid down procedure they follow to manage and preserve their national historical records and other valuable information materials. It was clear Sigauke and Nengomasha's [32] study that understanding of the technologies used for digitisation was a problem for professionals.

In addition, Samir, Sharkas, Adly, and Nagi [33] observed that the Alexandria Library and other memory institutions in Egypt faced a huge challenge of managing the digitisation of more than 800,000 pages of press articles. Thus, they developed a digitisation workflow that supported the digitisation process massively. Yet, memory institution in Egypt still face the challenges of associating the accessible online archive with a multidimensional search engine. Although many people are showing interest in, and using the new digital technologies, access to these technologies is difficult for memory institutions in Africa. Lack of funding is identified to be the main hindrance for acquiring the technology [31].

There is also access issues that relate to how to use the technology. People with the skills to operate digital technologies are lacking. Training in ICT for professional in memory institutions is not encouraging in most countries in Africa. It has been found that most people in Africa lose the desire in training in ICT because of the challenges they face with accessing the technologies. Also, other related challenges such as lack of access to electricity to operate digital technologies put most people off from spending their scare resources to train in skills they may find it difficult to put into use. In the last couple of years, Ghana for instance, attained international recognition for the use of the term "dumsor" (which is used daily on-and-off electricity supply and power rationing) because of the number of times the people searched the term in Google and described discussed it in Wikipedia. As a result of dumsor, many institutions that rely on electricity to operate their equipment were bad affected. Most memory institution lost the few digital technologies (such as computers, scanners, printer, etc.) at their disposal because of inconsistent power supply, affecting most of the digitisation projects, which are in their very early stages [34].

Certain attitudes by stakeholders who are involved in memory institutions and their activities also create challenges. In most developing countries, there is little stakeholder interest in investments in digitisation and digital preservation. Most of these instances of lack of interests can be attributed to the fact that there are other pressing needs that take priority of the use of scare resource. For instance, in places where the people are struggling to get enough food, clean water, good education, proper health-care, etc. decision makers will give little attention to investments in digitisation projects and memory institutions have to make do with what is made available for the. In most of these developing countries, activities of memory institutions rely on funding from governments.

Apart from this, there is lack of collaboration among the GLAM institutions. Libraries do their own things separate from what archives do and museums do their own things separate from what galleries do. When exploring digitisation initiatives in Malaysia Zuraidah [35] observed that such a situation of individual digitisation processes can result in duplication and ineffectiveness in the management and preservation of digital resources. In agreement, Boamah [34] indicates that there is a crucial need for an orderly scholarly investigation to understand the nature and state of the management of digitisation initiatives by cultural heritage institutions in Ghana. In addition, there is disregard for Information and Cultural Heritage Management laws. Boamah [34] observed that a little over a decade ago, organisations in the UK for instance were observed to be motivated to embark on digital preservation activities by factors including legal requirements, accountability, protecting the long-term view, protecting investments, enabling future reuse opportunities, fear of losing information, user expectations of information and business efficiency [36]. But while the fear in the UK motivates the institutions to digitise and preserve their heritage resources, the fear in developing countries rather hinders digitisation because, owners of cultural heritage resources also fear that the may lose ownership of their cultural heritage forever. Hence, they resist submitting their heritage objects and resources to memory institutions to be digitised.

There are also some tensions among information management authorities and decision makers when it comes to decision making regarding information management issues and projects that can lead to digitisation of heritage resources in developing countries. In Ghana for instance, the Ghana Library Board (GLB) executes national library responsibilities and the Ghana Library Association (GLA) is the leading professional association for library and information professionals in the country. There is also the Ghana Library Authority who has mandate to develop and oversee library related activities, policies and projects. Top decision makers in these organisations do not agree in ideas about the establishment of a national library for Ghana. Their views on the nature and purpose of a national library for Ghana were conflicting, creating tension between them. This tension is preventing the Ghanaian government from releasing funds and rolling out plans for the development of a national library for the country. Hence, stalling all-important projects including the development of a national heritage digitisation programme [34].

The tension issues among decision makers in memory institutions is very similar to the issues of power structure in indigenous African communities. African traditional systems are based on customary leadership and kinship. Such traditional leaders include kings, chiefs, clan heads and traditional priests etc. have control of the various heritage resources in their traditional areas. In Ghana for instance, each of the over 100 tribal groups have their specific heritage resources that are controlled by the traditional leaders. This separate control over heritage resources makes it difficult for memory instances to collect, and build a national heritage collection that can be digitised to establish a national digital memory. This issue become even more complex when a dominant tribe controls most of a country's heritage resources. Boamah for instance, found that one of the many challenges hindering Ghana from establishing a national heritage repository is because most of the country's heritage resources are controlled by the Asante tribe because they are the biggest traditional group. But, Asante is not prepared to release their heritage resources to be made national because they want the resources to be still recognised as Asante's. The other cultural groups also feel Asante will feel supreme if their heritage resources are used as national heritage. These tensions (which have their roots from ancient tribal wars) have created a lot of animosities and bitterness among the traditional groups. It is also creating fear permanent loos of tribal heritage resources in the various tribal groups [34].

There appears to no formidable long-term digital preservation strategies and policies in place at both national and institutional levels, to have African heritage materials still available and accessibly in the future. Le Roux [37] analysed a group of literature and suggest a need for a working group to look into the real need of policy for digital preservation in Africa. When Imo and Igbo [38] reviewed institutional policies and the management of institutional repositories in Nigerian, they found that out of 129 registered university libraries in Nigeria, only one had some policy for the management of it institutional repository. Observing that the fast improving technology and its concomitant enhancement of digital resources has brought about a myriad of new challenges faced by memory institutions generally, McGreal [39] analysed the specific challenges faced by academic librarians and found that many academics are reluctant to offer their research output to be published in electronic journals.

Boamah [34] found that while Ghanaian university libraries had good institutional repositories and some policies around their use, there were no institutional policy for any of the public memory institutions. Ghana has a policy on ICT for accelerated development (ICT4AD), which is the main policy that relate to digital activities in the country. However, the policy lacks associated strategies and has many issues affecting its implementation [34]. For instance:

- lacks achievable goals and targets because all the miles-stones set in the policy were not achieved
- there are no strategies for DPM accompanying the policy. None of the strategies that come with the policy focus on information management
- the policy lacks adequate resources to enhance its effective implementation
- there is no complementary policy to provide multipath actions and outcomes which the PSR troika model suggests as the effective way of achieving policy goals.
- as a result of political influences, the ICT policy in Ghana was not collaboratively developed. So, it lacks the input of all stakeholders and largely contains the interest of some key players.
- incumbent governments are not willing to continue with other policies initiated by previous governments
- relevant stakeholders are not even aware of the policy
- it is not reviewed on an on-going basis to meet current needs
- it is not effectively promoted [34].

5 Differences Between the Challenges Faced by Memory Institutions in Developed and Developing Countries

Most of the issues facing memory institutions are common in developed and developing countries. Nevertheless, there are specific issues faced by memory institutions in developing countries that are uncommon to their counterpart in developed countries. Table 1 outlines a summary of the various challenges facing memory institutions in developed and developing countries.

Table 1. Summary of challenges facing memory institutions in developed and developing countries

Issues in developed countries	Issues in developing countries
• Ownership issue	• Ownership issue
• Access issue	• Access issue
• Content selection/prioritization issue	• Inadequate funding
• Pressure/higher expectation for memory institutions	• Lack of policy/strategies
	• Power structure
• Tension between information management and information technology experts	• Tension between decision makers in relevant memory institutions, bodes ad authorities
• Inadequate collaboration	• Electricity/infrastructure problems
	• Lack of skilled personnel
	• Inadequate technology/equipment
	• Inadequate collaboration
	• Lack of a controlling body/institution
	• Animosities among tribes
	• Fear of permanent loss of tribal heritage

6   A Conceptual Framework for Digital Preservation Management

The cultural heritage digitisation and preservation management phenomenon can achieve progress when memory institutions as well as their respective governments or governing bodies give careful consideration to all the issues that influence every aspect of digital preservation management in their countries.

6.1   Strategic

Within the Krtalic and Hassenay [3] preservation management model, the strategic and theoretical component provides basic elements to consider for any effective digital preservation management programme. Factors in this category influence the planning and development of strategies and policies to manage preservation programme within current contemporary skills, ideas and knowledge, following good practice preservation activities. These strategies and policies include those developed at both national and institutional levels within a country. Attention should be paid to the national context within which memory institutions in the country operate - how preservation is organised at the national level and how national level plans and strategies affect institutional level preservation activities; and how institutions collaborate with national and international stakeholders to enable effective preservation programme [3]. Analysis of the literature reveals that most developed countries have strong policies and strategies at both national and institutional levels. These policies and strategies provide a general context in which their memory institutions operate which have enabled them to achieve progress in their digitisation and digital preservation management activities. There is also a defined corpus of knowledge about preservation, taking into account specific practical digitisation activities [25, 27–29]. In contrast, the literature also shows that most developing countries do not have strong national and institutional policies and strategies for their preservation management [32, 34], which means there is lack of defined context for memory institutions to operate. This also makes it difficult for them to cooperate with one another and collaborate effectively to develop digital preservation programmes.

6.2 Economic and Legal

Digital preservation management is typically costly and there can be issues with how to identify and analyse various financial sources both at local, national and international levels and once some funds become available, how to properly allocate or spend it towards the programme. Factors in this category also includes the development and implementation of legal documents, dealing with copyright issues relevant for regulating and guiding preservation management and dealing with roles and responsibilities (i.e. who should be responsible for developing these documents and who should be abiding by them, etc.) From the literature, most memory institutions in developed countries have established economic infrastructure and are typically better resourced than their counterparts in developing countries. They have overall support from their national governments and memory institutions draw on national resources to support their digital preservation management programmes. The same cannot be said of memory institutions in developing countries unfortunately. There is generally inadequate funding, basic infrastructure (e.g. electricity and power problems and inconsistent network connectivity) that make digital preservation management challenging for memory institutions in these countries.

6.3 Educational

The factors influencing the educational component of the conceptual preservation management framework relate to elements that help to define a body of knowledge about preservation within a particular country's context. Some of these issues include how key stakeholders within a country come together to create a forum to discuss what ideas about preservation management are necessary to develop knowledge for inclusion in their educational curriculum. In New Zealand for instance, professional bodies like LIANZA, ARANZ, RIMPA and the National Digital Forum gather together to discuss area of preservation management that are necessary for education and training. The professional bodies develop bodies of knowledge around those areas and provide professional training for their members. Educational institutions collaborate with employers, professionals and other key stakeholders to incorporate the necessary areas in their curriculum. The situation is different in developing countries where institutions generally lack trained workforce for preservation management.

6.4 Technical and Operational

The state of the national infrastructure of a country determines the conditions or challenges memory institutions within that country will face when it comes to the managing digital preservation. Considerations include factors that influence access and use of broadband, storage conditions, preservation, preservation equipment and method for their handling, risk management, techniques for ensuring the preservation of digital assets etc. Evident in the literature, memory institutions in developing countries lack appropriate technological infrastructure and tools to handle effective digital preservation management programme compared to their counterparts in developed countries.

6.5   Cultural and Social

The factors identified by Krtalic and Hassenay [3] to be affecting the cultural and social component of preservation management include the establishment and application of evaluation and selection criteria. Considerations include what materials need to be preserved and how they should be selected, who should be in charge of the selection process, who the target users are; how to determine the local, national and international value of the heritage resources selected for preservation. These issues affect memory institutions in both developed and developing countries. The challenges in determining which specific aspect of the culture should be prioritise for preservation within limited resources is a common dilemma faced by memory institutions around the world.

6.6   Attitudinal Factors

Our analysis of the literature also reveals various attitudinal issues that can have an impact on digital preservation. We found that in most developing countries, there is little stakeholder interest in investments in digitisation and digital preservation because of lack of awareness and education around them. Issues of power tension are also evident in both developed and developing countries albeit in different forms. Power tension could be observed among leading national memory institutions. In developing countries, there is also traditional power tension (e.g. between clans and tribes). Issues of ownership also affect people's attitude – e.g. fear of permanent loss of heritage resources through digital preservation management and animosities among various tribes or people from the source communities. Even though attitudinal issues have been mentioned in previous studies, they are often treated more at an implicit level. We argue that especially in the context of digitising and preserving cultural heritage preservation involving source communities and various stakeholders, the attitudinal dimension ought to be a key consideration and as such, should be made explicit in a framework. The attitudes of governments, policy makers, opinion leaders, cultural heritage experts, memory institutions staff, members of source communities and all other stakeholders in digital preservation management can affect the success of policy development, strategies and implementations, both in developed and in developing countries.

7   Conclusion

Contemporary challenges faced by memory institutions in terms of digitising heritage resources are many and varied. They are generally common in both developed and developing countries. However, memory institutions in each context face different circumstantial issues that make digitisation of cultural heritage resource particularly challenging for them. Memory institutions in both developed and developing countries are now feeling pressured by challenges brought about by the fast-developing digital technologies to digitise their heritage collections in order to stay current. The pressure faced by institutions in developed countries are particularly pressing given the general lack of infrastructure and funding. There appears to be good policies and strategies in place for institutions in developed countries and most of their stakeholders understand the cultural heritage digitisation process. Governments in developed countries are typically supportive (i.e. in terms of funding) digitisation projects. The main challenge for memory institutions in developed countries appears to be how to navigate the enormity of the collections that need to be prioritised for digital preservation.

Memory institutions in developing countries face a different kind of pressure. They fear the risk of losing access to relevant heritage resources in a modern world, where fast and significant access to heritage resources are rapidly moving to the digital space. They see the need to move their heritage resources into the digital realm. Yet, they are challenged by the lack of proper policies and appropriate strategies for effective digitisation. Different kinds of negative attitudes are also having an impact on cultural heritage digitisation projects in developing countries. While governments, decision makers and opinion leaders lack interest in heritage digitisation, owners of the heritage resources fear permanent loss of ownership and control of their cultural heritage or indigenous knowledge to outsiders. Professionals in the memory institutions in these countries also have conflicting ideas on how to go about the digitisation process, thus creating a lot of tension among them. These attitudes hinder progress. Although some memory institutions in the developed countries also face some of these challenges, the issues appear much more profound in developing countries. Memory institutions in developing countries therefore find it very difficult to manage their respective national cultural heritage resources both in physical and digital forms, especially in areas where tribal tensions also lead to further complications.

In this paper, we have built on findings from the literature to discuss the various issues facing memory institutions and we have outlined the differences in the challenges facing institutions in developing and developed countries. Following the analysis of the differences in the challenges, we suggest that attitudes have significant influence on the development of policy, implementation of strategies and allocation of resources for digital preservation management. Even though attitudinal issues have been mentioned in previous studies, they are often treated more at an implicit level. We argue that especially in the context of digitising and preserving cultural heritage preservation involving source communities and various stakeholders, the attitudinal dimension ought to be a key consideration and as such, to be made explicit in a framework. Further research should examine the attitudinal dimension, in relation to other dimensions that have been tested more extensively.

References

1. Liew, C.L.: Digital cultural heritage 2.0: a meta-design consideration. In: 8th International Conference on Conceptions of Library and Information Science, Information Research, vol. 18, no. 3, Copenhagen, Denmark. 19–22 August 2013 (2013). http://www.informationr.net/ir/18-3/colis/paperS03.html
2. Boamah, E., Liew, C.L.: Involving source communities in the digitisation and preservation of indigenous knowledge. In: 18th International Conference on Asia-Pacific Digital Libraries, ICADL 2016, Proceedings, Tsukuba, Japan, 7–9 December 2016, pp. 21–36 (2016)
3. Krtalić, M., Hasenay, D.: Exploring a framework for comprehensive and successful preservation management in libraries. J. Doc. **68**(3), 353–377 (2012). doi:10.1108/00220411211225584
4. Cleveland, G.: Digital libraries: definitions, issues and challenges (1998). https://www.ifla.org/archive/udt/op/udtop8/udtop8.htm
5. Greenstein, D.: Digital libraries and their challenges. Libr. Trends **49**(2), 290–303 (2000)
6. Kuny, T., Cleveland, G.: The digital library: myths and challenges. IFLA J. **24**(2), 107 (1998). doi:10.1177/034003529802400205
7. Mishra, R.K.: Digital libraries: definitions, issues, and challenges. Innov. J. Educ. **4**(3), 1–3 (2016)
8. Museum of New Zealand Te Papa Tongarewa: Planning a new museum-how god is your idea? Setting up a new museum (2007). https://www.tepapa.govt.nz/sites/default/files/32-planning-a-museum.pdf
9. Rosati, E.: Copyright issues facing early stages of digitization projects. Mobile collection projects (2013). http://www.digitalhumanities.cam.ac.uk/Copyrightissuesfacingearlystagesofdigitizationprojects.pdf
10. Simon, N.: Museum 2.0: what are the most important problems in our field (2011). http://museumtwo.blogspot.co.nz/2011/10/what-are-most-important-problems-in-our.html
11. Holcomb, J.L.: Preserving digital archives, preserving cultural memory. J. Assoc. Hist. Comput. **3**, 3 (2000). http://hdl.handle.net/2027/spo.3310410.0003.320
12. Picot, A.: Digital archives: Here's the problem – how would YOU address it? Report back from the Recordkeeping Roundtable Workshop at #ARANZASA in Christchurch, NZ. (2014). https://rkroundtable.org/2014/10/14/digital-archives-heres-the-problem-how-would-you-address-it/
13. Wright, J.: Challenges of appraising records in the digital age. In: The Bigger Picture: Exploring Archives and Smithsonian History (2012). https://siarchives.si.edu/blog/challenges-appraising-records-digital-age
14. Kaiser, J.F.: Richard Hamming: "You and Your Research". Transcript of the Bell Communication Research Colloquium Seminar (1986). http://www.cs.virginia.edu/~robins/YouAndYourResearch.html
15. Mallan, K.: Is digitisation sufficient for collective remembering? Access to and use of cultural heritage collections. Can. J. Inf. Libr. Sci. **30**(3/4), 201–220 (2006)
16. Huvila, I.: Archives, libraries and museums in the contemporary society: perspectives of the professional. In: iConference 2014 (2014). doi:10.9776/14032
17. Cathro, W.: Collaboration across the collecting sectors (2010). https://www.nla.gov.au/content/collaboration-across-the-collecting-sectors
18. Cimasi, R.J., Zigrang, T.A.: The four pillars of healthcare: part IV technological advancements in the healthcare industry. In: The Value Examiner, January/February 2017, pp. 17–24 (2017). AN: 121978019

19. Walker, I., Vlok, A.J., Kamat, A.: A double-edged sword: the effect of technological advancements in the management of neurotrauma patients. Br. J. Neurosurg. **31**(1), 89–93 (2017). doi:10.1080/02688697.2016.1220504

20. Burris, C.: Technical services and digital literacy. Technicalities **37**(1), 13–16 (2017). AN 120933179

21. Kumar, N.: Transforming libraries through information and communication technology. Int. J. Inf. Dissemination Technol. **6**(3), 174–178 (2016). AN 119763982

22. Barker, S.K.: New opportunities for research libraries in digital information and knowledge management: challenges for the mid-sized research library. J. Libr. Adm. **46**(1), 65–74 (2007). doi:10.1300/J111v46n01_05

23. Peacock, A.: Auckland a melting pot - ranked world's fourth most cosmopolitan city (2016). http://www.stuff.co.nz/auckland/75964986/Auckland-a-melting-pot-ranked-worlds-fourth-most-cosmopolitan-city

24. Ladiges, C., Bruenig, M.: Australian museums must innovate or risk becoming 'digital dinosaurs' (2014). http://www.csiro.au/en/News/News-releases/2014/Australian-museums-risk-becoming-digital-dinosaurs

25. Sansom, M.: Go digital or die, Australia's cultural institutions told (2014). http://www.governmentnews.com.au/2014/09/digitalise-die-australias-cultural-institutions-told/

26. Carnaby, P.: Libraries as a common denominator: a view from New Zealand of the citizen, country and global perspective. Electron. Libr. Inf. Syst. **43**(3), 251–263 (2009)

27. National Library of New Zealand: Digitisation Strategy 2014–2017 (2014). https://natlib.govt.nz/about-us/strategy-and-policy/digitisation-strategy-2014-2017

28. Moran, J.: Born digital in New Zealand report of survey results (2017). https://natlib.govt.nz/files/reports/research-borndigital2017-report.pdf

29. Crookston, M., Oliver, G., Tikao, A., Diamond, P., Liew, C.L., Douglas, S.L.; Kōrero Kitea: Ngā hua o te whakamamatitanga: the impact of digitised te reo archival collections (2016). https://interparestrust.org/assets/public/dissemination/Korerokiteareport_final.pdf

30. Boamah, E., Tackie, S.N.B.: The state of heritage resources management in Ghana. In: 4th International conference on African Digital Libraries and Archives. (ICADLA). University of Ghana, 29 May 2015 (2015). http://hdl.handle.net/10539/18396

31. Asamoah, C., Akusah, H., Mensah, M.: Funding memory institution in Ghana: the case of Public Records and Archives Administration Department (PRAAD) (2015). http://wiredspace.wits.ac.za/xmlui/bitstream/handle/10539/18395/Asamoah_Akussah_Mensah_Final.pdf?sequence=1&isAllowed=y

32. Sigauke, D.T., Nengomasha, C.T.: Challenges and prospect facing the digitisation of historical records for their preservation within the national archives of Zimbabwe. In: 2nd International Conference on African Digital Libraries and Archives (ICADLA) at The University of Johennesburg, South Africa (2014). http://wiredspace.wits.ac.za/handle/10539/11533

33. Samir, A., Sharkas, A., Adly, N., Nagi, M.: Digital preservation: handling large collections case study: digitizing Egyptian press archive at Centre for Economic, Judicial, and Social Study and Documentation (CEDEJ). In: 4th International conference on African Digital Libraries and Archives (2014). http://hdl.handle.net/10539/18635

34. Boamah, E.: Towards effective management and preservation of digital cultural heritage resources: an exploration of contextual factors in Ghana (2014). http://hdl.handle.net/10063/3270

35. Zuraidah, A.M.: The state of digitisation initiatives by cultural institutions in Malaysia; an exploratory survey. Libr. Rev. **56**(1), 45–60 (2007)

36. Waller, M., Sharpe, R.: Mind the gap; Assessing digital preservation needs in the UK (2006). http://www.dpconline.org/search.html?q=1975+NASA+data+problem

37. Le Roux, A.: Indigenous knowledge in a virtual context: sustainable digital preservation, a literature review. In: 4th International Conference on African Digital Libraries and Archives (ICADLA), University of Ghana, 29 May 2015 (2015). http://hdl.handle.net/10539/18402

38. Imo, N.T., Igbo, H.U.: Institutional policy and management of institutional repositories in Nigerian universities. In: 4th International Conference on African Digital Libraries and Archives (ICADLA), University of Ghana, 29 May 2015 (2015). http://hdl.handle.net/10539/18399

39. McGreal, R.: Stealing the goose: copyright and learning. In: Caswell, J., Haschak, P.G., Sherman, D. (eds.) New Challenges Facing Academic Librarian Today: Electronic Journals, Archival Digitisation, Documents Delivery, Etc. Lewiston, New York (2005)

A Metadata Model to Organize Cultural Heritage Resources in Heterogeneous Information Environments

Chiranthi Wijesundara[1]([⊠]), Winda Monika[1], and Shigeo Sugimoto[2]

[1] Graduate School of Library, Information and Media Studies,
University of Tsukuba, Tsukuba, Japan
chiranthis@gmail.com, windabi.wm@gmail.com
[2] Faculty of Library, Information and Media Science,
University of Tsukuba, Tsukuba, Japan
sugimoto@slis.tsukuba.ac.jp

Abstract. Cultural Heritage Information (CHI) is scattered among memory institutions, and connecting them together is an important issue for their continued discovery, access, and use. This study proposes a generalized model named Cultural Heritage in Digital Environments (CHDE), which enables the organizing of both tangible and intangible cultural heritage in heterogeneous information environments. The model collects all related digital resources into one instance, which can be later digested into a single digital archive on the networked environment, based on the One-to-One Principle of Metadata. We specially focus on organizing intangible cultural heritage through their instantiations. The proposed model is mapped to renowned cultural heritage models to identify the component entities and to clarify their strengths and the weaknesses. We use South and Southeast Asian cultural heritage information to evaluate the suitability of this model, which is a novel approach in the region.

Keywords: Cultural heritage information · Information organization · Metadata models · Linked Open Data · One-to-One Principle of Metadata

1 Introduction

Cultural Heritage is a unique asset that belongs to a certain community. In the networked information environment developed on the Web, there are large digitized collections of cultural heritage, which we refer to as Digital Archives in this study. Cultural heritage, which may be digital or non-digital, is described through information expressed as a metadata. This study mainly focuses on organizing this Cultural Heritage Information (CHI) from the viewpoint of a data model for CHI.

CHI is being considered as difficult to deal with from the viewpoint of interoperability on the Web because of its heterogeneity. Nevertheless, memory institutions, for instance, Libraries, Archives and Museums (LAM or MLA) accept this challenge and intervene into this process. They collect cultural heritage resources and digitize them, organize the digital cultural heritage resources as a part of their collections, and provide these information resources to their patrons via the Web and/or their in-house services.

© Springer International Publishing AG 2017
S. Choemprayong et al. (Eds.): ICADL 2017, LNCS 10647, pp. 81–94, 2017.
https://doi.org/10.1007/978-3-319-70232-2_7

With the advancement of the Web technologies LAM is now trying to find novel approaches to link these collections built by individual institutions and present them as a single, complete information portal. For instance, the Europeana data portal which has developed to collect and disseminate digital cultural heritage on the Web is a typical example of such an effort. Europeana uses a model-based information aggregation process and their model is known as the Europeana Data Model (EDM) [11].

The CHI scenario of the developing regions such as South and Southeast Asia is not as bright as the developed countries. According to our previous study, we have identified several basic problems related to LAM in the region [20]. It is obvious that South and Southeast Asian memory institutions also intervene in the CHI creation, management and dissemination, but they stand out as individual data silos without any interconnection. On the other hand, lack of widely accepted standards to share their information among the institutions leads to many barriers when linking information on the Web. Metadata is known as a key technology to lower these barriers.

Metadata at LAM is basically created for every item in their collections. On the other hand, there are many Web resources created by third parties, e.g., Wikipedia which is a very widely used encyclopedia among end-users on the Web. Those Web resources are useful for many end-users to understand contextual information about the cultural heritage resources. It is crucial for LAM to link their metadata and those Web resources to add values of CHI provided by LAM using the information provided by the third-parties. A significant problem for this issue is that the objectives of the LAM metadata description and those of Web resources are quite different. One of the primary contributions of this study is to clearly identify the objectives of metadata description to help linking between the LAM's metadata and Web resources based on One-to-One Principal of Metadata [15].

This paper tries to investigate the existing CHI issues learned in our previous study [20] and proposes a suitable model to collect and enrich the CHI. The model is designed to provide a generalized framework to describe digital collections of cultural heritage objects. This model can be introduced as a generalized model because it is essential to capture both tangible and intangible heritage assets, and because the generalized model helps connect heterogeneous LAM's metadata and Web resources. The proposed model is aligned with renowned cultural heritage models and is evaluated through use case scenarios related to the cultural heritage domain.

2 Cultural Heritage Information (CHI)

2.1 Cultural Heritage Facets

The term 'Cultural Heritage' has changed rapidly during past few decades. As defined by the UNESCO, "Cultural heritage is the legacy of physical artefacts and intangible attributes of a group or society that are inherited from past generations, maintained in the present and bestowed for the benefit of future generations" [19]. Basically, cultural heritage has two facets.

   i. Tangible Cultural Heritage: "objects significant to the archaeology, architecture, science or technology of a specific culture" [19].

  ii. Intangible Cultural Heritage: "traditions or living expressions inherited from our ancestors and passed on to our descendants" [18].

Tangible cultural heritage can be further subdivided into *Movable* objects such as paintings, coins, sculptures in a museum and *Immovable* objects as archaeological sites and monuments. Furthermore, intangible cultural heritage can be split into five main categories as follows [18].

    i. Oral traditions
   ii. Performing arts
  iii. Social practices, rituals, festive events
  iv. Knowledge and skills to produce traditional crafts
   v. Knowledge and practices concerning nature and the universe

2.2 Cultural Heritage Information in Heterogeneous Information Environments and Their Existing Problems

CHI is the primary factor which makes the cultural heritage meaningful and usable. CHI can be in various forms and can record in various means. Many scholars identify CHI as a unique type of information. According to Lanzi [12], CHI has ten characteristics. Similarly, Hyvönen [10] defines five features of cultural heritage data.

    i. Multi-format: contents are presented in various formats
   ii. Multi-topical: contents concern various topics
  iii. Multi-lingual: content is available in different languages
  iv. Multi-cultural: content is related and interpreted in terms of different cultures
   v. Multi-targeted: contents are targeted to different people

Because of this diversity, it becomes problematic to make this CHI interoperable specially within the semantic environment. The multi-organizational nature of collecting, maintaining and organizing CHI is the main reason for this issue [10].

However, for information creation, organization and dissemination need to employ metadata standards into the CHI process. In addition, standards improve the quality and interoperability of the information. Following list shows some CHI related standards.

   i. CARARE Metadata Schema: A harvesting schema intended for delivering metadata about an organisation's online collections, heritage assets and their digital resources.[1]

  ii. CDWA (Categories for the Description of Works of Art): A set of guidelines for the description of art, architecture, and other cultural works.[2]

  iii. LIDO (Lightweight Information Describing Objects): An XML schema for describing museum objects.[3]

---

[1] http://pro.carare.eu/doku.php?id=support:metadata-schema.
[2] http://www.getty.edu/research/publications/electronic_publications/cdwa/.
[3] http://network.icom.museum/cidoc/working-groups/lido/what-is-lido/.

iv. MIDAS Heritage: A British cultural heritage standard for recording information on buildings, monuments, archaeological sites, shipwrecks and submerged landscapes, parks and gardens, battlefields, artefacts and ecofacts.[4]

v. Object ID: An essential information about archaeological, artistic and cultural objects in order to facilitate their identification in case of theft.[5]

vi. SPECTRUM: A standard describes how to manage collections and what to do with artefacts at each stage of their lifecycle in a collection.[6]

Correspondingly, there are many local standards developed by each country depending on their own institutional requirements. Alternatively, Data standards used by other domains, for example, Dublin Core, MODS (Metadata Object Description Schema) and VRA (Visual Resources Association) Core Categories etc. are also utilized by the CHI domain where necessary. To give an instance, Cultural Heritage Metadata Task Group of Dublin Core Metadata Initiative (DCMI) tried to identify the challenges of metadata for cultural heritage by developing a simple cross-community metadata model for cultural heritage objects. Besides they intended to give a recommendation for the development of DCMI Application Profiles based on the above task [7].

Finally, there are Data Models specifically designed for CHI arena, which can be used to organize data and define their relationships on par with real world entities. Some of these well-known CHI models will be discussed in Sect. 3.1 of this paper.

Nevertheless, none of these standards could completely cover the entire cultural heritage domain to describe its properties. Previously mentioned standards are developed to capture tangible objects only. Thus, there is always a void between tangible and intangible heritage data standards which has yet to be filled.

When considering the LAM environment, they mostly record CHI related to a single object. In particular, museums who collect most tangible cultural heritage objects present their information as single items. When considering the intangible cultural heritage, it is difficult to express intangible assets as individual items. Similarly, intangible cultural Heritage can be realized if it is recorded only. Memory institutions cannot curate a concept such as a *skill* or a *performance* related to an intangible cultural heritage, but they can use various mediums to capture intangible heritage and record them as individual records. Whether there is a deviation of tangible and intangible heritage sometimes these assets are interrelated. Unfortunately, current CHI on the Web provided by various means does not deliver such contextual information to patrons.

Based on this observation about CHI, this study defines a data model for digital archives of cultural heritage based on the One-to-One Principle of Metadata [15], which should be applicable to any type of cultural heritage – either tangible or intangible, movable or immovable. We discuss the proposed model by comparing it with CIDOC-CRM and FRBRoo, both of which are known as standard ontologies for describing museum resources.

---

[4] http://heritage-standards.org.uk/midas-heritage/.

[5] http://archives.icom.museum/object-id/.

[6] http://collectionstrust.org.uk/spectrum/.

2.3 Goal and Methodology

The main goal of this research is to develop a model to aggregate diverse CHI resources on the Web based on One-to-One Principle of Metadata. The One-to-One Principle helps to distinguish digital copies and their source related to cultural heritage objects.

The platform for this research is the Linked Open Data and Semantic Web environment [2]. Metadata aggregation based on the Linked Open Data technologies is the main method assumed in this study because to collect and aggregate CHI from various information resources in different aspects is a key factor.

First, we investigated existing models used in the CHI domain such as EDM, which defines a metadata aggregation model for Europeana, CIDOC-CRM as a general-purpose ontology specifically for museums and FRBRoo as an extension of CIDOC-CRM. Also, we tried to do a crosswalk between proposed model classes and some of these existing model classes in Sect. 5, aiming for a harmonization between models. A crosswalk allows to identify the shortcomings and strengths of current models which gives insights to develop new models. This paper shows the CHDE model and discuss it in comparison with those standard metadata models. Implementation issues of CHDE are left for the future study.

3 Related Works

3.1 Models for Data Organization

Researches related to model-based data organization are varied. Some are directly connected with CHI and some are related to other information domains such as bibliographic or geographic data. In addition, the technologies behind the data organization are also important consideration.

Europeana Data Model (EDM). Europeana is an ideal example for model based CHI organization and aggregation. This is a large-scale CHI portal which is dedicated to aggregate, enrich and disseminate digital cultural heritage across memory institutions in the European Union. At present, it connects over 3,000 institutions across Europe and these institutions contribute their resources to Europeana data portal. Europeana portal is based on Europeana Data Model (EDM) which supports and manage the functionality of the system. EDM Primer states "EDM is not built on any particular community standard but rather adopts an open, cross-domain Semantic Web-based framework that can accommodate the range and richness of particular community standards such as LIDO for museums, EAD for archives or METS for digital libraries" [11].

CIDOC-Conceptual Reference Model (CRM). This can be identified as an ontological approach to harmonize the cultural heritage resources. CIDOC-CRM "... provides definitions and a formal structure for describing the implicit and explicit concepts and relationships used in cultural heritage documentation" [6]. The latest published version of the CIDOC-CRM consists of 94 classes and 168 properties [13]. Primarily, this model enables information exchange and integration between heterogeneous sources of CHI. It provides the semantic definitions and clarifications needed to transform disparate and localized information sources into a coherent global resource.

FRBR-object oriented (FRBRoo) Model. FRBRoo is another model formed by joining CIDOC-CRM and Functional Requirements for Bibliographic Records (FRBR). Therefore, it considers as an extension of the CIDOC-CRM. The aim of this model is to establish "… a formal ontology intended to capture and represent the underlying semantics of bibliographic information and to facilitate the integration, mediation, and interchange of bibliographic and museum information" [5].

3.2   Model Based Cultural Heritage Studies

Various studies have been conducted using above models to organize CHI aiming for the semantic interoperability in the networked environment. CARARE is one such project which brings heritage agencies, organizations, archaeological museums, research institutions etc. together to establish a service that will make digital content for Europe's unique archaeological monuments and historic sites interoperable with Europeana [8]. CARARE harvest metadata from content providers and store them in a repository. Content providers map their original data into CIDOC-CRM and MIDAS standards using a special web interface. Then CARARE maps those data to EDM as it should be harmonized with European data. This system aggregates special CHIs such as 2D and 3D information and geographic information as well.

Hu et al. [9] used CRM as a framework for describing *Pang Wang Festival* in China and provided an analysis for mapping their data to CIDOC-CRM. Similarly, Tan et al. [16] constructed an ontology model based on CIDOC-CRM to represent *Dragon Boat Festival*, China. Finally, they proposed a Browser/ Server architecture to implement a prototype, which involves several key functionalities such as semantic knowledge retrieving etc. Unfortunately, either of them does not discuss the significance of the festivals or define any contextual elements that describe the intangible asset.

Chen et al. used FRBRoo as an ontological approach to aggregate diverse metadata and transform it from human-understandable format to machine-understandable format for semantic query [4]. They have collected data (accompanied by Dublin Core terms) from two collections and mapped them into the FRBRoo classes and properties to make heterogeneous metadata integration possible.

In 2016 Carboni & de Luca [3] published a paper called *Towards a conceptual foundation for documenting tangible and intangible elements of a cultural object*. The main claim of this paper was analyzing the dichotomy between tangible and intangible heritage and proposing a way to document the same. The authors used CIDOC-CRM as the base and modelled information using a use case to show that cultural object has multiple facets and dimensions that incorporate both tangible and intangible elements.

Apart from renowned CHI models, some scholars propose their own models for organizing and describing heritage resources. Amin et al. [1] proposed a knowledge repository model for intangible culture heritage as a framework and guideline to archiving *Malay Intangible Culture Heritage* in Malaysia. They proposed to convert intangible to tangible heritage through digitizing the contents without losing their originality and archived them using the proposed model for future usage.

Compared with these studies the model presented in this paper uses the One-to-One Principle of Metadata to clearly identify of physical and digital objects, which is the key issue to aggregate metadata for a single cultural heritage object and to link item-based metadata and Web resources.

4 A Model to Organize Cultural Heritage Information (CHI): Cultural Heritage in Digital Environment (CHDE) Model

Figure 1 represents CHDE model which defines instances and their relationships in a cultural heritage collection. The CHDE model can have two main deviations: the *Physical Space* and the *Digital Space*. Whether tangible or intangible, any cultural heritage can physically exist or occur in the real world. On the other hand, LAM develop their digital collections simply by digitizing those physical instances. CHDE defines one metadata for each of these instances based on the One-to-One Principle. Thus, CHDE is designed to clearly split metadata for a physical object and metadata for its digitized object.

Starting from bottom (Fig. 1), *Physical Space* can have *Curated Objects* which consists of various types of physical *Recording Objects* recorded on different Mediums. Conventional LAM collects these *Recording Objects* such as *Image, Sound* or *Textual* formats which expresses cultural heritage. The upper half of the model embodies the *Digital Space* which belongs to the networked digital environment. The records in those physical mediums can be converted into digital records known as *Digital Objects*. For instance, *printed photo* and *VHS video* can be converted to *JPEG and MPEG images*. In addition, there can be born digital resources for example, *Virtual Reality (VR) data* and *digital photos* which can be directly created from cultural heritage object in the *Physical Space*. CHDE model assumes one or more recording objects for a physical cultural heritage object from which digital objects put in the digital space is created. Those recording objects may be analog or digital. Subsequently, all these digital objects created or converted from the physical objects are organized as an archived collection of *Digital Resources*, which we call a digital archive (s). The uppermost circle labeled *Curated Digital Instance* which acts as an aggregated instance in *Digital Space* is created from cultural heritage

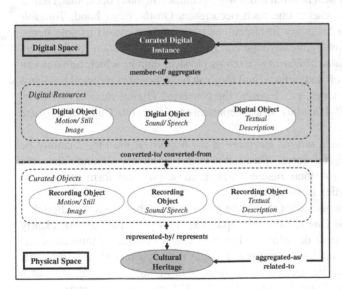

Fig. 1. CHDE model to organize digital resource of cultural heritage

objects in the *Physical Space*. So, Digital Archive is a collection *of Curated Digital Instances* to be maintained over time.

Figure 2 represents a model for intangible cultural heritage. In Fig. 2, *Intangible Cultural Heritage* denotes conceptual entity related to a *dance performance, traditional skill* or a *ritual* while *Tangible Cultural Heritage* represents as an *artefact* or a *monument*. *Intangible Cultural Heritage* is associated with an *Agent*, e.g., *dancer* or *singer* and *craftsman*, who owns the skill and knowledge needed for a performance.

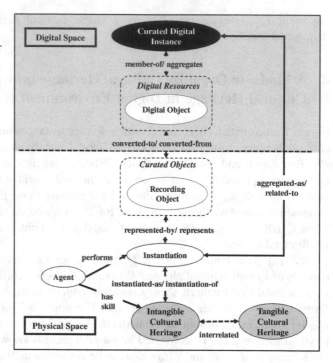

Fig. 2. CHDE model to organize intangible cultural heritage

Intangible cultural heritage does not exist as a single physical item but is usually instantiated in many occasions. Here in the model, *Instantiation* represents one such occurrence. On the other hand, *Tangible Cultural Heritage* does not have any instantiations because they consist as sole items. Additionally, tangible and intangible heritage can have some *Interrelation*. Both *Instantiation* and the *Tangible Cultural Heritage* exist as physical entities which humans can directly touch, see, hear, smell and/or taste, and they can be recorded in physical mediums such as video tapes, audio tapes, etc. Finally, the converted *Digital Resources* will be aggregated as *Curated Digital Instance* which represents an *Intangible Cultural Heritage* asset in the *Physical Space*.

In this model, *Intangible Cultural Heritage* at the bottom of the Fig. 2 cannot be directly converted into digital form. Thus, the model explicitly distinguishes the intangible heritage assets and their instantiation in some physical form in order to identify classes and properties in metadata.

In the CHDE model, one metadata should be given to each object either in digital or physical space based on the One-to-One Principle [15]. This principle helps us clearly identify objectives of metadata description. For instance, if consider a museum catalogue related to a tangible object it can have a single metadata record related to that object. The same thing can be applied to an intangible heritage instance such as a *performance* [21], but the issue is conventional LAM metadata is created for a *recording of the performance* and it does not clearly distinguish *a recording, a specific performance* and *performance as an intangible cultural heritage*. So, the CHDE model provides an answer to overcome this issue.

Figure 3 represents CHDE model applied to a real-world example *"Kandy Esala Perehara"* which is a historical festival in Sri Lanka. From bottom-Right, *"Kandy Esala Perehara"* is representing the main intangible cultural event. This is a religious parade performed by dancers and musicians along with decorated elephants. However, this intangible entity can have many instantiations such as *Performance in 2016* which is a Temporal instantiation. *Performers* denotes the dancers and musicians who involved in the same performance.

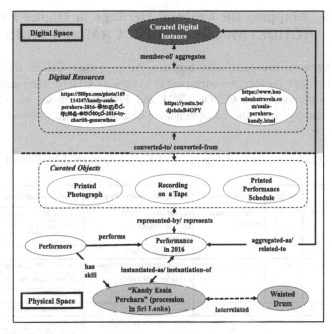

Fig. 3. CHDE model replaced by "Kandy Esala Perehara"

Then Fig. 3 shows the physical records related to the *Performance in 2016* such as a *video/audio tape, parade schedule* as a leaflet and a *printed photograph* of the parade. In the *Digital Space*, we can find similar resource in digital formats primarily hosted by LAM. Then can present the *"Kandy Esala Perahara"* as a *Curated Digital Instance* by aggregating metadata of these resources. In Fig. 3, bottom- right oval represents a tangible object which is interconnected with the intangible "Kandy Esala Perehara" parade. *Waisted Drum* (or *Membranophone-double-headed*) used to produce music during the performance is a tangible object in this model. According to Fig. 3, the *Digital Space* shows a hypothetical museum collection because there is no existing museum in Sri Lanka that provides a digital archive of intangible cultural heritage. This collection includes a *YouTube video* and *other resources* accessible on the Web as a virtually collected resource.

The advantage of CHDE is that we can identify every object separately and create metadata for each object, which is the primary difference from existing databases of cultural heritage objects at LAMs. In particular, this feature is crucial to collect various type of records about intangible cultural heritage such as *videos* showing a *festival* or a *skill*, and *data captured* from *body motion of a dancer* or a *craftsman*, because we can explicitly separate a single *performance* and his/her/their *skill* which is the body of intangible cultural heritage. Another crucial point is that, most of the metadata for those objects both in digital and physical spaces are available on the Web such as LAM metadata created for collected items, UNESCO's Web page and Wikipedia articles about cultural heritage, etc. Though, we need to develop technologies to properly link these metadata.

5 Mapping the Cultural Heritage in Digital Environment (CHDE) Model to CIDOC-CRM and FRBRoo

Seeking interoperability between the proposed CHDE model and existing cultural heritage models, we attempted to crosswalk CHDE main cultural heritage classes and instantiations to CIDOC-CRM and FRBRoo classes as follows (Tables 1 and 2). Findings from these mappings are discussed in the following section.

Table 1. Crosswalk between CHDE main heritage classes with CIDOC-CRM and FRBRoo

	Category	Main Classes	AFS/ AAT Related Terms	CIDOC-CRM Classes	FRBRoo Classes
1	TCH	Movable cultural heritage	cultural artifacts (AFS)	E22 Man-Made Object	
			arfifacts (AFS/AAT)	E18 Physical Thing	F7 Object (=)
			specimens (AAT)		
			natural objects (AAT)		
2	TCH	Immovable cultural heritage	archaeological sites (AFS/AAT)	E24 Physical Man-Made Thing	F4 Manifestation Singleton (*)
			monuments (AFS/AAT)	E25 Man-Made Feature	F53 Material Copy (*) (≠)
				E27 Site	
3	ICH	Oral traditions	oral traditions (AFS/AAT)	E28 Conceptual Object	F6 Concept (=)
4	ICH	Performing arts	performing arts (AFS/AAT)	E7 Activity	F31 Performance (*)
				E29 Design or Procedure	F25 Performance Plan (=)
5	ICH	Social practices, rituals, festive events	social ethics (AAT)	E7 Activity	F31 Performance (*)
			civic rituals (AFS)	E28 Conceptual Object	F6 Concept (=)
			rituals (events) (AAT)	E29 Design or Procedure	F25 Performance Plan (=)
			festivals (AFS/AAT)		
6	ICH	Knowledge and skills to produce traditional crafts	traditional knowledge (AFS)	E28 Conceptual Object	F6 Concept (=)
			knowledge (AAT)	E29 Design or Procedure	F25 Performance Plan (=)
			crafts (AFS)	E77 Persistent Item	
			ability (AFS)		
7	ICH	Knowledge and practices concerning nature and the universe	traditional ecological knowledge (AFS)	E28 Conceptual Object	F6 Concept (=)
			knowledge (AAT)		
			language (AAT/AFS)	E56 Language	
			visual art (AAT)	E36 Visual Item	
				E77 Persistent Item	

Key :   TCH: Tangible Cultural Heritage   ICH: Intangible Cultural Heritage
AAT: Art & Architecture Thesaurus (Getty)   AFS: American Folklore Society Ethnographic Thesaurus

(*) Subclass   (=) Equal Class   (≠) Not Equal

According to Table 1, starting from left-hand side, title *Category* denotes mainly the *Tangible* and *Intangible Cultural Heritage (TCH and ICH)*. Then it identifies the main heritage classes such as *Movable cultural heritage*, *Oral traditions* etc. defined by UNESCO [18, 19]. Apart from the main deviation, it is further divided into sub-classes which are not revealed in Table 1. Somehow, through these sub-classes, *Related Terms* were selected from AAT and AFS thesauruses [17, 14] which explains the content of the *Main Classes*. Subsequently, we matched these classes to CIDOC-CRM and

FRBRoo classes. Symbols used in the tables *(Subclass: *, Equal Class: = , Not Equal: ≠)* show the relationships between CIDOC-CRM and FRBRoo classes.

Table 2 represents the *Instantiation Classes* related to *Intangible Cultural Heritage*. Instance classes are realized according to questions covering *Temporal, Location, Category, Agent* and *Activity Classes*. Apart from these, another instance class was added to represent the conceptual entities named as *Concept Class*.

Table 2. Crosswalk between CHDE instance classes with CIDOC-CRM and FRBRoo

Instance Classes	AFS/ AAT Related Terms	CIDOC Classes	FRBRoo Classes
Temporal	time (AAT/AFS)	E2 Temporal Entity	
	time-related attributes (AAT)	E4 Period	F8 Event (=)
		E5 Event	
Location	location (AAT)	E53 place	F9 Place (=)
Category	_	E55 Type	F3 Manifestation Product Type (*) (≠)
Agent	agents (AAT)	E21 Person	F10 Person (=)
		E39 Actor	
Activity	activities (AAT)	E7 Activity	F31 Performance (*)
Concept	concepts (AFS)	E28 Conceptual Object	F6 Concept (=)

Key: AAT: Art & Architecture Thesaurus (Getty)   AFS: American Folklore Society Ethnographic Thesaurus

(*) Subclass   (=) Equal Class   (≠) Not Equal

6 Discussion

Museum portals or catalogues exhibit some limited information related to a single cultural object. As identified in Sect. 2, LAMs cannot curate intangible cultural heritage as physical objects. In addition, regardless of intangible or tangible, they have contextual information which is essential to recognize the heritage as a full entity. Moreover, existing metadata standards and models are not sufficient to manage CHI, such as intangible CHI. Aiming these issues, we proposed this CHDE model as a generalized model to gather information related to both tangible and intangible heritage domains.

This model distinguishes between the *Digital* and *Physical Spaces*. This feature is introduced based on the One-to-One principle to clearly split metadata for a heritage object in the physical space and a digital object created from the physical object. Here, we discuss this feature comparing CIDOC-CRM and EDM. CIDOC-CRM can be used to represent both digital and physical settings. It defines classes and properties of heritage objects, i.e., ontology for cultural heritage objects. EDM works to aggregate mainly the digital contents related to heritage assets. CHDE model tries to collect information related to specific cultural heritage instances such as a *performance* or a *dance*. Nevertheless, EDM focuses towards item oriented information. According to EDM, *Mona Lisa* by Leonardo da Vinci is a single item and its digital images may be collected from more than one institution. These are collected using *edm:hasView* and *edm:aggregatedCHO* properties [11]. Europeana's metadata aggregation is a top-down approach where data providers submit their CHI as packages to the Europeana in the form conforming EDM. However, memory institutions in South and Southeast Asia do not have a common basis to share cultural heritage information. This fact led us to design CHDE model (Figs. 1 and 2). CHDE model uses a bottom-up approach which relies on scattered and disorganized CHI. Anyone can clearly identify objectives of metadata descriptions in the CHDE model and properly describe metadata about the objectives based on the One-to-One Principle of metadata. In particular, clear identification is crucial to describe intangible cultural heritage assets.

In Sect. 3, we discussed related studies which utilized CIDOC-CRM and FRBRoo to represent intangible cultural Heritage properties as well [3, 9, 16]. These studies utilized CIDOC-CRM to create a single ontology or to illustrate a specific use case scenario related to intangible cultural heritage instance. However, CIDOC-CRM does not provide underlying model to explicitly express relationship between digital objects and their source objects which may be tangible or intangible.

If a model is proposed without any acceptable reasoning it becomes obsolete. To avoid this, we presented a use case example (Fig. 3) using the CHDE model and then created a crosswalk between the proposed models with CIDOC-CRM and FRBRoo classes (Tables 1 and 2).

This use case (Fig. 3) gives insight to the proposed CHDE model. Since intangible cultural heritage has *Instantiations* which depends on *Temporal, Location, Activity* etc. in Fig. 3, it was represented as a single instance class known as *Performance in 2016* which related to the *Temporal Class* in Table 2. Additionally, the tangible cultural heritage which was embodied as a *Waisted Drum* has an abstract relationship with the intangible cultural heritage which we need to further investigate.

Subsequently, through the crosswalk given in Sect. 4, we identified few characteristics significant to this study. By examining Table 1, we identified some CIDOC-CRM classes (such as *E22 Man-Made Object, E18 Physical Thing, E27 Site*) to represent the tangible heritage properties. Yet, it is not easy to find appropriate classes which represent all the intangible cultural heritage assets. Mostly *E28 Conceptual Object, F6 Concept, E29 Design or Procedure* and *F25 Performance Plan* continuously repeating in the table. Specially, when identifying related CIDOC-CRM and FRBRoo classes for intangible cultural heritage such as 'Social practices, rituals, festive events', 'Knowledge and skills to produce traditional crafts' and 'Knowledge and practices concerning nature and the universe' it is difficult to match suitable classes which completely explain the categories.

Table 2 shows a few instance classes related to intangible cultural heritage as explained earlier. This can be mapped to CIDOC-CRM classes without much effort. For example, classes, such as *E53 Place, E21 Person, E39 Actor* and *E7 Activity* correctly match with the meanings of the instantiation classes developed for the CHDE model. FRBRoo had handful classes which can be directly mapped to the same instance classes (e.g., *F8 Event* and *F9 Place*). Some classes can be mapped but they do not convey the same meanings of the instantiation classes. For instance, *E55 Type* can be mapped to *category* instance class. Also, *F3 Manifestation Product Type* is a subclass of the CIDOC *E55 Type* class. Nevertheless, *F3 Manifestation Product Type* real meaning is not compatible with the intangible instance class *category*. Therefore, it was marked using the *(≠)* sign. A similar case can be identified in Table 1 between *E25 Man-Made Feature* and *F53 Material Copy*. According to FRBRoo, *F53* is a subclass of *E25*. Nevertheless, *F53* description is about a *physical material of an information career* such as a book or a CD [5, 13]. Therefore, it is not equal to the CHDE Main classes such as *monuments* or *archaeological sites*.

7 Conclusions and Future Work

This paper has proposed the CHDE model to collect CHI, which is primarily designed to organize digital collections of cultural heritage. The resource identification and integration was done along with the One-to-One Principle of metadata and it gives a clear discrimination between the CHI and its original object. Through the crosswalk done between CHDE model and CIDOC-CRM and FRBRoo we sought to identify the CHDE classes and their relationships. However, it is possible to understand and express the CHDE classes through the existing CIDOC classes as well. Deviation of tangible and intangible cultural heritage and their physical, digital resources are not entirely expressed through these existing models. Therefore, developing a generalized model such as the CHDE model can be a solution to distinguish physical and digital entitics of a cultural heritage asset in diverse environment.

This would be a novel approach to the CHI domain in the region and this paper will be a foundation for that effort. The interrelation between intangible and tangible CHI, the method of collecting physical and digital records and their metadata, and the metadata aggregation process are still under investigation and that will be the future direction of this study.

Acknowledgements. This study has been partially supported by JSPS Kaken Grant-in-Aid for Scientific Research (A) #16H01754. The authors wish to express their appreciation to professors Atsuyuki Morishima, Mitsuharu Nagamori and all members at the Metadata Lab of the Graduate School of Library, Information and Media Studies, University of Tsukuba, for the guidance and support provided.

References

1. Amin, R., Baker, O.F., Deraman, A., Yatim, N.F.M.: Transforming model to meta model for knowledge repository of Malay intangible culture heritage of Malaysia. Int. J. Electr. Comput. Eng. **2**(2), 231–238 (2012). doi:10.11591/ijece.v2i2.205
2. Bizer, C., Heath, T., Berners-Lee, T.: Linked data-the story so far. In: Semantic Services, Interoperability and Web Applications: Emerging Concepts, pp. 205–227. IGI Global, USA (2009)
3. Carboni, N., de Luca, L.: Towards a conceptual foundation for documenting tangible and intangible elements of a cultural object. Digital Appl. Archaeol. Cult. Heritage **3**(4), 108–116 (2016). doi:10.1016/j.daach.2016.11.001
4. Chen, Y.N., Ke, H.R.: FRBRoo-based approach to heterogeneous metadata integration. J. Doc. **69**(5), 623–637 (2013)

5. Chryssoula, B., Doerr, M., Le Bœuf, P., Riva, P. (eds.): Definition of FRBROO a Conceptual Model for Bibliographic Information in Object-Oriented Formalism. International Working Group on FRBR and CIDOC CRM Harmonisation, version 2.4 (2015)
6. CIDOC-CRM. http://www.cidoc-crm.org/
7. DCMI: Cultural heritage metadata task group. http://dublincore.org/archive/mediawiki_wiki/Cultural_Heritage_Metadata_Task_Group/
8. Hansen, H.J., Fernie, K.: CARARE: connecting archaeology and architecture in Europeana. In: Ioannides, M., Fellner, D., Georgopoulos, A., Hadjimitsis, Diofantos G. (eds.) EuroMed 2010. LNCS, vol. 6436, pp. 450–462. Springer, Heidelberg (2010). doi:10.1007/978-3-642-16873-4_36
9. Hu, J., Lv, Y., Zhang, M.: The ontology design of intangible cultural heritage based on CIDOC CRM. Int. J. U-and E-Serv. 7(1), 261–274 (2014)
10. Hyvönen, E.: Publishing and using cultural heritage linked data on the semantic web. Synth. Lect. Seman. Web: Theor. Technol. 2(1), 1–159 (2012)
11. Isaac, A. (ed.): Europeana data model primer (2013). http://pro.europeana.eu/files/Europeana_Professional/Share_your_data/Technical_requirements/EDM_Documentation/EDM_Primer_130714.pdf
12. Lanzi, E.: Introduction to Vocabularies: Enhancing Access to Cultural Heritage Information. Getty Publications, Los Angeles (1999)
13. Le Boeuf, P., Doerr, M., Ore, C.E., Stead, S. (eds.): Definition of the CIDOC conceptual reference model. ICOM/CIDOC Documentation Standards Group and CIDOC CRM Special Interest Group, version 6.2.1 (2015)
14. Library of Congress: American Folklore Society Ethnographic Thesaurus. http://id.loc.gov/vocabulary/ethnographicTerms.html
15. Miller, S.J.: The one-to-one principle: challenges in current practice. In: International Conference on Dublin Core and Metadata Applications, pp. 150–164 (2010)
16. Tan, G., Hao, T., Zhong, Z.: A knowledge modeling framework for intangible cultural heritage based on ontology. In: Knowledge Acquisition and Modeling, KAM 2009, vol. 1, pp. 304–307. IEEE (2009). doi:10.1109/KAM.2009.17
17. The Getty Research Institute: Art & Architecture Thesaurus® Online. http://www.getty.edu/research/tools/vocabularies/aat/index.html
18. UNESCO: Intangible cultural heritage. https://ich.unesco.org/en/what-is-intangible-heritage-00003
19. UNESCO: Tangible cultural heritage. http://www.unesco.org/new/en/cairo/culture/tangible-cultural-heritage/
20. Wijesundara, C., Sugimoto, S., Narayan, B., Tuamsuk, K.: Bringing cultural heritage information from developing regions to the global information space as linked open data: an exploratory metadata aggregation model for Sri Lankan heritage and its extension. In: 7th Asia-Pacific Conference on Library and Information Education and Practice (A-LIEP), pp. 117–132 (2016)
21. Winda, M., Wijesundara, C., Sugimoto, S.: Modeling digital archives of intangible cultural heritage based on one-to-one principle of metadata. In: 8th Asia-Pacific Conference on library and Information Education and Practice (A-LIEP). Manuscript submitted for publication

Data Sharing and Retrieval

Is Data Retrieval Different from Text Retrieval? An Exploratory Study

Maryam Bugaje and Gobinda Chowdhury(✉)

iSchool, Faculty of Engineering and Environment,
Northumbria University, Newcastle, UK
{maryam.bugaje,gobinda.chowdhury}@northumbria.ac.uk

Abstract. The fundamental characteristics of and form of user interaction with research datasets differ considerably from those of research publications. Notwithstanding these differences, however, the majority of currently available research data repositories use the same retrieval engines for research data (datasets) as for publications (text), which retrieval engines, inevitably, are ill-suited as long-term solutions for sustainable data retrieval and use. This paper, through a systematic experiment, demonstrates the fundamental and deep-rooted differences between retrieval of research publications (predominantly text) and research data (i.e. datasets), and justifies the need for more research to build more efficient and effective data retrieval systems.

Keywords: Data retrieval · Text retrieval · Research data management

1 Introduction

Data, regarded as the world's most valuable resource [1], and the lifeblood of research [2], transcends all domains of scholarship, and could take on a variety of forms including text, sound, still images, moving images, models, games, and simulations as well as structured databases [3, 4]. Studies show several benefits of research data sharing [5]. As a result, governments and research funding bodies are increasingly pushing for open access and sharing of research data, especially when such data is generated through publicly funded research. This is all very positive, but until researchers and interested parties are able to find and use data as and when they need it and with tolerable ease, the vision of open access and sharing of data cannot be fully realized. Data retrieval systems are presently still at a relatively early stage of development, with the majority of research data repositories using the same or slightly tweaked versions of text retrieval engines for data retrieval. The fundamental characteristics of research data, and the form of its user interaction, differ considerably from research publications (text), both of which points make it impractical to expect standard text retrieval engines to adapt well to data. While both text and datasets can be tagged with metadata, the task of tagging the latter is often more complex; and unlike the indexing of research papers by services like Web of Science, the indexing of research datasets is not standardized or controlled. One of the key challenges of data retrieval arises from this lack of use of standard metadata and documentation to contextualize data sufficiently for discovery and reuse [2–7]. This paper does not aim to expound on the theoretical differences between text retrieval and

© Springer International Publishing AG 2017
S. Choemprayong et al. (Eds.): ICADL 2017, LNCS 10647, pp. 97–103, 2017.
https://doi.org/10.1007/978-3-319-70232-2_8

data retrieval, but to enquire into the following research questions through an exploratory study:

1. Are there any major differences between the search results of text retrieval and data retrieval services, particularly in terms of:
   a. The nature and volume of files retrieved; and
   b. The currently supported functionalities for interacting with the retrieved files; and
2. What are the implications of the above, resource-wise and otherwise? and
3. What measures could be taken to improve the efficiency of data retrieval services?

2   Research Methodology

The research reported in this paper is based on a controlled experiment that aimed to demonstrate some fundamental differences between text retrieval and data retrieval from the point of view of interaction and retrieval features of a typical text retrieval system and some commonly used data retrieval systems. Wikipedia[1] organizes all academic disciplines into 5 broad domains: Arts, Humanities, Social sciences, Natural sciences, and Applied sciences. For the purpose of this experiment we have slightly re-organized these further into four broad disciplines by merging together Arts and Humanities, and having Computer & Information Science represent its parent discipline of Applied Sciences. As each of the domains in the original Wikipedia classification is still well-represented, neither reshuffle is likely to affect the results of the experiment, being done mainly for convenience in the former case and to put the authors' subject knowledge to full advantage in the latter case. Five keywords and/or phrases were selected at random from the Wikipedia homepage of each respective discipline, and a search was conducted on the keyword/phrase in both data retrieval and text retrieval contexts. Thomson Reuters Web of Science[2] database, being the most comprehensive database for research publications, was employed for the text retrieval portion of the experiment; while a total of three research data repositories, viz. UK Data Service[3], DataOne[4], and Dryad[5] were used for the data retrieval portion. The selection of repositories was based on recommendations by re3data.org and Nature[6]; i.e. UK Data Service for Arts, Humanities, and Social Sciences data; DataOne for Natural Sciences data; and in the absence of a special Computer & Information Sciences data repository, Dryad, which is generalist. For both the data retrieval and text retrieval halves of the experiment, only the first 10 items of search results were considered, except in instances when an item so obviously departs from the intended topic, in which case the item is skipped and the next item is considered in its stead. As we have

---

[1] https://www.wikipedia.org.

[2] https://www.webofknowledge.com/.

[3] https://www.ukdataservice.ac.uk/.

[4] https://www.dataone.org/.

[5] datadryad.org/.

[6] https://www.nature.com/sdata/policies/repositories.

tried to mimic a typical search scenario of a researcher in a real world situation, the choice of only 10 items emanates from research on user search behavior which shows that well over half of search engine users do not go past the first page of search results [8–10]; and 10 just happens to be the default minimum number of results on a single page that is common to most search engines [11, 12], including, in our present case, Thomson Reuters Web of Science and UK Data Service. File sizes and formats were noted for each of the items considered: for publications (text retrieval) this constitutes full research papers; and for datasets (data retrieval) this constitutes the dataset itself as well as all of its documentation files, if any. A uniformity of file format was noted in the text retrieval portion of the experiment, all of the research papers being in PDF format, viewable on the web browser, and downloadable at the user's discretion. The journals featured include IEEE Xplore, Sage, ScienceDirect, Taylor & Francis, PLOS One, and JSTOR among others. Conversely for the data retrieval part, over 20 different file formats were noted, notwithstanding the more or less homogenizing effect of our decision to always give preference to non-propriety formats (e.g. txt, CSV, tab-delimited) over propriety formats (e.g. STRATA, SPSS, XLS, MATLAB) wherever possible. Also, as there have been variations in file sizes for the same dataset on account of the aforementioned multiplicity of file formats, preference was given to the rendering that is smaller in size. Unlike their publication counterparts, datasets cannot be viewed on the web browser, but must be downloaded first before even a first or cursory glimpse of their content could be had.

3 Findings

Figure 1 shows, for each keyword in each discipline, what proportion of the total file size retrieved constitutes research datasets and research publications. It could be seen that on average the file sizes of research datasets generally and significantly exceed those of research publications, so that, in some cases (i.e. search behavior, face recognition, computer vision, 'renewable energy', and 'ultraviolet light'), the whole appears to be composed entirely of research datasets; but that is not really so: the observation merely demonstrates the overwhelming disproportionateness in average file size of research datasets to research publications (text) in those subjects. Table 1 provides a more accurate representation, where the average file size of a single research dataset may in some cases be observed to amount to as much as 900 times over the average file size of a single research publication

Other key observations of this study with regards to the first research question are:

1. Average file size of retrieved datasets is several times larger than that of retrieved research publication files; and these in turn vary from one discipline to another.
2. Unlike publications, the retrieved datasets may be of different file types or formats.
3. Whereas research publications comprise of only the publication itself, research datasets are almost always accompanied with separate documentation files (up to 22 have been noted in this experiment). Each piece of documentation furnishes further information about the dataset in question, and may be necessary for its potential re-use. These documentation files tend be include code snippets, original survey

questions, file descriptions, READ MEs, appendices, variable coding information, user guides, instructions, index files, consent forms, ethical clearance certificates, etc.

4. A single dataset item record may constitute several composite files (as many as 524 have been noted in this experiment) comprising fragments of the dataset broken up into smaller file sizes; or versions of the dataset at different stages of processing or under different conditions of observation. This is in contrast with research publications whereby a single item record comprises only one file representing a whole.

5. Unlike research publications which may be read online in abstract or full text form, research datasets often must be downloaded before they can be read or used.

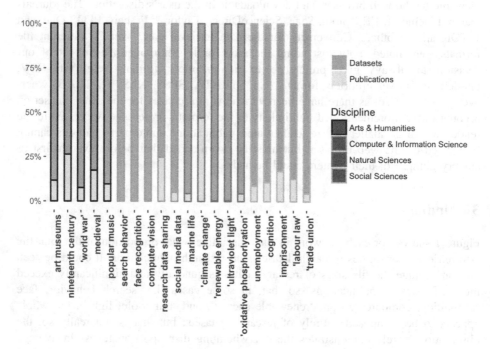

Fig. 1. The relative file size proportions for research datasets and research publications out of the overall total file size of all the files retrieved for each keyword.

For the second research question, it may thus be argued that the currently available research data retrieval services are unsustainable (for details on sustainability of information see [13, 14]). They involve an unnecessarily high consumption of valuable resources – both in terms of the network and researcher time – given evidence from Table 1, and seeing as research datasets must first be downloaded before their contents could even be viewed. These unnecessary downloads of large volumes of data will additionally involve energy, which could have severe environmental and economic implications in terms of server costs, etc. (see [13, 14] for details). In addition, these empty downloads present a major stumbling block to the reliability of research data impact indicators which cite download count as a measure of the impact, usefulness,

Table 1. Average sizes of files retrieved for research datasets and research publications.

Discipline	Keywords	Data Retrieval*	Text Retrieval*	Approx. ratio of text to data
Arts & Humanities	Art museums	6.205 MB	0.820 MB	1:8
	Nineteenth century	2.898 MB	1.042 MB	1:3
	"World war"	6.158 MB	0.508 MB	1:12
	Medieval	5.158 MB	1.091 MB	1:5
	Popular music	9.334 MB	1.000 MB	1:9
Social Sciences	Unemployment	4.729 MB	0.455 MB	1:10
	Cognition	13.340 MB	1.612 MB	1:8
	"Labour law"	2.827 MB	0.410 MB	1:7
	"Trade union"	15.939 MB	0.748 MB	1:21
	Imprisonment	2.444 MB	0.503 MB	1:5
Computer & Information Science	Search behavior	657.707 MB	0.731 MB	1:900
	Face recognition	**1.394 GB**	1.535 MB	1:908
	Computer vision	**1.339 GB**	2.782 MB	1:481
	Research data sharing	1.574 MB	0.521 MB	1:3
	Social media data	19.597 MB	1.078 MB	1:18
Natural Sciences	Marine life	32.318 MB	1.491 MB	1:22
	"Climate change"	2.808 MB	2.497 MB	1:1
	"Renewable energy"	766.432 MB	3.606 MB	1:213
	"Ultraviolet light"	496.745 MB	1.991 MB	1:250
	"Oxidative phosphorlyation"	41.177 MB	1.895 MB	1:22

*Average File Size, inclusive of documentation
**Average File Size

and/or popularity of a dataset. To resolve these issues, and to achieve sustainability in data access and reuse, not only should data retrieval services aim to improve search precision and prevent unnecessary data downloads by furnishing adequate contextual information to help users make informed decisions about download choices; but provision should be made, additionally, of features which allow datasets to be previewed before download.

In view of the aforementioned findings, we offer the following suggestions which also pertain to the third research question:

1. The conventional approach to information (text) retrieval may not be the best for data retrieval, and unless the efficiency of the data retrieval systems is improved the services cannot achieve sustainability (as discussed in the paper);

2. The efficiency of data retrieval systems can be achieved through a combination of:
   a. Providing adequate contextual information for retrieved datasets in the form of metadata specific to that discipline and thorough documentation. However, this would be highly resource-intensive if done manually, and therefore new automated and software-assisted means must be developed;
   b. Better training for researchers on the use of metadata and other tagging methods;
   c. The development of improved functionalities for data repositories, with interactive options allowing datasets to be previewed on the browser before download;
   d. Undertaking more research in the area of data retrieval with user-centered focus to better understand the data seeking and use behavior of researchers, and to develop models of users and usability for data retrieval; and
   e. Building reliable weighting and ranking methods for research datasets to guide users.

4 Conclusion

This study provides some useful insights on data retrieval, and is methodologically designed such that the experiment could be repeated with different parameters and variables to gain further insight. The average file size of research datasets is often several times larger than that of research publications. Moreover, often the retrieved datasets cannot be read or used online, but must be downloaded first before anything can be done with them; as a result of which users end up downloading files without full knowledge of the files' contents or usefulness. This is further compounded by the differences in file types, size, format, and/or documentation; all of which have major implications for search efficiency and resource requirements. Also, besides wastefully consuming large amounts of storage disk space and network resources, the unnecessary downloading of multitudes of large datasets (with all associated documentation) falsely spikes up download count, effectively rendering this metric unreliable as an indicator data impact, usefulness, or popularity. What's more, as a pre-requisite to reusing a research dataset, the user often spends a considerable amount of time wading through the dataset and its documentation to gain an understanding of it; an endeavor that is exacerbated by the lack of standardized tagging and documentation system for research datasets.

Research shows that energy consumption increases with increase in server load because energy is consumed during both phases: while doing computing work and while waiting for database data to arrive [15]. Hence, a reduction in the volume of data downloaded will reduce the energy consumption of IT infrastructure of data services as well as the universities and research institutions, thereby reducing the environmental costs of research data management. This may be achieved by building more efficient, user-centered, and perhaps discipline-specific data retrieval services.

References

1. The world's most valuable resource. The Economist, p. 9, 6–12 May 2017
2. Borgman, C.L.: The conundrum of sharing research data. J. Am. Soc. Inf. Sci. Technol. **63**(6), 1059–1078 (2012)
3. Borgman, C.L.: Big Data, Little Data, No Data: Scholarship in the Networked World. The MIT Press, Cambridge (2015)
4. Borgman, C.L., Wallis, J.C., Mayernik, M.S.: Who's got the data? Interdependencies in science and technology collaborations. Comput. Support. Coop. Work **21**(6), 485–523 (2012)
5. The Data harvest: How sharing research data can yield knowledge, jobs and growth. An RDA Europe report, December 2014. https://rd-alliance.org/sites/default/files/attachment/The%20Data%20Harvest%20Final.pdf. Accessed 11 June 2017
6. MacMillan, D.: Data sharing and discovery: what librarians need to know. J. Acad. Librarianship **40**(5), 541–549 (2014)
7. Wallis, J.C., Rolando, E., Borgman, C.L.: If we share data, will anyone use them? Data sharing and reuse in the long tail of science and technology. PLoS ONE **8**(7), e67332 (2013). doi:10.1371/journal.pone.0067332
8. Jansen, B.J., Spink, A.: How are we searching the world wide web? A comparison of nine search engine transaction logs. Inf. Process. Manag. **42**(1), 248–263 (2006)
9. Spink, A., Wolfram, D., Jansen, B.J., Saracevik, T.: Searching the web: the public and their queries. J. Am. Soc. Inf. Sci. **53**(2), 226–234 (2001)
10. Richardson, M., Dominowska, E., Ragno, R.: Predicting clicks: estimating the click-through rate for new ads. In: Proceedings of the 16th International Conference on World Wide Web, WWW 2007, pp. 521–530 (2007)
11. Malcy, C., Baum, N.: Getting to the top of google: search engine optimization. J. Med. Pract. Manag. MPM **25**(5), 301–303 (2010)
12. Wu, M., Marian, A.: A framework for corroborating answers from multiple web sources. Inf. Syst. **36**(2), 431–449 (2011)
13. Chowdhury, G.G.: Sustainability of Scholarly Information. Facet Publishing, London (2014)
14. Chowdhury, G.G.: How to improve the sustainability of digital libraries and information services? J. Assoc. Inf. Sci. Technol. **67**(10), 2379–2391 (2016)
15. Boru, D., Kliazovich, D., Granelli, F., Bouvry, P., Zomaya, A.Y.: Energy-efficient data replication in cloud computing datacenters. Cluster Comput. **18**(1), 385–402 (2015)

Preparedness for Research Data Sharing: A Study of University Researchers in Three European Countries

Gobinda Chowdhury[1(✉)], Joumana Boustany[2], Serap Kurbanoğlu[3],
Yurdagül Ünal[3], and Geoff Walton[4]

[1] iSchool, Northumbria University, Newcastle upon Tyne, UK
gobinda.chowdhury@northumbria.ac.uk
[2] DICEN-IdF EA 7339, UNIVERSITE PARIS-EST MARNE-LA-VALLEE
(UPEM), Champs-sur-Marne, France
jboustany@gmail.com
[3] Department of Information Management, Hacettepe University,
Ankara, Turkey
{serap,yurdagul}@hacettepe.edu.tr
[4] Department of Languages, Information and Communications,
Manchester Metropolitan University, Manchester, UK
g.walton@mmu.ac.uk

Abstract. Many government and funding bodies around the world have been advocating open access to research data, arguing that such open access can bring a significant degree of economic and social benefit. However, the question remains, do researchers themselves want to share their research data, and even if they do how far they are prepared to make this happen? In this paper we report on an international survey involving university researchers in three countries, viz. UK, France and Turkey. We found that researchers have a number of concerns for data sharing, and in general there is a lack of understanding of the requirements for making data publicly available and accessible. We note that significant training and advocacy will be required to make the vision of data sharing a reality.

Keywords: Research data management · Data sharing · Metadata · Ethics · User education

1 Introduction

Researchers have described data as the glue of a collaboration [1], and the lifeblood of research [2]. Several benefits of research data sharing have been highlighted including for example, economic growth, increased resource efficiency and securing public support for research funding [3, 4]. It is reported that: "in the US, one study estimated the $13 billion in government spending on the Human Genome project and its successors has yielded a total economic benefit of about $1 trillion. A British study of its public economic and social research database found that for every £1 invested by the government, an economic return of £5.40 resulted" [5]. Given these benefits, various governments and funding bodies are pushing for OA to research data. However,

S. Choemprayong et al. (Eds.): ICADL 2017, LNCS 10647, pp. 104–116, 2017.
https://doi.org/10.1007/978-3-319-70232-2_9

take-up of the concept of OA and sharing amongst researchers has been low. This may be attributable to a lack of skills and knowledge in making data discoverable, accessible, and reusable for others' research; or it may be attributed to issues related to trust, reputation, and ethics [5–9].

The exploratory research reported in this paper addresses the following questions:

1. Are university researchers willing to share their research data and what concerns do they have with regard to research data sharing?
2. Are university researchers familiar with various activities and preparation needed to make data shareable and usable?

2   Research Data Management

The UK Data Archive [4] proposes a research data lifecycle that comprises six major sets of activities some of which, such as data creation, data access, analysis and re-use, are undertaken or primarily driven by researchers in a specific discipline. Researchers, therefore, also have some important roles in research data management activities. However, not much is known about how researchers go about managing their data and whether they are willing to share data with others outside of the immediate research collaboration [10]. Often researchers are preoccupied by immediate issues of backing up data rather than the longer term question of preservation [11]. In fact, the sharing of data even within interdisciplinary projects is also highly problematic [12], and incentives to release data are lacking, the adopting of data repositories remain slow and there are questions regarding their design in that they are optimised for performance rather than scientific enquiry [2]. This is especially troublesome as the advent of "big science" and the emergence of the "fourth paradigm" which is a "computational data-intensive approach to science that constitutes a new set of methods beyond empiricism, theory and simulation" [10]. However, this appears to be less of a problem for large well-established and long-lasting collaborations than it is for small-scale, short-lived collaborative projects which is often called the "long tail of science and technology" [10]. In these small teams methods tend to be local and specific to the research at hand, where reusing this data requires a great deal of contextual knowledge about procedure. Without contextual information, where data have been separated from context, reuse can become "difficult or impossible" [13]. Within the "long tail" research projects data sharing is described as a "gift culture" [10] where data is bartered between colleagues in trusted relationships. Therefore, providers of data will overcome problems of context and documentation for trusted others but this is clearly unsustainable in the longer term.

One of the key challenges of data sharing is that it requires standard metadata and documentation to contextualise data sufficiently for re-use [2] and discovery [13, 15] outside of the collaboration for which it was intended. MacMillan [14] notes that, very few researchers (22%) use metadata, preferring to use their own laboratory standards instead, a view supported by Carlson et al. [11]. An underlying technical issue is the decreasing lifespan of data storage formats, which require more sustainable data management practices [14]. Furthermore, researchers lack the data curation skills and these are not addressed at undergraduate level [16]. There is also a lack of academic credit or reward for data curation [10, 14], and for developing common data structures, metadata formats and ontologies to support data mining [2, 13, 15]. The role of education should not be underestimated here. In a study of researchers in the area of health for example, 77% of researchers reported that they had, "never received any formal training" and reported their expertise as "very low" in data management [17, p. 54]. Another survey amongst over 2000 academics and researchers from around the world noted that, "researchers do not know how open they have made their data - 60% of respondents are unsure about the licensing conditions under which they have shared their data, and thus the extent to which it can be accessed or reused" [18, p.14]. This clearly indicates that there is a significant gap in awareness and understanding which needs to be addressed [11, 19].

3 Research Method

This research is based on an international survey conducted amongst university academics and researchers in three countries. The chosen countries – UK, France and Turkey – are all in Europe but they are different in terms of their current state of development and policies towards RDM.

Amongst the three countries chosen for this study, the UK is arguably the most advanced in terms of research and development of technologies, tools and policies for RDM. Researchers led by agencies like JISC, DCC and specific universities have been engaged in research in different areas of RDM for nearly a decade. A significant move towards management and research data sharing is also evident through various policies recently introduced by government funding agencies in UK. For example, the RCUK (research councils UK) Common Principles on Data Policy states that "publicly funded research data are a public good, produced in the public interest, which should be made openly available with as few restrictions as possible in a timely and responsible manner" [20].

In France, the interest in research data was stated publicly in 2011 when the Ministry of Higher Education and Research implemented a platform for monitoring and providing information about research data, and for raising awareness and encouraging a debate around challenges related to research data. Two years later, under the aegis of the same Ministry, a research infrastructure Huma-Num was created which provides research teams in the Human and Social sciences to facilitate the processing, access, storage and interoperability of various types of digital data. It also offers a platform, NAKALA, to archive and share research data. In 2016, the French URFIST Network that had already organized many national seminars on research data in collaboration with the National Center for Scientific Research and the digital scientific library lunched DoRANum project. Many academic libraries created specific services on RDM.

In Turkey, due to lack of necessary policies, strategies and regulations for RDM, the majority of research data is not archived and cannot be accessed and re-used. Neither the national funding agency for scientific research (TUBITAK: The Scientific and Technological Research Council of Turkey) nor other funding agencies or universities have any RDM policy and/or mandate, and do not require a data management plan from research they fund. As a result, none of the research institutions have yet implemented services for research data storage, analysis and curation. There are no units within research institutions which provides support to researchers who would like to store and share their research data [21, 22]. However, starting from 2012, there have been several initiatives which aim to increase awareness towards the importance of the subject and address the current situation in Turkey.

It is clear that RDM technology and policy developments are at varying levels in the UK, France and Turkey. The choice of the universities was based on a slightly different criterion: the three chosen universities have similarity in their nature such as; emphasis is given both to teaching and research, but all of them has increasing demand for national and international researches in different fields. This approach was employed to gain a sense of the awareness of, and preparedness for, RDM amongst academics and researchers in universities of similar nature but from three different countries that have different levels of progress in overall RDM activities.

The survey was developed by the researchers and a pilot study was carried out first to make sure that all questions were clear and understandable. Based on the pilot study results, the survey instrument was developed. E-mail invitations were sent out to the academics and researchers in the three chosen universities. There were 26 questions to collect data on: researcher information – role, discipline, gender, experience, etc.; nature of data collected, created, etc.; data sharing practices, concerns; familiarity with data management practices and policies/challenges including knowledge of metadata, training, etc. The research reported in this paper addresses only those questions in the questionnaire that are related to data sharing practices, concerns, and researchers' awareness and familiarity with for example, various RDM tools, techniques and policies. SPSS was used to analyse the dataset, and Chi-Square tests, at 0.05 signifi- cance level, were conducted to find out correlation between researchers' behaviour in different areas of RDM especially with regard to data tagging and storage, sharing and re-use of research data, etc., and researchers' characteristics such as country, discipline, age, gender and years of experience.

4 Data Sharing

Conducted in the summer of 2016 this survey received a total of 215 completed responses. Tables 1 and 2 present the general demographic data by country and years of experience. The OECD classification of disciplines [23] was provided as a list for the respondents to choose from.

Table 1. Respondents' status by country (%)

Country	Academic staff	Research student	Research staff	Total
France	16	22	69	21
Turkey	35	16	0	27
UK	50	63	31	52
Total	101	101	100	100

Note: The percentage of the total is not 100% due to rounding.

Table 2. Respondents' years of experience by discipline (%)

Years of experience	Science	Social science	Humanities	Total
<5	27	28	31	28
5–10	19	25	19	22
11–15	15	18	13	16
16–20	15	12	12	12
>20	25	18	25	21
Total	101	101	100	99

Note: 1 - The percentage of the total is not 100% due to rounding.
2 - Three respondents did not answer the question related to
discipline. Therefore the total is 212.

Table 3. Data sharing behaviour of researchers

Data sharing behaviour	%
Collaboration with researchers in the same team	56
Collaboration with researchers in the same university	40
Collaboration with researchers in other institutions	45
Not shared	29

However, in order to be able to run correlation tests, subject categories were merged under larger groups such as sciences, social sciences and humanities: 53% were from social sciences, 25% from humanities and 23% from sciences. Table 3 shows the user behaviour in relation to data sharing. Statistically significant differences were detected between specific behaviours with regard to *sharing data with others* and *country (C), years of experience (E), discipline (D)*, e.g. *sharing with own team* $(C-\chi^2_{(2)} = 41,858$; $p = 0,000, E-\chi^2_{(4)} = 22,305; p = 0,000, D-\chi^2_{(2)} = 9,376; p = 0,009)$, *sharing with researchers in the same university* $(C-\chi^2_{(2)} = 14,382; p = 0,001, E-\chi^2_{(2)} = 14,931; p = 0,005)$, *sharing with researchers in other institutions* $(C-\chi^2_{(2)} = 6,419$; $p = 0,040, E-\chi^2_{(4)} = 24,445; p = 0,000, D-\chi^2_{(2)} = 7,108; p = 0,029)$, and *not sharing data* $(C-\chi^2_{(2)} = 28,539; p = 0,000, E-\chi^2_{(4)} = 34,924; p = 0,000, D-\chi^2_{(2)} = 7,171; p = 0,028)$. A significant difference was detected between researchers' behaviour for *not sharing data* and *country* $(\chi^2_{(2)} = 28,539; p = 0,000)$. Whilst nearly half (45%) of the UK researchers claim that they do not collaborate in data sharing, this is significantly less for the other two countries: approximately 13% in France and 11% in Turkey. A statistically significant difference was also detected between *sharing data with own team* and *country* $(\chi^2_{(2)} = 41,858; p = 0,000)$, *sharing data with researchers in the same university* $(\chi^2_{(2)} = 14,382; p = 0,001)$, *sharing data with researchers in other institutions* $(\chi^2_{(2)} = 6,419; p = 0,040)$ and *country*.

5 Metadata and Tagging of Datasets

Researchers use different coding or tagging for their datasets (Table 4). However, not all of them are familiar with the concept of metadata, nor do they always use standard metadata (Table 5). Nearly a third of the researchers are either uncertain or are not familiar with the concept of metadata (Table 6). Nearly 95% of the researchers are either uncertain or do not know whether their university has a prescribed metadata set for uploading data onto the repository. However, nearly 60% of researchers feel that a formal training on metadata would be useful for managing research data.

Table 4. Data tagging done by researchers

Type of tag/added information	%
Administrative information (creator, date of creation, file name, access terms/restrictions, etc.)	47
Discovery information (creator, funding body, project title, project ID, keywords, etc.)	31
Technical information (file format, file size, software/hardware needed to use the data, etc.)	24
Description of the data file (file/data structure, field tags/descriptions, application rules, etc.)	29
No assignment	37

Only one metadata related behaviour in relation to data use, viz. *using datasets that are tagged with standard metadata* had a significant correlation with researchers' experience; and no significant correlation was found between researchers' metadata related behaviour and their gender. No significant correlations were found between researchers' status and tagging of datasets. Only one tagging behaviour (*description of the data file*, $\chi^2_{(2)} = 13,048; p = 0,001$) correlated with discipline: descriptions of a data file are used more by researchers in science (48%) and least by researchers in humanities (15%). Correlations were also detected between country and some tagging behaviour (such as *no assignment*, $\chi^2_{(2)} = 10,559; p = 0,005$; *administrative information*, $\chi^2_{(2)} = 9,318$; $p = 0,009$; *discovery information*, $\chi^2_{(2)} = 13,508; p = 0,001$; and *technical information* $\chi^2_{(2)} = 14,434; p = 0,001$). The number of researchers who do not assign tags and metadata to their datasets is higher in the UK (46%); and assigning administrative (38%), discovery (20%) and technical (15%) information to datasets is the lowest in UK.

Table 5. Use of standard metadata (%)

Use of standard metadata	Almost always	Often	Sometimes	Rarely	Never
Using metadata standard for tagging data	7	5	13	16	59
Using own/in-house (research team) tags and metadata	12	9	14	11	54
Using datasets that are tagged with standard metadata	5	10	16	15	54

Table 6. Familiarity with metadata (%)

Metadata issue	Yes	Uncertain	No
I am familiar with the term metadata	68	11	21
A formal training on metadata would be useful for managing research data	60	36	5
My university have a prescribed metadata set	5	83	12

Note: The percentage of the total is not 100% due to rounding.

6 Open Access and Data Sharing Issues

Only 23% of researchers agree that their university encourages OA and data sharing, and only 31% of researchers are familiar with the OA requirements (Table 7). Researchers have different views on the potential benefits and challenges of OA and data sharing (Table 8); only 55% of researchers are comfortable and willing to share research data; 67.5% of researchers perceive that data ethics could be an issue for data sharing. Researchers do have a number of concerns for making data available in open access mode (Table 9); and some of the key concerns of researchers include: legal and ethical issues, misuse and misinterpretation of data, and fear of losing the scientific edge (Table 10).

Table 7. Familiarity with OA policies (%)

Familiarity with OA policy	Yes	Uncertain	No
Your university encourage to share data on open access	23	43	34
I am familiar with funding body's requirements with regard to data storage	31	30	39

Table 8. Views on OA policies (%)

Views on OA	Strongly agree	Agree	Neither agree or disagree	Disagree	Strongly disagree
Familiar with the OA requirements	16	38	26	15	5
Comfortable/willing to share research data with others	15	40	26	17	1
Foresee no problems with sharing research data	11	23	31	28	7
Perceive data ethics could be an issue when research data is shared with others	21	47	23	8	2

Table 9. Data sharing practices

Data sharing practices	%
My data is openly available to everyone	20
My data is openly available only to my research team	34
My data is available openly upon request	47
My data has restricted access (e.g. only some parts of the dataset is accessible)	21
My data is not available to anyone else	20

A correlation was detected between researchers' country and familiarity with metadata ($\chi^2_{(4)} = 16,214; p = 0,003$): researchers in Turkey displayed the lowest score for familiarity with metadata (50%). A correlation was also detected between researchers' discipline and their *familiarity with the OA requirements* ($\chi^2_{(8)} = 16,162; p = 0,040$), *willingness to share their research data with others* ($\chi^2_{(8)} = 19,818; p = 0,011$) and *foreseeing no problems with sharing research data* ($\chi^2_{(8)} = 34,266; p = 0,000$). More than half of the researchers in all countries claim to be familiar with OA requirements: combined figures for *strongly agree* or *agree* on this were 61% for France, 56% for Turkey and 50% for UK. Researchers in France seem to be more willing to share their research data (74%) and they see data sharing less problematic (54%) compared to the other two countries.

Table 10. Data sharing concerns

Data sharing concerns	%
No concerns	26
Fear of losing the scientific edge	20
Legal and ethical issues	52
Misuse of data	37
Misinterpretation of data	39
Lack of resources (technical, financial, personnel, etc.)	12
Lack of appropriate policies and rights protection	19

Table 11. Availability and awareness of a DMP (%)

Data Management Plan	Yes	Uncertain	No
Your institution have a DMP	32	59	9
I used a DMP for my research	23	17	61
I have a DMP for my current research project(s)	25	17	59
A DMP helps researchers in managing research data	40	52	8

Table 12. File naming system (%)

File naming system	Yes	Uncertain	No
My research community use a standard file naming system	9	39	53
My university have a standard file naming system	3	50	47

Table 13. Use of standard file naming conventions (%)

Data file management	Almost always	Often	Sometimes	Rarely	Never
Using file naming convention or standard	16	21	14	13	37
Having different versions of the same dataset(s)	15	25	19	14	26
Using systems/techniques for version control to recognise a specific version	18	16	15	14	37

A significant correlation was detected between researchers' discipline and data sharing practices such as making their research *data available to everyone* ($\chi^2_{(2)} = 6,158; p = 0,046$) and making it *available only to own research team* ($\chi^2_{(2)} = 7,264; p = 0,026$). Only 13% of researchers in social sciences are willing to make their data open to everyone and only 19% in humanities are willing to make it available only to their own research team. Some correlations were also detected between researchers' country and certain data sharing practices (*making it available openly upon request* ($\chi^2_{(2)} = 8,716; p = 0,013$), *providing restricted access* ($\chi^2_{(2)} = 7,158$; $p = 0,028$), *not making it available to anyone else* ($\chi^2_{(2)} = 8,492; p = 0,014$). Researchers in the UK had the highest score for reluctance to share data: 28% for *making data available with restricted access* and 27% for *not making data available to anyone else*. They also show the lowest score for *making data available upon request* (38%).

7 Data Management Plans (DMP): Issues and Awareness

Despite various government and funding body mandates, researchers still appear to be not quite familiar with DMP: two-thirds or more researchers are either uncertain or do not know whether their institution has a DMP, and only a quarter of researchers have or used a DMP for their research (Table 11). However, on a positive note, 40% of researchers believe that a DMP helps researchers manage their data. Tables 12 and 13 show that very few researchers practise or use standard file naming systems which is a key requirement of a good data management system. Very few people had any formal training on different aspects of data management that are essential for research data sharing and use (Table 14):

- Only 6.5% had any formal training on DMP;
- Only 10% had a formal training on metadata;
- Only 2.8% had any training on version control, etc.

However, over 77% of researchers are willing to take formal training on these topics. A significant correlation was observed between the researchers' country and their opinion about the role of the universities for *recommending a standard file naming system* ($\chi^2_{(8)} = 41,927; p = 0,000$). Turkish researchers had the highest score (53%) in this regard. Some correlations were discovered between researchers' country and the *use of standard file naming system* $(\chi^2_{(4)} = 15,711; p = 0,003)$, *use of standard style for citing research data* $(\chi^2_{(4)} = 14,214; p = 0,007)$, *being recommended a specific guideline for citing data by the university* $(\chi^2_{(4)} = 29,136; p = 0,000)$ and *owning a unique researcher ID* $(\chi^2_{(4)} = 13,390; p = 0,010)$. More than 40% of researchers in UK own a unique researcher ID, while this is only 17% in France. Whilst approximately 60% of researchers in both the UK and Turkey claim that their universities recommend some guidelines for citing data, for France it is only 15%. Nearly half (46%) of the researchers from France also claimed that they do not use a standard style for citing research data.

Table 14. Formal training (%)

Formal training subjects	Have had a formal training	Willingness for a formal training
Data Management Plan	7	58
Metadata	10	51
Consistent file naming	7	39
Version control of data sets	3	44
Data citation styles	23	36
No, I haven't had training on any of the above	71	78

8   Discussions and Conclusion

This study shows that the culture of OA and data sharing is not yet common: only about 40% of researchers do almost always or often use OA data, and only about 23% work with datasets with restricted access. In most cases (80%) researchers have to put in some effort before they can make use of OA data. There may be several reasons such as data may not be tagged properly or standard metadata set has not been used, or for example, researchers may not be familiar with tagging or data management. In general, nearly 80% of researchers do not want to share data with anyone. Less than a quarter of researchers agree that their university encourages OA and data sharing, and only 31% of researchers are familiar with the OA requirements of the funding bodies. Nearly 95% of researchers are either uncertain or do not know whether their university has a prescribed metadata set. Despite various government and funding body mandates, majority (about 80%) of the researchers do not want to share data with others; and the key concerns for OA and data sharing include: legal and ethical issues, misuse and misinterpretation of data, and fear of losing the scientific edge. In total, 40% of researchers do not use a standard data citation style, and only 50% universities have a recommended citation style; 61% are familiar with the concept of DOI, but only a third of the researchers have a unique researcher ID; and researchers do not always find appropriate systems for version control of datasets.

Although UK is ahead of the two other countries in terms of research and development in RDM, the willingness for data sharing is still low: 45% of the UK researchers claim that they do not collaborate in data sharing. UK researchers appeared to be more reluctant to share data: 28% said they would make *data available with restricted access* and 27% will *not make data available to anyone else*. They also show the lowest score for *making data available upon request* (38%). Researchers in France seem to be more willing to share their research data (74%) and they see data sharing less problematic (54%) compared to other two countries. The number of researchers who do not assign tags and metadata to their datasets is higher in the UK (46%); whilst assigning administrative (38%), discovery (20%) and technical (15%) information to datasets is also the lowest in UK. However, researchers in Turkey displayed the lowest score for familiarity with metadata. More than 40% of researchers in UK own a unique researcher ID, while this is only 17% in France. Nearly 60% of researchers in both the UK and Turkey claim that their universities recommend some guidelines for citing data, but for France it is only 15%; 46% of the researchers from France also do not use a standard style for citing research data. Two-thirds or more of researchers are either uncertain or do not know whether their institution has a data management plan (DMP), and only a quarter of the researchers have used a DMP for their research. Over 70% of researchers did not have any formal training in DMP, metadata, consistent file naming and version control or data citation. This corroborates previous research [17] which noted that 77% of researchers never received any formal training in data management.

Overall, this research demonstrates that a significant number of gaps exist between researchers' perceptions and behaviours with regard to research data creation and sharing, and the ambition of funding bodies and academic institutions with regard to OA data. The gap in the skill sets required for university researchers can be filled by developing data literacy which is broadly defined as, "knowing how to select and synthesise data and combine them with other information sources and prior knowledge" [13, p. 405].

The purpose of this study was to explore whether differences exist amongst countries, disciplines, and years of the experience of the researchers with regard to their awareness and behaviour in relation to RDM. The findings show a range of interesting behaviours in research data sharing and various RDM practices displayed by university academics and researchers that may provide valuable insight for the development of data literacy training programmes. However, given the relatively small sample size and response rate, the results, especially the comparison at country, discipline and experience level, should be taken with some caution. More detailed studies with larger and more representative samples should be undertaken in order to make reliable comparisons amongst these variables.

References

1. Borgman, C.L., Wallis, J.C., Mayernik, M.S.: Who's got the data? Interdependencies in science and technology collaborations. Comput. Support. Coop. Work **21**(6), 485–523 (2012)
2. Borgman, C.L.: The conundrum of sharing research data. J. Am. Soc. Inf. Sci. Technol. **63**(6), 1059–1078 (2012)

3. Beagrie, N., Houghton, J.: The value and impact of data sharing and curation: A synthesis of three recent studies of UK research data centres, JISC (2013). http://repository.jisc.ac.uk/5568/1/iDF308_-_Digital_Infrastructure_Directions_Report%2C_Jan14_v1-04.pdf. Accessed 11 June 2017
4. UK Data Archive: Create & manage data. Research data lifecycle. Concordat on open access data Version 10, 17 July 2015. http://www.rcuk.ac.uk/documents/documents/concordatopenresearchdata-pdf/. Accessed 11 June 2017
5. The Data harvest: How sharing research data can yield knowledge, jobs and growth. An RDA Europe report, December 2014. https://rd-alliance.org/sites/default/files/attachment/The%20Data%20Harvest%20Final.pdf. Accessed 11 June 2017
6. Faniel, I.M., Kriesberg, A., Yakel, E.: Data reuse and sensemaking among novice social scientists. Proc. Am. Soc. Inf. Sci. Technol. **49**(1), 1–10 (2012). doi:10.1002/meet.14504901068. Accessed 11 June 2017
7. Faniel, I., Kansa, E., Kansa, S.W., Barrera-Gomez, J., Yakel, E.: The challenges of digging data: a study of context in archaeological data reuse. In: JCDL 2013 Proceedings of the 13th ACM/IEEE-CS Joint Conference on Digital Libraries, pp. 295–304. ACM, New York, NY (2013)
8. Yakel, E., Faniel, I.: Virtuous circles: circulating old data through new collaborations. In: 17th ACM Conference on Computer Supported Cooperative Work and Social Computing Workshop: Sharing, Re-Use and Circulation of Resources in Cooperative Scientific Work. Baltimore, MD, 15 February 2014
9. Borgman, C.L.: Big Data, Little Data, No Data: Scholarship in the Networked World. The MIT Press, Cambridge (2015)
10. Wallis, J.C., Rolando, E., Borgman, C.L.: If we share data, will anyone use them? Data sharing and reuse in the long tail of science and technology. PLoS ONE **8**(7), e67332 (2013). doi:10.1371/journal.pone.0067332
11. Carlson, J., Fosmire, M., Miller, C.C., Nelson, M.S.: Determining data information literacy needs: a study of students and research faculty. Portal: Libr. Acad. **11**(2), 629–657 (2011)
12. Mayernik, M.S., Wallis, J.C., Borgman, C.L.: Unearthing the infrastructure: humans and sensors in field-based scientific research. Comput. Support. Coop. Work **22**(1), 65–101 (2013). doi:10.1007/s10606-012-9178-y
13. Koltay, T.: Data literacy: in search of a name and identity. J. Documentation **71**(2), 401–415 (2015). doi:10.1108/JD-02-2014-0026
14. MacMillan, D.: Data sharing and discovery: what librarians need to know. J. Acad. Librarianship **40**(5), 541–549 (2014). doi:10.1016/j.acalib.2014.06.011
15. Verbaan, E., Cox, A.M.: Occupational sub-cultures, jurisdictional struggle and third space: theorising professional service responses to research data management. J. Acad. Librarianship **40**(3–4), 211–219 (2014). doi:10.1016/j.acalib.2014.02.008
16. Frank, E.P., Pharo, N.: Academic librarians in data information literacy instruction: a case study in meteorology. Coll. Res. Libr. **77**(4), 536–552 (2016)
17. Federer, L.M., Lu, Y.L., Joubert, D.J.: Data literacy training needs of biomedical researchers. J. Med. Libr. Assoc. **104**(1), 52–57 (2016)
18. Fane, B., Treadway, J., Gallagher, A., Penny, D., Hahnel, M.: Open season for open data: a survey of researchers. In: Digital Science Report, The State of Open Data: A Selection of Analyses and Articles About Open Data, Curated by Figshare, Digital Science, pp. 12–19, October 2016. https://figshare.com/articles/The_State_of_Open_Data_Report/4036398. Accessed 11 June 2017
19. Prado, J.C., Marzal, M.Á.: Incorporating data literacy into information literacy programs: Core competencies and contents. Libri **63**(2), 123–134 (2013)

20. RCUK Common Principles on data Policy, Research Councils UK. http://www.rcuk.ac.uk/research/datapolicy/. Accessed 12 Sept 2017
21. Tonta, Y.: Açık erişimin geleceği ve araştırma verilerine açık erişim, (Future of open access and open access to research data). http://library.bilkent.edu.tr/activities/librarianship-seminars/presentations/yasar-tonta.pptx. Accessed 12 Sept 2017
22. Aydınoğlu, A.U.: Araştırma verileri yönetimi: Türkiye, (Reserach data management: Turkey). Paper Presented at the 5th National Open Access Conference in Ankara, Turkey (2016)
23. Frascati Manual: Proposed Standard Practice for Surveys on Research and Experimental Development, 6th edn. http://www.oecd.org/sti/inno/frascatimanualproposedstandardpractice forsurveysonresearchandexperimentaldevelopment6thedition.htm

Lexical and Discourse Analysis

Deep Stylometry and Lexical & Syntactic Features Based Author Attribution on PLoS Digital Repository

Saeed-Ul Hassan$^{(\boxtimes)}$ ⓘ, Mubashir Imran ⓘ, Tehreem Iftikhar ⓘ,
Iqra Safder ⓘ, and Mudassir Shabbir ⓘ

Information Technology University, Ferozepur Road, Lahore 54000, Pakistan
`saeed-ul-hassan@itu.edu.pk`

Abstract. In this paper, we address the problem of author attribution through unsupervised clustering using lexical and syntactic features and novel deep learning based Stylometric model. For this purpose, we download all available 158918 publications accessible till 1 July 2015 from PLOS.org - an open access digital repository of full text publications. After pre-processing, out of these, we use 803 single authored publications written by 203 unique authors. For unsupervised modeling, stylometric markers such as lexical and syntactic features are used as a distance matrix by employing k-Means clustering algorithm. For supervised modeling, we present a novel long short-term memory (LSTM) based deep learning model that predicts the testing accuracy of a given publication written by an author. Finally, our unsupervised model shows that 88.17% authors are classified into correct cluster (all papers written by the same author) with at most 0.2 coefficient of Entropy error. While our deep learning based model consistently shows above 95% accuracy across all the given testing samples of publications written by an author with an average loss of 0.21.

Keywords: Stylometry · Deep learning · Clustering · Long short-term memory (LSTM) · PLoS

1 Background

Authorship attribution is defined as the science of inferring characteristics of an author from the features of texts written by that author [1]. It relies on the distinctiveness of individual writing styles by identifying the unique patterns in their written work. There is a fundamental assumption that every author has a habit of using certain words unconsciously which makes their writing distinguishable from others. According to Rudmen [2], every author has a unique style of writing which may be considered as the fingerprint of author. This style includes the word selection, average word length, words frequency, function words and the arrangement of sentences that author made for achieving an effect. Therefore, by analyzing style and writing patterns, one may identify the author of a given document. In this process, authors claiming the ownership of the disputed or anonymous text with their writing samples are considered. Then using these writing samples, suitable features are extracted which help in determining

© Springer International Publishing AG 2017
S. Choemprayong et al. (Eds.): ICADL 2017, LNCS 10647, pp. 119–127, 2017.
https://doi.org/10.1007/978-3-319-70232-2_10

the writing style of authors. These features, termed as *style markers*, are considered to differentiate the writing style of one author from another [3].

Stylometry has a vast scope for academic purpose - it has been used for author name disambiguation [4], citation pattern matching [5], bibliometric [6] and plagiarism detection [7]. Recently, a new field of Forensic Stylometry has been introduced that focuses to identify the mental health of patient after analyzing his/her writing style [8]. In addition, it has been used to solve cybercrimes by analyzing the language in order to identify the actual author of suspicious messages, tweets or Facebook profile etc. [9]. Deep learning techniques have been vastly adopted for authorship identification tasks [10]. Both vocabulary based cues as well as sequential patterns are provided to the model [11, 12], which then identifies a pattern for authorship attribution. Recently deep learning techniques have been widely adopted in the field of Stylometry, due to their extensive classification power [13].

In this paper, we address the problem of authorship attribution through Stylometry on the scientific publications downloaded from PLOS.org [14], having more than 200 unique authors. In contrast with the existing models that use different features such as average word length, most frequent words, function words [15–20], we identify the potential changes in writing style of different authors using lexical features (including *n*-gram and word frequency) and syntactic features (including parts of speech tagger). Using these stylometric markers, we deploy *k*-Means clustering algorithm with the goal that papers by unique authors be grouped in a single cluster. In addition, we also employ a novel long short-term memory (LSTM) based deep learning model to predict the author of a given publication. While the unsupervised model shows that 88.17% authors are classified into correct cluster (all papers written by the same author) with at most 0.2 coefficient of Entropy error, our LSTM deep learning based model consistently show above 95% accuracy across all the given testing samples of publications written by an author.

2 Data and Methodology

2.1 Dataset

We download all available (till July, 1 2015) 158918 full text publications from PLOS. org [10] in XML format. Further, we identify all single authored 1506 publications from the dataset. Among these publications, we select 803 publications authored by 203 unique authors with at least two publications each. For further processing, we extract <body> section from the xml files that contain full text of publication and converted them into the ".txt" file format. These "txt" files are then named with their respective author identification number including serial number of publication out of total available publication e.g. AU001_1_2.txt represent a paper written by author # 1 having total 2 publications). Further we pre-process the dataset by omitting few, seemingly superfluous, sections like tables and function words (such as *and*, *but*, *in*, *may* etc.). For function word removal we use Apache Open NLP - a machine learning based toolkit used for the pre-processing of the natural language text [21]. For stemming, Snowball stemmer is used - a common stemming algorithm for information retrieval pre-processing [22]. The Fig. 1 shows the distribution of publications with respect to authors. Our dataset ranges from 136 authors with at least 2 publications each to an author with 56 publications.

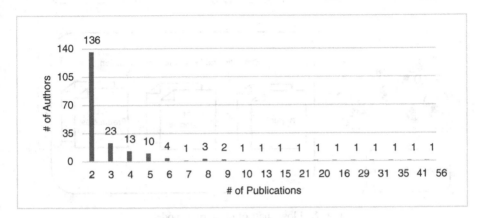

Fig. 1. Description of dataset used

Next sections describe the deployed unsupervised clustering technique and supervised deep learning models.

2.2 Unsupervised Clustering Model

We deploy a flat clustering algorithm, k-Means that determines all clusters at once instead of making a hierarchy. Since we already know the number of unique authors in our dataset, we set the value of k equal to the number of authors i.e. 203. For the clustering model (as shown in Fig. 2), we use the following style markers for feature set from lexical and syntactic:

n-**Gram.** For lexical features, we use n-gram technique for extracting features form the publications. We vary the value of n from 1 to 10 g to obtain n which gives the best result. For processing n-gram lexical feature, we applied Jaccard similarity coefficient. It is used in statistical analysis for getting similarity between two sets, by dividing the intersection and union between the available sample sets as shown in Eq. 1, where A and B represents two sets under consideration.

$$J(A, B) = \frac{|A \cap B|}{|A \cup B|}, \text{ where } 0 \leq J(A, B) \leq 1 \tag{1}$$

We apply n-gram on our dataset by varying the value of n from 1 to 10. Further, we also calculate Jaccard similarity on all 1 to 10 g to obtain similarity matrices of size 803 by 803.

Word Frequencies. We use another lexical feature i.e. word frequencies, to obtain frequency of each word in a publication - then arranged them in decreasing order of

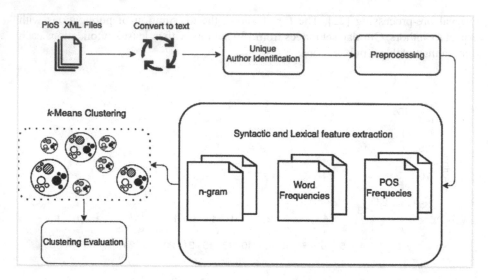

Fig. 2. Flow chart of clustering model

their frequencies. Then from these the top fifty most frequent words of each publication is compared with the top fifty most frequent words of every other publication in our dataset [20].

Frequency of Parts of Speech (POS). For syntactic feature, we use frequency of POS tags extracted by using Apache Open NLP library [21] for tagging all 36 POS tags [23]. After POS tagging we compute the frequency of each tag. Further, we compare the frequency of each tag across the publication in our dataset. For processing POS tag syntactic feature, we apply Euclidian distance between the publications across all 36 POS tags. Euclidean Distance is the distance between two points - it is the square root of sum of squares of two points as shown in Eq. 2. Here q_i and p_i are two identical POS tags in publication p and q and n ranges from 1 to 36.

$$d(p, q) = \sqrt{\sum_{i=1}^{n} (q_i - p_i)^2} \qquad (2)$$

We obtain multiple distance matrices of size 803 by 803. For n-gram: 10 matrices, each for 1 to 10 g. For frequency of POS: A matrix for POS tagger and a matrix for the comparison of top 50 most frequent.

Evaluation Indices for Clustering Accuracy. Finally, to evaluate the clustering accuracy, we use Dunn's index to evaluate our k-Means based model. In addition, we also employ Entropy based model to evaluate the effectiveness of unsupervised cluster models used to group the publications that belong to a given author. Well known Dunn's index identifies all sets of clusters that are cohesive and well separated from each other such that the means of different clusters are sufficiently far apart, as compared to the intra-cluster variance, as shown in Eq. 3, where $X_{i,j}$ is the average dissimilarity between the clusters i and j and Y_k is the average dissimilarity within cluster k.

$$\text{Dunn's} = \frac{min(X_{i,j})}{max(Y_k)} \qquad (3)$$

The Entropy measures the information spread - greater the value of Entropy more the information spread be. For instance, if all the publications that belong to an author are grouped in a single cluster then the contribution to Entropy index for this cluster would be 0 – implying the correct grouping of *related* publications into a single cluster. In contrast, if all the publications of an author are uniformly spread in all 203 clusters then the value of Entropy index would be 1 – an evidence for maximum error in grouping. Equation 4 shows the Entropy index, where n is the number of cluster, $P(x_i)$ denotes the probability of a publication in a given cluster i, and H(A) is Entropy of a given author. The value of Entropy ranges from 0 to 1.

$$\text{H}(A) = - \sum_{1}^{n} P(x_i) \log_n P(x_i) \qquad (4)$$

2.3   Supervised Deep Stylometric Model

Writing style of specific author can be determined by applying numerous text mining techniques. LSTM is an effective neural network in determining and constructing sequential text. More recently, the LSTM has proven to be an important tool in authorship identification [24]. For our problem of authorship attribution, we define an LSTM model with hidden layer memory of 256 units. The 256 hidden memory units can keep the text sequence up to 256 characters. Afterwards, for each distinct character (letter), we apply the *softmax activation function* as shown in Eq. 5.

$$\sigma(z)_j = \frac{e^{z_j}}{\sum_{j=1}^{k} e^{z_j}} for\, j = 1, \dots, k \qquad (5)$$

Where z is a vector of inputs to output layer and j is the number of output units. Here e^{z_j} represents an exponential function, whose value increases the probability of maximum value of previous layer. The value of $\sigma(z)_j$ are real values between 0 and 1.

In our case, this function is used to represent categorical distribution. For better understanding, Fig. 3 shows the flow chart of LSTM based employed model.

Baseline Stylometric Model. Further, to compare the results of our LSTM based model with baseline, the following steps were considered. At first, we compute word frequency of training and testing sets (i.e. publication) of a given author. We chose top 40% most frequent words from the training and testing set and mark them as the true class. Further a confusion matrix is computed which is used to calculate evaluation indices. Finally, the results of our baseline method are compared with that of state-of-the-art LSTM based deep learning model.

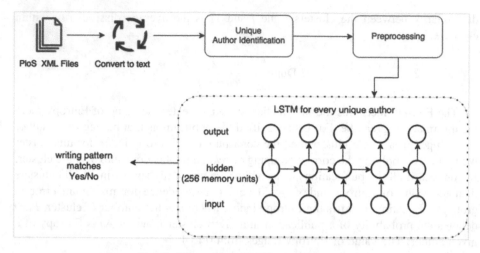

Fig. 3. Flow chart of LSTM based model

3   Results and Discussion

This section presents the results of our deployed unsupervised clustering technique and supervised deep learning models.

3.1   Results of Unsupervised Clustering Model

In this section we show the results of all three features when deployed on our dataset using k-Means clustering with the value of k set as 203. Table 1 shows the results of all three features implemented with k-Means clustering. The n-Gram appears to be best clustering feature. Note that we compute accuracy score, using Dunn's, for each gram from 1 to 10 for k-Means. We achieve best clustering accuracy of 0.96 at 5-gram. While the Word frequency achieves only 0.02 accuracy, POS provides up to 0.12 accuracy. This indicates that while grouping the publications into relevant groups, the key task is to separate the publications w.r.t. authors.

Table 1. Comparison of features used for k-Means

Features	Clustering accuracy
5-Gram	0.96
Word-frequency	0.02
POS	0.12

In addition, we also show clustering errors by deploying Entropy index with k-Means clustering. Here lower the value of Entropy coefficient means less error in grouping the publications that belong to an author. Figure 4 shows very encouraging results with 88.17% author classify into correct groups with at most 0.2 coefficients of

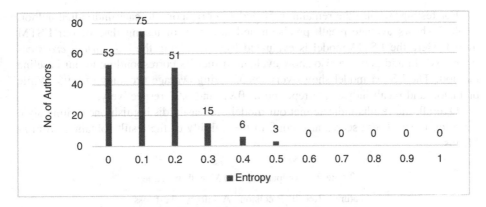

Fig. 4. Clustering errors using entropy

Entropy (error). Interestingly, 53 authors are perfectly grouped together in their respective clusters. Only 23 authors show coefficient of Entropy (error) above 0.2.

3.2   Results of Deep Stylometric Model

We run our LSTM model for 100 epochs having a batch size of 128 characters for each author in our dataset. As training input, we provide 50% publications of an author (only ASCI characters are considered and sequence length of 20 characters). Figure 5 shows average training accuracy of our LSTM model for 100 epochs run for each author. The y-axis shows the training accuracy along with epochs in x-axis. In first 50 epochs, model starts learning very quickly. Afterwards, it shows the gradual increase in accuracy and reach up to 0.89. Whereas the average training loss is achieved up to 0.21.

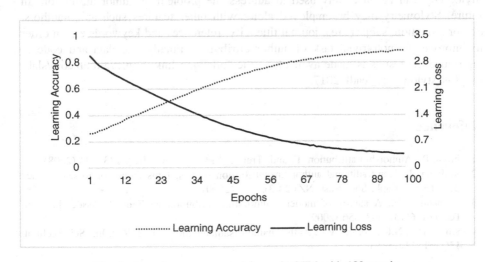

Fig. 5. Learning accuracy and loss of LSTM with 100 epochs

For testing, we use the remaining 50% data correspond to each individual author. Table 2 shows average recall, precision and accuracy of testing data of our LSTM model. Here the LSTM model is evaluated by minimizing the *categorical cross-entropy* loss. In addition, we also show evaluation metrics corresponding to our baseline method. The LSTM model shows very encouraging average accuracy of 0.96. While precision and recall indices are reported as 0.92 and 0.93 respectively.

Overall, the results indicate that our model can easily distinguish one writing style from the other. These scores also confirm the validity of the results obtained from *k*-Means.

Table 2. Comparison LSTM with baseline

Features	Recall	Precision	Accuracy	Test loss
Baseline	0.47	0.46	0.49	N/A
LSTM	0.92	0.93	0.96	0.12

4 Concluding Remarks

In this paper, we have addressed author attribution problem through unsupervised clustering using lexical and syntactic features and novel deep learning based Stylometric model. The unsupervised modeling reveals that *n*-gram shows better clustering accuracy and can be considered important lexical features for stylometric analysis as compared to word frequency and POS. We have shown that 88.17% authors are classified into correct cluster (all papers written by the same author) with at most 0.2 coefficient of Entropy error. While the supervised deep learning based LSTM model consistently show above 95% accuracy across all the given testing samples of publications written by an author.

We conclude that the deployed supervised and unsupervised approaches based on Stylometry can be effectively used to address the problem of author attribution. In future, Stylometry may be employed along with other features such as co-authors, author affiliation, subject area, journal title, city, references and keywords etc. in order to improve the non-trivial task of author attribution. Finally, the data and code to reproduce the results is made available at the following link: https://github.com/slab-itu/plos_stylometric_icadl_2017.

References

1. Juola, P.: Authorship attribution. Found. Trends® Inf. Retrieval 1(3), 233–334 (2008)
2. Rudman, J.: Non-traditional authorship attribution studies: Ignis Fatuus or Rosetta stone? Bull. (Bibliograph. Soc. Aust. NZ) 24(3), 163 (2000)
3. Stamatatos, E.: A survey of modern authorship attribution methods. J. Assoc. Inf. Sci. Technol. 60(3), 538–556 (2009)
4. Smalheiser, N.R., Torvik, V.I.: Author name disambiguation. Annu. Rev. Inf. Sci. Technol. 43(1), 1–43 (2009)

5. Gipp, B., Meuschke, N.: Citation pattern matching algorithms for citation-based plagiarism detection: greedy citation tiling, citation chunking and longest common citation sequence. In: Proceedings of the 11th ACM Symposium on Document Engineering, pp. 249–258 (2011)
6. Bergsma, S., Post, M., Yarowsky, D.: Stylometric analysis of scientific articles. In: Proceedings of the 2012 Conference of the North American Chapter of the Association for Computational Linguistics: Human Language Technologies, pp. 327–337 (2012)
7. Eissen, Z.M.S., Stein, B.: Intrinsic plagiarism detection. In: European Conference on Information Retrieval, pp. 565–569 (2006)
8. Smith, M.W.: Forensic stylometry: a theoretical basis for further developments of practical methods. J. Forensic Sci. Soc. 29(1), 15–33 (1989)
9. Zheng, R., Qin, Y., Huang, Z., Chen, H.: Authorship analysis in cybercrime investigation. In: Chen, H., Miranda, R., Zeng, Daniel D., Demchak, C., Schroeder, J., Madhusudan, T. (eds.) ISI 2003. LNCS, vol. 2665, pp. 59–73. Springer, Heidelberg (2003). doi:10.1007/3-540-44853-5_5
10. Wang, L.Z.: News authorship identification with deep learning. https://cs224d.stanford.edu/reports/ZhouWang.pdf. Accessed 4 Jan 2017
11. Macke, S., Hirshman, J.: Deep Sentence-Level Authorship Attribution. https://cs224d.stanford.edu/reports/MackeStephen.pdf. Accessed 5 Feb 2017
12. Liu, P., Qiu, X., Huang, X.: Recurrent neural network for text classification with multi-task learning (2016)
13. Surendran, K., Harilal, O.P., Hrudya, P., Poornachandran, P., Suchetha, N.K.: Stylometry detection using deep learning. In: Behera, H., Mohapatra, D. (eds.) Computational Intelligence in Data Mining, pp. 749–757. Springer, Singapore (2017). doi:10.1007/978-981-10-3874-7_71
14. PLOS.org. https://plos.org/. Accessed 3 Jan 2017
15. Nirkhi, M.S.: Stylometric approach for author identification of online messages. Int. J. Comput. Sci. Inf. Technol. 5(5), 6158–6159 (2014)
16. Mustafa, T.K., Mustapha, N., Azmi, M.A., Sulaiman, N.B.: Dropping down the maximum item set: improving the stylometric authorship attribution algorithm in the text mining for authorship investigation. J. Comput. Sci. 6(3), 235 (2010)
17. Chakraborty, T.: Authorship identification in Bengali literature: a comparative analysis. arXiv preprint arXiv:1208.6268 (2012)
18. Bozkurt, I.N., Baglioglu, O., Uyar, E.: Authorship attribution. In: 22nd International Symposium IEEE Computer and Information Sciences, pp. 1–5 (2007)
19. Eder, M.: Style-markers in authorship attribution a cross-language study of the authorial fingerprint. Stud. Pol. Linguist. 6(1), 99–114 (2011)
20. Voyer, D.: Word frequency and laterality effects in lexical decision: right hemisphere mechanisms. Brain Lang. 87(3), 421–431 (2003)
21. OpenNLP. https://opennlp.apache.org/. Accessed 1 Feb 2017
22. Porter, M.F.: Snowball: a language for stemming algorithms. snowball.tartarus.org/texts/introduction.htm. Accessed 17 June 2017
23. List of part-of-speech tags. https://www.ling.upenn.edu/courses/Fall_2003/ling001/p-enn_treebank_pos.html. Accessed 17 June 2017
24. Bagnall, D.: Author identification using multi-headed recurrent neural networks. arXiv preprint arXiv:1506.04891 (2015)

Automatic Answering Method Considering Word Order for Slot Filling Questions of University Entrance Examinations

Ryo Tagami$^{(\boxtimes)}$, Tasuku Kimura, and Hisashi Miyamori

Division of Frontier Informatics, Graduate School of Kyoto Sangyo University,
Kyoto-shi 603-8555, Japan
{i1788124,i1658047,miya}@cse.kyoto-su.ac.jp

Abstract. Recently, automatic answering technologies such as question answering have attracted attention as a technology to satisfy various information requests from users. In this paper, we propose an automatic answering method considering word order for the slot filling questions in the university entrance examination world history problems. In particular, when in analyzing the question sentence, the answer category is estimated from the surrounding words of the filling slot and used for extracting the answer candidates. Also, these candidates are evaluated by introducing the indicator using the consistency with the category and the occurrence situation of the surrounding words. In the experiment, we first compare the accuracy of the word prediction models. Then, we compare the proposed method with the baseline method and clarify what kind of change is observed in the correct answer rate.

Keywords: Factoid question answering · Automatic answering · University entrance examination · Distributed representation · word order

1 Introduction

Recently, automatic answering technologies such as question answering (QA) have attracted attention as a technology to satisfy various information requests from users. Questions handled by QA can be categorized into two types: factoid type, which requires facts with short words such as person's name as the answer, and non-factoid type, which needs to explain definitions or procedures in the answer. Many researches have been conducted on factoid type QA so far, whereas it is difficult to say that these technologies can adequately respond to the diverse and complicated questions in realistic situations including university entrance examinations handled in NTCIR-13[1] QA Lab-3.

Figure 1 shows an example of factoid type questions in the university entrance examination world history problems of Japan. If we exclude multiple-choice questions, they can be classified into slot-filling type and response type. In general

---

[1] NTCIR-13:http://research.nii.ac.jp/ntcir/ntcir-13/.

© Springer International Publishing AG 2017
S. Choemprayong et al. (Eds.): ICADL 2017, LNCS 10647, pp. 128–141, 2017.
https://doi.org/10.1007/978-3-319-70232-2_11

(a)Slot-Filling Type Question (Excerpt)

空欄の(A)〜(H)に適切な語句を入れ,
また下記の【設問】に答えなさい。
Enter the appropriate words from (A) to (H).

1. ボスニアの(A)を訪問中の帝位継承
者夫妻が暗殺されたため, その一か月
後にセルビアに対して宣戦を布告した。
The couple who were in charge of the
throne who was visiting (A) in Bosnia
were assassinated, and declared war on
Serbia in a month.

Correct answer: (A)サライェヴォ Salavevo

(b)Response Type Question (Excerpt)

(2) 前13世紀前半にシリア北部のカデシュ
でヒッタイトと戦い, 戦いの後ヒッタイト王と
講和条約を結んだ新王国時代の王は誰か。
Who was the King of the New Kingdom who
fought with Hittite in Kadesh in the
northern part of Syria in the first half of the
previous 13th century and signed peace
treaty with King Hittite after the battle?

Correct answer: (2)ラメス2世 Ramesh II

Fig. 1. Example of factoid-type question in university entrance examination (World history, Faculty of Letters, Chuo University, 2015)

factoid type QA, response type questions as shown in Fig. 1(b) are often targeted. In previous studies, to automatically answer such questions, many QA systems adopt the method to acquire various clues from the question and select the answer based on them. For example, predicting the answer category such as the name of a person, the region name, etc. is often introduced in the conventional methods, whereas they assume the sentence structure of the restriction-type questions, meaning that these conventional methods cannot be applied to the slot-filling questions as it is. For this reason, it is necessary to introduce the optimal method into QA systems to answer automatically to slot-filling questions.

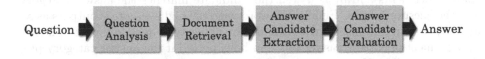

Question ▶ **Question Analysis** ▶ **Document Retrieval** ▶ **Answer Candidate Extraction** ▶ **Answer Candidate Evaluation** ▶ Answer

Fig. 2. Basic processing steps of factoid QA system

Figure 2 shows the basic processing steps of factoid type QA. When one question is input, the modules are executed in the order of "question analysis", "document retrieval", "answer candidate extraction" and "answer candidate evaluation", to output the final answer. The process of obtaining clues from the question mentioned above corresponds to the question analysis module. Also, the process of selecting the answer based on the clues is performed in the answer candidate evaluation module. Hence, it is necessary to introduce the optimal method into these modules to cope with slot-filling questions.

In this paper, we propose an automatic answering method considering word order for the slot filling questions in the university entrance examination world history problems, based on the process of Fig. 2.

2   Related Research

Many researches on QA systems have been conducted so far [1–3]. In NTCIR, question answering tasks have been frequently held. The system developed by Murata et al. [3] gave the best results at NTCIR-5^2 QAC-3 for factoid type QA. The feature of this system is that the evaluation score of the answer candidate for each document are finally added up by using multiple documents. The system also estimates the answer category using a rule-based method. That is, even with a rule-based method, certain correct answer rate can be achieved in factoid type QA. However, as detailed in Sect. 4.1, it is expected that the definition of the rules becomes complicated and the range that can be covered is limited with the rule-based method in case of the slot filling problems, because questions in the university entrance examination use complex phrases and the structure of the question sentence is different from that used in the conventional factoid type QAs.

Research on the QA system for questions of university entrance examination has also been conducted in recent years. Sakamoto et al. [4] identifies response type questions with slot-filling type questions, as the same word answer questions. The basic processing steps of this system is also in accordance with Fig. 2. In question analysis module, the system predicts the answer category such as the name of a person or the region name, by focusing on the interrogative of the question, and also estimates the question's focus such as the name of king or the name of god, by focusing on the word just before the interrogative (after the interrogative in case of English). In answer candidate evaluation module, each answer candidate is scored by how frequent the candidate word appears in the source documents and by how well the candidate matches the answer category and the question's focus. Finally, the word with the highest score is outputs as an answer. Also in automatic answering of slot-filling type question, we think that improvement of correct answer rate can be expected if the answer category prediction is possible. However, the sentence structure is different between response type and slot-filling type, so the same method as Sakamoto et al. cannot be used.

There are also various studies on distributed representation of words.

The word2vec developed by Mikolov et al. [5] is famous as learning tool of distributed representation of words. Continuous Bag-of-Words (CBOW) model is one of the learning models used in this tool. In this model, the central word is predicted from its surrounding words. This is similar to the way of thinking by humans when answering slot-filling type questions. It is, however, difficult to predict the central word suitable for the context because CBOW model doesn't consider the word order. In the first place, word2vec does not necessarily intend the task to predict the central word from its surrounding words using the model generated by this tool.

Ariga et al. [6] proposed a new learning model with word order information added to CBOW model. In particular, they proposed two methods: Left and Right (LR) model distinguishing between front and back words of the central

---

^{2} NTCIR-5: http://research.nii.ac.jp/ntcir/ntcir-ws5/.

word, and Word Order (WO) model that distinguishes all positions of the surrounding words. They reported that the accuracy of predicting the central word was improved by the proposed model. Unlike the CBOW model, the WO model is given word order information, which makes it easier to predict the central word suitable for the context.

3 Automatic Answering Method

In this paper, the QA system is based on the basic steps shown in Fig. 2. This section explains the specific steps used by the system. Based on that, Sect. 4 explains our proposal method to be incorporated into the system.

3.1 Summary of Slot-Filling Type Question in World History Problem

Figure 3 shows an example of slot-filling type question in the university entrance examination world history problems. The question is basically composed of instruction part and context part, regardless of university or year. The instruction part has one or more sentences ordering the way of answering. The context part has multiple sentences and slots.

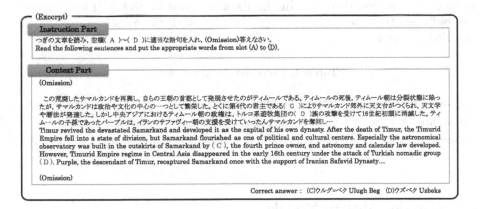

Fig. 3. Example of descriptive slot filling question in university entrance examination world history problem (World history, Faculty of Letters, Chuo University, 2014)

3.2 Dictionary and Knowledge Source Regarding World History

We prepared some dictionaries and knowledge sources for developing the automatic answering to world history problems.

We use MeCab[3] for Japanese morphological analysis engine in automatic answering process. We introduced mecab-ipadic-NEologd developed by Sato [7] for the system dictionary of the engine. In addition, we used a user dictionary [8] containing proper nouns specialized in world history to correctly analyze words of world history.

Next, we use the following books as knowledge sources to be stored in the document retrieval module. The data of four textbooks were provided from the organizer of QA Lab-3, while the data of a reference book were prepared by ourselves.

Textbook 詳説 世界史 (Detailed World History. *Yamakawa Shuppansha, 2008*)
Textbook 世界史 B (World History B. *Tokyo Shoseki, 2007*)
Textbook 新選世界史 B (New World History B. *Tokyo Shoseki, 2007*)
Textbook 世界史 A (World History A. *Tokyo Shoseki, 2007*)
Reference Book 山川一問一答世界史 (World History Question Answer by Yamakawa. *Yamakawa Shuppansha, 2015*)

We registered documents in knowledge source in two ways shown in Table 1. When retrieving in the document retrieval module, it is necessary to select either set.

This system is based on the assumption that the answer of the question can always be found in the knowledge source. Therefore, if the answer does not exist in the knowledge source in the first place, it is impossible for this system to answer the question correctly. In the data set used in Sect. 5 (Experiments), we confirmed that the correct answers for almost all the questions exist in the knowledge source.

Table 1. Prepared document set

Name of document set	Register method of documents	# Documents
Sentence set	One sentence in a book is one document	18,209
Paragraph set	One paragraph in a book is one document	3,642

3.3 Question Analysis Module

This module inputs the context part, generates a query for document retrieval and predicts the answer category for each sentence containing a slot.

When generating a query q, all nouns are extracted from the sentence containing a slot, by morphological analysis. The query is generated using all the nouns for OR search.

In this paper, the prediction of the answer category means to predict the category of the word to be filled in the slot. For example, for questions asking a person's name, the category should be "person's name". The proposed method of category prediction is explained in Sect. 4.1.

---

[3] MeCab: http://taku910.github.io/mecab/.

3.4 Document Retrieval Module

This module obtains document set containing answer candidates by retrieving document by query q against knowledge source introduced in Sect. 3.2. For the search engine, we use Apache Solr[4], an open source full text search system. Also, Okapi BM25 [9] were used for weighting documents at the retrieval process.

$RankingResult(q)$ is defined as a set of documents obtained by retrieval by query q, and sorted in descending order of the score of BM25. As explained in Sect. 3.2, it is necessary to select either of the set in Table 1 when retrieval process.

The top 50 items in case of sentence set, or the top 5 items in case of paragraph set, of $RankingResult(q)$ are input to the answer candidate extraction module.

3.5 Answer Candidate Extraction Module

This module extracts the answer candidate word w from the set of document d obtained in Sect. 3.4. Since we think that the correct word of slot-filling type question of world history is necessarily proper noun, all the proper nouns are extracted as answer candidates from each document d. The set of w obtained under above condition is defined as C. C is a set of all proper nouns included in the top 50 or top 5 documents d of $RankingResult(q)$.

3.6 Answer Candidate Evaluation Module

This module evaluates the likelihood of answers for each candidate word w obtained in Sect. 3.5 and determines the final answer word. In the system of this paper, for each w, $Score(w)$ is calculated using several indicators. Finally, the system outputs the answer based on the ranking of the score.

4 Proposed Method

4.1 Prediction of Answer Category and Category Mismatch Judgement

As explained in Sect. 2, the correct answer rate is expected to be improved if the system can accurately predict the answer category of slot-filling type questions.

A rule-based method can be taken as a basic method to estimate the answer category. However, the method requires humans to find patterns and create rules while referring to past questions and is extremely difficult to guarantee that the rules cover new phrases. Therefore, we propose a method using the word prediction model as a method to estimate the answer categories for any given phrases in the question.

Before executing the automatic answering process, we construct a word prediction model that predicts a center word from its surrounding words and their word order.

---

[4] Apache Solr : http://lucene.apache.org/solr/.

Word Prediction Model. We adopt the WO model proposed by Ariga et al. Chainer [10], one of the popular deep learning frameworks, was used to construct the model.

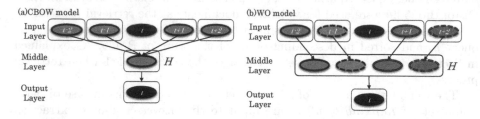

(a)CBOW model   (b)WO model

Fig. 4. Two learning models used to acquire distributed representation of words

Figure 4 shows the outline of each layer for both CBOW and WO model. t is the center word to be predicted. $t \pm x$ indicates that it is the xth surrounding word before and after t, respectively. Unlike the CBOW model, the WO model produces the vector H in the middle layer while keeping the positional relationship of words, meaning that t can be predicted considering the word order.

The word prediction model is constructed based on the WO model. When the surrounding words are input to this model, candidates of the center word are output in descending order of possibility. The number of words to be input depends on the window size x at model construction.

Prediction of Answer Category. In the question analysis module, we introduce a process to predict answer categories from input questions using the model constructed in previous section. In the user dictionary described in Sect. 3.2, 18 kinds of categories such as "person", "place", "ethnic group", etc. are given to proper nouns in world history field. As an example, the procedure for predicting the answer category in Fig. 3 (D) is shown in Fig. 5. For the word "ウズベク族 (Uzbek Tribe)" which is the correct answer to this question, the "ethnic group" category is labeled. When inputting the surrounding words of the slot into the model, the set of the center word candidates is output. Incidentally, words other than nouns are ignored and are not counted as candidate words. Categories assigned to each word in the set are collated, and all matched is set as the category of the question.

If the word immediately after the slot is a noun, the word is exceptionally not included in the input of the model, because in Japanese, the word which should be in the slot and the nouns just after the slot should be often considered as one compound noun.

The number of words output by the model can be arbitrarily set. When it is set to two or more, predicted categories may be plural as shown in Fig. 5.

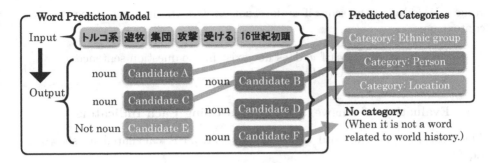

Fig. 5. Prediction of answer category.

Category Mismatch Judgement. As one of the indicators explained in Sect. 3.6, we introduce the index based on category mismatch judgement as shown in Eq. (1). This indicator collates the category of w and subtracts the positive value a if it does not match any one of the categories predicted in previous section.

$$f_{category}(w) =$$
$$\begin{cases} -a \text{ (if the category of } w \text{ does not match any categories predicted)} \\ 0 \text{ (otherwise)} \end{cases} \quad (1)$$

4.2   Backward Match Judgement

In Japanese, if a noun exists immediately after the slot, the string of the noun is likely to match the backward string of the correct word. Accordingly, as one of the indicators explained in Sect. 3.6, we introduce an index based on the backward match judgement as shown in Eq. (2). This indicator adds a positive value b if the backward string of w matches the word next to the slot.

$$f_{backward}(w) =$$
$$\begin{cases} b \text{ (if the backward string of } w \text{ matches the word next to the slot)} \\ 0 \text{ (otherwise)} \end{cases} \quad (2)$$

For example, as shown in Fig. 3 (D), b is added to the score since the backward part of the candidate word is "族 (tribe)" which exists immediately after the slot.

4.3   Non-existence Word Judgement

In the case of the university entrance examinations, it is very unlikely that the words already appearing in the question sentences become their correct words. Accordingly, as one of the indicators explained in Sect. 3.6, we introduce an index based on non-existence word judgement as shown in Eq. (3). The positive value c is added to the score if w does not exist in the instruction part or the context part.

$$f_{existence}(w) = \begin{cases} c \text{ (if } w \text{ does not exist in the question sentences)} \\ 0 \text{ (otherwise)} \end{cases} \tag{3}$$

4.4 Evaluation of Answer Candidates Using Each Indicators

The $Score(w)$ of each word explained in Sect. 3.6 is calculated as shown in Eq. (4).

$$Score(w) = \max_{w \in d} Score_{BM25}(q, d) + f_{category}(w)$$
$$+ f_{backward}(w) + f_{existence}(w), \forall w \in C \tag{4}$$

$\max_{w \in d} Score_{BM25}(q, d)$ in Eq. (4) is an indicator that represents the potential possibility that w is an answer. The score represents the maximum of BM25 of the documents d including w for the query q. This is the base score of w, and the final score of w is determined by applying the indicators described in Sects. 4.1, 4.2 and 4.3 to this base score.

5   Experiments

5.1   Experiment 1: Change in Precision Due to Different Word Prediction Models

Purpose. The prediction accuracy of the category is considered to change depending on the parameters set at the time of the model construction and on the output word count of the model. By this experiment, we find more appropriate conditions such as parameters.

Method. First, Table 2 shows the list of conditions for constructing the model.
The format of the model name is a combination of the learning model and the window size. The learning model is the name of the learning model used to

Table 2. Construction condition of word prediction model used by experiment (x: window size)

Model name	Learning model	x	Model name	Learning model	x
CBOW-3	CBOW	3	WO-3	WO	3
CBOW-4	CBOW	4	WO-4	WO	4
CBOW-5	CBOW	5	WO-5	WO	5
CBOW-6	CBOW	6	WO-6	WO	6
CBOW-7	CBOW	7	WO-7	WO	7

construct the word prediction model. It is either CBOW or WO. As explained in Sect. 4.1, the WO model considers the word order, while the CBOW does not. Window Size is the number of the surrounding words to be used when learning. For example, if $x = 4$, 4 words are used before and after the center word, respectively.

For the training data, we use four textbooks from among the knowledge sources introduced in Sect. 3.2.

Next, consider the case where the number of outputs of the central word candidate is 1,5,10 in each model, respectively. The prediction accuracy of the category under each condition is calculated.

Of the data provided in NTCIR-12[5] QA Lab-2, only slot-filling type questions are used as the data set of the experiment. In the experiment 1, use the following 57 questions.

- Hokkaido University, 2003 (9 questions)
- The University of Tokyo, 2003 (4 questions)
- Chuo University, 2003 (15 questions)
- Waseda University, 2003 (15 questions)
- Kyoto University, 2003 (14 questions)

We use MAP (Mean Average Precision) of each question as an indicator showing the accuracy of the predicted answer category. Thus, it is possible to know how many words in the correct category are appearing in the upper part of the output of the model.

Table 3. Accuracy (MAP) of category prediction by each condition

Model	# Output			Model	# Output		
	Top 1	Top 5	Top 10		Top 1	Top 5	Top 10
CBOW-3	0.175	0.241	0.235	WO-3	0.035	0.102	0.124
CBOW-4	0.281	0.343	0.335	WO-4	0.211	0.332	0.318
CBOW-5	0.175	0.268	0.260	WO-5	0.404	0.380	0.344
CBOW-6	0.175	0.293	0.268	WO-6	0.070	0.183	0.221
CBOW-7	0.123	0.229	0.248	WO-7	0.088	0.287	0.288

Result. The results of the accuracy of the prediction categories under each condition are shown in Table 3 and Fig. 6.

They indicate that $x = 4$ in CBOW model and $x = 5$ in WO model gave more accurate results than others. In CBOW-4, the MAP value when the number of output candidates is five is higher than that when it is one. As for WO-5, the MAP value gets decreased as the number of output candidates becomes 1, 5, and 10.

---

[5] NTCIR-12: http://research.nii.ac.jp/ntcir/ntcir-12/.

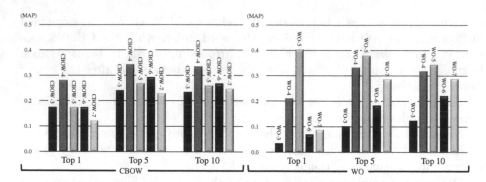

Fig. 6. Accuracy (MAP) of category prediction by each condition.

5.2 Experiment 2: Change in Correct Answer Rate Due to Different Methods

Purpose. In this experiment, we will clarify the change of the correct answer rate by different methods used in the system.

Method. The data set is the same as the one used in Sect. 5.1. In the experiment 2, the following 54 questions were used.

- Hokkaido University, 2011 (9 questions)
- Chuo University, 2011 (15 questions)
- Waseda University, 2011 (8 questions)
- Kyoto University, 2011 (22 questions)

We compared four methods shown in Table 4. First, two methods in Table 1 were compared in order to investigate the differences in the target document set. Next, other two methods were compared depending on whether the prediction model considers the word order or not. As for the models, we used CBOW-4 (word order not considered) and WO-5 (word order considered), according to the result of the highest MAP in Sect. 5.1. For both models, the number of output candidates was set to one.

Next, we set the parameters used in each indicator of scoring within the answer candidate evaluation module. As a preliminary experiment, we examined

Table 4. Answering methods to be compared

Method name	Target document set	Word prediction model
Method 1	Sentence set	CBOW-4
Method 2	Sentence set	WO-5
Method 3	Paragraph set	CBOW-4
Method 4	Paragraph set	WO-5

the value of the parameter that makes the correct answer rate highest when automatically answering the data set of questions used in Sect. 5.1. The result showed that the correct answer rate became highest when $a = 10$, $b = 30$, $c = 50$. Therefore, these values are used for parameters in the following experiments.

Finally, Table 5 shows the definitions of correct and wrong answers in this experiment. Each question is classified into one of the sub classes depending on the relationship between the scoring result and the true correct word.

Table 5. Definition of correct/wrong answer in experiment

Classes	Sub classes	Definition
Correct	Single	The word with the highest score is the correct word and the same score does not exist
	Same rate	The word with the highest score is the correct word but the same score word exist
Wrong	Existence	The correct answer word is included in the answer candidates (not the highest score)
	None	The correct answer word is not included in the answer candidate

Result. Table 6 shows the breakdown of the answer results

Table 6. Breakdown of answer results by difference in answering methods (Correct or incorrect number of questions / total number of questions in parentheses)

Method	Correct		Wrong	
Name	Single	Same rate	Existence	None
Method 1	0.24 (13/54)	0.19 (10/54)	0.41 (22/54)	0.17 (9/54)
Method 2	0.19 (10/54)	0.17 (9/54)	0.48 (26/54)	0.17 (9/54)
Method 3	0.22 (12/54)	0.32 (17/54)	0.28 (15/54)	0.19 (10/54)
Method 4	0.19 (10/54)	0.24 (13/54)	0.39 (21/54)	0.19 (10/54)

6 Discussion

6.1 Discussion 1: Predictive Accuracy of Answer Category

In experiment 1, it was found that the accuracy of the answer category prediction greatly varies depending on the method of constructing word prediction models and the number of output words.

Looking at the results in terms of the window size, the accuracy becomes the highest when the window size is four in case of CBOW, and when it is five in case of WO. If the window size is too small, the accuracy is considered to get decreased because the number of clues are reduced. In contrast, if the size is too large, the accuracy is also considered to get decreased because the number of clues increase and more irrelevant words will be included.

As for CBOW, the highest accuracy was given by the CBOW-4 model with five output words, and the MAP was 0.343. By contrast, in case of WO, the highest accuracy was achieved by the WO-5 model with one output word, and the MAP was 0.404. Therefore, the prediction accuracy gets better when the word order is taken into consideration. Additionally, WO has high accuracy when the number of output words is one. From this, it is expected to further improve the category prediction accuracy by further strengthening the WO learning.

6.2   Discussion 2: Correct Answer Rate of Automatic Answering

Experiment 2 examined the change in the correct answer rate of the automatic answer depending on the different target document set to be searched and on the different word prediction models.

As for the document set to be retrieved, the overall correct answer rate gets higher with the paragraph set than the sentence set. Specifically, there was no improvement in the "single" correct answer rate, whereas the "same rate" correct answer rate became higher. The reason for this is because the documents related to the question sentence in the paragraph set tend to be ranked with higher score of BM25 than those in the sentence set, and because many answer candidates w exist having the same base score.

Regarding the word prediction model to be used, the correct answer rate became higher when the word order is not taken into consideration. The reason for this is probably because the accuracy of the current category prediction itself is low, predicting incorrect categories, and adversely affecting scoring.

7   Conclusion

In this paper, we proposed an automatic answering method for the slot filling questions in the university entrance examination world history problems.

In the experiments, we examined the accuracy of the category prediction using word prediction models, the correct answer rate of automatic answer by different methods, and the effect of each indicator in the answer candidate evaluation module. As a result, we confirmed that the prediction accuracy of category prediction becomes better for models considering word order.

In the future, in order to improve the accuracy of the category prediction, we plan to improve the method of constructing models and propose new methods. We will also consider structuring slot-filling questions and introducing a new scoring indicator that takes advantage of its characteristics.

Acknowledgment. A part of this work was supported by Kyoto Sangyo University Research Grants.

References

1. Ferrucci, D., Brown, E., Chu-Carroll, J., Fan, J., Gondek, D., Kalyanpur, A.A., Lally, A., Murdock, J.W., Nyberg, E., Prager, J., et al.: Building Watson: an overview of the DeepQA project. AI Mag. **31**(3), 59–79 (2010). doi:10.1609/aimag. v31i3.2303
2. Iyyer, M., Boyd-Graber, J.L., Claudino, L.M.-B., Socher, R., Daumé III, H.: A neural network for factoid question answering over paragraphs. In: EMNLP, pp. 633–644 (2014)
3. Murata, M., Utiyama, M., Isahara, H.: Japanese question-answering system using decreased adding with multiple answers at NTCIR 5. In: NTCIR-5 Workshop Meeting (2005)
4. Sakamoto, K., Ishioroshi, M., Matsui, H., Jin, T., Wada, F., Nakayama, S., Shibuki, H., Mori, T., Kando, N.: Forst: question answering system for second-stage examinations at NTCIR-12 QA lab-2 task. In: 12th NTCIR Conference on Evaluation of Information Access Technologies, pp. 467–472 (2016)
5. Mikolov, T., Chen, K., Corrado, G., Dean, J.: Efficient estimation of word representations in vector space. CoRR (2013)
6. Ariga, S., Tsuruoka, Y.: Synonym extension of words according to context by vector representation of words (in Japanese). In: 2015 The Association for Natural Language Processing, pp. 752–755 (2015)
7. Sato, T.: Neologism dictionary based on the language resources on the web for MeCab (2015)
8. Kimura, T., Nakata, R., Miyamori, H.: KSU team's multiple choice QA system at the NTCIR-12 QA lab-2 task. In: 12th NTCIR Conference on Evaluation of Information Access Technologies Conference on Evaluation of Information Access Technologies, pp. 437–444 (2016)
9. Robertson, S., Zaragoza, H., et al.: The probabilistic relevance framework: BM25 and beyond. Found. Trends® Inf. Retr. **3**(4), 333–389 (2009)
10. Tokui, S., Oono, K., Hido, S., Clayton, J.: Chainer: a next-generation open source framework for deep learning. In: Proceedings of Workshop on Machine Learning Systems in NIPS (2015)

A Pilot Study on Comparing and Extracting Impact Relations

Yejun Wu[1](✉) and Li Yang[2]

[1] School of Library and Information Science, Louisiana State University,
Baton Rouge, LA 70808, USA
`wuyj@lsu.edu`
[2] School of Computer Science, Southwest Petroleum University,
Chengdu 610500, Sichuan, China
`yangli0027@163.com`

Abstract. Documents often contain knowledge about who did what to whom under what conditions, which can be expressed as relations between two entities. Impact relations between two entities express the impacts of one entity on the other. The goal of this pilot study is to examine whether impact relations are similar across domains or not, and investigate how to extract impact relations from unstructured documents using existing techniques. Impact relations in three domains – medical science, international relations, and environmental science (particularly oil spill) are collected and examined. Impact relations account for a significant percentage of semantic relations in all the three domains. The three domains share a common set of impact relations, and each two of the three domains share a significant number of common impact relations. An approach to applying the knowledge to extract impact relations from environmental science documents is proposed. The common impact relations and synonyms of two very different domains can be applied to extract impact relations of a third domain.

Keywords: Impact relation · Semantic relation · Relation extraction

1 Introduction

Impact relation is a new concept we use in this pilot study. Extraction of concepts and relations is studied in the natural language processing and knowledge organization communities. Relation extraction is the task of extracting semantic relations between two entities from unstructured documents. Impact relations between two entities express the impacts of one entity on the other. Human beings are naturally interested in the impact of an event or activity, such as the impact of the 2010 Gulf of Mexico Deepwater Horizon oil spill incident on the coastal states in the United States of America, and the impact of climate change on the earth.

Relations between entities are usually represented as verb phrases. Impact relations are represented by a group of verb phrases. People in different domains tend to be interested in different things and their impacts. For examples, economists discuss economic events (e.g., the end of quantitative easing may raise interest rates), and

S. Choemprayong et al. (Eds.): ICADL 2017, LNCS 10647, pp. 142–149, 2017.
https://doi.org/10.1007/978-3-319-70232-2_12

medical professionals care about drugs and diseases (e.g., a drug is used to treat a disease). Understanding the major activities and their impacts in a profession is one of the major tasks of the profession. Understanding and extracting impact relations from unstructured documents aims to extract knowledge (in the form of relations between two entities) from documents in a digital library and help professionals reduce the information explosion problem.

The goal of this pilot study is to examine whether impact relations are different across domains or not, and investigate how to extract impact relations from unstructured documents using existing techniques. To proof-test the new concept, we collected the impact relations in three domains – medical science, international relations, and environmental science (particularly oil spill), and examined whether impact relations are domain sensitive or not, and then proposed to apply the knowledge to extract impact relations from environmental science (particularly oil spill related) documents.

2 Significance of the Study

Relation extraction has many applications in information retrieval, question answering, and knowledge organization (such as ontology construction). Bertaud et al. [1] found that using verbs (i.e., to show, to confirm) in MEDLINE queries can improve the retrieval of findings. Green [2] identified an inventory of 26 basic relations structured by investigating the general relationships underlying the 1,250+ verbs, and hypothesized that frame-based index should have the potential of contributing to precision and recall. Relations have proved valuable in question-answering [3]. Ontologies represent entities and their relationships, so relation extraction is an important part of automatic development of ontologies.

Studying all the relations (i.e., verb phrases) can be too complicated to find useful patterns. We propose that impact relations are the most important relations between entities. Therefore, we plan to study impact relations first. It's unknown whether impact relations are domain sensitive or not. However, understanding the impact relations in selected domains can help information retrieval, question answering, and ontology construction in those domains directly.

Impact relations also facilitate knowledge discovery through inference. Swanson and Smalheiser [4] discovered numerous undiscovered implicit relationships within the biomedical literature. For example, if one article reports that *substance A causes disease B* and another reports that *disease B causes disease C*, then we can infer that *substance A might cause disease C*. Impact relations facilitate the grouping of relations and inference of concept relationships through the specified relationship chains.

3 Related Work

This section provides a brief review of impact relation lexicons and main approaches of information extraction and relation extraction.

3.1 Impact Relation Lexicons

The concept of "influence" (of A on B) in the medical domain can be expressed by a group of verb phrases, including *increase, decrease, attenuate, reduce, promote, inhibit, ameliorate, exacerbate, enhance, cause, accelerate, facilitate, trigger, catalyze, compete with, interfere with,* or *act synergistically* [4]. The Unified Medical Language System (UMLS) Semantic Network [5, 6] defines 54 types of semantic relations between medical entities. We propose that impact relations can be roughly classified into two categories: direct/strong impact and indirect/weak impact. Direct/strong impact types in UMLS include: *affect, be result of, bring about, cause, complicate, interact with, disrupt, manage, prevent, produce,* and *treat*. Indirect/weak impact types include: *be associated with, be adjacent to, be branch of, be connected to, be part of, be an ingredient of, be tributary of, consist of, contain, interconnect, surround, traverse,* etc. Indirect/weak impact types can be used to assist the inference of direct impacts, but they are not included in this study.

The Conflict and Mediation Event Observation (CAMEO) [7] project defines 20 categories of verb phrase patterns in the international relation domain: (01) make public statement, (02) appeal, (03) express intent to cooperate, (04) consult, (05) engage in diplomatic cooperation, (06) engage in material cooperation, (07) provide aid, (08) yield, (09) investigate, (10) demand, (11) disapprove, (12) reject, (13) threaten, (14) protest, (15) exhibit military posture, (16) reduce relations, (17) coerce, (18) assault, (19) fight, (20) attack with weapons of mass destructions. Direct impact relation categories include: 03, 05-08, 10-20. Indirect/weak impact relation categories include: 02 and 04.

As a result of our oil spill topic map project, we have created the Oil Spill Semantic Relation Taxonomy (OSSRT). The taxonomy has ten categories of verb phrases in the oil spill domain [8, 9].

More generally, Levin [10] proposes 193 English verb classes. The FrameNet project defines 230 semantic frames [11], and the WordNet contains over 21,000 verb word forms and approximately 84,000 word meanings [12].

3.2 Information Extraction (IE) and Relation Extraction

Extraction of structured information from unstructured sources is a challenging task [13]. Relation extraction has been an active, research topic since 2000 [14, 15], and no mature solution has been established. The accuracy is around 50-70% even in benchmark datasets such as ACE [16].

Major components of modern information extraction (IE) systems can include: name/nominal extraction, entity coreference resolution, relation extraction, event mention extraction and event coreference resolution [17]. There are pattern learning based approaches in which patterns are automatically learned based on an annotated corpus preprocessed by syntactic and semantic analyzers [18], supervised learning based approaches in which supervised machine learning methods are applied to address each component of an IE system separately [19], and rule-based information extraction approaches (such as Proteus [20]) in which rules are defined manually by domain experts or automatically generated by using machine learning methods from an annotated corpus [21].

Relation extraction aims to extract the semantic relations between two entities. It has two settings. The first setting is to extract all relationships between a given (marked) pair of entities in a natural language document. There are three methods: feature-based methods, kernel-based methods, and rule-based methods [16]. Feature-based methods extract a flat set of features for use by conventional classifiers such as decision tree or SVM [22]. Kernel-based methods use kernel functions to capture the similarity between two structures such as trees and graphs for use by a SVM classifier to predict the relation type [16]. Rule-based methods create propositional and first order rules over structures around the two entities [16]. The second setting is to extract entity pairs in a corpus given a relation type. There is no labeled unstructured training data in this setting. Instead, we are given a corpus with a set of relation types and entity types forming arguments of these relation types, and a seed set of relation-entity pair examples indicating that the entity pair has a specified relation. There are three steps to solving the problem in this setting [16]. The first step is to learn extraction patterns from seed triplets (i.e. relation-entity pair examples) by bootstrapping [14, 16]. The second step is to apply the learned extraction patterns to extract candidate entity pairs that support the given relation types. The third step is to validate the extracted relations using additional statistical tests.

Bootstrapping-based information extraction system [14] requires only a small number of seed triplets, which are used to generate extraction patterns, which in turn extract new triplets from the corpus. This approach is to be used in this study.

4 Objectives and Methodology

This study has three objectives: (1) to collect and compare the impact relations in three domains – medical science, international relations, and environmental science (related to oil spill, particularly), (2) to apply the knowledge to extract impact relations and entities from oil spill related documents, and then to expand the oil spill entity lexicon and impact relation lexicon, and (3) to evaluate the lexicons with annotated documents. We selected these three domains because they are different domains (although medical science and environmental science share some common topics) and we have linguistic resources in these domains.

To fulfill the first objective, we collected the CAMEO lexicon, the Oil Spill Semantic Relation Taxonomy (OSSRT), and UMLS semantic relation types which are used as a small semantic relation lexicon in this study. By comparing each two of the three lexicons or taxonomies, we generated a common impact relations lexicon for each pair. We hypothesized that the common impact relations lexicon that appear in two very different domains (e.g., medical science and international relations) should also appear in a third domain (i.e., the oil spill domain). We implemented the following two research tasks to test the hypothesis:

a. studying whether impact relations in different disciplines are mainly different or similar by comparing the impact relation lexicons in the three disciplines.
b. studying whether the common impact relation lexicon that is generated from CAMEO and UMLS can be applied to the oil spill domain.

As the result of our oil spill topic map project, we have created a set of triplets (entities and relations) in the oil spill domain [23]. Therefore, we use the oil spill domain as a test bed. To fulfill the second objective, we plan to supply the common impact relation lexicon and the oil spill entity lexicon to the TextRunner information extraction system to verify whether a relation exists between two entities. TextRunner can extract the relationship between two entities from the Web with 80.4% accuracy [15]. It takes three query terms: Argument 1, Predicate, and Argument 2. A program can be written to formulate a query using a pair of arguments and a predicate, issue the query to TextRunner, and crawl the result page, which presents the relation between the two arguments, and example sentences. The HTML file will be processed to identify the relations between the two arguments.

If an impact relation between two entities is extracted, its existence is verified. The verified impact relations can be added to the oil spill impact relation lexicon. The extended impact relation lexicon and one entity of the oil spill triplets can be supplied again to TextRunner to extract the other entity. The extracted entity can be added to the oil spill entity lexicon. This bootstrapping process is described in Fig. 1.

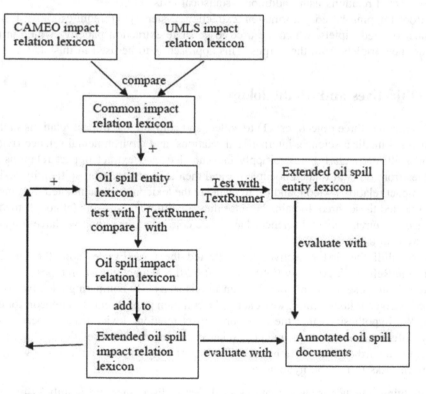

Fig. 1. A bootstrapping process of extracting impact relations and entities

To fulfill the third objective, for evaluation purpose, we plan to manually annotate a small set of oil spill related documents that present impact relations between entities. The TABARI coding system [24] can be customized to code the oil spill documents using the oil spill entities and impact relation lexicons. Text2Onto [25] can also be used to extract entities and relations. Based on our approach, providing any bootstrapping-based information extraction system with the oil spill entities and any three impact relation lexicons (including OSSRT) will tell the value of the lexicons and the accuracy of the system.

5   Preliminary Findings and Implications

UMLS has defined 54 semantic relation types [5, 6], and 11 (or 20%) of them are direct impact relation types. CAMEO has 1,835 effective verb phrases [9], and 540 (or 29.4%) of them are direct impact relations. The Oil Spill Semantic Relation Taxonomy (OSSRT) has 900 semantic relations, and 263 (or 29.2%) of them are direct impact relations. Therefore, direct impact relations account for about 20-30% of semantic relations in the three domains respectively. Impact relations play a significant role in all the three domains.

By comparing the direct impact relations in CAMEO and OSSRT, we found 72 common direct impact relations and 75 direct impact relation synonyms, so 55.9% of direct impact relations and synonyms in OSSRT appear in CAMEO, or 27.2% of direct impact relations and synonyms in CAMEO appear in the OSSRT. Synonyms were judged according to the Merriam-Webster online dictionary [26]. Ten out of 11 (91%) UMLS direct impact relations appear in OSSRT. They are *affect, be result of, bring about, cause, disrupt, interact with, manage, treat, prevent,* and *produce*. The only verb that does not appear in OSSRT is *complicate*. Eight out of 11 (73%) UMLS direct impact relations appear in CAMEO. They are *affect, cause, complicate, disrupt, interact with, manage, prevent,* and *produce*. The UMLS verb phrases that do not appear in CAMEO are *be result of, bring about,* and *treat*.

This indicates two direct findings. Different domains share a significant number of direct impact relations although every domain may have some unique impact relations, such as "*extradite*" and "*assault*" in CAMEO. The hypothesis that the common impact relations of two very different domains (i.e., medical science and international relations) should also appear in a third domain (i.e., oil spill) is not fully supported, because "*complicate*" which appears in UMLS and CAMEO does not appear in OSSRT. A reason for the issue is probably that the OSSRT lexicon is not big enough and has missed the verb "*complicate*." However, the hypothesis can be revised as the following: most of the common impact relations and synonyms of two very different domains should appear in a third domain. Consequently, the common impact relations and synonyms of two very different domains can be used to guide the extraction of impact relations of a third domain. Furthermore, two semantic relation lexicons (i.e., CAMEO and OSSRT) contain semantic relations that are not impact relations. The non-impact relations of the two domains can also be used to guide the extraction of impact relations of a third domain because they are less likely to be impact relations of the third domain and so are often recommended to be ignored if they are extracted by the impact relation extraction system.

The findings suggest three generalized hypotheses. First, there is a common set of direct impact relations across different domains. Second, whether impact relations are domain sensitive or not may depend on the scope of the domain. The impact relations of a narrow-scope domain (e.g., medical science) may not be as sensitive to the domain as a wide-scope domain (e.g., international relations). Third, every domain may have some unique impact relations.

6 Summary and Future Work

This pilot study compares impact relations of three domains: medical science (UMLS), international relations (CAMEO), and oil spill (OSSRT). Impact relations account for a significant percentage (about 20-30%) of semantic relations in the three domains. Most (73-91%) of the UMLS impact relations appear in CAMEO and OSSRT whereas OSSRT and CAMEO share a significant number (27-47%) of common direct impact relations. Each domain may have some unique impact relations. The scope of a domain may affect the size of its semantic relations. A wide-scope domain may have a bigger set of direct impact relations than a narrow-scope domain. The study indicates a revised hypothesis that most of the common impact relations and synonyms of two very different domains should also appear in a third domain. Consequently, the common impact relations and synonyms of two very different domains can be applied to guide the extraction of impact relations from unstructured documents of a third domain because they are very likely to appear in the third domain. The semantic relations of two different domains that are not impact relations can also be applied to guide the extraction of impact relations in the third domain because they are less likely to be impact relations of the third domain.

The research project is the initial stage and much work remains to be completed in the future. The project has three objectives. For the first objective, the UMLS semantic types need to be expanded to be an impact relation lexicon. For the second and third objectives, the impact relation extraction approach needs to be implemented and evaluated.

References

1. Bertaud, V., et al.: The value of using verbs in Medline searches. Med. Inf. Internet Med. **32** (2), 117–122 (2007)
2. Green, R.: A relational thesaurus: modeling semantic relationships using frames. Annu. Rev. OCLC Res., 94–97 (1996)
3. Wang, Y., et al.: Relational thesauri in information retrieval. JASIS **36**(1), 15–27 (1985)
4. Swanson, D., Smalheiser, N.: Implicit text linkages between Medline records: using Arrowsmith as an aid to scientific discovery. Libr. Trends **48**(1), 48–59 (1999)
5. UMLS: About the UMLS (2016). https://www.nlm.nih.gov/research/umls/about_umls.html. Accessed 9 Sept 2017

6. UMLS: Current relations in the semantic network (2016). https://www.nlm.nih.gov/research/umls/META3_current_relations.html. Accessed 9 Sept 2017
7. Schrodt, P. et al.: The CAMEO actor coding framework. In: Annual Meeting of the International Studies Association (2008)
8. Wu, Y., Yang, L.: Construction and evaluation of an oil spill semantic relation taxonomy for supporting knowledge discovery. Knowl. Organ. **42**(4), 222–231 (2015)
9. Wu, Y., Yang, L.: Expanding an oil spill semantic relations taxonomy with a foreign policy semantic relations taxonomy. In: Proceedings of the Association for Information Science and Technology (2015)
10. Levin, B.: English Verb Class and Alternations: A Preliminary Investigation. University of Chicago Press, Chicago (1993)
11. Baker, C., et al.: The Berkeley FrameNet project. In: Proceedings of the 17th International Conference on Computational Linguistics, pp. 86–90 (1990)
12. Fellbaum, C.: English verbs as a semantic net. Int. J. Lexicography **3**(4), 278–301 (2010)
13. Zhang, C., Cafarella, C.R.M., Ratner, A., et al.: DeepDive: declarative knowledge base construction. Commun. ACM **60**(5), 93–102 (2017)
14. Agichtein, E., Gravano, L. Snowball: extracting relations from large plain-text collections. In: 2000 International Conference on Digital Libraries
15. Banko, M., Etzioni, O.: The tradeoffs between open and traditional relation extraction. In: Proceedings of ACL 2008
16. Sarawagi, S.: Information extraction. Found. Trends Databases **1**(3), 261–377 (2007)
17. Grishman, R.: Information extraction: techniques and challenges. In: Proceedings of SCIE, pp. 10–27 (1997)
18. Muslea, I.: Extraction patterns for information extraction tasks: a survey. In: AAAI-99 Workshop on Machine Learning for Information Extraction (1999)
19. Ji. H.: Information extraction: techniques, advances, and challenges (2012). http://nlp.cs.rpi.edu/paper/IE_2012.pdf
20. NYU: The proteus project, http://nlp.cs.nyu.edu/index.shtml. Accessed 6 Sept 2017
21. Shahab, E.: A short survey of biomedical relation extraction techniques (2017). https://arxiv.org/pdf/1707.05850.pdf. Accessed 9 Sept 2017
22. Jiang, J., Zhai, C.: A systematic exploration of the feature space for relation extraction. In: Human Language Technologies 2007: The Conference of the North American Chapter of the Association for Computational Linguistics, Proceedings of the Main Conference, pp. 113–120 (2007)
23. Wu, Y., Dunaway, D.: Creating a large topic map by integrating Wandora and Ontopia. Libr. Hi Tech **31**(1), 64–75 (2013)
24. O'Connor, B., Stweard, B., Smith, N.: Learning to extract international relations from political context. In: ACL 2013
25. Cimiano, P., Völker, J.: Text2Onto: a framework for ontology learning and data-driven change discovery. In: NLDB 2005, pp. 227–238 (2005)
26. Merriam-Webster online dictionary (2017). https://www.merriam-webster.com. Accessed 9 Sept 2017

Measuring Discourse Scale of Tweet Sequences: A Case Study of Japanese Twitter Accounts

Shuntaro Yada[✉] [iD] and Kyo Kageura

Graduate School of Education, The University of Tokyo, 7-3-1 Hongo,
Bunkyo-ku, Tokyo 113-0033, Japan
{shuntaroy,kyo}@p.u-tokyo.ac.jp

Abstract. In this study, we measure the discourse scale of tweet sequences and observe their characteristics, for 80 × 3 Japanese Twitter accounts that deal with books, films, and other interests. For each account, a sequence of 3,000 tweets is regarded as the overall textual unit for which the discoursal scale is evaluated. To measure the discourse scale, we first selected 50 words that we call "discourse keywords" and observed how they occur in each of the Twitter accounts. The results showed that the discourse scale is about 15 tweets, regardless of their interests.

Keywords: Twitter · Discourse scale · Interval measuring

1 Introduction

In this study, we analyse the discourse scale of tweet sequences and examine their characteristics, for Japanese Twitter accounts that have a record of referencing books, films, and other interests (interests other than books and films).

Existing work on Twitter has mainly focused on its two characteristic features, i.e. network connections among accounts (follower and followee relationships) and tweets (through RTs, replies, and likes) [5, 15, 25, 32], and transitions of tweet topics in time scale, the typical application of which is trend detection [12, 23, 27]. Some textual and multimodal characteristics of tweet texts have also been observed and analysed [10, 24], either descriptively or in relation to such applications as maximising dissemination of information. Emotion detection has recently been an important topic [8, 26, 30]. Characteristics of individual Twitter accounts have been observed from the point of view of posting behaviour, user profiles, and follower-followee characteristics, including identification of spam accounts [4, 33].

To the best of our knowledge, however, there has been little work, if any, that analysed the discoursal characteristics of tweets for different Twitter accounts or account type. By "discoursal characteristics", we mean to observe the set of all tweets with the temporal order of tweets as one textual unit and to observe its discoursal features such as coherency. We observe that some people successively post tweets on the same topic, following the previous tweets with later tweets and construct an argument about the topic. This is especially observable in Japanese tweets, which can

S. Choemprayong et al. (Eds.): ICADL 2017, LNCS 10647, pp. 150–157, 2017.
https://doi.org/10.1007/978-3-319-70232-2_13

contain nearly twice as much information as English tweets due to the nature of character sets [22]. These tweets are often posted in the form of self-replies, but this is not necessarily the case. Taking into account this kind of successive tweeting behaviour, we set out observing how different people make different discoursal scales using their Twitter accounts. Some people may tweet on different topics in succession, while others may construct a coherent discourse over a span of successive tweets.

The present study is descriptive, but it can contribute to some Twitter-based applications. For instance, the authors are currently developing a book-recommendation system using Twitter [31]. The system delivers users a package of information related to books that are mentioned in Twitter accounts' timelines registered by the system's users. What sort of information related to books should be packaged into the unit of information to be delivered to users is a topic that involves difficult decisions. One hypothesis is that those who tend to follow Twitter accounts that have heavy and long discoursal scales are more likely to accept in-depth, analytical information about books, while those who prefer "lighter" accounts do not want heavy loads of information accompanying the book information that the system provides. We recognise that knowing the discoursal characteristics of Twitter accounts is not only interesting on its own but could potentially be useful to a range of applications, such as ours, since the discoursal characteristics can be utilised for user profiling.

The rest of the paper is organised as follows. In Sect. 2, we briefly introduce related work from the view of discourse analysis methods. In Sect. 3, we define the concept of discourse scale and introduce indices to measure the discourse scale. We also elaborate on how we actually apply these indices in measuring the discourse scale of tweet sequences. In Sect. 4, we discuss the result of the analysis. Section 5 concludes the study.

2 Related Work

We shall introduce studies related to the method we adopted in this paper.

Units larger than sentence units have been studied in the field of text linguistics [3, 13] and the study of discourse analysis [9]. The range of topics addressed in these fields in general are too numerous to cover here; we summarise computational approaches to discourse analysis that are of relevance to our study. In automatic text summarisation, understanding discourse structure constitutes a critical part. Mani et al. [16] adopted cohesion and coherence, and Barzlay & Elhadad [2] and Silber & McCoy [28] used lexical chains for automatic summarisation. Automatic analysis of discourse structure itself has also been proposed [17]. More recently, topic modelling has been applied to extract the topical structure of texts [1, 6, 7]. Dascalu [11] gives an accessible overview of the computational approaches to discourse analysis.

Compared to these works, we are more concerned with analysing surface discourse scale (rather than topical or coherency structures), and doing so descriptively. In relation to our immediate concern, a series of studies carried out by Montemurro et al. on measuring the semantic scale of texts was particularly relevant [19–21]. The measure introduced in these studies and how we applied it to clarifying the discourse scale will be elaborated on the next section.

3   Method

We investigated the "discourse scale"—which can be observed from the point of view of the number of successive tweets that constitute a coherent unit of topical discourse— of Japanese Twitter accounts. We chose Twitter accounts that explicitly list books as one of their interests, as we are developing the book recommendation system mentioned earlier. In particular, we are interested in whether book lovers have a characteristic discourse scale. For purposes of comparison, we also analyse Twitter accounts that deal with film, and accounts that deal with other interests. Films are chosen as a similar media-related interest to books or reading. The accounts enjoying other interests are collected for a simulation of average Twitter users because interests other than books and films can cover almost any type of interest. This will show whether a difference in interests relates to discourse scales of accounts or not.

We explain below how we chose accounts and collected basic tweet data, taking book-related Twitter accounts as an example. From approximately 1,000 Japanese Twitter accounts that state that they are book lovers in their profile, or accounts whose profile (or user name) contain both "interest" and "reading" in Japanese, we selected 80 accounts randomly. Note that the initial 1,000 accounts were already biased by Twitter's recommendation algorithm as related to the starting account we prepared. For each of these accounts, we collected 3,000 recent original tweets and selected the 50 most frequently occurring content words (nouns, verbs, and adjectives) in the 3,000 tweets[1]. Thus each account has a different set of 50 content words[2]. Hereafter, we refer to these as "discourse keywords". Note also that the discourse keywords may not necessarily be related to books or reading, but this is valid because what we are concerned with is the discoursal scale of Twitter accounts, and not the discoursal scale for book-related content.

Twitter accounts that deal with films were collected in the same manner. Those that deal with other interests were regarded as accounts whose profile contains the word "interest" but not "reading" or "films" in Japanese. For each account, intervals and discoursal spans are observed for each of the 50 words. We explain below how we measured the interval and the discoursal span.

3.1   Measuring Interval

For each word, we count the number of tweets that intervene between two occurrences of the word in the sequence of 3,000 tweets. For instance, if the word occurs for the first time in the i-th tweet and for the second time in the j-th tweet ($j > i$), then the interval is simply $j - i - 1$. We calculated this for all successive occurrences of each word. We can analyse many interesting features, including differences in intervals for different group of topics, personal differences, and their correlations. Here, however,

---

[1] In order to infer the Part-of-Speech tags of Japanese words, we adopted the Japanese morphological analyser MeCab (https://github.com/taku910/MeCab), with a dictionary enhanced for neologisms frequently appearing online [29]. The version we used was released on 24th April 2017.

[2] In any set of content words, we removed Japanese stop-words suitable for content analysis [14], which enables us to exclude delexical words among nouns, verbs, and adjectives.

due partly to space limitations and partly to the fact that we are interested in gaining insight into the general discoursal characteristics of Twitter accounts that deal with books in contrast to accounts that deal with different interests such as films or other interests, we focus on the differences between different groups, i.e. those accounts that are interested in books, in films, and in other interests. For that, we only give summary figures of the intervals. That is, we first obtain the mean intervals of 50 discourse keywords per user, and then further calculate the mean of these mean intervals among each user group. We also calculate their maximum, minimum, quantiles, and standard deviation values.

Table 1 shows the summary figure for the accounts dealing with books, films, and other interests.

Table 1. Descriptive statistics on user-wide mean values of mean tweet intervals among the top 50 frequent content words in the accounts dealing with books, films, and other interests.

	Books	Films	Other
Mean	63.17	64.91	60.32
Std.	31.11	38.60	27.58
Min.	5.55	9.67	6.67
25%	42.98	44.09	40.16
50%	56.96	57.19	59.27
75%	80.39	78.50	73.53
Max.	153.60	317.64	135.20

3.2 Discourse Span

Intervals can be affected by the frequency of words (which can be easily understood if we assume equi-interval occurrences stretching over the 3,000 tweets evenly). To compensate, we introduced information theoretic measures that can measure, so to speak, the "discourse span" for each word.

Roughly speaking, the optimal discourse span of a given word can be defined as the span or sequence of tweets (in the current setup) that maximises the information for the occurrence of the word. We simply call this optimal discourse span the "discourse span". More specifically, this amount of information is calculated as the difference between the mutual information for the discoursal unit and the actual occurrence of the word, and the mutual information for the discoursal unit and the random occurrence of the word. By calculating the difference in this mutual information for different discoursal units (i.e. a single tweet, a sequence of two tweets, a sequence of three tweets) and comparing the amount of information for the different units, we can obtain the unit that maximises this information, which is the discourse span of the word [19].

The formal definition and algorithm to calculate the discourse span are given below. First, we define the following notations.

- P: the number of discoursal units (if we set the unit as consisting of a single tweet, we have $P = 3,000$;
- n: the frequency of the word w in the account;

- n_j: the frequency of the word w in the j-th unit;
- N: the length of all the tweet data as counted by the token frequency of words;
- N_j: the length of j-th unit as counted by the token frequency of words;
- J: the random variable for the unit $(1, \ldots, P)$.

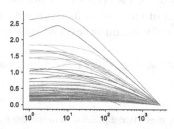

Fig. 1. Tweet length per discourse unit (x-axis) and ΔMI (y-axis) of book lover users.

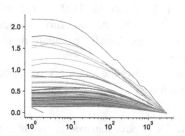

Fig. 2. Tweet length per discourse unit (x-axis) and ΔMI (y-axis) of film lover users.

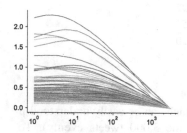

Fig. 3. Tweet length per discourse unit (x-axis) and ΔMI (y-axis) of users interested in the other interests

Table 2. Descriptive statistics of mean discourse spans per user group.

	Books	Films	Other
Mean	14.34	17.76	14.80
Std.	12.86	11.28	14.00
Min.	1.00	1.00	1.00
25%	3.75	10.00	5.00
50%	12.00	20.00	12.00
75%	20.00	25.00	20.00
Max.	60.00	50.00	75.00

The discoursal span for a word w for each user account is calculated as follows:

1. Divide the 3,000 tweets into P units.
2. For each word w among the 50 most frequent words (discourse keywords):
   a. Calculate the mutual information between w and J for the original text:

$$\mathrm{MI}(w, J) = p(w) \sum_{j=1}^{P} p(j|w) \log_2 \frac{p(w)p(j|w)}{p(w)p(j)}$$

$$= p(w) \sum_{j=1}^{P} p(j|w) \log_2 \frac{p(j|w)}{p(j)};$$

b. Calculate the mutual information between w and J for randomly reordered text:

$$\langle \text{MI}(w,J) \rangle = p(w) \sum_{j=1}^{P} \langle \hat{p}(j|w) \rangle \log_2 \frac{\langle \hat{p}(j|w) \rangle}{p(j)};$$

c. Take the difference ΔMI between $\text{MI}(w,J)$ and $\langle \text{MI}(w,J) \rangle$;
3. Take the mean for the 50 words.

ΔMI for each Twitter account was obtained by the above procedure. Figures 1, 2, and 3 plot ΔMI, in which the x-axis shows the discourse unit and the y-axis shows ΔMI. The value of the x-axis that corresponds to the largest ΔMI is the discourse span for the account. Table 2 shows the mean, maximum, minimum, standard deviation, and quantiles for the discoursal span for the accounts that deal with books, films, and other interests.

4 Discussion

First, from Table 1, we can say that there is little outstanding difference among user groups of different interests. This result describes the distributions of mean tweet intervals at which the top 50 frequent content words appear within each user's tweet sequences. This roughly means, for a mean user in each user group, a mean discourse keyword appears once in a sequence of around 60 tweets. Second, from Table 2, we found that the user group of film lovers has relatively longer mean discourse spans than the others, whereas book lovers and accounts with other interests have similar distributions. We chose these interests for comparative purposes, and the accounts dealing with other interests can be regarded as a group of average users because people with any specific interests excluding books and films cover a much wider variety than people who specifically like books or films. Thus, the results can be interpreted as signifying that film lovers on Twitter behave differently to average accounts while book lovers behave more similarly. We informally observed that the discourse keywords among the accounts dealing with films tend to contain more film-related words than those among the other two user groups. That is, accounts listing books as their interest seem to mention book/reading-related words much less in comparison to accounts that like films.

Another finding of the discourse span analysis is that outlier accounts that produced high information amounts of ΔMI were all bot accounts and accounts that mainly tweet via tweet-automation services. This is because such bot accounts tend to pack many words into one tweet, which causes larger texts within each discoursal unit of tweets in the calculations for Sect. 3.2.

The figures of discourse spans suggest that users in each group can be segmented into several groups according to their ΔMI values. These segmentations can be related to users' tweeting behaviours such as tweet frequencies per day.

5 Conclusion

In this study, we analysed the discourse scale of tweet sequences and examine their characteristics, for Japanese Twitter accounts that declare their interests to be books, films, and some other interests. We prepared 80 accounts for each of the above three groups and gathered 3,000 tweets per user. Applying discourse scale calculation to the top 50 content words (discourse keywords) of each account, we found that, regardless of their interests, Twitter users seem to mention their favourite topics at intervals of around 15 tweets long.

We plan to conduct further analyses on the discourse scale of Twitter, which remains to be clarified in this research. We will examine the effects of individual discourse keywords in terms of their types and topics. We are also going to investigate the characteristic of users segmented by tweet frequencies per a certain time span.

Acknowledgement. This work was supported by JSPS KAKENHI Grant Number JP 16K12542.

References

1. Adams, P.H., Martell, C.H.: Topic detection and extraction in chat. In: 30th International Conference on Software Engineering, pp. 581–588 (2008)
2. Barzlay, R., Elhadad, M.: Using lexical chains for text summarization. In: ACL Workshop on Intelligent Scalable Text Summarisation, pp. 111–121 (1997)
3. de Beaugrande, W., Dressler, W.U.: Introduction to Text Linguistics. Longman, London (1981)
4. Benevenuto, F., Haddadi, H., Gummadi, K.: The world of connections and information flow in Twitter. IEEE Trans. Syst. Man Cybern. Part A Syst. Hum. **42**(4), 991–998 (2012)
5. Bi, B., Cho, J.: Modeling a retweet network via an adaptive Bayesian approach. In: 25th International World Wide Web Conference, pp. 459–469 (2016)
6. Blei, D.M., Ng, A.Y., Jordan, M.I.: Latent Dirichlet allocation. J. Mach. Learn. Res. **3**(4–5), 993–1022 (2003)
7. Blei, D.M., Lafferty, J.: Topic models. In: Srivastava, A., Sahami, M. (eds.) Text Mining: Classification, Clustering, and Applications, pp. 71–93. CRC, London (2009)
8. Bollen, J., Mao, H., Pepe, A.: Modeling public mood and emotion: Twitter sentiment and socio-economic phenomena. In: Fifth International AAAI Conference on Weblogs and Social Media, pp. 450–453 (2011)
9. Brown, G., Yule, G.: Discourse Analysis. Cambridge University Press, Cambridge (1983)
10. Can, E.F., Oktay, H., Manmatha, R.: Predicting retweet count using visual cues. In: 22nd ACM International Conference on Information and Knowledge Management, pp. 1481–1484 (2013)
11. Dascalu, M.: Analyzing Discourse and Text Complexity for Learning and Collaborating. Springer, Heidelberg (2014)
12. Guzman, J., Poblete, B.: On-line relevant anomaly detection in Twitter stream: an efficient bursty keyword detection model. In: 19th ACM SIGKDD Conference on Knowledge Discovery and Data Mining, pp. 31–39 (2013)
13. Halliday, M.A.K., Hasan, R.: Language, Context and Text. Deaking University Press, Geelong (1985)

14. Kokubu, H., Yamazaki, H., Nosaka, M.: Japanese stopword list making for keyword extraction suitable for semantic interpretation. Trans. Japan Soc. Kansei Eng. **12**, 511–518 (2013). [in Japanese]

15. Luo, Z., Osborne, M., Tang, J., Wang, T.: Who will retweet me? Finding retweeters in Twitter. In: 36th International ACM SIGIR Conference on Research and Development in Information Retrieval, pp. 869–872 (2013)

16. Mani, I., Bloedorn, E., Gates, B.: Using cohesion and coherence models for text summarisation. AAAI technical report (1998)

17. Marcu, D.: The theory and practice of discourse parsing and summarization. MIT Press, Cambridge, Mass (2000)

18. Mathioudakis, M., Koudas, N.: TwitterMonitor: trend detection over the Twitter stream. In: 2010 ACM SIGMOD International Conference on Management of Data, pp. 1155–1158 (2010)

19. Montemurro, M.A., Zanette, D.: Towards the quantification of the semantic information encoded in written language. Adv. Complex Syst. **13**(2), 135–153 (2009)

20. Montemurro, M.A., Zanette, D.: The statistics of meaning: Darwin Gibbon Moby Dick. Significance **6**(4), 165–169 (2014)

21. Montemurro, M.A.: Quantifying the information in the long-range order of words: semantic structures and universal linguistic constraints. Cortex **55**, 5–16 (2014)

22. Neubig, G., Duh, K.: How much is said in a Tweet? A multilingual, information-theoretic perspective. In: AAAI Spring Symposium: Analyzing Microtext, pp. 32–39 (2013)

23. Paris, C., Wan, S.: Listening to the community: social media monitoring tasks for improving government services. In: The ACM CHI Conference on Human Factors in Computing Systems, pp. 2095–2100 (2011)

24. Paris, C., Thomas, P., Wan, S.: Differences in language and style between two social media communities. In: 6th International AAAI Conference on Weblogs and Social Media (2012)

25. Pezzoni, F., An, J., Passarella, A., Crowcroft, J., Conti, M.: Why do I retweet it? An information propagation model for microblogs. In: 5th International Conference on Social Informatics, pp. 360–369 (2013)

26. Roberts, K., Roach, M.A., Johnson, J., Guthrie, J., Harabagiu, S.M.: EmpaTweet: annotating and detecting emotions on Twitter. In: 8th International Conference on Language Resources and Evaluation, pp. 3806–3813 (2012)

27. Sakaki, T., Toriumi, F., Matsuo, Y.: Tweet trend analysis in an emergency situation. In: ACM the Special Workshop on Internet and Disasters, no. 3 (2011)

28. Silber, G., McCoy, K.: Efficiently computed lexical chains as an intermediate representation for automatic text summarization. Comput. Linguist. **28**(4), 487–496 (2003)

29. Toshinori, S.: Neologism dictionary based on the language resources on the web for Mecab (2015)

30. Wan, S., Paris, C.: Understanding public emotional reactions on Twitter. In: 9th International AAAI Conference on Weblogs and Social Media (2015)

31. Yada, S.: Development of a book recommendation system to inspire "infrequent readers". In: 16th International Conference on Asia-Pacific Digital Libraries, pp. 399–404 (2014)

32. Yang, Z., Guo, J., Cai, K., Tang, J., Li, J., Zhang, L., Su, Z.: Understanding retweeting behaviors in social networks. In: 19nd ACM International Conference on Information and Knowledge Management, pp. 1633–1636 (2010)

33. Zhao, D., Rosson, M. B.: How and why people Twitter: the role that micro-blogging plays in informal communication at work. In: ACM International Conference on Supporting Group Work, pp. 243–252 (2009)

Mobile Applications

Tracking Smartphone App Usage
for Time-Aware Recommendation

Seyed Ali Bahrainian$^{(\boxtimes)}$ and Fabio Crestani

Faculty of Informatics, University of Lugano (USI), Lugano, Switzerland
{bahres,fabio.cerstani}@usi.ch

Abstract. Mobile personal assistants aim at addressing users' information needs by anticipating their actions at different points in time. One such application which has been the focus of researchers recently, is regarding the anticipation of users' app usage patterns on their smartphones. The rapid proliferation of smartphone applications, have changed these mobile devices from mere communication tools to means for accessing personalized content that fit various needs and tastes. In this paper, we propose a novel method that given a user's previous smartphone activities and their contexts, predicts the user's activity at different times and under certain contexts. Such prediction could be used to organize content on a mobile phone in a personalized fashion such that users would need less time to access their desired content. Our temporal model captures local patterns of actions of a user over consecutive time slices. Our experimental results using an app usage dataset demonstrate the efficacy of our proposed method outperforming two major state-of-the-art baselines, namely, the Singular Value Decomposition (SVD), and the Author Topic Model (ATM).

Keywords: Time-aware app recommendation · Personal information management · Topic models

1 Introduction

In recent years, with the substantial growth of smartphone apps market, millions of people use smartphones as their primary device not only for communication, but also for accessing information regarding bus schedules, maps, events, news or even for entertainment and other specialized apps. This pertains to people carrying smarphones throughout their every day and using them. The interaction of users with their smartphones can be a wealthy source of information about users' habits and interests and can have application in recommending apps to users [12], retrieving a desired app and showing it in the lock screen just in time the user needs it (similarly to what personal assistants such as Apple's Siri do), or even logging one's life for summarizing one's activities in order to increase one's self-awareness and self-organization. The latter example has been the focus of several productivity apps.

© Springer International Publishing AG 2017
S. Choemprayong et al. (Eds.): ICADL 2017, LNCS 10647, pp. 161–172, 2017.
https://doi.org/10.1007/978-3-319-70232-2_14

"An empirical study conducted by the Yahoo Aviate team shows that on average there are 96 apps installed on each mobile device. This large number of apps installed calls for the design of new paradigms for the management of the installed apps" [8].

Therefore, its necessary to organize apps as a form of personal information management and accessing the right app at the right time or rearranging the apps such that the ones that are more likely to be used would be easily accessible.

Furthermore, such data can be utilized for Just-In-Time Information Retrieval (JITIR), e.g., predicting the next app that a user is going to use and show it in the home screen just before you try to access it. Such prediction can be useful because: (1) a user who has hundreds of apps installed on her smartphone would not need to go through the cumbersome process of finding an app on her device, as it could be opened or placed in a notification bar at the right time. (2) modeling a user and showing how she behaves can bring increased self-awareness. (3) in case a user is distracted and forgets to interact with a certain app, it can aid her memory and remind her about the event. The latter motivation originates from studies that show the effectiveness of presenting information to a user which could serve as memory cues [5,6].

Baeza-Yates et.al. [3] discusses that "given the large number of installed apps and the limited screen size of mobile devices, it is often tedious for users to search for the app they want to use. Although some mobile OSs provide categorization schemes that enhance the visibility of useful apps among those installed, the emerging category of homescreen apps aims to take one step further by automatically organizing the installed apps in a more intelligent and personalized way". We follow the same aim in this paper. Most of the current models for predicting app usages focus primarily on frequency and co-occurrence of patterns in order to recommend apps that are likely to be used at a specific time. However, the decisions that people make in exhibiting certain behaviors and habits are also influenced by complex cognitive memory functions in their minds. A person's memory can recall certain behaviors at different times depending on time, mood, the surrounding environment, etc. Thus, we design a time-aware app recommendation system based on the psychology of human memory [13] that tracks a person's app usage log in order to assist her with organizing apps.

In this paper we specifically would like to solve a problem which is formally defined as: given the app usage behavior of a user from time slices $t_1, t_2, \ldots, t_n$ and the corresponding contexts, predict the app that the user will use during a future time slice. That is:

$$\arg \max_{app} P(app_{usage}|t, c) \tag{1}$$

where t shows a specific time and c represents a specific context for time t. Thus, the aim is to find an app which maximizes the probability of it being used by a user under a certain context and time.

This goal is based on the belief that users have repeating behaviors in using certain apps at a specific time and under a specific context. As an example, Fig. 1 shows the behavior of a user in using communication apps. From the

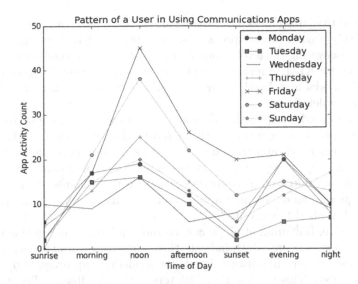

Fig. 1. The behavior of a user from the Frappe dataset in using communication apps

figure we observe that this user has significantly more communications around noon times, afternoons and in the evenings. From this we can infer that this user is maintaining regular office hours. Additionally, we observe that the user is more inclined to using communications apps on Fridays and Saturdays. We notice that just by looking at the statistical pattern of this user. We therefore hypothesize that by looking at usage patterns of all apps that this user has installed on her smartphone, we would be able to predict the next app that she is going to use. Therefore, our goal is to develop a model that can predict the app usage behavior of a user. Such models can be beneficial in assisting users in their everyday lives by sending them relevant information and notifications. Moreover, a person's memory could be augmented with relevant information just in time one needs the information. This goal motivates this paper. We present a model, that not only can predict the app usage behavior of a user but also, if trained with a different dataset, can predict other aspects of a user's behavior.

The remainder of this paper is organized as follows: Sect. 2 briefly discusses previous related work. Furthermore, Sect. 3 describes two state-of-the-art methods that we use in this paper as baselines. Section 4 presents our proposed model. Section 5 describes our experimental setup and initial evaluation. Finally, Sect. 6 concludes this paper and presents insights into future work.

2   Related Work

Predicting the next app usage has been studied before in the literature. Do et al. [12] proposed applying the Author Topic Model (ATM) to the problem of next app usage prediction. They used the Nokia Challenge dataset [15] in their work.

They showed that this model was capable of modeling users' app usage behavior and effectively predict future app usages. They use a bag-of-apps approach with the aim of discovering the level of phone usage over specific times of a day, using the probabilistic ATM to represent each user as a mixture of different patterns. We use this model as a baseline for our work. In Sect. 3 we describe the ATM model in more detail.

Another related work in this domain is [3] which studies how to improve homescreen apps' usage experience through a prediction mechanism that allows to show to users which app they are going to use in the immediate future. The prediction technique they propose is based on a set of features representing the real-time spatiotemporal contexts sensed by their homescreen app. They model the prediction of the next app as a classification problem and propose a personalized method to solve it.

Furthermore, Baltrunas et al. [8] carried out a related study in-the-wild with users' app usage patterns which indicate that contextual variables, such as location and time are very important signals for modeling app usage and providing recommendations. This is while they also report that feedback collected in their small scale user study shows that, while users understand the value of context dependent adaptation, their expectations in this regard are also very high. They provide a set of lessons learned which outline important considerations for designing, deploying and evaluating mobile context-aware recommender systems in-the-wild with real users.

Another study [9] which also motivates studying user's app usage patterns, aims at modeling the life cycle of a user using a certain app. This life cycle include phases such as first view, installation, direct usage and long-term usage. Based on the user app usage behavior they then try to recommend new apps to the users. For achieving this goal they designed a usage-centric evaluation considering different phases of application engagement.

Furthermore, [10] carried out a large-scale deployment-based research study that logged detailed application usage information from over 4,100 users of Android-powered mobile devices. They also study app usage patterns based on contextual factors such as time of the day and location. They present some interesting findings based on their large-scale user study. For instance, they found out that people are most likely to use news apps in the mornings and games in the night. They also mention that communication applications are almost always the first used upon a device's waking from sleep.

Deerwester et al. [11] proposes applying the Singular Value Decomposition (SVD) method to a very different but related problem. SVD or Latent Semantic Indexing (LSI) have been extensively used in the literature to identify semantic patterns in a dataset to recommend items to users [19]. SVD-based models have been long a state-of-the-art in collaborative recommender systems. Therefore, we use SVD as a second baseline for identifying the times of the day that a user is more likely to use a certain app.

Use of user profiling and personalization has been explored in the past, not only for app recommendation but also in other domains. For instance a recommender system in an e-store which adapts the recommendations to a user's current interests [4], or a contextual and personalized venue recommender system that based on user profiles finds places that match a user's taste [1,2]. Here we also rely on the concept of personalization.

Finally, time series modeling has been used in the literature [7] for various applications such as modeling the evolution of topics over time. In this paper, we also use time series for just-in-time app recommendation.

3   Baselines

3.1   Author Topic Model

Since it was shown that ATMs are effective in addressing the problem of next app prediction [12], we include this model to be compared against our model as a baseline. In the following we briefly explain the ATM model.

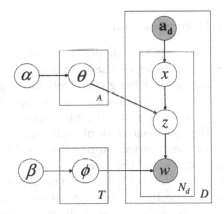

Fig. 2. The graphical representation of the Author Topic Model.

Topic models are defined as hierarchical Bayesian networks of discrete data where a topic is a set of words drawn from a fixed vocabulary that together represent a high-level concept [18]. These probabilistic methods represent a dataset with reduced dimensions. Do et al. [12] state that "from an applicative viewpoint, topic model is a tool for extracting emergent hidden patterns from a collection of data". Since ATM utilizes ownership information, it can distinguish between persistent behaviors of a user and the rare ones (which are more of a temporary nature and my not be reliable information for inferring a pattern).

The ATM was originally proposed by [17] and used for recommending items to users.

Here, similarly to our assumption in designing our model in Sect. 3 and also analogously to [12], for each user we train one ATM model, where we try to recommend a certain app to a user depending on a specific time of the day.

In other words, lets say we divide different times of a day over different days in a week into multiple time buckets. Assume that in each of the time buckets a user is required to use a different app. The ATM model can identify which apps are actually triggered as a function of a specific time bucket and which app usages are just random occurrences which could be seen as noise. Hence, it assigns those apps that strongly correlate with a certain time and context to its corresponding time bucket.

Figure 2 illustrates the graphical model of ATM. In the figure, x indicates the time bucket responsible for a given app chosen from a_d. Each time bucket is associated with a distribution over topics θ, chosen from a symmetric Dirichlet (α) prior. The mixture of weights corresponding to the chosen author are used to select a topic z and a word (i.e. app word) is generated based on the distribution ϕ drawn from a symetric Dirichlet (β). For further details about this model and our implementation of it, we refer to [12]. The only difference between our implementation and that of [12] is that we use variational inference as opposed to Gibbs sampling.

3.2   Singular Value Decomposition

Singular Value Decomposition (SVD), famously known in the topic modeling community as Latent Semantic Indexing (LSI) [11,14], is a technique for reducing the dimensionality of data for identifying the most salient patterns in the data. SVD has been frequently used in collaborative recommender systems due to its capability of modeling co-occurrences of certain features in a dataset. We use this model to be trained on the app usage data of each user and use a collaborative filtering approach to recommend certain apps to be used by the user at certain times of the day on different days of the week.

Latent semantic indexing (LSI) [11] is the very first topic model that was introduced and patented in the 1980's. The algorithm of LSI was based on the idea of data dimensionality reduction. One of the most famous techniques used for dimensionality reduction is the Singular Value Decomposition (SVD). LSI is also based on SVD. It reduces documents of a corpus to a matrix of the most important terms that co-occur together, i.e. topics. The process decomposes the (words * documents) matrix as shown in Fig. 3. In our app recommendation problem, a document is an app usage record, and the words are name of the app, context words such as location, time, etc.

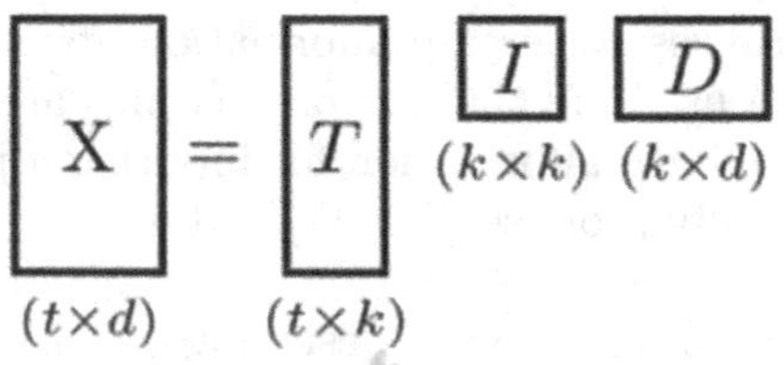

$$X = T \quad \boxed{I} \quad \boxed{D}$$
$$(t \times d) \quad (t \times k) \quad (k \times k) \quad (k \times d)$$

Fig. 3. Illustration of Singular Value Decomposition

Figure 3 shows the matrix decomposition of SVD. In this case k topics will be extracted from t words presented in matrix T. Furthermore, the diagonal of matrix I presents the rank or strength of each topic. Hence, using this simple matrix decomposition technique the dimensionality of documents in a corpora are reduced and topics are extracted. Additionally, matrix D presents the similarity of each document to each topic. One advantage of this model is that it is deterministic, meaning that the resulting topics are always the same in different runs of the algorithm on the same dataset. Another advantage of this model is that it is simple to interpret and understand.

Analogous to the ATM, we train one LSI per each user. After a model is trained, we query it with unseen test data to compute a ranked list of other similar app usage entries under the model. As it will be explained later, for each ranked list we find the top 5 highest ranked app names to examine the correctness of the result. We then compare the highest ranked apps with the ground truth data to assess the performance of this model. This process will be explained elaborately in Sect. 5.

4 Methodology

In this section we introduce a novel method for predicting the next app that one is likely to use. Our method considers the passage of time in order to model change in the behavior of a user. We want to identify those user behaviors that have persisted over time. That is because a behavior which is both frequent and persistent over time is more likely to be repeated in the future.

We base our model on the SVD/LSI topic model. However, by using a time series we model the changes in behavior of a user with respect to a certain app over time.

For this purpose we break down the data containing sequences of app usage of one user into n partitions or time slices. Then we apply an SVD/LSI to each partition. By doing so, we strive for modeling a user in different time slices and then aggregate the results in a time series fashion. The rationale behind our method is that applying a single SVD/LSI to the entire dataset will result in a global model of the user. Such model would treat each app usage as words in a bag-of-words model. Furthermore, the time factor is not considered at all. Therefore, the strategy behind our model assumes that there might be some local changes in a user's behavior due to certain needs or state of mind. Under our model, there is the assumption that a user does not necessarily behave the same over different consecutive time slices.

As explained, SVD/LSI can identify the most frequent patterns of a user. By modeling the most salient behavioral patterns of a user's app usage behavior over time, we can further identify those behaviors that are established over time. In simple terms, our model assumes that there is a high chance that a user would repeat a behavior that not only has been frequent in the entire dataset, but also is persistent over time. We visualize our model in Fig. 4.

After n models are trained for each user for n consecutive time slices, we query each of the n models with an unseen test data which describes a context

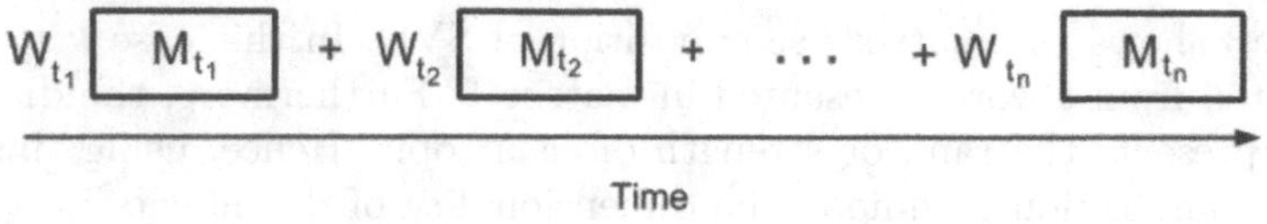

$$W_{t_1} \boxed{M_{t_1}} + W_{t_2} \boxed{M_{t_2}} + \cdots + W_{t_n} \boxed{M_{t_n}}$$

Time

Fig. 4. Our time-aware model for predicting app usage

and time (e.g. Spain-home-Sunday-afternoon-cloudy-weekend) and get a ranked list of other app usage entries closest to the query in the LSI space. By keeping a list of all app names we can then find the highest ranked apps with their corresponding probability score under each of the models. Thus, we have computed n ranked vectors of similarity between the query and the training data from the n LSI models. We note that for modeling the structure presented in Fig. 4, in each of the ranked vectors we assign only the highest corresponding probability score of an app, hence building a vector with one similarity score per each unique app. Subsequently, we compute the element-wise similarity score for each app over all n time slices according to Eq. 2.

In other words, we modify the probability scores in each of the similarity vectors based on persistence over time. We use the following equation for modifying the probability scores of each of the computed ranked vectors computed for each query:

$$P_{w,c} = \sum_{n=1}^{n} \sum_{w_i \in v} \frac{e^{-(n-1+\lambda)} * |P(w_{i,n})|}{(n)} \tag{2}$$

where n is the time slice sequence number, $w_{i,n}$ is the probability of app name w derived from the n_{th} time slice. The resulting constructed vector is an average representation of probability of all app names present in all n models where the most persistent behaviors are weighted higher. Finally, λ is the persistence (i.e. establishment of a behavior) rate which models an exponential factor of time. The use of an exponential factor is due to findings of psychology research [13] which shows that forgetting is an exponential function of time. This finding has been used by information retrieval researchers [16] which have modeled user behavior over time. Therefore, since every time a user repeats a behavior it shows that the user memory recalls this behavior, we multiply it by an exponential factor of time. In this research we set λ to 1.5. As a future work, we plan to test the effect of this parameter.

Finally, based on the final ranked list of apps computed by the above equation, we can predict the app usage behavior of users. A higher rank shows a higher likelihood of a user using the corresponding app at the time specified in the query.

5   Experimental Setup

5.1   Dataset Description

We use the dataset presented in [8] for our experiments. The original dataset contains over 96,000 entries of app usage from 957 users. However, in our analysis of the dataset we observed that for many of the users there are as many as a few app usage entries. Therefore, we reduced the dataset to those users with at least 200 app usage entries.

The resulting dataset contains 69,787 app usage entries belonging to 176 users. For the experiments reported in this paper we used this dataset. A full description of the dataset is available in [8]. Out of all the attributes collected for each app usage we are only interested in the day of the week, time of the day, whether or not the day is a weekend, location, weather, category of app and the app name. For training the models we use these entries, but for testing the models we issue queries without the app categories and app names.

As explained earlier, we treat the data of each user independently from other users. That is, for each user we train a separate model. In order to train and test each model we need to divide the data of each user into two sets of training data and testing data. Since we are dealing with data that are in sequence, we can not divide the data merely on a random basis. Instead, we take a 20% sample of the data in the original sequence and use it as test data. That means that out of every 5 app usage entries we put aside the last entry for testing the trained models. The remainder of the data, is then used for training the models.

The data is also pre-processed such that all the blank spaces in between app name and categories are removed and also all letters are lower-cased. Additionally, if one of the attributes always remained the same, e.g. a user always stayed in Spain, that attribute was removed from the data as a stop word. These steps are necessary for training the topic models in an effective way.

We present our evaluation based on the presented dataset in Sect. 5.3.

5.2   Evaluation Metric

Our goal in this study is to develop models that given a specific time and situation, can predict which app a person will use in that specific time and rearrange the order of the apps such that those that are more likely to be used by the user at that specific time would show on the home screen of a smartphone. Since most current smartphones have screens big enough to show 5 apps in the home screen, we evaluate our models based on whether or not the app that a user used at a specific point in time was shown among the 5 apps in the home screen.

Therefore, our evaluation metric computes the accuracy (i.e. correctness) of a recommended app at a certain point in time such that:

$$Accuraccy = \frac{\#of Correctly Predicted Apps}{\#of All Examined Apps} \tag{3}$$

where $\#ofCorrectlyPredictedApps$ indicate the apps that were shown in the home screen of a smartphone and were predicted by the model, and $\#ofAllExaminedApps$ is the total number of apps in the test data. In the next section we present the results of our experiment.

5.3   Evaluation

In this section, we present the results of our evaluation of the models presented. We first train the models for each user and test them using the evaluation metric described in Subsect. 5.2. For this purpose, we set the number of topics across all models to 10 so that the models are comparable. Also, we set the number of time slices n of our novel time-aware model to 4.

Then we compute the accuracy of the three presented models and compare them. Table 1 shows the results of our experiment.

Table 1. Results of comparison between our time-aware model, the Author Topic Model (ATM) and the Singular Value Decomposition (SVD/LSI) based on accuracy.

	ATM	SVD/LSI	Our model
Acc. (%)	38.78	37.45	43.30

As it could be seen in the table, our model outperforms both the ATM and the SVD/LSI models in terms of accuracy. Our intuition from observing these results is that our model not only finds a generalized pattern based on the frequency of usage of certain apps at certain times, but also finds a pattern which is generalizable over time. In other words, our model removes noisy observations which are not persistent over time.

That may be the reason why our method has shown better results as compared with ATM and SVD/LSI. Our proposed models could be used to manage and organize the apps that a user has installed on her mobile phone by rearranging the apps customized to the behavior of the user at each specific time.

In a second experiment, we would like to assess the impact of the sampling rate of the training data. As described in Sect. 5.1, we took a 20% sample of the sequential app usage as test data. In this experiment we would like to analyze the effect of increasing the sample rate so that we reduce the amount of training data. In this experiment, for each 3 app usage entries we hold the last entry out

Table 2. Results of the comparison between all models with an increased sampling rate of 33% for the test data.

	ATM	SVD/LSI	Our model
Acc. (%)	35.43	34.68	40.11

as test data. Therefore, we have increased the sampling rate to slightly more than 33% (Table 2).

As we see in the table the performance of all three models in terms of accuracy drop. However, our model still outperforms the other two baseline models despite the reduced amount of training data.

6 Conclusion

With the rapid proliferation of smartphones and the variety of apps developed for them, there is a need for managing and organizing such content. In this paper, we tackled the problem of predicting users' app usage behavior and time-aware organization of apps in a personalized way. We first presented two baseline methods which could be used for solving such problem. Then, we proposed a time-aware model for the same task. Our results demonstrate that our model is superior to the baseline methods in terms of accuracy.

In the future we plan to extend the current work to analyzing all interactions between users and smartphones. Additionally, we would like to assess the content that users interact with on smartphones in greater depth for designing models that can retrieve user information needs proactively just-in-time they need it. The retrieved information could be shown to the user on the smartphone home screen, or in the form of notifications and reminders.

References

1. Aliannejadi, M., Mele, I., Crestani, F.: Personalized ranking for context-aware venue suggestion. In: SAC, pp. 960–962 (2017)
2. Aliannejadi, M., Rafailidis, D., Crestani, F.: Personalized keyword boosting for venue suggestion based on multiple LBSNs. In: Jose, J.M., Hauff, C., Altıngovde, I.S., Song, D., Albakour, D., Watt, S., Tait, J. (eds.) ECIR 2017. LNCS, vol. 10193, pp. 291–303. Springer, Cham (2017). doi:10.1007/978-3-319-56608-5_23
3. Baeza-Yates, R., Jiang, D., Silvestri, F., Harrison, B.: Predicting the next app that you are going to use. In: Proceedings of the Eighth ACM International Conference on Web Search and Data Mining, WSDM 2015, pp. 285–294 (2015)
4. Bahrainian, S.A., Bahrainian, S.M., Salarinasab, M., Dengel, A.: Implementation of an intelligent product recommender system in an e-store. In: An, A., Lingras, P., Petty, S., Huang, R. (eds.) AMT 2010. LNCS, vol. 6335, pp. 174–182. Springer, Heidelberg (2010). doi:10.1007/978-3-642-15470-6_19
5. Bahrainian, S.A., Crestani, F.: Cued retrieval of personal memories of social interactions. In: Proceedings of the First Workshop on Lifelogging Tools and Applications, LTA 2016, pp. 3–12 (2016)
6. Bahrainian, S.A., Crestani, F.: Towards the next generation of personal assistants: systems that know when you forget. In: Proceedings of the 2017 ACM International Conference on the Theory of Information Retrieval, ICTIR 2017 (2017)
7. Bahrainian, S.A., Mele, I., Crestani, F.: Modeling discrete dynamic topics. In: Proceedings of the Symposium on Applied Computing, SAC 2017, pp. 858–865 (2017)

8. Baltrunas, L., Church, K., Karatzoglou, A., Oliver, N.: Frappe: Understanding the usage and perception of mobile app recommendations in-the-wild. arXiv preprint arXiv:1505.03014 (2015)
9. Böhmer, M., Ganev, L., Krüger, A.: Appfunnel: a framework for usage-centric evaluation of recommender systems that suggest mobile applications. In: Proceedings of the 2013 International Conference on Intelligent User Interfaces, IUI 2013, pp. 267–276 (2013)
10. Böhmer, M., Hecht, B., Schöning, J., Krüger, A., Bauer, G.: Falling asleep with angry birds, facebook and kindle: a large scale study on mobile application usage. In: Proceedings of the 13th International Conference on Human Computer Interaction with Mobile Devices and Services, MobileHCI 2011, pp. 47–56 (2011)
11. Deerwester, S., Dumais, S.T., Furnas, G.W., Landauer, T.K., Harshman, R.: Indexing by latent semantic analysis. J. Am. Soc. Inf. Sci. **41**(6), 391 (1990)
12. Do, T.-M.-T., Gatica-Perez, D.: By their apps you shall understand them: mining large-scale patterns of mobile phone usage. In: Proceedings of the 9th International Conference on Mobile and Ubiquitous Multimedia, MUM 2010, pp. 27:1–27:10 (2010)
13. Ebbinghaus, H.: Memory: A contribution to experimental psychology (1985). Translated in 1913
14. Hofmann,T.: Probabilistic latent semantic indexing. In: Proceedings of the 22nd Annual International ACM SIGIR Conference on Research and Development in Information Retrieval, SIGIR 1999, pp. 50–57 (1999)
15. Laurila, J.K., Gatica-Perez, D., Aad, I., Bornet, B.J.O., Do, T.M.T., Dousse, O., Eberle, J., Miettinen, M.: The mobile data challenge: big data for mobile computing research. In: Pervasive Computing (2012)
16. Li, W., Eickhoff, C., de Vries, A.P.: Probabilistic local expert retrieval. In: Advances, Information Retrieval, pp. 227–239 (2016)
17. Rosen-Zvi, M., Griffiths, T., Steyvers, M., Smyth, P.: The author-topic model for authors and documents. In: Proceedings of the 20th Conference on Uncertainty in Artificial Intelligence, pp. 487–494. AUAI Press (2004)
18. Wang, C., Blei, D., Heckerman, D.: Continuous time dynamic topic models. In: Proceedings of Uncertainty in Artificial Intelligence (2008)
19. Zhou, Y., Wilkinson, D., Schreiber, R., Pan, R.: Large-scale parallel collaborative filtering for the netflix prize, pp. 337–348 (2008)

Use of Mobile Apps for Teaching and Research – Implications for Digital Literacy

Annika Hinze[1(✉)], Nicholas Vanderschantz[1], Claire Timpany[1],
Sarah-Jane Saravani[2], Sally Jo Cunningham[1], and Clive Wilkinson[2]

[1] Computer Science Department, University of Waikato,
Hamilton, New Zealand
{hinze, vtwoz, ctimpany, sallyjo}@waikato.ac.nz
[2] University Library, University of Waikato, Hamilton, New Zealand
{saravani, cwilkins}@waikato.ac.nz

Abstract. This paper reports on the results of an online survey about mobile application (app) use for academic purposes, i.e. teaching and research, by Higher Degree Research (HDR) students and academic staff at one of the eight New Zealand universities. Two thirds of the 138 respondents reported they used apps for academic purposes. In teaching, apps were reported to be used as a means to push information to students. In research, apps appeared to be used to self-organise, collaborate with colleagues, store information, and to stay current with research. This paper presents the survey results and discusses implications for personal information management in education context and opportunities for university library services.

Keywords: Mobile apps · Research methodology · Information behaviour · Teaching practice · Information management · Academia

1 Introduction

Mobile learning has been claimed as the Future of Learning (Bowen and Pistilli 2012). Mobile apps are a fundamental feature of mobile devices and can be valuable in higher education for such activities as gathering and using information, accessing content, promoting communication, collaboration and reflection (Bowen and Pistilli 2012; Beddall-Hill et al. 2011). They also offer extended capacity to undertake *research* across a wider range of locations than traditionally possible and enable the collection, manipulation and sharing of data in real time (Hahn 2014). The intervention of technology has the potential to prompt new practices in research, both expanding and constraining relationships with the research process and methodological approaches (Goble et al. 2012). This is not necessarily a smooth path. According to Makori and Mauti (2016), usage of digital technologies is negatively impacted on by a range of crucial factors, including inadequate social computing facilities, insufficient information infrastructure coupled with weak institutional and physical structures, lack of enough information resources, and inadequate knowledge, skills and competencies. Digital literacy is increasingly on the agenda of higher education organisations as they commit

© Springer International Publishing AG 2017
S. Choemprayong et al. (Eds.): ICADL 2017, LNCS 10647, pp. 173–184, 2017.
https://doi.org/10.1007/978-3-319-70232-2_15

to delivering graduates who are capable of demonstrating technology competency and equally able to contribute to modern, digitally-oriented, fast-paced economies.

We believe that libraries, particularly academic libraries, enter a new service field of making available not the information itself (in form of books and documents) but also the means to acquire, manage and develop relationships with information in digital form, such as via mobile apps. This paper examines the current use of mobile apps for teaching, learning and research at our local university. We analyse the implications for personal information management in education context and opportunities for the university library and future service requirements.

The remainder of this paper is structured as follows: Sect. 2 discusses current literature and related work; Sect. 3 gives an overview of our study methodology; Sect. 4 presents the findings from our survey; and Sect. 5 discusses implications.

2   Literature and Related Work

The research literature on using mobile apps for education and research purposes is extremely sparse and significant potential for research in this area is evident in the related work that we are able to present here. Discussion of digital tools for research has focused on opportunities and challenges, ranging from technical issues to complex concerns involving implications for future research processes (Carter et al. 2015; Davidson et al. 2016; Garcia et al. 2016; Raento et al. 2009). Several studies have been conducted on the selection, use or development of mobile apps by or for libraries (Wong 2012; Hennig 2014; van Arnhem 2015), mainly focusing on delivery of information or data about the library services. Mobile apps for libraries are often featured by these authors—an example being apps for ethnographic field research (van Arnhem 2015). One of the pitfalls of writing about apps with respect to education is the tendency to merely describe app functionalities. The University of Chester observed the ready adoption of mobile note-taking software by undergraduate students (Schepman et al. 2012). The previously held concern that not all students have access to a smartphone is not supported by recent data (Anderson 2015). However, McGeeney (2015) observed a number of logistical and technical constraints for using mobile apps, compared to Web browsers, for surveys, including lower response rates, increased costs applied by some survey apps vendors and more design constraints which can involve limiting options such as navigation buttons and check boxes. Due to time and effort required to learn how to use an app effectively, using apps resulted in lower response rates than web-based data collection (Pew Research Center 2015). Carlos (2012) identified the advent of mobile research tools as a useful supplement to the desktop computer. Within the academic environment, provision of technical infrastructure is an accepted service for both research and teaching/learning. Adopting an analogous view of mobile technology may assist in exploring its potential. MacNeill (2015) suggests that academic staff make use of apps for teaching and research purposes, with initial focus on keystone apps around which to build the body of supporting apps (MacNeill 2015, p. 241).

3 Methodology

An online survey was conducted to investigate how mobile apps were being used for teaching, research and learning purposes across the university.

Data Collection. The data collection used an online, self-administered survey intended as a snapshot of the situation across all faculties of a single university. The university's research office forwarded invitations to all departmental administrators, who distributed the survey invitation to all the university's academics and researchers via email. For the higher-degree students, the School of Graduate Research emailed their student body and posted the invitation on the School's Facebook page. The potential sample size was about 1400 participants (including 820 students and 580 academics). Responses were anonymous and external participation was excluded through the use of location-restriction in the Qualtrics Survey Software.

Survey Questions. The survey used a 24-item survey utilising Likert scales, radio buttons, and free text questions; for details see (Hinze et al. 2017). The first section comprised four demographic questions, followed by a short section on whether mobile apps had been used, the third section focused on device and operating system used, the following, main section, depending on role and type of academic purpose (teaching or research), sought reflection on aspects of mobile apps use and whether such use had influenced research or teaching practice. For those respondents who had not used, and were not intending to use, mobile apps information was sought on the reason for this situation.

Data Analysis. The results were analysed using a variety of reports, both default and cross-tabulation for measuring association, within Qualtrics. A basic descriptive statistical analysis was applied to the data.

4 Results and Analysis

Demographic. The survey was completed by 138 respondents (9.8% of potential sample), with 58 academic staff, 73 doctoral students, 6 Master's students and 16 others (general staff, librarian, postgraduate certificate student, doctoral assistant, research fellow, research assistant, tutor, contracted Professional Learning and Development, management, support, graduate diploma and a PhD graduate). Respondents could select more than one category and 16 of 138 people did so. The gender breakdown of respondents was 60% female (N = 82), 40% male (N = 55) and one person who did not specify a gender; the age bands were equally distributed between 20–30, 31–40, 41–50 and 51 and over. The respondents represented a range of faculties, the largest groups being from Science and Engineering ($\sim$28%), Arts and Social Sciences ($\sim$20%), Education ($\sim$20%) and Computing and Mathematics ($\sim$16%).

Use of Mobile Apps. Sixty-five percent of respondents (90 of 138) had used mobile apps for academic purposes (71% of academic and 67% of student respondents); with a composition of 73% of male and 60% of female respondents. Of those who had used mobile apps for academic purposes, most were in the Faculty of Computing and Mathematical Sciences, followed by the Faculty of Education. Respondents showed a clear preference for smartphones (twice as likely as the second preference of iPad); further options were android tablets, cellphones and wearable devices. Most were using android devices (>60%), followed by iOS (48%); Mac, Windows and others made up (~26%); multiple selections were possible.

Non-users. Thirty-five percent of respondents (48 of 138) had not used mobile apps for academic purposes; half of these indicated they were not planning to do so either. When asked what was stopping them, 23 people responded, some noting more than one impediment. Nearly half considered their own lack of knowledge about how apps might be used as the leading factor. Approximately one third of the responses indicated that the responder was uninterested in apps and/or viewed them as irrelevant to their teaching or research. Other responses included the opinion that computers offer better options than mobile devices, with a lack of support also being stated as reason for future non-use. The 50% of non-users who might use apps in future named a range of potential uses, such as document sharing (64%), communication (45%), note taking (42%), storage (36%) and access to course information and data collection (both 32%). These respondents were also asked to rate factors in increasing app usage; the question was answered by 21 participants (see Fig. 1).

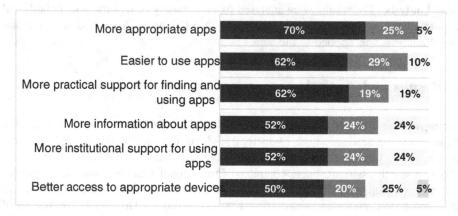

Fig. 1. Factors to encourage apps use: from very helpful (dark) to very unhelpful (blue) (Color figure online)

Non-use factors. In their further comments, non-users expressed technical concerns ("new apps have a track record of failure in their first years: this does not look good to students if suddenly the app for their course falls over") data safety concerns ("need to be reliable enough that researchers can be confident that they will not suffer data losses if they use just apps"), pedagogical usefulness ("[...] we have gone into more and more web based teaching [...] use of white board and limited amount of notes uploaded will work well, with lot of laboratory type hands-on elements. I strongly believe that if we [lose] the "human touch" in classroom setting, it will gradually and negatively affect the quality of the graduates we produce"), and being concerned that "one can only move as fast as students are able [...] you have built a learning task on a particular resource and then find that half the class cannot even access it". Some respondents expressed reservations about institutional support and felt "it would also be great if there was some sort of online resource on the uni website that lists and briefly explains some of the apps that might be useful when conducting research". Some respondents found apps inconvenient ("I despise having to download and constantly update several apps, plus they come with intrusive permissions") or they felt, at the present time, apps were "Only useful where use of a real computer is impossible". Several participants noted that "it is challenging to find the most appropriate app to meet a specific teaching purpose" or "to modify existing apps to suit the purpose of the user and the context of the user". Some of the comments by participants reveal concerns that seem born out of a lack of practical experience with apps (e.g., having to constantly update apps and student not willing or able to engage with apps).

Purpose of App Usage. All of the 90 people who had used apps, responded to a question about the purpose (multiple selections possible): 36 (40%) had used them for teaching/supervision and 80 (89%) for research purposes. Figure 2 shows the distribution of roles of the users of mobile apps.

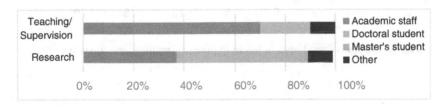

Fig. 2. Mobile app user role and purpose

Apps for Teaching/Supervision. The 36 respondents using apps for teaching and supervision were asked to select which apps they used from a list. They were also asked to indicate if the app was for their own use or if they had asked students to use the app (see Fig. 3). There were 19 other options named, not shown in the figure: Skype (2), Facebook (2), Feedly (1), Viber (1), Kahootz (1), Trello (1), Kindle (2), and Google apps (9). The same respondents were asked about the specific aspects of their teaching practice the apps were used for (see Fig. 4). Twenty-five of 36 had also asked their students to use mobile apps (for purposes see Fig. 5).

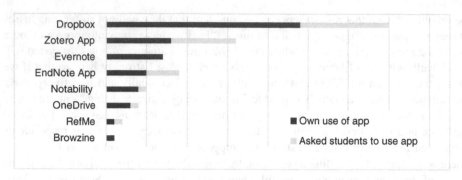

Fig. 3. Apps used for teaching/supervision purposes (multiple selections possible)

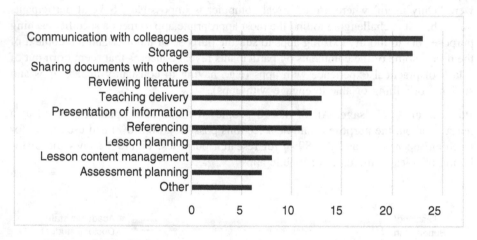

Fig. 4. Purpose of used apps in teaching practice (multiple selections possible)

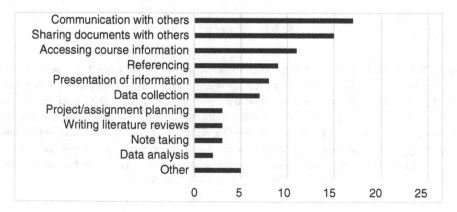

Fig. 5. Purpose of used apps requested of students (multiple selections possible)

Apps for Research. Eighty of the 90 app-using respondents did so for research purposes. They were asked what mobile apps they had used for research, with results summarized in Fig. 6. The 40 others include Mendeley (3), ToDo (1), Keynote (1), iBook (2), Spotify(1), Facebook (1), Skype (4), Compass (1), Trello (1), Mindmeister (1), NoteIt (1), and Google apps (17). The research purposes are summarized in Fig. 7.

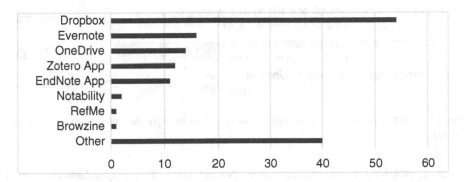

Fig. 6. Apps used for research purposes (multiple selections possible)

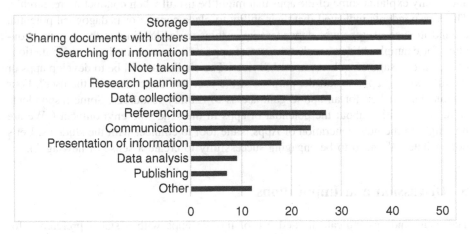

Fig. 7. Research purpose for mobile apps (multiple selections possible)

Impact of Apps on Academic Experience. The users of apps for academic purposes rated the impact of the app usage, see Fig. 8. Nearly 80% felt their academic activity had benefitted from mobile apps. Half the users believed their academic activity had been conducted differently as a consequence of using apps. Eighteen percent had experienced difficulties.

Additional Factors. Thirty-eight responses were received covering instructional support, (in)convenience, technical aspects, pedagogical and contextual viewpoints. Several respondents were neutral regarding the inclusion of mobiles apps into their

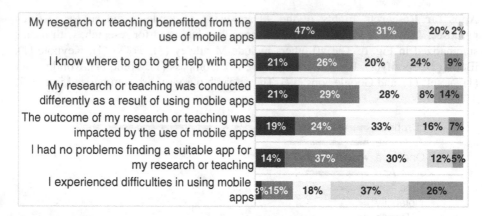

Fig. 8. Impact of app use: from strongly agree (dark) to strongly disagree (blue) (Color figure online)

academic practice ("I just used the camera. No big deal"). Five respondents mentioned the need or benefit of training ("Would be great to get some training on this☺", or "It would be great if there was some sort of online resource on the uni website that lists and briefly explains some of the apps that might be useful when conducting research"). These respondents indicated that their ability to place context or pedagogical potential around the use of apps was dependent upon their understanding of the app functionality, for example, "I can see that the use of apps will increase in line with predictions of increased usage of web-connected devices. The challenge will be to develop apps or modify existing apps to suit the purpose of the user and the context of the user". Four respondents wished for an app to gain access to Library resources. Some respondents were very positive about the potential of apps in the academic environment ("We are moving into the new generation of Apps is the tool to connect with the students. Let's not hesitate. We need to be engaging successfully to create a sense of new age").

5   Discussion and Implications

The main findings indicate limited use of mobile apps with a stated preference for organisational provision of information training and support to enable greater engagement. This has implications for support areas of the university, including library service planning and delivery, and their involvement in academic information behaviour and information management including the use of mobile apps.

5.1   Summary of Main Findings

Naturally, a response rate of less than 10% of the potential sample size was less than hoped for, and constitutes a limitation of the collected data. Online surveys are not noted for high response rate, even when they are more targeted, as in our case. We cannot draw definitive conclusions but rather read these as indicators, such as that a core of mobile app activity is occurring across the university which may be built upon and which would benefit from a platform of co-ordinated support. Further research in this area is required to strengthen the recommendations possible from the snapshot results. Here we list the main findings:

Apps for Research. Where mobile apps were used, most participants had used apps for research, with the majority being post-graduate students. The main purposes were storage, document sharing, searching, referencing and note taking. While nearly 30% had used mobile apps for data collection, only eight percent had moved beyond this to analyze their data in this manner.

From this study the reasons for this lack of use of apps during the research planning and research analysis phases is unclear. However, comparison between the results of app user and non-user respondents reveals both groups demonstrated preference for apps enabling document sharing, communicating and note taking. It is interesting to note this mirroring of preference for app functionality. Additionally, neither app users nor non-users expressed strong preference for data analysis, referencing, or presentation apps. This co-incidence of preference may be a reflection of the identified lack of support and training available across the university campus.

Apps for Supervision/Teaching. For teaching/supervision purposes, a clear preference was on apps for communication or document and data sharing with colleagues and for storage. Some of the apps were used for both teaching and research purposes. Academic staff used apps for teaching/supervision (26%) to almost the same degree as for their research activities (30%). Teachers/supervisors asked their students to use apps mainly for the purposes of communicating and sharing information. Apps for planning were barely used nor were apps for research tasks such as reviewing literature, data collection or analysis. Responses indicate that use of apps in both teaching and research practices focused upon the purposes of sharing documents, storage and communication with colleagues. It is, therefore, unsurprising that teachers/supervisors requested their students to engage in app usage for similar purposes, rather than venturing into areas of app use with which they, themselves, were unfamiliar. This indicates that students collecting field data for course work were expected to do so using traditional tools and techniques.

More Support Requested by Non-users and Users. Among those not considering apps, lack of knowledge was the primary stumbling block followed by a lack of interest. They also challenged the university to determine the most useful apps and how best to use them effectively. Potential users were nearly all interested in having more appropriate or easier to use apps available, indicating that this group of respondents has attempted to access or use apps in the past but had been discouraged. Potential app users also wanted more practical support for finding and using apps. It appears that non-users could move to mobile app use if they had access to information and support on technical specifications and purpose or application. It remains the need to convince of the overall usefulness of mobile apps "to suit the [academic] purpose and the context of the user".

Those respondents using apps for academic purposes had a positive attitude – nearly 80% perceived a benefit from app use. The majority did encounter difficulties, however, less than half the users knew where to go to get sufficient help. Only half had found the experience of locating a suitable app for their teaching or research to be problem-free. One participant observed that "many of the apps I now use would have been extremely useful had I known about them when I began this degree."

Impact Needs Further Study. Fifty percent perceived a change in research conduct and almost as many felt their teaching was impacted. This is an area that would benefit from further study to gather empirical evidence on the application of technology to traditional pedagogies or research methodologies and processes.

5.2 Implications

This study provides a small snapshot of the current state of mobile app use across a university. The following implications arise from this study and are offered for consideration:

- The data indicates that academic staff and students involved in using mobile apps are personally driven and motivated rather than supported by clearly-planned, identified and integrated infrastructure across the institution.
- While some aspects of using apps for communication were reported, the majority of usages was related to management of documents, text, and data. This indicates an opportunity to frame and explore academic app use as an issue of personal information management. It may also indicate a need to explore scholarly workflows and which role apps could play when their use was embraced and supported by the academic institution.
- Introduction to the possibilities and limitations of mobile apps for non-users provided by the institution may serve to increase the uptake of tools during teaching and research.
- There are implications for the way in which support areas, such as libraries, are keeping abreast of initiatives and developing trends across the institution. To ensure teaching and learning is occurring effectively, identified information management and digital literacy support needs to be interwoven from the earliest stages of planning.
- It is institutional strategy to invest in innovative applications of digital technology in research and teaching. The use of apps for academic endeavour is currently underutilised. A coordinated approach is needed to enable digital technology acceptance to transform digital innovation in education.

6 Conclusion

Some indicators were drawn from the survey as outlined above and they serve a useful purpose of guiding future work in this area. Mobile apps are being used by teachers and researchers to a limited degree, both in staff numbers and in range of mobile apps and there is a clearly-identified need for a strong platform of support for staff and students. It appears that non-users would consider using mobile apps if there were suitable apps available and if training or support was offered. Similarly, app users expressed that they would welcome more information and guidance. We propose that libraries, particularly academic libraries, are in a position to address this particular problem. Today, libraries and librarians are uniquely placed to provide patrons with the means to acquire, manage and develop relationships with information in digital form, such as via mobile apps. Investigation into best-practices around the provision of this next generation of support is required. Mobile apps were more likely to be used for research than teaching purposes, but for both practices the ability to communicate, collaborate and share with others were primary motivators for use. Users were able to perceive the benefit of including mobile apps in their teaching or research practice but were uncertain as to the impact of the apps upon the conduct or outcomes of their practice.

The present snapshot indicates a tertiary education environment experimenting with technology within teaching and research practices. The use of mobile apps is an essential component of digital literacy and has huge potential for changing teaching and research practice. The response of our participants indicate that both individual and shared workflows in the field, the classroom, and the office may be enhanced by these mobile apps should appropriate digital literacy programmes be present to enable effective use within teaching and research. However, the survey highlights that addressing the needs of users and potential users of mobile apps for academic purposes is an area yet to be fully explored. A larger study of academic use of mobile apps is currently underway, with additional universities to be invited in future.

References

Anderson, M.: Technology device ownership: 2015. Report by Pew Research Center (2015). http://www.pewinternet.org/2015/10/29/technology-device-ownership-2015/

Beddall-Hill, N.L., Jabbar, A., Al Shehri, S.: Social mobile devices as tools for qualitative research in education: iPhones and iPads in ethnography, interviewing, and design-based research. J. Res. Cent. Educ. Technol. 7(1), 67–90 (2011)

Bowen, K., Pistilli, M.D.: Student preferences for mobile app usage. Educause Research Bulletin (2012)

Carlos, A.: Research on the go: Mobile tools for conducting research. Ref. Librarian 53(4), 433–440 (2012)

Carter, A., Liddle, J., Hall, W., Chenery, H.: Mobile phones in research and treatment: ethical guidelines and future directions. JMIR Mhealth UHealth 3(4), e95 (2015)

Davidson, J., Paulus, T., Jackson, K.: Speculating on the future of digital tools for qualitative research. Qual. Inq. 22(7), 606–610 (2016)

Garcia, B., Welford, J., Smith, B.: Using a smartphone app in qualitative research: the good, the bad and the ugly. Qual. Res. 16(5), 508–525 (2016)

Goble, E., Austin, W., Larsen, D., Kreitzer, L., Brintnell, E.: Habits of mind and the split-mind effect: when computer-assisted qualitative data analysis software is used in phenomenological research. Forum: Qual. Soc. Res. 13(2) (2012)

Hahn, J.: Undergraduate research support with optical character recognition apps. Ref. Serv. Rev. 42(2), 336–350 (2014)

Hennig, N.: Apps for librarians: using the best mobile technology to educate, create and engage. Libraries Unlimited (2014)

Hinze, A., Vanderschantz, N., Timpany, C., Cunningham, S.J., Saravani, S.-J., Wilkinson, C.: Use of mobile Apps for Teaching and Research, Working paper 01/2017, University of Waikato (2017)

MacNeill, F.: Approaching apps for learning, teaching and research. In: Middleton, A. (ed.) Smart Learning: Teaching and Learning with Smartphones and Tablets in Post Compulsory Education, pp. 238–264 (2015)

Makori, E.O., Mauti, N.O.: Digital technology acceptance in transformation of university libraries and higher education institutions in Kenya. Library Philos. Pract. 0_1, 1–20 (2016)

McGeeney, K.: What we learned about surveying with mobile apps. Report by Pew Research Center, April 2015. http://www.pewresearch.org/fact-tank/2015/04/02/what-we-learned-about-surveying-with-mobile-apps/

Pew Research Center: App vs. web for surveys of smartphone users: experimenting with mobile apps for signal contingent experience sampling method surveys (2015). http://www.pewresearch.org/2015/04/01/app-vs-web-for-surveys-of-smartphone-users/

Raento, M., Oulasvirta, A., Eagle, N.: Smartphones: an emerging tool for social scientists. Sociol. Meth. Res. 37(3), 426–454 (2009)

Schepman, A., Rodway, P., Beattie, C., Lambert, J.: An observational study of undergraduate students' adoption of (mobile) note-taking software. Comput. Hum. Behav. 28, 308–317 (2012)

van Arnhem, J.-P.: Apps and gear for ethnographic field research. Charleston Advisor 17(2), 58–64 (2015)

Wong, S.H.R.: Which platform do our users prefer: website of mobile app? Ref. Serv. Rev. 40 (1), 103–115 (2012)

Motivational Difference Across Gameplay Mechanics: An Investigation in Crowdsourcing Mobile Content

Ei Pa Pa Pe-Than[1(✉)], Dion Hoe-Lian Goh[2], and Chei Sian Lee[2]

[1] Institute for Software Research, School of Computer Science,
Carnegie Mellon University, Pittsburgh, PA 15213, USA
eipapapt@cs.cmu.edu
[2] Wee Kim Wee School of Communication and Information,
Nanyang Technological University, Singapore, Singapore
{ashlgoh,leecs}@ntu.edu.sg

Abstract. The convergence of crowdsoucing and gaming has led to the rise of new game genres that leverage the collective intelligence of online players. These are called crowdsourcing games, and they have become a viable option for garnering georeferenced metadata for digital library projects. Understanding the phenomenon of these games requires consideration of gameplay mechanics and their effects on players' motivations. Given the scarcity of research in this area, this study investigates how gameplay mechanics—collaboration and competition—influence motivations for playing and sharing mobile content. We conducted a between-subjects experiment using a non-game app and two virtual-pet-themed games with the collaborative and competitive mechanics respectively. Results indicate that crowdsourcing games lead to a higher level of enjoyment, immersion, and socializing. Moreover, the collaborative and competitive games were found to differ with respect to achievement, relaxation, task efficiency, and skills development.

Keywords: Crowdsourcing games · Human computation · Mobile content · Collaboration · Competition · Gameplay mechanics · Motivation

1 Introduction

Crowdsourcing organizes online users to generate output as a joint computation between computer and humans [2]. It is also known as an inexpensive and more efficient alternative to the traditional approach of finding and hiring human experts to generate content or tackle problems, such as image tagging, corpus annotation, language translation, georeferenced data and metadata creation [6, 13, 21].

The phenomenon of crowdsourcing is largely driven by the ubiquity of social computing that enables not only experts but also ordinary online users to participate in publishing content based on their knowledge or experience. *Amazon Mechanical Turk* (AMT) is one prominent example in which users perform a computational task with monetary incentives [19]. *OpenStreetMap* is another example, which constructs an online map based on data about different geographical locations contributed by its users [17].

© Springer International Publishing AG 2017
S. Choemprayong et al. (Eds.): ICADL 2017, LNCS 10647, pp. 185–196, 2017.
https://doi.org/10.1007/978-3-319-70232-2_16

With the prevalence of mobile devices providing location awareness and Internet connectivity, people can now perform crowdsourced tasks anytime and anywhere, and accordingly, crowdsourcing in the mobile or location-based context is likely to accelerate. Additionally, being able to carry mobile phones gives people the opportunity to perform crowdsourced tasks that require physical presence. For instance, people can instantly document their experience at/about their current locations. Such documentation serves not only as a personal record but also as real-time information and history about the associated locations that other people can retrieve and learn [17]. Although promising, a more engaging experience would attract users and encourage sustained usage.

The game-based approach to crowdsourcing could be a viable alternative for two main reasons. First, games are no longer an entertainment medium solely for young males and have finally achieved a critical mass of players. This is exemplified in recent statistics published by the Entertainment Software Association that suggest that the average game player is 35 years old and is 41% likely to be female [7]. Second, it is believed that tasks that require human perceptual capability and creativity can better be accomplished by collaboration between humans and computer, rather than performed alone by either party. Accordingly, games are used in the crowdsourcing context in which players perform a given crowdsourced task through enjoyable gameplay, known as crowdsourcing games, human computation games or games with a purpose [6, 9, 21]. These games are used in various application areas to harness human intelligence, including the creation of metadata for online images and videos, sentiments of given statements, shapes of proteins, annotations of real-world locations, and many more (e.g., [1, 3, 10, 17]). Hence, beyond the traditional approach of recruiting users, crowdsourcing enables the digital libraries community to reach out to potential participants to tackle library-related problems on a larger scale.

One important feature of games is their gameplay mechanics, which refers to the set of rules driving how players behave in a game [20]. Collaboration and competition are two commonly used gameplay mechanics [24], and the specific behavior induced by such mechanics may affect players' motivations. Hence, understanding players' motivations is an important first step toward developing games that cater to the needs of potential players. Furthermore, developing crowdsourcing games that attract users and sustain their usage imposes another challenge because such games serve dual purposes—generating output and entertaining [9]. More specifically, players' motivations may arise from their desire to fulfill either or both purposes.

This study presents the argument that research on gameplay mechanics and players' motivations is important for two primary reasons: (1) the empirical evidence on the effect of such mechanics is limited. It is necessary to investigate whether incorporating games into crowdsourced tasks can better motivate players, and if so, how different gameplay mechanics are in influencing motivations derived from the dual purposes of crowdsourcing games. Moreover, (2) findings from prior research on games for pure entertainment (e.g., [18, 23]) may not be readily applicable to crowdsourcing games because of the contextual difference. These games are unique in that they blend gaming with content creation; hence, this dual purpose might interplay in influencing players' motivations.

Therefore, we aim to answer the research question regarding how gameplay mechanics are different in motivating individuals to play and share mobile content in crowdsourcing games. To achieve our research goal, we first developed two different games for mobile content sharing, each utilizing different gameplay mechanics (i.e., collaborative or competitive), and a non-game version that acted as a control. A total of 73 participants were recruited for a between-subjects experiment in which they used an assigned app for a week, and completed a questionnaire. Based on findings, we provide recommendations to guide the design of crowdsourcing games and other similar game-based apps.

2 Background

We will begin by presenting two commonly-used gameplay mechanics in crowd-sourcing. This is followed by a discussion of motivations in crowdsourcing for mobile content.

2.1 Gameplay Mechanics

Gameplay refers to the experience of interaction between the player and the game [5]. Specifically, gameplay is directed by a set of rules that players abide by while trying to achieve the goal [20]. Typically, games use collaboration and competition to organize the goal setting, and then specific game rules are constructed to achieve the specified goal [24]. In crowdsourcing, games can be structured in such a way that players either compete or collaborate with others while performing the crowdsourced tasks. In fact, collaboration and competition are regarded as two different goal structures in social science and psychology literature [22], and hence they may induce varying levels of motivating behaviors.

Collaboration occurs when people work toward a collective goal [24]. In crowd-sourcing games, the collaborative situation happens when players work together as a team to achieve the game objective, and the outcome is typically shared among team members. One well-known example is the *ESP Game* [21], which embeds an image-labeling task into gameplay in which two randomly-paired players create labels for given images within a time limit. They both earn points for every matching label. The *Gopher Game* [1] is another example in which players collaboratively create content about real-world locations. Specifically, a player creates a gopher (a game agent) that seeks information about the player's current location. The other player who picks up this gopher must create the requested information.

Competition is another commonly used gameplay mechanic, and it occurs when only one person accomplishes the goal while the others do not [24]. Players develop strategies to play against others, and only one player can win at a time. For example, *KissKissBan* [12] approaches the image-labeling problem from a competitive perspective. A player acts as a blocker and competes with a group of two players with a rule that the blocker prevents the group from reaching an agreement (i.e., matching image labels). Another example is *CityExplorer* [15], in which players conquer a city segment by placing markers for their chosen categories, such as food, café, and so on. The player who creates the most categories wins the game.

The effects of collaboration and competition have been examined in several contexts including learning and entertainment (e.g., [20, 22]). Collaboration is believed to promote positive behaviors, which in turn influence enjoyment and performance in the task performed, whereas competition is said to promote negative behaviors and outcomes [24]. In entertainment-oriented games with competition as their central element, players were found to be motivated primarily by achievement [8]. In contrast, collaborative situations may promote mutual affiliation and social interaction among players [23]. Hence, depending on the gameplay mechanics used, crowdsourcing games may differ in affording motivations. Understanding the effects of gameplay is important because its misuse may hinder players' motivation to participate, thereby diminishing performance and content quality. This study therefore investigates the potential differences in motivations afforded by collaborative and competitive gameplay mechanics in crowdsourcing mobile content.

2.2 Motivations

Motivation refers to a psychological state that directs individuals' actions toward a desired goal [10]. Prior research (e.g., [16, 18]) has regarded several basic human needs as motivators for playing games. These include the need for autonomy, competence, relatedness, achievement, power, and affiliation. As these needs are innate to human beings, it can be argued that games that fulfill psychological needs are enjoyable for players. Based on a study of players of a massive multiplayer online game, [23] identified three categories of motivations: achievement, socializing, and immersion.

In the context of content sharing, motivation pertains to the desire or willingness of an individual to contribute content while he/she is on the move [9]. Several motivations for sharing content were reported in prior studies, including entertainment, relationship maintenance, information discovery, relaxation, socializing, task performance, competition, and self-presentation (e.g., [4, 8, 10, 14]). Furthermore, altruism, self-efficacy, sense of community, and causal importance were identified as significant motivators for participation in crowdsourcing [11].

Taking an integrative perspective, this study considers motives relevant to both playing and sharing content in games for crowdsourcing mobile content. Research in this area is important for the design of game-based apps that better motivate desired behaviors. Therefore, a key contribution of this study is to shed light on the relationships between two gameplay mechanics—collaboration and competition—and motivation for playing and sharing in crowdsourcing mobile content.

3 Method

3.1 Applications Developed

Three mobile apps for mobile content creation were developed: *Share*, a non-game app; *Collabo*, a collaborative game; and *Clash*, a competitive game. All three apps have a similar purpose of collecting location-based data, which are known as comments in our apps. Each comment comprises title, tags, descriptions, media elements, and ratings. Using custom-deveoped apps enables us to have a better control over the look and feel of the interfaces and the accessibility of the collected crowdsourced data.

Our apps are designed for people to contribute content about real-world locations while being entertained by the gameplay. Each app is built around a core design that uses Google Maps and the GPS functionality on an Android phone. As people move around, they can browse the map, which is overlaid with mushroom houses, indicating places in their vicinity (Fig. 1). People can tap on houses to see several units, each of which holds comments that have been created. In the game-based apps, players create comments by means of feeding the virtual pet (i.e., in-game character), which lives in each unit, whereas users submit comments in the non-game app.

People can rate each other's comments in the apps. This rating feature of our apps serves as a quality control mechanism, where highly rated comments are socially acceptable. Further, our apps use a visualization technique to facilitate the quality judgment of crowdsourced data. The appearances of the pet or houses are dependent on four attributes of data—quantity, quality, sentiment, and recency. Specifically, the sizes of pets and houses are determined by the amount of content while their color is dependent on ratings. The mood of pets and weather around the houses depend on the number of positive or negative comments, and the age of the pets is determined by the creation dates of comments. Comments and ratings generated by people are updated in real time to reflect participants' ongoing activities in the apps.

Share serves as a control, and it uses all the functionality described above except that it does not have virtual pets. Moreover, participants are not awarded with any game points or rewards for their activities. Instead, they can view statistics, such as the number of comments and ratings. *Share*, therefore, serves as a representative app for crowdsourcing mobile content through which to compare the perceived motivation of game-based apps. Figure 2 shows a list of comments created in *Share*.

Collabo uses all the functionality described above, but unlike *Share*, it also incorporates collaborative mechanics and a points-based system. This game asks players to search for starving pets in their vicinity and team up with other players to rescue these pets. The starving pets appear sad and have a darker tone compared to healthier pets (Fig. 3). The pets become starved if their strength is lower than 50. To save the pets, players need to feed them with comments or rate those comments created by others on a five-star scale. Every new comment created increases the pet's strength by five, and the rating value (i.e., 1 to 5) is directly added to the strength. Bonus points are awarded every time a new member joins the team. Once a pet is rescued, the game allocates an equal amount of points to the team members, and at the same time, a winning message is displayed (Fig. 4).

In *Clash*, players compete with others for pet ownership. The current pet owner's name is shown underneath the pet (Fig. 5). During gameplay, players build up their strength by creating and rating comments. They can then challenge the pet owner to a duel (Fig. 6). He/she will win if the total score of his/her strength and daily luck (i.e., a random number generated at the first login of each day) is greater than that of the challenged player. The game also considers the rating value and recency of comments in calculating players' strengths, so that the pet is winnable by new players. The game allows owners to retain the ownership status securely for a 15-minute period. This feature was included based on the results of the pilot testing in which players felt frustrated about losing the pet immediately after a win.

Fig. 1. Places on the map overlaid with houses.

Fig. 2. A list of comment in *Share*.

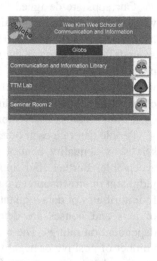

Fig. 3. A list of pets residing in a location.

Fig. 4. A winning message in *Collabo*.

Fig. 5. A pet owned by "ca122" in *Clash*.

Fig. 6. A player trying to challenge "ca122" in *Clash*.

3.2 Participants

Seventy-three participants (42 males and 31 females) were recruited from two local universities. Their ages ranged from 21 to 35 years. Among our participants, 19.18% of them had a background in computer science or information technology, 49.32% were from engineering disciplines, and the remainder were from disciplines such as arts, humanities, and social sciences, education, and business. Further, 63.01% have used social network apps, and 45.21% have used the location check-in feature of such apps. The majority of participants (86.30%) used mobile phones to share multimedia information. Additionally, slightly above half of the participants (54.79%) had experience with online games, and 17.81% reported to be regular players.

3.3 Experimental Procedure

This study adopted a between-subject design, and participants were randomly assigned to play either *Share*, *Collabo*, or *Clash*—24, 22, and 27 participants respectively. The experiment was conducted across separate sessions, with each having five to seven participants. This helped us create simulated collaborative or competitive environments, and also made the study manageable. Before the actual experiment, a briefing was done in which participants were given instructions on how to use the assigned app together with a short practice session. They then completed a questionnaire that elicited demographic information, mobile phone usage, and experience with games and location-based apps. Participants were then asked to use the assigned app on Android phones for a week, and create a minimum of 10 comments per day. Usage scenarios were provided, which include joining a team to save a pet (in *Collabo*), winning a pet (in *Clash*), and creating and rating comments (in *Share*). At the end of the experiment, participants completed a questionnaire that measured their motivations for using the assigned app and creating content on it.

A pilot study was carried out with 24 graduate students, and they were divided into two groups and randomly assigned to play either *Collabo* or *Clash*. They then rated the extent to which they felt competitiveness in the game they played on a 5-point Likert scale. An independent sample t-test was then and as expected, the results showed that participants who played *Clash* ($M = 3.80$) felt significantly higher levels of competitiveness than those who played *Collabo* ($M = 2.64$), suggesting that these two gameplay mechanics were appropriately perceived as such by the study's participants. Although the majority of participates reported that the questionnaire was largely clear and comprehensive, certain parts of it were revised to improve clarity.

3.4 Measures

The dependent variables of this study were motivations for playing and sharing content, and the independent variable was the app type. All question items were drawn from previous studies (e.g., [9, 14, 16]) and adapted to suit the study's context, and they were all measured on a 5-point Likert scale ranging from 1 (strongly disagree) to 5 (strongly agree). A total of 15 question items was used to measure motivations for playing and they are: achievement–individuals' desire to win and make progress;

socializing–individuals' desire to engage with others; relaxation–individuals' desire to combat boredom or escape from real life stress; enjoyment–individuals' desire to seek pleasurable experience; and immersion–individuals' desire to get involved completely or feel absorbed in the app.

Again, 15 question items were used to measure motivations for sharing content, and these constructs are: altruism–individuals' desire to express concerns for and help others; task efficiency–individuals' desire to accelerate information seeking; competitive play–individuals' desire to compare and compete with others; improving skills–individuals' desire to improve information-related skills; and social influence–individuals' desire to use the app is directed by concerns over social rewards.

4 Results

Table 1 shows the means and standard deviations of the study's dependent variables. One-way analysis of variance (ANOVA) was performed on these variables. The results indicated that there were significant differences with respect to the following constructs: achievement [$F(2,70) = 13.67$, $p < 0.001$], socializing [$F(2,70) = 7.55$, $p < 0.001$], relaxation [$F(2,70) = 3.91$, $p < 0.05$], enjoyment [$F(2,70) = 5.13$, $p < 0.01$], immersion [$F(2,70) = 6.73$, $p < 0.01$], task efficiency [$F(2,70) = 4.26$, $p < 0.05$], competitive play [$F(2,70) = 7.40$, $p < 0.001$], and improving skills [$F(2,70) = 5.36, p < 0.001$]. There were, however, no statistically significant differences among the three apps for altruism [$F(2,70) = 0.002, p = 0.99$] and social influence [$F(2,70) = 0.21, p = 0.81$].

Table 1. Means and standard deviations for participants' motivations for playing and sharing.

Constructs	Collabo (N = 22)		Clash (N = 27)		Share (N = 24)	
	M	SD	M	SD	M	SD
Achievement**	2.71	0.87	3.74	0.74	2.72	0.83
Socializing*	3.57	0.95	3.48	0.97	2.58	1.01
Relaxation**	3.07	1.01	3.69	0.77	3.07	0.98
Enjoyment*	3.43	1.18	3.35	0.94	2.57	0.98
Immersion*	3.67	1.10	3.46	0.67	2.72	1.01
Altruism	3.74	0.86	3.75	0.74	3.75	0.62
Task efficiency**	4.10	0.71	3.56	0.81	3.57	0.66
Competitive play**	2.90	1.08	3.60	0.65	2.74	0.83
Improving skills**	3.01	0.94	3.74	0.81	2.93	1.16
Social influence	3.25	1.22	3.35	1.01	3.44	0.88

Note. ** Statistically significant difference between games,
* Statistically significant difference between games and the non-game app.

Post-hoc comparisons using Tukey's test were then conducted, which uncovered the following results.

- **Achievement**. Participants who played *Clash* ($M = 3.74$) were more satisfied with their achievement in the game, compared to those who used either *Collabo* ($M = 2.71$) or *Share* ($M = 2.71$).
- **Socializing**. Participants reported that they were better able to socialize with others when playing *Collabo* ($M = 3.57$) and *Clash* ($M = 3.48$) than the non-game app, *Share* ($M = 2.58$). No significant difference was found between games.
- **Relaxation**. In contrast to socializing, participants stated that they were more like to play *Clash* ($M = 3.69$) for a relaxation purpose than *Collabo* and *Share*.
- **Enjoyment**. Participants who played *Collabo* ($M = 3.43$) and *Clash* ($M = 3.35$) reported to experience higher level of enjoyment than those used *Share* ($M = 2.57$).
- **Immersion**. Similar to enjoyment, participants were more likely to get immersed in *Collabo* ($M = 3.67$) and *Clash* ($M = 3.45$) than in *Share* ($M = 2.72$).
- **Task efficiency**. With regards to information seeking and retrieval, *Collabo* ($M = 4.10$) was more likely to be used by participants than *Clash* and *Share*.
- **Competitive play**. As expected, *Clash* ($M = 3.60$) outperformed *Collabo* and *Share* regarding fostering a sense of competition among players.
- **Improving skills**. Again, participants reported that they were more likely to use *Clash* ($M = 3.74$) to improve their ability in commenting about locations.
- **Social Influence**. There were no statistically significant differences in perceived social influence across three apps—*Collabo* ($M = 3.25$), *Clash* ($M = 3.35$), and *Share* ($M = 3.44$).

5 Discussion

Our results suggest that collaborative and competitive gameplay mechanics differ in affording motivations with respect to achievement, socializing, relaxation, enjoyment, and immersion. In particular, the competitive game, *Clash*, was better able to foster a sense of accomplishment or achievement among players. This finding may imply that players appreciate more of a reward obtained for being able to edge over other players because such rewards are unique to them. In *Clash*, participants had to try on one's own to outperform the current pet owners to win the game, whereas in *Collabo*, the rewards were equally distributed across players, perhaps diluting the sense of achievement. Next, participants of both *Collabo* and *Clash* were more motivated to socialize with others than those used the non-game app. Games for crowdsourcing mobile content can use either collaborative or competitive mechanics to garner meaningful outputs as a by-product of interaction among players.

Participants also reported that they were more likely to use *Clash* as a means to escape from real life stress compared to *Collabo* and *Share*. This is interesting because competition is a win and lose dichotomy, and that it can create tensions and stressful situations [22]. Perhaps as competition demands attention and involvement, participants may have experienced a greater sense of satisfaction when they were closer to win *Clash* or after a win, thereby leading to a more relaxation experience. Finally, participants experienced a higher level of enjoyment and immersion in games compared to the non-game counterpart. In our games, we encourage players' involvement by having pets that need to be nurtured over time. This finding, therefore, implies that the crowdsourced tasks and games need to be purposefully blended in such a way that people can use them as a source of entertainment.

With regards to motivation for sharing, this study found significant differences in task efficiency, competitive play, and improving skills across apps. Participants favored *Collabo* over *Clash* when creating content with an intention to seek information from others (e.g., raising a question), possibly indicating that people approach sharing content as a collaborative act. In other words, competition may encourage people to focus on one's own benefit [22], and such perception may have discouraged participants to use *Clash* for task efficiency. In contrast, participants were more likely to play *Clash* to improve their content creation ability. Here, the findings of task efficiency and developing skills imply that participants of *Clash* exert more effort in generating content, but they determine the content type based on their self-interest rather than explicitly creating content to support the needs of others. With regards to altruism, which refers to the selfless intention to benefit others [8], this study found no significant difference between crowdsourcing apps. Based on this finding, we speculate that games with either collaborative or competitive mechanics are comparable to non-game apps in terms of being able to inspire people to help others through crowdsourcing. Moreover, this finding implies that collaboration and competition add a dimension of enjoyment to crowdsourcing without diluting people's desire to participate in such projects.

6 Conclusion

This study examined the motivational differences between gameplay mechanics in the context of crowdsourcing mobile content. Findings of this study also provide several implications for research and practice. First, this study adds evidence to the differential effects of collaboration and competition on motivations in the crowdsourcing context. Depending on gameplay mechanics, games were found to perform differently in motivating with respect to playing and sharing content. This finding informs researchers of the necessary to investigate potential factors that influence motivations as well as the interplay between these factors. Second, while this study was conducted in games for crowdsourcing mobile content, our results may be generalizable to other contexts that use collaboration and competition to drive engagement and participation. For instance, to motivate people to engage in a task (e.g., learning, physical activity), they can be given a goal to compete or collaborate with others. Based on our findings, people in the competitive setting may try to improve their skills to achieve the goal. In contrast, people in the collaborative setting may be more likely to accomplish the task through interaction with others. Therefore, designers need to be aware of the tradeoff between the choice of collaboration and competition, and consider how to best utilize them.

Although our work yields important findings, it is not without limitations that offer opportunities for future research. First, this study relied on two commonly-used gameplay mechanics. Other alternative classifications of games exist, which include game genres, such as adventure and simulation as well as hybrid games that use a combination of collaborative and competitive mechanics [16]. Therefore, future research may investigate the differential effects of a larger set of gameplay mechanics on motivation. Second, given the motivational differences between games, this study calls for future research to examine whether different mechanics attract different content types. Third, the characteristics of the sample pose further limitations. Participants in this study were primarily undergraduate and graduate students from two local universities. A more diverse sample would validate the study's findings. Finally, this study was conducted in a single domain—mobile content creation. Different tasks may demand varying levels of cognitive abilities; hence, they may yield different perceptions. Further, studies of other domains are needed to verify the generalizability of our findings. Nevertheless, our findings provide deep insight on how collaboration and competition affect players' motivations in games for crowdsourcing mobile content. Given the growing popularity of apps that blend games with content creation, this study's findings augur well for digital libraries that wish to use game-based crowdsourcing to tackle library-related problems.

Acknowledgement. This work was supported by MOE/Tier 1 grant RG64/14.

References

1. Casey, S., Kirman, B., Rowland, D.: The gopher game: a social, mobile, locative game with user generated content and peer review. In: Proceedings of the International Conference on Advances in Computer Entertainment Technology, ACE 2007, Salzburg, pp. 9–16. ACM (2007)
2. Chen, Y., Ghosh, A., Kearns, M., Roughgarden, T., Vaughan, J.W.: Mathematical foundations for social computing. Commun. ACM **59**, 102–108 (2016)
3. Cooper, S., Khatib, F., Treuille, A., Barbero, J., Lee, J., Beenen, M., Leaver-Fay, A., Baker, D., Popović, Z.: Predicting protein structures with a multiplayer online game. Nature **466**(7307), 756–760 (2010)
4. Cramer, H., Rost, M., Holmquist, L.E.: Performing a check-in: emerging practices, norms and 'conflicts' in location-sharing using foursquare. In: Proceedings of the 13th International Conference on Human Computer Interaction with Mobile Devices and Services, Mobilehci 2011, Stockholm, pp. 57–66. ACM (2011)
5. Djaouti, D., Alvarez, J., Jessel, J.P., Methel, G., Molinier, P.: A gameplay definition through videogame classification. Int. J. Comput. Games Technol. **2008** (2008). Article No. 4
6. Doan, A., Ramakrishnan, R., Halevy, A.Y.: Crowdsourcing systems on the World-Wide Web. Commun. ACM **54**, 86–96 (2011)
7. ESA: Essential facts about the computer and video game industry (2016). Retrieved 5 February 2017. http://www.theesa.com
8. Espinoza, F., Persson, P., Sandin, A., Nyström, H., Cacciatore, E., Bylund, M.: *GeoNotes*: social and navigational aspects of location-based information systems. In: Abowd, G.D., Brumitt, B., Shafer, S. (eds.) UbiComp 2001. LNCS, vol. 2201, pp. 2–17. Springer, Heidelberg (2001). doi:10.1007/3-540-45427-6_2
9. Goh, D.H.L., Ang, R.P., Lee, C.S., Chua, A.Y.: Fight or Unite: investigating game genres for image tagging. J. Am. Soc. Inf. Sci. **62**, 1311–1324 (2011)

10. Goh, D.H.-L., Lee, C.S., Low, G.: "I played games as there was nothing else to do" Understanding motivations for using mobile content sharing games. Online Inf. Rev. **36**, 784–806 (2012)

11. Goncalves, J., Hosio, S., Rogstadius, J., Karapanos, E., Kostakos, V.: Motivating participation and improving quality of contribution in ubiquitous crowdsourcing. Comput. Netw. **90**, 34–48 (2015)

12. Ho, C.J., Chang, T.H., Lee, J.C., Hsu, J.Y.J., Chen, K.T.: KissKissBan: a competitive human computation game for image annotation. In: Proceedings of the ACM SIGKDD Workshop on Human Computation, HCOMP 2009, Paris, pp. 11–14. ACM (2009)

13. Holley, R.: Crowdsourcing: How and why should libraries do it? D-Lib Mag. **16**(3/4 Ma) (2010)

14. Lee, C.S., Goh, D.H.L., Chua, A.Y., Ang, R.P.: Indagator: investigating perceived gratifications of an application that blends mobile content sharing with gameplay. J. Am. Soc. Inf. Sci. **61**, 1244–1257 (2010)

15. Matyas, S., Matyas, C., Schlieder, C., Kiefer, P., Mitarai, H., Kamata, M.: Designing location-based mobile games with a purpose: collecting geospatial data with CityExplorer. In: Proceedings of the 2008 International Conference on Advances in Computer Entertainment Technology, ACE 2008, Yokohama, pp. 244–247. ACM (2008)

16. Pe-Than, E.P.P., Goh, D.H.L., Lee, C.S.: Making work fun: investigating antecedents of perceived enjoyment in human computation games for information sharing. Comput. Hum. Behav. **39**, 88–99 (2014)

17. Procyk, J., Neustaedter, C.: GEMS: the design and evaluation of a location-based storytelling game. In: Proceedings of the 17th ACM Conference on Computer Supported Cooperative Work and Social Computing, CSCW 2014, Baltimore, pp. 1156–1166. ACM (2014)

18. Przybylski, A.K., Rigby, C.S., Ryan, R.M.: A motivational model of video game engagement. Rev. Gen. Psychol. **14**, 154 (2010)

19. Quinn, A. J., Bederson, B.B.: Human computation: a survey and taxonomy of a growing field. In: Proceedings of the SIGCHI Conference on Human Factors in Computing Systems, CHI 2011, pp. 1403–1412. ACM, Vancouver, May 2011

20. Siu, K., Zook, A., Riedl, M.O.: Collaboration versus competition: design and evaluation of mechanics for games with a purpose. In: Proceedings of the 9th International Conference on the Foundations of Digital Games, FDG 2014 (2014)

21. von Ahn, L., Dabbish, L.: Designing games with a purpose. Commun. ACM **51**, 58–67 (2008)

22. Waddell, J.C., Peng, W.: Does it matter with whom you slay? The effects of competition, cooperation and relationship type among video game players. Comput. Hum. Behav. **38**, 331–338 (2014)

23. Yee, N.: Motivations for play in online games. Cyberpsychology Behav. **9**, 772–775 (2006)

24. Zagal, J.P., Rick, J., Hsi, I.: Collaborative games: lessons learned from board games. Simul. Gaming **37**, 24–40 (2006)

Search Results Presentation and Visualization

Interactive Displays for the Next Generation of Entity-Centric Bibliographic Models

Trond Aalberg[1]([✉]), Tanja Merčun[2], and Maja Žumer[2]

[1] Norwegian University of Science and Technology, Trondheim, Norway
trondaal@ntnu.no
[2] University of Ljubljana, Ljubljana, Slovenia

Abstract. The model of bibliographic entities defined in the IFLA Functional Requirements for Bibliographic Records (FRBR) represents a major transition from the digital card catalog to databases containing a rich structure of entities and relationships with well-defined semantics. However, the question of how to best search and present this entity-centric bibliographic data remains a challenge. In this paper we present a system for entity-centric search and a user study on how the displays of the FRBR entities compare in their ability to support different user tasks.

Keywords: Search · User interface · User study · Library reference model

1 Introduction

Libraries worldwide are in the process of adopting the next generation of bibliographic information models to meet the expectations of modern end users, support new ways of search and exploration as well as increase the long-term value of the data. The E-R model of bibliographic entities defined in the IFLA Functional Requirements for Bibliographic Records (FRBR) [1] – soon to be superseded by IFLA Library Reference Model (IFLA LRM) [22] – represents a major transition from the record-oriented digital card catalog to entity-centric catalogs with rich and semantically well-defined structures of entities and relationships. The core entities introduced in FRBR; *work, expression, manifestation* and *item*, have slowly made their way into the common understanding of the bibliographic universe and are now aligned with current cataloguing practice (Resource Description and Access – RDA) [12]. Additional interesting new developments include BIBFRAME [16], a project exploring new formats for bibliographic data, and FRBRoo [18], which is the result of the harmonisation of FRBR with CIDOC CRM [17]. However, the modernization of library catalogs worldwide has been surprisingly slow and the question of how to best display FRBR or other entity-centric data in search results remains a challenge [4,14].

Entity-centric bibliographic data, describing intellectual and artistic products as entities at different levels of abstraction, inherently complicates the process

© Springer International Publishing AG 2017
S. Choemprayong et al. (Eds.): ICADL 2017, LNCS 10647, pp. 199–211, 2017.
https://doi.org/10.1007/978-3-319-70232-2_17

of indexing, querying and presenting results compared to the traditional digital card catalog, which is displaying a list of publications (manifestations) as the result of all queries. A list of manifestations is not appropriate for all contexts; users might be focused on the work level or on the expression level. They might wish to get a very specific answer or they might want to explore and learn about the opus of a particular person or about various adaptations of a particular work. As a consequence, the one-size-fits-all approach does not work.

To address this challenge, we have implemented the BIBSURF search system [19] to research design issues and conduct systematic studies of bibliographic search in entity-centric catalogs. In this paper, we give a presentation of the displays implemented in BIBSURF, which offers three different views of the graph structure: focusing on works, expressions and manifestations respectively. A user study was conducted to measure how the different displays compare in their ability to support different user tasks. The contribution of this research includes a novel bibliographic search system, a new methodological approach to evaluation of entity-centric bibliographic search and display, and insight into the effects of different display strategies for the FRBR model.

2   Background

Improved search experience was early recognized as the key contribution of FRBR [2] and this has been the main motivation for research and experimental prototypes applying the model [3,6,8,11,20]. Unfortunately most systems developed so far are based on existing data, automatically transformed from MARC records into a FRBR-based representation [15]. Due to missing and inconsistent information, frbrization is incomplete, resulting in simple pragmatic systems, focusing only on works and manifestations (such as OCLC Fiction Finder or data.bnf.fr). Even locating works throughout multiple records in current catalogs is a major challenge as addressed by Carlyle [7]. The actual effect of the FRBR model on the user experience, or the fundamental design issues that need to be addressed are thus hard to study in these implementations. The need for more user studies was recognized by Salaba and Zhang [14], who performed (1) user evaluation of three FRBR-based catalogs, (2) user participatory design of a prototype FRBR-based catalog, and (3) user evaluation of the resulting catalog.

The lack of research of how to adapt the display of FRBR-based information to different contexts is the main motivation for the research presented in this paper. Our previous work on display of FRBR-based information resulted in the development of the FRBRVis prototype and extensive user testing [20,21]. There the focus was on supporting browsing and exploration and choosing the best visualization technique. The results show that the visualized displays in general rated better compared to the baseline traditional faceted display in all elements of usability, i.e. efficiency, effectiveness and user experience. The limitation of that study was that it did not include searching and was focused on graphical visualizations. What is presented here is a logical continuation and has a focus on the search experience and result lists presented using UI features that are commonly found in search interfaces.

3 Design

FRBR is often presented as a model with a hierarchical structure, but is in reality a network consisting of typed nodes for the bibliographic entities and typed links for bibliographic relationships. Each bibliographic entity is described using attributes – which in a graph-context can be defined as typed node values. The main challenge when implementing searching and displaying results for such data is (a) how to index and query the data so that a user can retrieve information relevant to a query, and (b) how to display what is found in order to enable the user to understand and explore the results.

The BIBSURF system utilizes an indexing strategy based on dividing the graph into *indexing units* that loosely correspond to dynamically created metadata records which can be indexed using a text search engine. Works, expressions, manifestations, and even agents represent different perspectives of the same graph and are possible main (or root) entities for such dynamic metadata records (see Fig. 1). Each created metadata record needs to include the attribute values from the main entity as well as the attribute values from related entities that are needed to support querying and retrieval. A dynamic metadata record for a specific work will e.g. include the attributes of the work such as title and type of work, as well as the attributes of all related agents such as names. A search using specific keywords will then return all units for which these keywords appear in any of the attribute values. Determining the boundaries of an indexing unit is a question of tuning for precision and recall in the context of an application. Expanding the graph will add more terms to the indexing unit with increased recall but possibly reduced precision because of more irrelevant terms.

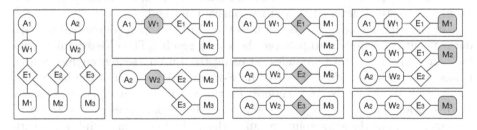

Fig. 1. Transforming a bibliographic graph into indexing units. The source graph to the left followed by the subsets used in the indexing of works, expressions and manifestation, with the main (root) entity in each unit highlighted.

A search performed on the index will find the set of units matching the query and return the identifier of the main entity of the index unit, which then can be used to construct *display units* for the result listing. Each display unit is essentially a subgraph selected for a presentation of the main entity. The choice of entities to include in the integrated display unit will impact the understanding

and contextualization. Determining the boundaries of each display unit is based
on principles of strong and weak links comparable to what is explored in [13].
Some relationships represent strong connections and indicate entities that should
naturally be integrated in the same display unit. Other relationships are weaker
and better represented as links to other display units in the user interface. A
self-contained display unit of an expression e.g. needs to integrate information
about the work as well as agents associated with the expression and the work,
and combine it with a presentation of all manifestations that embodies this
expression.

Distinguishing between indexing units and display units for the concepts
of interest to end-users in the search and exploration process, and the notion
of entities that are integrated in a display unit vs. entities that are interlinked,
forms a framework that is reusable across models. Our focus in the current setup
of the interface has been on the work, expression and manifestation entities as
defined in the initial FRBR model.

4   Implementation

The BIBSURF system is designed as a generic keyword-based bibliographic
search web interface where a user can enter terms or a phrase in a single field,
and retrieve a ranked listing of units found. The main elements of the user
interface is the search box and the result display. A filtering feature is added
to enable users to refine the listing based on names or categorical values in the
result set. Additional elements in the search interface are oriented towards the
researchers, such as an option to choose between display views, select a ranking
mechanism, and examine the underlying data. The user interface is developed
using the component-based React framework and the React Bootstrap UI-widget
library to create an interactive and responsive front-end.

On the backend side, the system uses the eXistdb[1] open source native XML
database utilizing xquery to produce the search results. The eXist database has
built-in support for full text indexing using the Lucene search engine. Search
is based on an intermediary index of RDF-fragments for each of the index unit
types, mainly because dynamic support for this would add an expensive processing overhead. The technology is chosen to enable rapid development and easy
management, but the same solution can in theory be based on a triple store with
flexible support for full text indexing of RDF such as described in [9].

Our test collections have been created by enhancing and transforming existing MARC 21 records into rich and well-structured FRBR data coded in RDF
using the RDA vocabularies[2]. Records have been retrieved from different library
catalogs using Z39.50, and have been manually enhanced to make the inher-
ent structure more explicit, based on the techniques identified in [10]; e.g. by
adding missing uniform title and relator codes, or coding information in note
fields or responsibility statements using explicit fields. Afterwards, the data has

---

[1] http://exist-db.org/exist/apps/homepage/index.html.
[2] http://www.rdaregistry.info.

been transformed using a rule-based FRBRization process [5]. Collections used in the experiments presented in this paper include crime fiction novels and short stories and other works related in different ways, and a collection of publications of Don Quixote in various languages and editions.

To enable comparative evaluation of alternative indexing and display units, we have separate search and result views for works, expressions and manifestations units. The views have the same visual "look and feel", but are different to account for the nature and structure of the units and required interactive support. See Fig. 2 for examples of result presentations.

In the **work display** each unit consists of a header with the title and type of the work and agents associated with the work. A tabbed display is used to present subordinate groups of expressions of the same type and language, with a listing of manifestations grouped according to agents associated with those expression in each tab window. An additional tab for related works is included next to the expression tabs. A "show more" feature for each manifestation allows the user to explore the table of contents. Each content item is a header describing the expression and work and their associated agents.

For the **expression display** each display unit consists of a header with the title, the work and expression type, as well as all related agents. We are using the same tab display to create a presentation consistent with the work display, and include the same related works tab. In this view, the manifestations are listed directly under each expression, and the same "show more" feature for table of contents is included.

The **manifestation display** is based on display units that are visually comparable to those for work and expression, but does not include a tabbed display. The header is based on the publication title and statement of responsibility. As for other displays, we have included an expandable "show more" feature for the table of contents, which is where the user will find details about all embodied expressions and works.

A query performed using a specific view will search the corresponding index, and present the corresponding display units. Due to different decomposition of the bibliographic graph into indexing units as illustrated in Fig. 1, the returned result list may differ in what is returned and how it is presented in the display. The different display units reflect a different "starting point" and reflects a particular way of viewing, interpreting and interacting with the bibliographic graph. Another difference will be the replication of information across units. In the manifestation view, the same expressions and work descriptions may appear in the contents listings of many manifestation. In the work view, replication of manifestation listing will occur for manifestations that embodies multiple expressions and works. The displays also represent different choices in implicit and explicit description of entities. In the work display, we explicit describe the work and list and describe expressions individually. In the expression display, we describe each expression and work as one unit.

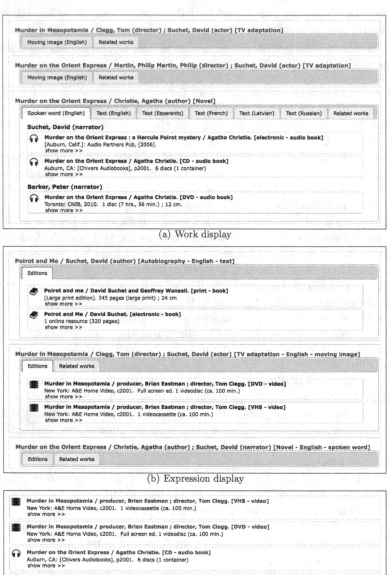

(a) Work display

(b) Expression display

(c) Manifestation display

Fig. 2. Selection from the different displays

5   User Study Methodology

An exploratory user testing of the three displays was conducted in March 2017 with 15 volunteer students from the Faculty of Arts at University of Ljubljana. The study design was set up as a between-subjects experiment, where each participant was randomly assigned to work with one of the three displays. This means that 5 participants solved the tasks using manifestation view, 5 participants using the expression view and 5 with the help of work-oriented view. All participants were given 5 tasks which were recorded and analysed using Tobii Studio and eye tracking equipment. The results in this paper focus on the measured aspects of participants' interaction with the system, such as (a) the time needed to complete the task, (b) successful completion of the task and (c) the user understanding of the results. By looking at those measures, our aim was to analyse how manifestation, expression and work view compare in terms of:

- their ability to support different user tasks,
- users' understanding of what is displayed,
- what users learn about the entity they are interested in, and
- users' effort needed to identify and make sense of specific information?

As the aim of this experiment was to test only the displays, the participants were only presented with the scenario for each task and a list of results that were retrieved for the predefined search. Although the interface and the bibliographic data were predominantly in English language, all students who participated in the study had a high level of English comprehension and were not distracted by the foreign language. The results in this paper do not include eye tracking data or participants' perceptions of the task difficulty.

For each scenario, researchers assigned the following measures to evaluate how well the display supported users in discovering the correct answer and to assess participant's understanding of the displayed entities for the given scenario:

Success score noted whether the participant found the correct answer where 5 = complete success, 3 = partial success and 1 = no success

Description score reflected the quality of participant's description regarding the retrieved set of results: 5 = complete description, 4 = one element of description missing, 3 = two elements missing; 2 = three elements missing; 1 = no relevant description

Time needed to complete the task (the overall mean task time for each scenario was afterwords calculated only for those tasks with success score 5 or 3).

To give context and explain the content of each result listing, we have implemented a simple notation to show the core W-E-M chains with numbers indicating how many of each entity type that is found in a result set (as shown in Table 2). The rightmost E is for expressions in the contents listing and the corresponding work count is redundant due to the 1:1 relationship from an expression to its parent work.

Scenario 1: "Chekhov Murder"

A professor asked you to read an English translation of a short story by Anton Pavlovich Chekhov that was translated into English under the title Murder. You have made a query "Chekhov Murder" in the library catalog and retrieved a list of results.

Task: Explain what is presented in the list of results. Is this short story available in the library collection?

Objective: In the data set, Chekhov's short story Murder appears only in manifestations that embody multiple expressions of different works - collections of short stories. Additionally, the title "Murder" represents an expression title (work title is in Russian) and differs from the manifestation titles that represent a collection of stories (for example "Peasants and other stories"). The user needs to find among the results of a search resources that embody a manifestation of the expression sought. In the work display, the manifestations are grouped under a work title in Russian, which can make it difficult for the user to recognize what the search result represents.

Scenario 2: "Don Quixote Charles Jarvis"

You would like to read an English edition of Don Quixote that was translated by Jarvis. You have made a search "Don Quixote Charles Jarvis" and got a list of results.

Task: How many different editions can you choose from and how do the editions differ based on their content?

Objective: The user needs to identify manifestations embodying a particular expression (Jarvis' translation of Don Quixote) and compare how these manifestations differ. In the expression and manifestation display, the list of results provides the user with an exact match to the query, while the work display shows the user also all other translations and versions.

Scenario 3 Query "Murder on Orient Express Agatha Christie"

You are interested a mystery story Murder on the Orient Express by Agatha Christie. You have made a search ...

Task: Explain what you got as the result of this search. What are the different versions you can choose from?

Objective: The query retrieves texts and narrated versions in English as well as some translations in different languages and TV adaptations of the novel Murder on the Orient Express. The user explores expressions and manifestations associated with the work and follows the derivation relationships between the progenitor work and other works adapted from it. In the expression display, information about the different versions is clearly visible as it is not obscured by numerous editions as in manifestation display or hidden in a single result which is the case in work display.

Scenario 4 Query "Agatha Christie"

You are interested in the works by Agatha Christie and would like to see the selection of her works in your library. You have made a search and got a list of results.

Task: How many different novels by Agatha Christie are available in the library?

Objective: The data set includes works about Agatha Christie, works by Agatha Christie and some adaptations of her works. Some of her novels appear only in manifestations that embody multiple expressions (collections of stories). The user needs to explore the entities associated with Agatha Christie and identify the novels written by Agatha Christie. In case of manifestation display, some of the novels can only be identified using the full content display, while other novels appear in numerous publications.

Scenario 5 Query "David Suchet"

You have recently seen a play starring David Suchet. You liked his performance and would like to discover what other works connected to David Suchet are available in your library.

Task: Explore the list and explain the results you got. Now write down what you have learned about Suchet and his repertoire.

Objective: In the data set, David Suchet appears in different roles (author, narrator, actor) and is often linked to the expression and not the work level. The user explores the works and expressions associated with the given agent and the roles played by that agent in their creation or realization. The expression display therefore gives the most comprehensive information about the roles and different endeavours.

6   Results

Our main research question is focused on the usefulness of each of the displays. The collected data can provide an insight and give some conclusions for the FRBR entity displays. Table 1 shows the final results of our test with end users for individual scenarios. As our main research question was focused on the usefulness of the three displays for different user tasks, the results were not analysed from the viewpoint of overall score per display, but individually for each scenario.

For scenario 1, the success score was highest for the manifestation display, while the descriptions of the retrieved results were most comprehensive using the expression display. The low score for the work display and higher scores for manifestation and expression display reflect the use case scenario where the main emphasis was to identify manifestations that embody expressions of the work in a particular language.

Scenario 2 also asked the user to identify manifestations that embody a specific expression. As shown in Fig. 1, this scenario is also well reflected in the high success and description scores that were the same for the manifestation and expression display. In the work view, some participants had difficulty locating the sought information as it was displayed among other expressions of the work.

Scenario 3 required the user to focus on the different versions of a chosen work and the results indicate that the expression view was the most appropriate for this task.

In contrast to all other use cases, the scores for scenario 4, where the user was primarily interested in the works of an author, reveal a high advantage of the work display, particularly in comparison to the manifestation display. In manifestation view, participants not only spent more time to identify individual works, but also made more errors, viewing some expressions (translations) and manifestations (collections) as new works written by Agatha Christie. A smaller difference in the scores appeared in scenario 5, but again the results from the user test, where the highest scores were achieved using expression view, coincide well with the scenario.

In some scenarios (for example scenario 4 and 2) low or high scores also correlate with the mean time needed to complete the task, but not in others (scenario 3). Overall however, it seems that participants needed more time using the expression display, which might be connected to the fact that such display is quite novel to the users (in contrast to manifestation display), but at the same time gives a longer list of results than the work display.

Table 1. A comparison of scores by display type for each scenario.

	Display type	Success score (max sum = 25)	Description score (max sum = 25)	Mean time (successful tasks)
Scenario 1	Manifestation (N = 5)	19	14	72
	Expression (N = 5)	15	16	110
	Work (N = 5)	13	8	90
Scenario 2	Manifestation (N = 5)	25	20	84
	Expression (N = 5)	25	20	70
	Work (N = 5)	19	14	127
Scenario 3	Manifestation (N = 5)	15	17	97
	Expression (N = 5)	19	19	150
	Work (N = 5)	15	14	76
Scenario 4	Manifestation (N = 5)	7	11	154
	Expression (N = 5)	17	17	135
	Work (N = 5)	23	21	67
Scenario 5	Manifestation (N = 5)	17	15	190
	Expression (N = 5)	23	22	205
	Work (N = 5)	17	17	210

Table 2. Complexity chains for each scenario result set.

Query	Work display	Expression display	Manifestation display
Scenario 1	W1-E4-M4-E39	E4-M4-E39	M4-E39
Scenario 2	W1-E21-M32-E58	E1-M5-E9	M5-E9
Scenario 3	W3-E9-M22-E31	E9-M22-E31	M22-E31
Scenario 4	W21-E30-M57-E117	E30-M57-E117	M46-E61
Scenario 5	W8-E14-M29-E43	E8-M11-E18	M9-E12

7   Conclusions and Future Work

The results of our preliminary user testing with the three displays indicate that a each type of display is useful for some scenarios, but not all of them. The work-oriented view, which has already been adopted in some FRBR-inspired catalogs, supported users well in exploring and learning about a repertoire of a selected agent, but made it somewhat more difficult for participants to identify specific manifestations or expressions they were looking for. The expression view was successful in cases where participants needed publications in a chosen language, while the manifestation view remained quite consistent, but did not really excel the other two views in any of the scenarios at least in terms of success and understanding of the presented bibliographic entities. In our future analysis, we will have to compare this usability data with user perception data, which might be more influenced by the familiar interactions and displays in current catalogs. While the presented test suggests that FRBR catalogs and digital libraries might need to adapt the results display to the user's query, more studies will be needed to confirm this hypothesis, further testing of the users' perception of different displays as well as analyzing how to automatically understand what the user is looking for in order to offer an optimal view.

Our experience in using the search prototype in this study also proves that research should be done using realistic search prototypes that can exploit the rich structure of the data and test collections which reflect how information is intended to be represented if it was originally created according to FRBR. In our research we have so far only focused on the basic FRBR-models, but the system can be adapted to related models such as BIBFRAME [16] which can be seen as a simplification of the initial FRBR model, or FRBRoo [18] which can be characterized as an elaborated and extended version of FRBR. Comparative studies on how these models perform within the setting of the same search user interface and use cases would be a valuable contribution to determine which model or features best fit the needs of end users.

Ranking of results is another topic we have identified as future work. Default ranking based on term frequency is rather unpredictable when indexing frag-ments due to the different number of entities that may be included. Currently we deploy a ranking solution that simply weights forewords, illustrations etc. lower than others, and we also support a ranking solution that includes a count of entities. Ranking strategies based on the structure of the nodes or based on the distance between the nodes that include the search terms, are other strategies worth exploring further.

By creating data that fully exploit FRBR, we have also come across challenges that have not been revealed in systems that utilize simpler FRBR data (the kind of data that is produced by transforming MARC records). Cataloguing all content as distinct expressions and works, including illustrations and forewords, tends to introduce noise in the result displays for users not primarily interested in this content. Different strategies for dealing with this could be default low ranking or default hiding of specific types of entities, leaving it to the user to decide when to put them in front. Another challenge is the representation of works that have parts, manifestation that have parts, or aggregates (e.g. collections of short murder stories by different authors or text augmented by illustrations). This is a topic that has been discussed in theory, but real world experiments are needed to establish best practice representation and determine which entities are needed to offer specific functionality – or not needed – to include and manage in the database.

References

1. Standing Committee and IFLA Study Group: Functional Requirements for Bibliographic Records: final report, vol. 19, K.G. Saur (1998)
2. Hegna, K., Murtomaa, E.: Data Mining MARC to Find: FRBR? (2002). http://folk.uio.no/knuthe/dok/frbr/datamining.pdf
3. Kilner, K.: The AustLit gateway and scholarly bibliography: a specialist implementation of the FRBR. Cataloging Classif. Q. **39**, 87–102 (2005)
4. Yee, M.: FRBRization: a method for turning online public finding lists into online public catalogs. Inf. Technol. Libr. **24**(3), 77–95 (2005)
5. Aalberg, T.: A process and tool for the conversion of MARC records to a normalized FRBR implementation. In: Sugimoto, S., Hunter, J., Rauber, A., Morishima, A. (eds.) ICADL 2006. LNCS, vol. 4312, pp. 283–292. Springer, Heidelberg (2006). https://doi.org/10.1007/11931584_31
6. Ercegovac, Z.: Multiple-version resources in digital libraries: towards user-centered displays. JASIST **57**(8), 1023–1032 (2006)
7. Carlyle, A., Ranger, S., Summerlin, J.: Making the pieces fit: little women, works, and the pursuit of quality. Cataloging Classif. Q. **46**(1), 35–63 (2008)
8. Dickey, T.J.: FRBRization of a library catalog: better collocation of records, leading to enhanced search, retrieval, and display. Inf. Technol. Libr. **27**, 23–32 (2008). ISSN 07309295
9. Minack, E., et al.: The Sesame LuceneSail: RDF Queries with Full-text Search. NEPOMUK Technical report (2008)
10. Aalberg, T., Merčun, T., Žumer, M.: Coding FRBR-structured bibliographic information in MARC. In: Xing, C., Crestani, F., Rauber, A. (eds.) ICADL 2011. LNCS, vol. 7008, pp. 128–137. Springer, Heidelberg (2011). https://doi.org/10.1007/978-3-642-24826-9_18
11. Notess, M., Dunn, J.W., Hardesty, J.L.: Scherzo: a FRBR-based music discovery system. In: International Conference on Dublin Core and Metadata Applications, pp. 182–183 (2011)
12. Riva, P., Oliver, C.: Evaluation of RDA as an implementation of FRBR and FRAD. Cataloging Classif. Q. **50**(5–7), 564–586 (2012). https://doi.org/10.1080/01639374.2012.680848
13. Sielski, K., Walkowska, J., Werla, M.: Methodology for dynamic extraction of highly relevant information describing particular object from semantic web knowledge base. In: Aalberg, T., Papatheodorou, C., Dobreva, M., Tsakonas, G., Farrugia, C.J. (eds.) TPDL 2013. LNCS, vol. 8092, pp. 260–271. Springer, Heidelberg (2013). https://doi.org/10.1007/978-3-642-40501-3_26
14. Zhang, Y., Salaba, A.: What do users tell us about FRBR-based catalogs? Cataloging Classif. Q. **50**(5–7), 705–723 (2012)
15. Aalberg, T., Žumer, M.: The value of MARC data, or, challenges of frbrisation. J. Documentation **69**(6), 851–872 (2013)

16. Kroeger, A.: The road to BIBFRAME: the evolution of the idea of bibliographic transition into a Post-MARC future. Cataloging Classif. Q. **51**(8), 873–890 (2013)
17. Ore, C.E., et al.: Definition of the CIDOC Conceptual Reference Model (2015). http://www.cidoc-crm.org/Version/version-6.2
18. Working Group on FRBR/CRM Dialogue: Definition of FRBRoo: A Conceptual Model for Bibliographic Information in Object-Oriented Formalism (2015). https://www.ifla.org/publications/node/11240
19. Aalberg, T., Merčun, T., Žumer, M.: BIBSURF: discover bibliographic entities by searching for units of interest, ranking and filtering. In: Proceedings of the 16th ACM/IEEE-CS on Joint Conference on Digital Libraries, pp. 207–208. ACM, New York (2016)
20. Merčun, T., Žumer, M., Aalberg, T.: Presenting bibliographic families: designing an FRBR-based prototype using information visualization. J. Documentation **72**(3), 490–526 (2016)
21. Merčun, T., Žumer, M., Aalberg, T.: Presenting bibliographic families using information visualization: evaluation of FRBR-based prototype and hierarchical visualizations. J. Assoc. Inf. Sci. Technol. **68**(2), 392–411 (2016)
22. Riva, P., Le Bœuf, P., Žumer, M.: IFLA Library Reference Model (LRM) (2017). https://www.ifla.org/publications/node/11412

Writers of the Lost Paper: A Case Study on Barriers to (Re-) Finding Publications

David Bainbridge[1], Sally Jo Cunningham[1],
Annika Hinze[1(✉)], and J. Stephen Downie[2]

[1] University of Waikato, Hamilton 3216, New Zealand
{davidb, sallyjo, hinze}@waikato.ac.nz
[2] University of Illinois at Urbana-Champaign, Urbana, Champaign, IL, USA
jdownie@illinois.edu

Abstract. We document the surprising hurdles that we encountered when attempting a known-item search to locate copies of four of our own published research papers, known to be archived in the ACM Digital Library and Google Scholar. The discoveries made in this exercise in 'search engine archaeology' are noteworthy as they are equally relevant to other users engaging with these and other digital libraries, to whom the pitfalls are much less readily apparent. We present details of our investigation together with a description of MEDDLE (a ModifiED Digital Library Environment), a proof-of-concept system that illustrates a technique to address some of these search issues for a target digital library. We conclude with suggestions on how scholarly digital libraries may avoid these issues in the future.

Keywords: Known-item search · Metadata quality · Re-finding

1 Introduction

This paper was inspired by the experiences of the authors as we met to plan an extension to our previous research on semantic search (the *Capisco* project). An obvious first step was to review our previously published work, but we quickly realized that none of us maintain a personal archive; instead, we rely on access to online digital libraries for the final, published version of our research. In this present paper, we detail the unexpected difficulties encountered when we attempted the seemingly straightforward task of locating copies of four papers detailing our own *Capisco* system, all known to be published in the ACM Digital Library (references [1–4], hereafter labeled [JCDL16A, JCDL16B, JCDL15, SIGWEB]).

These difficulties are primarily based on metadata errors that have crept into, and propagated across, scholarly document collections; related work investigating the scope and extent of these issues is summarized in Sect. 2. Section 3 presents a case study of problems that can be encountered when conducting known-item searches (here, while hunting for full text copies of our own papers), beginning with interface issues in the ACM DL that led to confusion as to whether or not full-text searching was being used (Sect. 3.1). We then report on the outcomes of searching through Google Scholar, where full-text search is the default, but the results returned could still miss returning a

S. Choemprayong et al. (Eds.): ICADL 2017, LNCS 10647, pp. 212–224, 2017.
https://doi.org/10.1007/978-3-319-70232-2_18

matching document, even when that lexical term appears in the full-text (Sect. 3.2). These exploratory searches turned up additional search issues caused by errors in document metadata (Sect. 3.3), by special characters (Sects. 3.4 and 3.5), and as a by-product of stemming in indexing (Sect. 3.6). Section 4 outlines a potential solution: a proxy-based approach that uses JavaScript for manipulation of the Document Object Model (DOM) to modify a user's queries so as to overcome the identified issues. Section 5 presents our conclusions.

2 Related Work

To place our findings in context, we here discuss briefly work on problems in metadata creation and correction.

Gladney [6] discusses different approaches of creating metadata and makes a strong case for using author-generated metadata, which could have resolved the problems detailed in Sect. 3.3. A lack of formal investigation into the metadata creation process has also been noted before (e.g., [9–11]). They point to similar issues as those observed in our case study, such as inaccurate data entry.

Currier [9] especially describes the issues that are faced in commercial resource discovery as a consequence of metadata errors, referring to the bargains to be had when searching for "Plam Pilots" on eBay. The problem of metadata quality has also been previously acknowledged by Beall [7], who observed the main types of data quality errors in digital libraries and particularly highlighted the problem of blocked access.

Bui and Park [8] evaluated metadata quality at the American National Science Digital Library (NSDL), analyzing more than one million Dublin Core metadata records. They found that for about 17% of the data the creator (i.e., author) of the resource was not specified at all and that there are whole collections without specified creator metadata.

Park & Tosaka [12] further acknowledged the challenges in creating metadata, especially for rapidly developing large-scale digital repositories. They identify as one of the issues that existing semi-automatic metadata tools often target only selected metadata elements, leading to the necessity for interoperability between tools and their output. An alternative, or addition, to automatically created metadata is the user-driven correction of available metadata: [5] describes a prototype system that allows users to correct disambiguation and collocation errors, while [13] argues for a combination of author-provided metadata with automatic data to improve findability.

3 Problems Encountered

This section details the problems that we encountered when attempting to locate copies of four papers ([JCDL16A, JCDL16B, JCDL15, SIGWEB]) summarizing progress to date on our *Capisco* project. All four were known to be archived in the ACM Digital Library and so are also included—through an information sharing agreement—in Google Scholar.

3.1   What Is Full Text Search?

A. Simple Search box. In our initial attempt to locate the four papers, we searched the ACM DL for the term Capisco (a common strategy for a known-item search is to use what is believed to be a relatively uncommon term in the document as a query term). We entered this search in the simple search box on the home page; given the similarity of this search box to that of Google and Google Scholar, together with the statement on that webpage that the underlying collection is, "The **Full-Text Collection** of all ACM publications" (emphasis in the original), we assumed that this query would match to all documents in the DL containing the term Capisco. This search uncovered [SIGWEB] and [JCDL15] papers but not [JCDL16A] and [JCDL16B]. Inspection of the two returned papers determined that they both include Capisco in the abstract and in the case of [SIGWEB], in the title also. The other two papers only used the term Capisco in the main text of the articles. After further experimentation with different searches we determined that the most readily encountered search box to the ACM Digital Library does not in fact search on the full text of the paper, but rather on the text of the metadata (title, keywords, abstract, etc.).

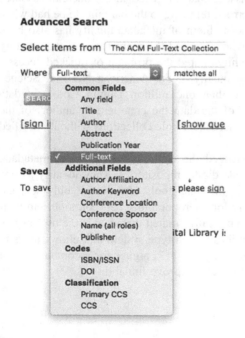

Fig. 1. Advanced Search options of the ACM DL.

B. Advanced Search: Any. We next attempted to use the Advanced Search facility, which defaults to the Full-Text Collection and 'Any Field'. This search again yielded the same two papers: [SIGWEB] and [JCDL15]. On closer inspection of the Advanced Search options (Fig. 1), we noticed that 'Full-text' is one of the options provided. Even though 'Full-text' is listed under 'Common *Fields*' (our emphasis), the observed result from searching was that it is not included in an 'Any field' search.

C. Advanced Search: Full text. On searching for Capisco with Advanced Search → Full-text, all four papers were retrieved. Through further experimentation we determined that 'Any field' refers to metadata fields but not the text of the documents, while a 'Full-text' search in some way combines both the metadata **and** the document text. We say 'in some way combines' because it is not clear whether this is actually a union operation of text and metadata, or if it just so happens that the processed full text contains title, abstract, keywords, etc. Certainly it is the case that for a search for the term Matamua (the name of an author for the [JCDL15] paper) and then using the 'result highlights' option on the results list (which displays and highlights the matches for the query), we see that the term *Matamua* is highlighted in both the document's extracted text and in the metadata (Fig. 2).

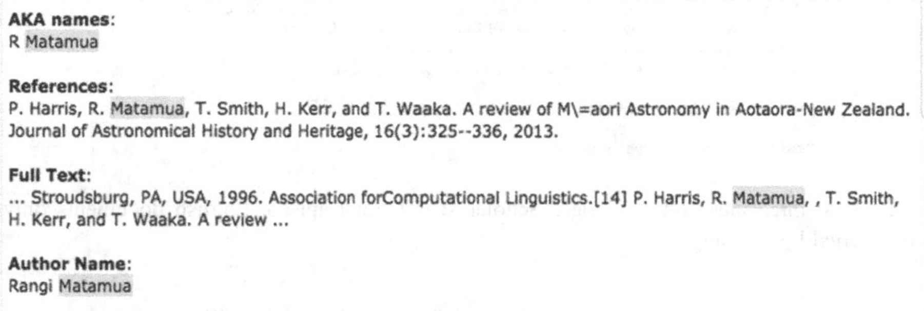

AKA names:
R Matamua

References:
P. Harris, R. Matamua, T. Smith, H. Kerr, and T. Waaka. A review of M\=aori Astronomy in Aotaora-New Zealand. Journal of Astronomical History and Heritage, 16(3):325--336, 2013.

Full Text:
... Stroudsburg, PA, USA, 1996. Association forComputational Linguistics.[14] P. Harris, R. Matamua, , T. Smith, H. Kerr, and T. Waaka. A review ...

Author Name:
Rangi Matamua

Fig. 2. Matches for search term Matamua – one of the co-authors of [3].

3.2 Full Text Search in Google Scholar

Knowing that the ACM digital library is a feed to Google Scholar, we switched to this digital library to see if it fared any better. The search strategy in Sect. 3.1: A (searching for the term Capisco to identify papers describing the system) is not useful in this case. The initial search for Capisco yielded approximately 19,500 results, not surprisingly many in Italian (*Capisco* is Italian for "I see/understand"). Re-running the search with document language restricted to English yields 842 results: the [SIGWEB] paper is result number 9 on page 1, [JCDL15] number 1 on page 4, and [JCDL16A] number 3 on page 4.

However, [JCDL16b] is not retrieved by this latter query. A search for "Semantic Bookworm" confirms that the document is indexed by Google Scholar, and the associated PDF contains the term Capisco—but only once, in the body of the document rather than the title, keywords, or other metadata. We conjecture that for short documents ([JCDL16b] is two pages), single occurrence terms might not be indexed. Further experimentation with searches including other terms that appear only once in the document (e.g., "semantic bookworm" orange) lend weight to that hypothesis.

We note further anomalies in the results list for the Capisco query, restricted to English language documents: the first two documents returned include Capisco as the institutional affiliation of the authors and in the authors' email address, but not in the body of the documents; and the third document returned—a citation with no associated link to the document and no further details beyond that shown in Fig. 3—does not include the term Capisco. This results ranking is particularly surprising given that the ranking mechanism is the default, 'by relevance'—which counter-intuitively weights institutional affiliation more heavily than author name and the appearance of a term in the title and body of the document. The third result is possibly highly ranked because

Discolouration of mechanical and chemimechanical pulps: influence of wood r material, process and ageing method
H Fjellström, H Höglund, M Paulsson... - Nordic Pulp & Paper ..., 2008 - diva-portal.org
... Mats Rundlöf (mats@**capisco**.se): **Capisco**, Nygatan 13, SE-602 34 Norrköping, Sweden. Corresponding author: Helena Fjellström ... Helena Fjellström and Hans Höglund, Mid Sweden University, Magnus Paulsson, Eka Chemicals AB, Sweden, Mats Rundlöf, **Capisco**, Sweden ...
Cited by 3 Related articles All 2 versions Web of Science: 2 Cite Save More

A novel method of studying the ability of coating layer to retard the photo-yellowing of the base paper
H Fjellström, H Höglund, S Forsberg... - Nordic Pulp & Paper ..., 2007 - diva-portal.org
... Magnus Paulsson (magnus. paulsson@eka.com): Eka Chemicals AB, SE-445 80 Bohus, Sweden. Mats Rundlöf (mats@**capisco**.se): AB **Capisco**, Nygatan 13, SE-602 34 Norrköping, Sweden. Corresponding author: Helena Fjellström ...
Cited by 3 Related articles All 3 versions Web of Science: 3 Cite Save More

[CITATION] **Romance Infinitival Particles as Specifiers of CP**
F Benucci - Proceedings of the XVII Meeting of Generative ..., 1991
Cited by 2 Related articles Cite Save

Fig. 3. First three hits from a Google Scholar search for Capisco, English documents only, results sorted by relevance.

the Google Scholar search engine conflates CP (Complementizer Phrase, a syntax tree structure) with Capisco—though it is not clear why it would occur for this paper and not for other linguistics papers.

3.3 Errors in the Metadata and Document Text

The ACM DL metadata for [JCDL15] includes a typo in the title: "Improving Access to Large-scale Digital Libraries ThroughSemantic-enhanced Search and Disambiguation". This error does not occur in the document itself. Conducting a string search (exact match) for the correct title does not locate the paper in the ACM Digital Library—a significant issue in terms of findability, as one common pattern of search is to copy the title out of the references of an already located paper, and paste it into the search box in quotes. A search for the correct title without quotes yields 2.4 M hits (fortunately in this case with the [JCDL15] paper as result number 3 on page 1, but this relative visibility for a non-exact match search is not guaranteed for papers with fewer distinctive terms in the title).

Improving Access to Large-scale Digital Libraries Through Semantic-enhanced Search and Disambiguation

Annika Hinze, Computer Science | Craig Taube-Schock, Computer Science | David Bainbridge, Computer Science

Fig. 4a. Title of [JCDL15] as it appears in print.

We note that this metadata error is propagated across some, but not all, digital libraries, repositories, and databases (e.g., the error is present in the University of

Illinois[1] archive and Scopus[2] but not in SemanticScholar[3]), and will have an unpredictable impact on searches for the paper. Google Scholar, for example, is more forgiving than the ACM DL; Google Scholar returns this paper as the sole result for all permutations of a query on the title (the correct title both with and without quotes; the title with Through and Semantic concatenated both with and without quotes).

Where could this error have come from? We note that the title of this paper runs to two lines on the printed page, with the break occurring between the two words concatenated in the ACM DL metadata (Fig. 4a). We conjecture that the error is related to line breaks on the printed page. To explore this hypothesis we searched for "DisambiguationAnnika" (the next potential concatenation error) and, consulting the 'result highlights', see further erroneous concatenations across both line and column breaks (Fig. 4b). We are at a loss as to why this issue occurs for the [JCDL15] paper and not for the other three.

> **Full Text:**
> Improving Access to Large-scale Digital Libraries ThroughSemantic-enhanced Search and DisambiguationAnnika HinzeComputer ScienceUniversity of WaikatoHamilton, New Zealandhinze@waikato.ac.nzCraig Taube-SchockComputer ScienceUniversity of WaikatoHamilton, ...

Fig. 4b. Further errors in the [JCDL15] extracted text.

3.4 Ligatures and Searching

Paper [JCDL2016B] includes an example of semantic analysis of Charles Dickens' classic *David Copperfield*. If we were to extend that paper then it would be natural to reference other papers that also perform a computational analysis of this book—and to find them, similar to copying titles from reference sections (Sect. 3.3), one might very well copy the novel's title from the existing document and then paste that phrase into the ACM DL search box (Fig. 5a).

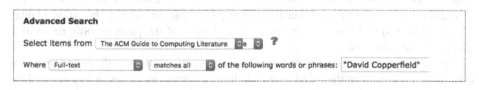

Advanced Search

Select items from [The ACM Guide to Computing Literature ◌◌e ◌] **?**

Where [Full-text ◌] [matches all ◌] of the following words or phrases: ["David Copperfield"]

Fig. 5a. Advanced search for *"David Copperfield"* in the ACM DL.

---

[1] https://experts.illinois.edu/en/publications/improving-access-to-large-scale-digital-libraries-throughsemantic.

[2] http://bit.ly/2kTTxd3.

[3] https://pdfs.semanticscholar.org/0936/fece67ba70cf263dcf8fdef6e2aa77ea1145.pdf.

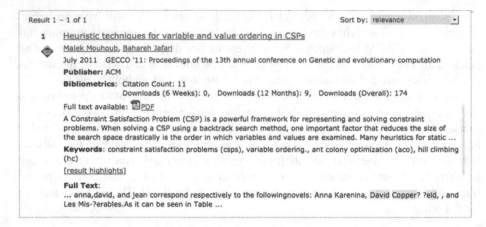

Fig. 5b. Search result for query inadvertently including the fi ligature.

We know from our experiences detailed in Sect. 3.1 to use the Advanced Search, Full-Text option, to pick up on mentions of the novel in the document text (since its title is unlikely to appear in the metadata for technical research papers). This search yields a single result—and it is not our [JCDL16B] paper (Fig. 5b). Inspecting the matched text, we realize that we were unlucky in our choice of source for the text to copy/paste; of the two mentions in our paper, we chose the italicized version that included a ligature between the f and the i (fi).

A search for *"David Copperfield"* without the ligature yields a more plausible 41 hits (including [JCDL16B], but not the paper in Fig. 5b. We note that searching for "*David Copperfield*" (ligature included) in Google Scholar returns documents both with and without the ligature.

3.5 Other Issues with Special Characters

As we created the Related Work section for this present paper (Sect. 3), we noticed an anomaly in the title of one of the references: a special character in the title of [5] displays differently in the print version of the paper (Fig. 6a) and in the ACM Digital Library (Fig. 6b) and Google Scholar, in their display of the paper in both result lists and in citation formats.

As with the case described in Sect. 3.3, a copy/paste of the title either from the document itself or from the ACM/supplied citation format, in quotes, into a search box will not return the paper in the ACM Digital Library.

That's 'é' not 'þ' '?' or '□': A User-driven Context-aware Approach to Erroneous Metadata in Digital Libraries

David Bainbridge   Michael B. Twidale   David M. Nichols
University of Waikato   University of Illinois   University of Waikato

Fig. 6a. Reference [5] title in the print version of the paper.

David Bainbridge, Michael B. Twidale, and David M. Nichols. 2011. That's 'é' not 'þ' '?' or '☻': a user-driven context-aware approach to erroneous metadata in digital libraries. In *Proceedings of the 11th annual international ACM/IEEE joint conference on Digital libraries* (JCDL '11). ACM, New York, NY, USA, 39-48. DOI=http://dx.doi.org.ezproxy.waikato.ac.nz/10.1145/1998076.1998084

Fig. 6b. Reference [5] citation format in the ACM DL.

3.6 Unexpected Stemming

We again attempted to search for what we believed would be relatively uncommon text to retrieve the [SIGWEB] paper: *"semantically-enhanced"* conducted as a phrase search using Advanced Search, Any Field (that is, metadata only) on the ACM DL. According to the DL's documentation,[4] a phrase search (query terms enclosed in double quotation marks) follows the common search engine convention of returning documents that contain that exact string. This interpretation of phrase searching is corroborated by the summary of the query as translated to the format of the ACM search engine (Fig. 7a).

Searched for *(+"semantically-enhanced")* [new search] [edit/save query]

Fig. 7a. Search engine representation of query "semantically-enhanced".

1   Addressing the RDFa publishing bottleneck
     Xi Bai
     March 2011   WWW '11: Proceedings of the 20th International conference companion on World wide web
     Publisher: ACM
     Bibliometrics: Citation Count: 2
                     Downloads (6 Weeks): 1,   Downloads (12 Months): 2,   Downloads (Overall): 114
     Full text available: PDF
     In the more dynamic environments emerging from ad hoc and peer-to-peer networks, our research has explored the extent to which Web-based knowledge sharing as well as community formation require automation to understand human-readable content in a more distributed manner. RDFa is a syntactic format which can leverage this issue by ...
     Keywords: semantic enhancement, federated markup, linked data, rdfa
     [result highlights]

     Keywords:
     semantic enhancement

Fig. 7b. Search result demonstrating that punctuation is stripped and query terms are stemmed.

57 documents were returned. An examination of the results shows that the hyphen in the phrase was stripped out, and that the terms in the phrase were stemmed (Fig. 7b). That hyphens are stripped is not surprising, as many search engines do not index

---

[4] http://dl.acm.org/documentation/Types.htm#phrases.

punctuation. It is, however, misleading for the transformed query to include the hyphen. It was completely unexpected to see that terms within a phrase are stemmed, contrary to convention and to the provided documentation. We do, however, note that in practice this implementation of phrase searching can be useful (in this case, the search retrieved both [SIGWEB] and [JCDL16]).

4   Introducing MEDDLE: A ModifiED Digital Library Environment

Seeking a pragmatic approach to finding papers 'lost' by the issues discussed in Sect. 3, we have developed a proxy-based solution combined with JavaScript for DOM manipulation which we call MEDDLE.[5] We chose the ACM Digital Library, Springer, and Google Scholar for our proof-of-concept implementation; the technique can be extended to other digital libraries as well (as discussed in Sect. 4.2).

4.1   The MEDDLE Interface and Implementation

Using our approach, a user visits the MEDDLE homepage and selects one of the listed digital libraries to search. MEDDLE then uses its proxying capability to serve up that digital library's home page and also to inject bespoke JavaScript into the page to help to address the issues covered in Sect. 3. Specifically, MEDDLE manipulates the user's query string to transform it to a query that more closely matches the user's intent.

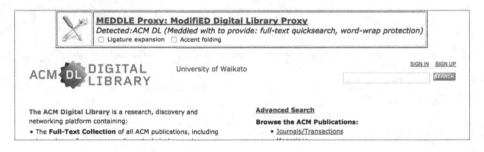

Fig. 8a. The ACM DL quick search page with MEDDLE.

Figure 8a shows a snapshot of the user visiting the ACM Digital Library through MEDDLE. The MEDDLE information box at the top of the page indicates that the quick search box has been modified to perform full text searching and to help find search terms that are accidentally concatenated due to line wrap issues (Sect. 3.3). Figure 8b shows the result of a search for Capisco where all four relevant documents are returned, as was originally expected by the authors (that is, MEDDLE has conducted a full-text search via the quick search box). Not shown in the figure, had the user

---

[5] https://bedrock.resnet.cms.waikato.ac.nz/meddle/.

searched using the intended title of the first document returned (with Through Semantic rather than ThroughSemantic) with MEDDLE then this too would result in a successful query. What MEDDLE does in this situation is deliberately add in additional query terms that are the concatenation of adjacent pairs of terms in the query that the user has entered.

A further feature of MEDDLE addresses issues connected with ligatures and accents. The bottom line of the MEDDLE information box (Fig. 8a) contains check boxes for ligature expansion and accent folding. If either or both of these check boxes are selected when a query is submitted then the injected JavaScript in the page checks the query terms for instances of these types of characters and substitutes suitable replacements (e.g., a query including *José Borbinha* will be changed to *Jose Borbinha*). Even if the user has not activated these options, MEDDLE still monitors and alerts a user if an accent or ligature is present in the search terms—giving the user the opportunity to enable the option for that query.

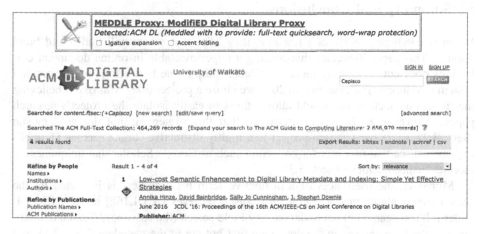

Fig. 8b. Results of a MEDDLE-ed search for Capisco.

4.2   Limitations of the MEDDLE Approach

Each MEDDLE solution must be hand-tailored to the target DL—and designing the solution might require a good bit of reverse engineering of the DL's indexing and search functionality implementations. However, we note that the time invested by one frustrated author/developer can benefit many; MEDDLE is available Open Source. Fortunately, even with the three digital libraries supported by MEDDLE so far, we have identified common adjustments that typically are beneficial to make (such as ligatures and accent folding) and these operations can be activated in a new MEDDLE implementation for a new DL in a straightforward manner. We also note that as digital libraries share their source documents and metadata that errors introduced in one digital library can easily propagate to others (as seen in Sect. 3.3, where the 'ThroughSemantic' error has spread from the ACM DL to Google Scholar)—hence the approach developed for one MEDDLE-ed digital library is likely to be needed by other digital libraries.

Changes in the way that a digital library handles indexing, text extraction, and search features may necessitate changes to its MEDDLE extension. These changes might make MEDDLE superfluous (a problem that the authors would welcome!) or necessitate modifications to the MEDDLE extension to achieve the same result. They may also introduce new issues for MEDDLE to address. The challenge then is to include monitoring functionality to help identify when a MEDDLE-ed with digital library has changed. One approach would be a form of digital library 'unit testing', where the monitoring software periodically conducts pre-determined queries and compares their expected results to the hits returned by that digital library.

And, of course, it might not be possible to develop a MEDDLE-based work-around for every issue identified. For example, the anomalies in full text searching in Google Scholar appear to be based in the implementation of the index and the matching algorithm, and as such are not amenable to correction by manipulating the query string.

5 Summary and Conclusions

When researchers publish their research, they hope that others will find it and build upon it. This paper illustrates that making a paper available in online document collections does not necessarily make it findable, despite the best efforts of authors and system developers. For example, in 2014 we chose a project title—*Capisco*—believing that it was distinctive and would allow others to easily isolate the project's research papers. However, in 2017 we discovered that this strategy is not domain-agnostic (Sect. 3.2): while our Capisco project is a highly distinctive 'brand' across IT publications, we see that in a broader collection such as Google Scholar that uniqueness is more difficult to achieve (Sect. 3.3).

Moreover, the usefulness of a distinctive term for searchers is impacted by the search engine algorithms: a search for Capisco retrieves [JCDL16b] in the ACM DL under full text search but not under an Any Field search (the Advanced Search default), because the term appears in the document text but not in the metadata (Sect. 3.1); and the search does not retrieve [JCDL16b] from Google Scholar for less clear reasons. The important lesson here appears to be that researchers should be much more careful in creating metadata—particularly author-specified keywords and abstract terms—and not rely on the presence of a term in the document body to support findability. Similarly, glitches in automated metadata extractions can also severely impact the findability of individual papers (Sect. 3.3). Text extraction errors are difficult to predict and can have erratic effects on search results, even—or especially—when the search terms are copy/pasted from the document or reference (Sects. 3.4 and 3.5).

Since metadata-related errors and general findability problems appear to resist simple automated solutions, we believe that involving human quality checks is warranted. We suggest that as a condition of inclusion in the ACM DL (or similar) that authors be required to verify the findability of their papers by reviewing metadata as seen in the DL prior to the paper being made available publicly. Adding this simple additional step to the publication cycle would provide low-cost improvements to DLs that would greatly enhance their value as research communication tools.

We also call for more transparency and clarity on the part of digital libraries, as to why a given document is returned as a match to a query and how the query is understood by the search engine. The ACM DL's 'results highlights' facility is a step in the right direction, as is its query summary—neither of which are provided by Google Scholar. However, our experiments indicate that, in their present implementation, these facilities do not provide sufficient detail for the searcher to fully understand the results displayed—and so can lead unwary searchers astray, thinking that they have a comprehensive set of papers on a given topic when it is in actuality incomplete.

As the authors have personally experienced, it can take quite an unusual search activity to realize that a digital library is not functioning as the user expects—but the MEDDLE approach is premised on knowledge of such issues. While Sect. 3 makes some inroads on generalizing the types of problems to look for, it cannot be claimed to be exhaustive; there is scope for a principled and comprehensive review of the major research digital libraries to identify further issues and techniques for addressing them. Key to that approach would be the compilation of queries that trigger these issues together with a set of ideal results for each query. Through this, as we have done in Sect. 3, one can reason about what the difference is between your understanding of the digital library's search capability and its actual implementation.

The MEDDLE approach described here is a refinement of the technique first developed in our collaboration with the HathiTrust Digital Library (HTDL): we created a web browser add-in to create a mashup of three websites—the HTDL and two web-based offerings operated independently by HTRC [14]. The user interacts with the HTDL as usual, and at strategic locations in the interface functionality drawn from the research systems—which take account of the user's current context—is seamlessly blended in. The advantage of the MEDDLE approach is that the user does not need to install extensions to their browser.

Additionally, we note that the identified issues and their suggested work-arounds could be offered to the digital library provider to suggest further refinements for that system. A prime example would be the MEDDLE identification and handling of accents and ligatures, which could be easily incorporated into a digital library.

References

1. JCDL16A: Hinze, A., Bainbridge, D., Cunningham, S.J., Downie, J.S.: Low-cost semantic enhancement to digital library metadata and indexing: simple yet effective strategies. In: JCDL 2016, pp. 93–102 (2016)
2. JCDL16B: Hinze, A., Coleman, M., Cunningham, S.J., Bainbridge, D.: Semantic bookworm: mining literary resources revisited. In: JCDL 2016, pp. 227–228 (2016)
3. JCDL15: Hinze, A., Taube-Schock, C., Bainbridge, D., Matamua, R., Downie. J.S.: Improving access to large-scale digital libraries through semantic-enhanced search and disambiguation. In: JCDL 2015, pp. 147–156 (2015)
4. SIGWEB: Hinze, A., Taube-Schock, C., Bainbridge, D., Cunningham, S.J., Downie. J.S.: Introducing capisco: a semantically-enhanced search and discovery system for large-scale text corpora. SIGWEB Newslett. 14, November 2015. Autumn 2015, Article 4

5. Bainbridge, D., Twidale, M.B., Nichols, D.M.: That's 'é' not 'þ' '?' or '□': a user-driven context-aware approach to erroneous metadata in digital libraries. In: Proceedings of the 11th Annual International ACM/IEEE Joint Conference on Digital libraries (JCDL 2011), pp. 39–48. ACM, New York, NY, USA (2011)
6. Gladney, H.: Preserving Digital Information. Springer, Heidelberg (2007). doi:10.1007/978-3-540-37887-7
7. Beall, J.: Metadata and data quality problems in the digital library. J. Digital Inf. **6**(3), 1368–7506 (2006)
8. Bui, Y., Park, J.-R.: An assessment of metadata quality: a case study of the national science digital library metadata repository. In: Proceedings of the Annual Conference of CAIS/Actes du Congrès Annuel de l'ACSI (2013)
9. Currier, S., Barton, J., O'Beirne, R., Ryan, B.: Quality assurance for digital learning object repositories: issues for the metadata creation process. ALT-J Res. Learn. Technol. **12**(1), 5–20 (2004)
10. Guy, M., Powell, A., Day, M.: Improving the quality of metadata in e-print archives. Ariadne **38** (2004)
11. Park, J.-R.: Metadata quality in digital repositories: a survey of the current state of the art. Cataloging Classif. Q. **47**(3–4), 213–228 (2009)
12. Park, J.-R., Tosaka, Y.: Metadata creation practices in digital repositories and collections: schemata, selection criteria, and interoperability. Inf. Technol. Libr. **29**(3), 104–116 (2010)
13. Maurer, M.B., McCutcheon, S., Schwing, T.: Who's doing what? Findability and author-supplied etd metadata in the library catalog. Cataloging Classif. Q. **49**(4), 277–310 (2011)
14. Bainbridge, D., Downie, J.S.: All for one and one for all: reconciling research and production values at the hathitrust through user-scripting. In: Joint Conference on Digital Libraries JCDL 2017, pp. 283–284 (2017)

Result Set Diversification in Digital Libraries Through the Use of Paper's Claims

José María González Pinto[⊠] and Wolf-Tilo Balke

Institut für Informationssysteme, Technische Universität Braunschweig,
Braunschweig, Germany
{pinto, balke}@ifis.cs.tu-bs.de

Abstract. Understanding the possible associations between two entities from a query is a hard problem. For instance, querying "coffee" and "cancer" even in a curated Digital Library is a challenge to the retrieval system that struggles to figure out the intention of the query. Maybe the user wants a consensus of what it is known? But how many different associations exist? How to find them all? Herein we introduce an approach to diversify the results retrieved from such queries aiming at re-ranking the result list. Our re-ranking models specifically one fundamental aspect of scientific papers: claims. Claims are the sentences that scientists use to report findings. In particular, we study claims that express associations between entities in the medical domain. More specifically, we focus on queries that involve two entities in which one of the entities has some effect on a disease. Thus, we work on a corpus obtained by querying PubMed to empirically assess our proposed solution. Moreover, we promote the idea of claims as an explicit key aspect to consider diversification in the result set of a query. We show the potential of our approach to ease the process of discovering representative associations between entities. Our approach relies on a representation of claims using neural embedding of word vectors and implements an algorithm to perform the re-ranking of the result set of a query. We empirically show the potential of our approach.

Keywords: Diversification · Embedding · Scientific claim

1 Introduction

A core functionality of Digital Libraries to satisfy information needs is to provide search capabilities that exploit key aspects of the documents. Delivering high quality results to a query is crucial because of the potential impact of user's decisions. However, as it has been shown in [1] biases are observed during search with respect to two aspects: (1) most of the results support the query while only a few disapprove it and (2) results supporting the query are ranked higher than results contradicting it. Previous work has shown that diversification of the results of a query can alleviate this problem. However, little attention has been paid to enable such mechanisms to cope with complex information needs in the medical domain where the health conditions of users could be compromised. In particular, when the user is trying to decide about the consumption of a product, a medicine or a drug regarding a specific disease. For this

© Springer International Publishing AG 2017
S. Choemprayong et al. (Eds.): ICADL 2017, LNCS 10647, pp. 225–236, 2017.
https://doi.org/10.1007/978-3-319-70232-2_19

type of information need no doubt that Digital Libraries have better quality content than the Web. For instance, today a user interested in discovering whether a drug is beneficial or not regarding a specific disease, she would have to do an exploratory search submitting several queries. For each query, the user will basically try to get a "consensus" of what the research community has found. Is there a better alternative? In this work, we explore the idea of diversification of the returned set of a given query to help the user in such a task. In particular, we focus on a key aspect of research papers to help the user in her quest: claims. By *claims* in scientific papers we mean statements that express associations between entities. This is of particular relevance in the medical domain where the consumption of a drug, a substance, a fruit, etc., has an effect on a disease. One of the challenges of considering the claims of papers is that the association between two entities can be subject to different *interpretations*. Thus, in this paper, we model a particular case that can arise when interpreting some of the associations between the entities: controversy. One instance of the existence of several controversial claims was found and reported first by [2]. The authors manually discovered, by submitting several queries to PubMed and analyzing the result set relating 50 substances to cancer, that basically most of the substances could increase the risk of cancer and decrease it! The existence of such cases motivates our work to ease the discovery of such cases. Herein, we propose to implement a mechanism to *diversify* the result set of a query to help the user discover entities that may be in a controversial case.

In this work, we aim at modeling the claims of research to perform a re-ranking of the result set of a query represented by two entities. Our approach consists of three basic steps given a pair of $<entity, disease>$: firstly, extract from research papers, associations between the pair; secondly, represent the associations using a neural embedding representation of documents and thirdly, deliver a re-ranking of the result set to ease the discovery of controversial claims.

Our proposed approach will bring several benefits: for the information's provider, it will add more value to its current retrieval mechanisms. For the user, the possibility of making an informed decision that can potentially save her life. Moreover, researchers in the medical domain who are in the quest of solving complex problems can also benefit from our approach: they will be able to find controversial claims that basically are in the need of further investigation.

Aiming at this challenge, in this paper, we focus on the design and implementation of a technique that can re-rank documents based on a fundamental aspect of research papers: claims. The remainder of this paper is organized as follows. Section 2 provides definitions and the problem we aim at solving in this paper. Section 3 overviews related work. Sections 4 and 5 describe the experimental setup and the evaluation of our proposed approach. Lastly, Sect. 6 presents our concluding remarks.

2   Model and Problem Definition

In this section, we provide definitions and the problem we aim at solving in this paper. Let's first define what a claim is:

Definition 1 (Claim): A claim is a sentence in a research paper that expresses an association between two entities. An association is any verb found in WordNet.

Definition 2 (Entity): An entity is the name of a substance, a fruit, vegetable, a drug or a disease.

For example, in the following claim: "lycopene increases the risk of cancer" The entities are "lycopene" and "cancer". The association between the two is "increases".

Now we can define our controversial claim problem below:

Problem Definition (Claim Diversification Problem): Given a collection of m documents $D = \{d_1, \ldots, d_m\}$ of a Digital Library, an initial query represented by a pair of entities $< entity, disease >$, we intent to rank documents in D to *diversify* the result set to cover the different interpretations of the associations between $< entity, disease >$ at the top t results.

Our definition resembles the general case [3] where it was proven to be NP-hard in its original form: aiming at maximum coverage with minimum redundancy. However, in our case, we aim at using claims as the proxy to represent an explicit aspect behind the user query instead of the implicit approach that makes the problem NP-hard. Thus, coverage in our work is in terms of the semantics of the associations of claims. And claims are represented as vectors using neural embedding.

We approach the problem by dividing it in the following tasks:

1. Find all the $d \in D$ where a pair of entities $entity, disease$ appear as a claim $< Claims >$ (Sect. 4.1).
2. Represent each claim $< Claims >$ in an embedding space $< EmbedClaims >$ (Sect. 4.2).
3. Perform a ranking of the documents using an adaptation of the List of Clusters Diversification algorithm (LCD) originally introduced in [4] and used to accomplish diversification by [5] (Sect. 4.3).

In the corresponding sections, we elaborate on the details of each of the tasks. The following section reviews related work.

3 Related Work

Our research is related to efforts found in the Web search community towards alleviating biases. Indeed, biases have been a constant problem on the Web and have received considerable attention from different aspects. For instance, in [6] domain bias was investigated in Web search. Domain bias is defined as the user's propensity to believe that a page is more relevant just because it comes from a particular domain. In [1] it was found that users show biases by favoring information that confirms what their beliefs when conducting a search. Researchers proved by a series of experiments the urgent need of search engines to cope with what they called bias and accuracy problem in the result set of a query. To deal with the problem of bias, several approaches to deliver result diversification have been proposed. These approaches could be categorized as either implicit or explicit [7]. Basically, they differ in how they account for the different query aspects that can help to diversify the result set for a given query.

Implicit approaches make the assumption that similar documents will cover similar aspects of the query and should therefore be in the final ranking. The challenge for these methods is to discover the possible different aspects in an unsupervised fashion. A pioneering example presented in [8] introduces a method that basically combines query-relevance with information-novelty in the context of retrieval and summarization. In a similar line of thought in [9] a method was introduced that exploits statistical language modeling to cope with redundancy and relevance. In their work, the problem of sub-topical retrieval is introduced. Basically, the idea is to find documents that cover different sub-topics (aspects) of a query. In [10] the use of clustering was introduced to improve the effectiveness of the diversification of the results of a query. Basically, the idea is to first cluster the candidate documents and then restrict the diversified approach to documents associated with clusters that potentially contain many relevant documents. A study comparing implicit diversification techniques with cluster based approaches that select cluster centroids as the representative documents in the final result list is given in [11]. They concluded that clustering is usually a better approach for single sub-topics of a given query. However, diversification implicit methods turned out to be better for quick coverage of distinct sub-topics. Another line of research takes diversification with a different perspective. These efforts model specifically the query aspects considered relevant for a specific domain. Usually, some type of external knowledge is exploited to account for these aspects. For instance, in [3] they look at the problem of diversification by assuming that a taxonomy exists. With this assumption, diversification is achieved by favoring documents from different categories and penalizing those that fall into already covered categories. A similar approach is used for product search in [12] where in addition to the categories of products, attributes within each category were considered. In [13] the query aspects were taken from the query log of a commercial search engine. Then, they proposed a ranking to satisfy each aspect of the original query. Another approach that exploits the idea of automatic query reformulations using TREC subtopics is the work of [7]. The researchers introduced a probabilistic approach that explicitly considers the aspects of the query as given by the sub-topics track in the TREC diversification task. The presented approach favors documents that cover those aspects that are not yet covered in the current results set of the generated candidate list. Our work is related to the explicit category of diversification. In our work, we promote claims as first-class citizens and how controversial claims, in particular, can raise in health-related queries.

4   Methodology

In this section, we introduce our methods to solve our novel problem of Claim Diversification, to explicitly rank the result set of a query represented as the pair $<entity, disease>$.

4.1 Dataset

To rely on high quality content, we used PubMed as our main source of documents. For each pair $<entity, disease>$, we submitted a query represented as the following query pattern in PubMed:

(help AND prevent) OR (lower AND risk) OR (increase OR increment AND risk) OR (decrease OR diminish AND risk) OR (factor AND risk) OR (associated AND risk) AND (entity AND disease).

The ranking provided from PubMed' retrieval system is our initial set of ranked documents . However, not all the documents retrieved from the query were used in our experiments. The main reason was that we wanted to be sure that a claim corresponds to the main contribution of a paper. Thus, we proceeded as follows: firstly, we filtered out documents with no conclusions metadata. Secondly, we split each document in sentences. And thirdly, for each sentence in each document, we selected as the claim of the document the sentence that contained $<entity, disease>$. This preprocessing step had a positive impact in the quality of the documents that we used.

4.2 Claim Representation

In this section, we provide details of how we represent claims of research papers and how we compute similarity between them for our proposed re-ranking mechanism. To represent the sentence with the $<entity, disease>$ pair, we used neural embedding of words. Following the success of word embedding representations that capture meaningful semantic relations between words from large text corpus, we opted to represent the claims using word2vec [14, 15]. One particular property that makes this representation useful for our task is that it has been demonstrated that not only are words with similar meanings embedded nearby, but also natural word arithmetic can be applied.

Claim embedding representation: Concretely, we represent each claim as the set of the word2vec representation of its words. For our experiments, we relied on the word2vec vectors trained on a combination of all publication abstracts from PubMed and all full-text documents from the PubMed Central Open Access subset [16]. As detailed from the authors, word2vec was run using the skip-gram model with a window size of 5, hierarchical softmax training, and a frequent word subsampling threshold of 0.001 to create 200-dimensional vectors. Another possible representation of words, Glove [17] could also be used for our particular problem.

Distance metric: Computing the distance between claims is a fundamental step for our proposed re-ranking mechanism. We decided to use the Word Mover's Distance (WMD) [18] after previous experimentation. As stated by the authors, the WMD distance measures the dissimilarity between two text documents as the minimum amount of distance that the embedded words of one document need to "travel" to reach the embedded words of another document. The proposed WMD was shown to deliver very successful results on document classification data. For our problem, we contrasted it with the cosine similarity and report only our results using WMD because it was superior.

4.3   List of Clusters Diversification (LCD)

The idea of List of Clusters Diversification was first introduced in [4]. Basically, the approach relies on the List of Clusters (LC) data structure. LC has been shown to be efficient in high-dimensional metric space searches [5]. In the following paragraphs we include a summary of the explanation of [5]. The idea of the algorithm is to build clusters (c, r). Each cluster has a center c with a covering radius r, so that documents in the cluster are within the covering radius of the center.

To diversify a ranking of documents that were initially retrieved from a query, we first need to choose a center c and a radius r. The cluster (c, r) comprises the subset of documents of D which are at distance of at most r from c. We define:

$$I_{D,c,r} \doteq \{d \in D\{c\} : \delta(c, d) \leq r\} \tag{1}$$

as the set of internal documents, i.e., which lie inside the cluster (c, r), and

$$\varepsilon_{D,c,r} \doteq \{d \in D\{c\} : \delta(c, d) > r\} \tag{2}$$

as the set of external documents. Clustering is applied recursively in the external set. The function δ in our case is WMD. The algorithm ends when all documents have been assigned to a cluster. Afterwards, the centers are promoted to the top of the ranking. Furthermore, a center chosen first has preference over the subsequent ones. After that, the remaining of the documents are returned in the order given by its internal membership with respect to its corresponding center. More formally, Algorithm 1 shows how to compute the List of Clusters Diversification (LCD).

$LCD[q, D = \{d_1, \dots, d_n\}, k]$

1. $C \leftarrow \{d_1\}$
2. $\varepsilon \leftarrow D\{d_1\}$
3. $c \leftarrow d_1$ #current center
4. while $|\varepsilon| > 0$ do
5.   for each $d_i \in \varepsilon$ do
           a.$V = V \cup \{\delta(d_i, c)\}$
6.   end for
7.   Sort V
8. $r \leftarrow V[k]$
9. $I \leftarrow \{d_j \in D\{c\} : \delta(c, d_j) \leq r\}$ (3)
10. $\varepsilon \leftarrow \varepsilon \backslash I$
11. $c \leftarrow \{d_i \in \varepsilon \; \delta(c, d_i) > \delta(c, d_j) \forall d_j \in \epsilon\}$
12. $C \leftarrow C \cup \{c\}$
13. $\varepsilon \leftarrow \varepsilon\{c\}$
14. end while
15. $C \leftarrow C \cup \{D \backslash C\}$

Algorithm 1. List of Clusters Diversification (LCD)

Let's clarify two important aspects of the algorithm. Firstly, the selection of cluster centers. The algorithm uses a ranked list of results and takes as the first cluster the top result. After that, to select cluster centers, line 11 of the algorithm, in [4] was extensively investigated using different heuristics. Experimentally, it was shown that the best strategy is to choose the next center as the object that maximizes the sum of distances to the previous centers. We used in our work the same heuristic. Secondly, the parameter k of the algorithm is used to set the size of the clusters. Empirically, it has been shown that when working with high dimensional metric spaces, the value of k can be dynamically increased as many documents may have the same distance to the center. This is helpful because the number of computations required to select the centers of the clusters can be dramatically reduced. Using a large value of k can help alleviate the cost of distance computations. In our experiments, we set k to six after evaluating a range of values and manually assessing the tradeoffs of the computational cost versus diversity of the result set.

5   Experiments

We are aware that the TREC09 and TREC10 collections [19], provide data samples and queries related to the diversification problem in Information Retrieval. Unfortunately, no such data is available for the novel problem presented in this paper where claims are first class citizens. Thus, to evaluate our results, we conducted a series of experiments by querying PubMed as indicated in Sect. 4.1. Moreover, we propose to use as a metric of our evaluation the Entropy at the top t documents to measure the amount of information expressed in the documents at each t. Basically, the idea is that if we achieve higher diversification than the initial result set delivered by PubMed, then we should have a higher entropy. In other words, our proposed method should more evenly divide its probability mass across the documents. Thus, a lower entropy would imply narrow focus of the result set (bias). More formally, entropy is defined as:

$$H(X) = - \sum_{i=1}^{m} p(x_i) \log p(x_i) \tag{4}$$

We performed experiments with 16 entities related to cancer: wine, tea, sugar, salt, potato, pork, onion, olive, milk, lycopene, lemon, egg, coffee, cigar, beef and bacon. We selected these entities for our analysis taken from the cases studied by [2]. We begin in the following paragraphs with a brief discussion of the three main cases found among the 16 entities we analyzed. More specifically, we explain three entities that reflect our main findings: tea, wine and coffee.

In Figs. 1, 2 and 3 we plot the entropies at the top 5, 10, 15 and 20 result set with three queries representing three different entities related to cancer: tea, wine and coffee. The label "no diversification" in the plots means the retrieved list of documents where our approach is not used. The label "with diversification" is the one that corresponds to our proposed approach.

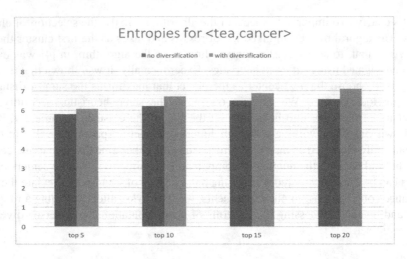

Fig. 1. Entropies for the query <tea, cancer>

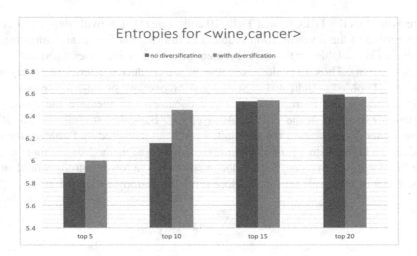

Fig. 2. Entropies for the query <wine, cancer>

The first case, tea and cancer are shown in Fig. 1. We can observe that when diversification is applied there is a constant positive difference with respect to the default result set. According to our hypothesis, when diversification is applied up to the top 20 results the user could be better informed.

The second case shown in Fig. 2 corresponds to wine and cancer. As it can be observed, it is a different situation: up to the top 10 results our approach could potentially help the user to be aware of a broader set of associations between the entities. However, beginning at the top 15 the differences can be neglected.

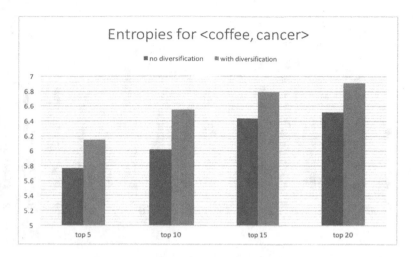

Fig. 3. Entropies for the query <coffee, cancer>

In Fig. 3 we have the case of coffee and cancer. It seems that our approach is able to diversify the result set. In this particular case, the differences between our approach and the default result set remain constant.

In summary, what we learned from these preliminary experiments is that up to the top 10 results diversification makes a different for this type of data. Even though the differences look small, please notice that our preprocessing step cleaned a lot of data. Because of this preprocessing, the differences do not seem to be as relevant as they could have been expected.

Comparison with MMR. To further validate our proposed solution, we also considered in our work the diversity-based re-ranking method called Maximal Margin Relevance (MMR) [8]. We proceeded as follows: we used two metrics to evaluate the differences between the two methods using top 10 results. Firstly, we used entropy as before. And secondly, we computed correlation of word frequencies between each method and the first 10 results with "no diversification". The idea behind this metric is simple but powerful: the performance of one method is worse than the other, the more correlated is with the set of "no diversification". In this work, we used Pearson's correlation with 95 confidence intervals.

To our surprise, the differences between the two methods when using entropy as our main metric are not statistically significant. In Fig. 4 we observe the comparisons with each entity and there is no clear winner: in some cases, MMR is better but in half of them LCD does a better job.

However, when we computed the correlation of word frequencies between each method and the top 10 results with no diversification, LCD turned out to be slightly better. In particular, it outperformed MMR in 10 out of the 16 entities.

Discussion. One limitation of our current analysis is that qualitatively speaking, we cannot evaluate our approach. We can only observe some differences using entropy as our metric in favor of the idea of allowing a user to get a better overview of a result set.

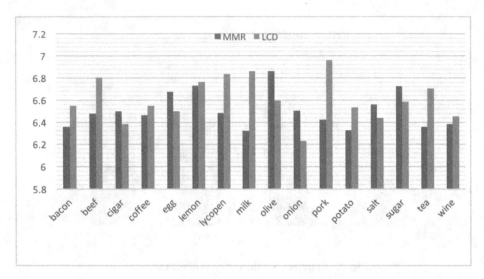

Fig. 4. Entropies of MMR (left bar in each pair) and the LCD model (right bar in each pair)

Nevertheless, this is a rather complicated and interesting query type and further work is needed to overcome our current limitations. On the other hand, we could manually observe examples where our approach seems promising. Consider for instance the following top 5 results of our approach for the pair <tea, cancer>:

1. "over consumption of fish sauce, pickled food, moldy cereals, irregularly taking meals and familial history of malignancy may be the local risk factors for high occurrence of gastric cancer, and fresh vegetables and fruits, green tea may have protective effects on it"
2. "our results did not show a protective role of tea in five major cancers"
3. "tea consumption protects against oral cancer in non-smokers or non-alcohol drinkers, but this effect may be obscured in smokers or alcohol drinkers"
4. drinking hot tea, a habit common in golestan province, was strongly associated with a higher risk of esophageal cancer
5. "we observed evidence to support a potential beneficial influence for breast cancer associated with moderate levels of tea consumption (three or more cups per day) among younger women".

6   Conclusions and Future Work

We motivated and presented the novel Claim Diversification Problem for Digital Libraries. In particular, for queries in the medical domain where one entity (a substance, a drug, a medicine, a product, etc.) has some influence with respect to a disease. We build on previous work on Web search where diversification was introduced to deal with the bias on the result set with complex ambiguous queries. In our case, we model specifically one key aspect of scientific papers: claims. Claims in this work are the sentences used in medical research papers to assess the association between two entities.

Our results look promising, and we envision future work to specifically assess the value of promoting claims as the text snippets to present to users from real world queries. Furthermore, we would like to validate the diversification approach that we proposed in this paper with user's feedback. Moreover, we would like to improve our current approach to account for more complex cases where the claims involve more than two entities. Currently, we do not support this type of queries. To accomplish such a task, we would investigate more sophisticated models of the Natural Language community to extract and represent semantically these cases.

We also believe that "time" in the medical domain should be considered as a relevant factor in the diversification process. Therefore, we will incorporate this important factor in our work.

References

1. White, R.: Beliefs and biases in web search. In: Proceedings of 36th International ACM SIGIR conference on research and development in Information Retrieval - SIGIR 2013, p. 3 (2013)
2. Schoenfeld, J.D.: Is everything we eat associated with cancer? A systematic. Am. J. Clin. Nutr. **97**, 127–134 (2013)
3. Agrawal, R., Gollapudi, S., Halverson, A., Ieong, S.: Diversifying search results. In: Proceedings of the Second ACM International Conference on Web Search and Data Mining - WSDM 2009, p. 5 (2009)
4. Chávez, E., Navarro, G.: A compact space decomposition for effective metric indexing. Pattern Recognit. Lett. **26**, 1363–1376 (2005)
5. Gil-Costa, V., Santos, R.L.T., MacDonald, C., Ounis, I.: Modelling efficient novelty-based search result diversification in metric spaces. J. Discret. Algorithms **18**, 75–88 (2013)
6. Ieong, S., Mishra, N., Sadikov, E., Zhang, L.: Domain bias in web search. In: WSDM 2012 Proceedings of Fifth ACM International Conference on Web Search and Data Mining, pp. 413–422 (2012)
7. Santos, R.L.T.T., Macdonald, C., Ounis, I.: Exploiting query reformulations for web search result diversification. In: Proceedings of 19th International Conference on World Wide Web, pp. 881–890 (2010)
8. Carbonell, J., Goldstein, J.: The use of MMR, diversity-based reranking for reordering documents and producing summaries. In: Proceedings of the 21st Annual International ACM SIGIR Conference on Research and Development in Information Retrieval - SIGIR 1998, pp. 335–336 (1998)
9. Zhai, C.X., Cohen, W.W., Lafferty, J.: Beyond independent relevance: methods and evaluation metrics for subtopic retrieval. In: Proceedings of the 26th Annual International ACM SIGIR Conference on Research and Development in Informaion Retrieval, pp. 10–17 (2003)
10. He, J., Meij, E., De Rijke, M.: Result diversification based on query-specific cluster ranking. J. Am. Soc. Inf. Sci. Technol. **62**, 550–571 (2011)
11. Carpineto, C., D'Amico, M., Romano, G.: Evaluating subtopic retrieval methods: clustering versus diversification of search results. Inf. Process. Manag. **48**, 358–373 (2012)

12. Chen, X., Wang, H., Sun, X., Pan, J., Yu, Y.: Diversifying product search results. In: SIGIR, pp. 1093–1094 (2011)
13. Radlinski, F., Dumais, S.: Improving personalized web search using result diversification. In: Proc. 29th Annual International ACM SIGIR Conference on Research and Development in Information Retrieval, SIGIR 2006, p. 691 (2006)
14. Mikolov, T., Corrado, G., Chen, K., Dean, J.: Efficient estimation of word representations in vector space. In: Proceedings of International Conference on Learning Representation (ICLR 2013), pp. 1–12 (2013)
15. Le, Q., Mikolov, T.: Distributed representations of sentences and documents. In: International Conference on Machine Learning - ICML 2014, vol. 32, pp. 1188–1196 (2014)
16. Pyysalo, S., Ginter, F., Moen, H., Salakoski, T., Ananiadou, S.: Distributional semantics resources for biomedical text processing. In: Proceedings of LBM 2013 (2013)
17. Pennington, J., Socher, R., Manning, C.: Glove: global vectors for word representation. In: Proceedings of the 2014 Conference on Empirical Methods in Natural Language Processing (EMNLP), pp. 1532–1543 (2014)
18. Kusner, M.J., Sun, Y., Kolkin, N.I., Weinberger, K.Q.: From word embeddings to document distances. In: Proceedings of 32nd International Conference on Machine Learning, vol. 37, pp. 957–966 (2015)
19. Hawking, D.: Overview of the TREC-9 web track. In: NIST Special Publication 500-249: The Ninth Text REtrieval Conference (TREC-9), pp. 87–102 (2001)
20. Manning, C.D., Raghavan, P.: An introduction to information retrieval (2009). http://dspace.cusat.ac.in/dspace/handle/123456789/2538

Identifying Key Elements of Search Results for Document Selection in the Digital Age: An Observational Study

Yasuko Hagiwara[1]($\boxtimes$), Emi Ishita[2], Emiko Mizutani[1],
Kana Fukushima[1], Yukiko Watanabe[2], and Yoichi Tomiura[3]

[1] Department of Library Science, Graduate School of Integrated Frontier
Sciences, Kyushu University, Hakozaki, Fukuoka 812-8581, Japan
2FS15060R@s.kyushu-u.ac.jp
[2] Kyushu University Library, Hakozaki, Fukuoka 812-8581, Japan
ishita.emi.982@m.kyushu-u.ac.jp
[3] Department of Informatics, Faculty of Information Science and Electrical
Engineering, Kyushu University, Motooka, Fukuoka 819-0395, Japan

Abstract. Academic database systems are vitally important tools for enabling researchers to find relevant, useful articles. Identifying how researchers select documents from search results is an extremely useful measure for improving the functions or interfaces of academic retrieval systems. This study aims to reveal which elements are checked, and in what order, when researchers select from among search results. It consists of two steps: an observational study of search sessions performed by researchers who volunteered, and a questionnaire to confirm whether extracted elements and patterns are used. This article reports findings from the observational study and introduces questions we developed based on the study. In the observational study we obtained data on nine participants who were asked to search for documents using information retrieval systems. The search sessions were recorded using a voice recorder and by capturing screen images. The participants were also asked to state which elements they checked in selecting documents, along with the reasons for their selections. Three patterns of order of checking were found. In pattern 1, seven researchers used titles and abstracts as the primary elements. In pattern 2, the others used titles and then accessed the full text before making a decision on their selection. In pattern 3, one participant searched for images and accessed the full text from the link in those pictures. We also found participants used novel elements for selecting. We subsequently developed items for a questionnaire reflecting the findings.

Keywords: Information retrieval · Document selection · Academic database · Empirical study

1 Introduction

Search engines are tools widely used by the public. Yet while academic databases remain an important information resource for researchers [1], the spread of search engines may affect personal preferences for search interfaces. Pajić [2] evaluated a

© Springer International Publishing AG 2017
S. Choemprayong et al. (Eds.): ICADL 2017, LNCS 10647, pp. 237–242, 2017.
https://doi.org/10.1007/978-3-319-70232-2_20

visualization-based and a text-based information retrieval system for document sear-ches performed by students. The study concluded the visualization-based one was more efficient. E-journal platforms have also become more common. Some academic data-bases now provide links that enable easy access to full-text versions in such platforms for each item listed in the search results. These adaptations influence processes for document selection. Knowing how researchers select documents from among the search results to obtain the full-text versions, and by using academic databases, can help improve interfaces to academic information retrieval systems. This knowledge also contributes to improving instructional programs on academic databases.

In the present study, we aimed to identify which elements are checked, and in what order, when researchers select documents from among search results. The study con-sisted of two steps. First, we observed search sessions by volunteer researchers to extract patterns of checked elements and order for document selection. Second, we plan to widely distribute a questionnaire among users to confirm whether extracted elements and patterns were used. This article describes the results of our observational study, that is, the checked elements and order in the search results. We also propose questionnaire items reflecting the observational study findings.

2   Related Research

Three similar published studies exist on clarifying which elements are used for doc-ument selection. Wang et al. [3] proposed six document selection components: doc-ument information elements, user criteria, document values, personal knowledge, decision rules, and decision. Macedo-Rouet et al. [4] observed researchers' search strategies when using the PubMed database. That study showed that 84% of the par-ticipants checked the abstracts after reviewing the titles. Xie et al. [5] also conducted an empirical study, also finding that most participants read the abstract prior to selecting a document. Nicolas et al. [6] used a questionnaire and found that abstracts were used in the present-day environment wherein users have complete full-text access. These results indicate reading the title and abstract are common elements in the process of document selection. Such studies have typically applied observational and/or used questionnaires in their methodology; therefore, we opted to use both.

3   Methodology

3.1   Study Design

The observational study comprised three steps: (1) pre-interviews, (2) search sessions conducted by the participants, and (3) follow-up interviews. In the pre-interviews, we asked participants their research theme, research duration, and search topic. After our first study, we revised the questions from those shown in the study plan [7]. In the pre-interviews, we subsequently only asked participants for details of their research theme and search topic. In the search session, the participants were asked to perform a document search in accordance with their search topic and using their academic databases of preference. After performing their searches, they selected the documents they wished to read in full based on the search results. During the search session, the participants were asked to describe which elements they were checking in the search results, which sentences they noted in abstracts, and their reasons for selecting particular documents. Audio of these statements was recorded, and a number of screen images were captured. During the session and in the follow-up interviews, we occasionally asked the participants to confirm which elements and sentences they checked.

The study was approved by the research ethics committee of the Department of Informatics, Graduate School of Information Science and Electrical Engineering, Kyushu University.

3.2   Data Collection

The preliminary study involved 10 researchers (five faculty members and five doctoral students) and was conducted from November 2015 to September 2016. We did not give any of the participants a specific search topic: each conducted a document search based on their own search topics. The maximum time permitted was 3 h; however, the participants were allowed to stop searching if and when they were satisfied with the results. The average time taken was 2 h, with a maximum of the full 3 h and minimum of 1 h. The study involving the first three researchers (participants A, B, and C) was reported elsewhere [8]. Subsequently, we conducted studies with an additional seven participants. However, we eliminated one student from the analysis because she had never used academic databases such as Web of Science and Scopus prior to the study. Table 1 shows the participants' research topics and the respective databases they used to assist their document searches.

Table 1. Research topics and databases used.

	Research topic	Database(s) used		Research topic	Database(s) used
A	Information retrieval	Web of Science	F	Organic electronic devices	Google Images, Google Scholar, Google, Web of Science
B	Bibliometrics	Scopus			
C	Machine learning	Scopus	G	Olfactory sensors	Web of Science
D	Information retrieval	Web of Science	H	E-learning	Web of Science
E	Record keeping	Web of Science, Scopus, Google Scholar	I	Gas-detection devices	Web of Science

4   Elements Checked by Participants

In the search results, we analyzed which elements were checked and in what order to select documents. Two main patterns of order of checking elements were identified in the nine participants, as shown in two representative samples in Fig. 1. Though the participants conducted multiple searches, we summarized them to focus on elements

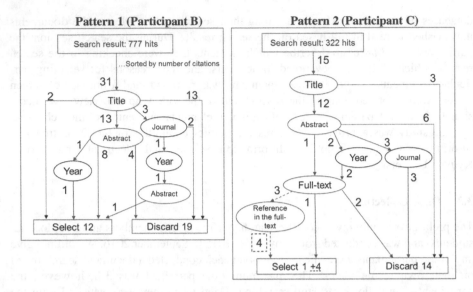

Fig. 1. Order of elements checked for document selection

checked and the order of checking. In representative pattern 1, participant B first obtained 777 search results and sorted them by the number of citations. He checked the first 31 document titles, then selected two documents and excluded 13. From among the remaining 16, he read 13 abstracts and checked the journal titles of the other three titles.

The primary element for pattern 1 was the title, followed by the abstract. These elements were also identified in other studies as the main criteria for document selection [3, 4]. Participants A, D, E, F, H, and I all fell under pattern 1. Participant B also checked the publication year and journal title. He explained that it was difficult to judge the documents' relevance only by author names, because he was not yet well-versed in the field, and he used the journal titles to judge the documents' relevance. Participant A's pattern was simpler—checking only the document title and abstract. Participant D checked other elements, such as number of pages, document type, and language. Participant E checked keywords and research fields. Although these six participants checked different elements, their orders of checking the title and abstract were the same, so we placed them under pattern 1.

Participant C represented pattern 2 (Fig. 1). This participant accessed three documents (full-text versions) without making a selection decision. He checked their references but not the body text. Moreover, he selected four documents from among the references. Participant G also accessed full-text versions after checking the abstracts. This participant mainly checked figures in the full text and used them to assist his selection. He stated he tended to rule out documents when he could not find their full-text version online. The patterns of participants C and G in accessing full-text versions were the same. We analyzed the reasons for the order they followed through their statements. They first identified that some documents in the search result list had links to the full-text versions. This process likely encouraged them to access the full text. As participant C's research topic was optimization for machine learning, it should be noted that researchers in this field are generally inclined to seek fundamental references. Furthermore, participant C mentioned he sought to source a few of the fundamental references because he had recently started his research and his knowledge of the topic was still quite limited. Participant G searched for documents regarding devices for experiments on his research topic. He mentioned he would determine which documents he wished to read by checking the figures showing each paper's device tests. Based on this approach, it appears the research topic, research phase, and particular aspects of the research field may affect some researchers' decisions on which elements are checked.

Participant F also conducted a process unique from the other participants and cannot therefore be categorized into pattern 1 or 2. He first searched for images of a device, specifically for chemical storage, on Google Images. He then clicked on images of devices that seemed related to his research. After that, he accessed the full texts or abstracts available on the publishers' websites linked to the pictures presented in the Google Images results. Finally, he decided on selection by reading the abstract or full text. He explained that by viewing images of the devices discussed in the documents he could judge the documents' relevance. Additionally, he noted his weekly search habits for gathering information in his research field were browsing contents of specific journals and glancing at search results using predetermined keywords.

5 Discussion

This observational study showed that titles and abstracts are highly important and among the primary elements in decision making when selecting relevant research documents. We also found some participants examined references, figures, and/or images from full-text versions. Decisions were also based on the online availability of the full text. From our analysis of participants' statements and from related research on document triage [9, 10], we can assume phases of research, i.e. topic familiarization and objectives of browsing, influence which elements are checked. However nine participants constitute a small sample that may restrict generalizability. We plan to conduct a questionnaire to confirm whether these findings on information retrieval are general or are behavior idiosyncratic to these respondents. We have developed two items for questionnaire inclusion in this regard.

(1) Which elements—including new elements such as full text, images, and online availability of full text—are checked when selecting documents from among search results? To confirm the relation between research phases and elements, we will ask respondents to select elements by using three objectives: (a) find previous research in an unfamiliar field, (b) learn current research trends in their fields, and (c) identify methods for adapting to their research problems. Respondents who select full text in the above question 1 will also be asked which part of the text they check (e.g., introduction, references, tables, figures, formulas).

(2) What types of patterns of checked elements and order are found? We will show orders of elements from the study results and ask respondents to select the closest ones that they normally employ. Options for example orders contain traditional patterns (e.g., title > abstract, title only), patterns including new elements found in the study

(e.g., title > full text, image search > full text, title > abstract > online availability of the full text), and unique patterns (e.g., document type > title > abstract, checking language only) to confirm generality.

We hope to fully uncover the entire process of researchers' information-seeking behavior. In the questionnaire items, we will also address areas such as which databases are used and from which forms of media documents are accessed. We plan to carry out such a questionnaire among researchers and clarify the current status of document selection using the most contemporary information retrieval system environments.

Acknowledgements. This work is supported by JSPS KAKENHI Grant Number JP15H01721.

References

1. Liyana, S., Noorhidawati, A.: How graduate students seek for information: convenience or guaranteed result? Malays. J. Libr. Inf. Sci. **19**(2), 1–15 (2014)
2. Pajić, D.: Browse to search, visualize to explore: who needs an alternative information retrieving model? Comput. Hum. Behav. **39**, 145–153 (2014)
3. Wang, P., Soergel, D.: A cognitive model of document use during a research project. Study I. Document selection. J. Am. Soc. Inf. Sci. **49**(2), 115–133 (1998)
4. Macedo-Rouet, M., Rouet, J.-F., Ros, C., et al.: How do scientists select articles in the PubMed database? An empirical study of criteria and strategies. Eur. Rev. Appl. Psychol. **62** (2), 63–72 (2012)
5. Xie, I., Benoit III, E.: Search result list evaluation versus document evaluation: similarities and differences. J. Documentation **69**(1), 49–80 (2013)
6. Nicholas, D., Huntington, P., Jamali, H.R.: The use, users, and role of abstracts in the digital scholarly environment. J. Acad. Librarianship **33**(4), 446–453 (2007)
7. Hagiwara, Y., Wu, M., Mizutani, E., et al.: An experiment to identify how researchers select documents from search results. In: Proceedings of CiSAP Workshop 2015, pp. 8–11 (2015)
8. Hagiwara, Y., Ishita, E., Mizutani, E., et al.: A preliminary study and analysis to identify key elements in document selection. In: Information Seeking in Context, ISIC 2016, Zadar (2016)
9. Bae, S., Marshall, C.C., Meintanis, K., et al.: Patterns of reading and organizing information in document triage. In: ASIST Proceedings, vol. 43, no. 1, pp. 1–27 (2007)
10. Stelmaszewska, H., Blandford, A.: From physical to digital: a case study of computer scientists' behavior in physical libraries. Int. J. Digit. Libr. **4**(2), 82–92 (2004)

Social Media

Information Seeking Behaviour of Aspiring Undergraduates on Social Media: Who Are They Interacting with?

Lara Dodd[1], Gobinda Chowdhury[1(✉)], Morgan Harvey[1], and Geoff Walton[2]

[1] Northumbria University, Newcastle upon Tyne NE1 8ST, UK
{laura.dodd,gobinda.chowdhury,
morgan.harvey}@northumbria.ac.uk
[2] Manchester Metropolitan University, Manchester M15 6BH, UK
g.walton@mmu.ac.uk

Abstract. In this paper we consider how aspiring undergraduates are utilising social media to meet their information needs during their application and transition into university. In particular, we ask who some of the prominent online actors are during this period. We want to know whether hopeful students are consulting social sources online, and if so, who these conversations are with, or, about. We use term frequency analysis to process a large sample (n = 494,180) of "tweets" (social media messages from Twitter) to determine who these main actors are. Our analyses provide insights into who students are interacting with during different stages of the decision-making process and, perhaps more importantly, who they are mostly failing to engage with. This leads us to a number of potentially useful conclusions and recommendations with regard to young people's information behaviour on social media in the context of university admission.

Keywords: Social media · Twitter · Information-seeking behaviour · Adolescents · Teenagers

1 Introduction

Information behaviour and HCI research has focused on understanding how people access, interact, use and share information in different contexts for decades; especially in the digital world. In addition to the traditional channels of scholarly communications, new platforms and media of communications have emerged in the recent past, which on one hand have immensely enlarged the scope and opportunities for information creation, access and sharing, but, on the other, have opened new challenges and opportunities for research to understand the changing or emerging information behaviour of people. Consequently, numerous research projects and activities have been undertaken over the past few years that have aimed to understand how people behave – communicate, access and share information – on the web and social media (e.g. [1]). The research reported in this paper is part of an ongoing project that aims to understand

© Springer International Publishing AG 2017
S. Choemprayong et al. (Eds.): ICADL 2017, LNCS 10647, pp. 245–255, 2017.
https://doi.org/10.1007/978-3-319-70232-2_21

the information behaviour of young people on social media, especially Twitter, in a specific context, viz. the university admission process in the UK.

Investigating the role social networks play on school/college leavers information-seeking behaviour in the UK can be considered timely on two fronts. Firstly, there is a potential information gap, which has resulted, in part, from a government decision in 2005 to place schools/colleges in charge of their own careers advice provision [2]. Secondly, for millennials, social networks are now an integral and intrinsic part of everyday life whether they are at home or at school [3]. These networks operate as information hubs, especially for those with similar interests [4], where information not merely exists but where they can also ask questions. Given that platforms, including Twitter, are increasingly being used as a primary method of communication [5] it is then perhaps natural to wonder that if an information gap does exist, to what extent they might be meeting this need through social media?

The key research questions addressed in the research reported here are as follows:

1. What is the typical pattern of communications on Twitter on issues related to the university admission process in the UK in terms of volume, content, etc.?
2. Do these change during different stages of the university admission cycle?
3. Who are the different stakeholders – information providers – and do their importance or roles change during the year?

2 The Wider Context and Related Research

2.1 Context

The period of transition that prospective students go through as they leave school/college requires them to make potentially life-changing decisions, repeatedly (detailed below), and in a time sensitive environment. In 2013 Ofsted, the British educational standards inspector and regulator, concluded that only 20% of learners aged 17 to 18 were receiving adequate levels of careers advice/support. However, contrary to what might then be suspected, the numbers of aspiring undergraduates applying for, and ultimately attending university has not dropped [6]. This raises intriguing questions. If the prospective undergraduates of the future are not getting their information through traditional in-house channels, how are they navigating this key period of progression? Perhaps more and more students are using the social media for acquiring and sharing the relevant information? These questions triggered a PhD research part of which is reported in this paper.

2.2 Related Research

Twitter is potentially well suited on a number of fronts to meet the career-related information needs of millennials, also known as Generation Y, and especially those who have grown up in the age of social media. Tweets are not only capable of providing specific and up-to-date information, but they can also provide insight from the personal experiences of others [7]. In a wider sense it also provides multiple channels for interpersonal feedback, peer acceptance and reinforcement of group norms [8].

Conversely the fact that people are central to many interactions on Twitter and behave like hubs that join up information [9], is potentially a double-edged sword. Critically, whilst most tweets are truthful they can also carry rumours and misinformation, albeit often unintentionally [10]. However, there is a risk in millennials adopting a default position of trust as it takes more effort to be proactively critical than trusting [11]. A study conducted by Flanagin and Metzger [12] also found that people rarely verified web-based information and considered it to be as credible as television, radio and magazines.

The nature of Twitter arguably facilitates some types and/or topics of conversation better than others. Users tend to communicate with like-minded people and are quicker to rebroadcast rather than address information and/or enter into a debate [13]. In addition students have been found to be reluctant to engage with educational organisations via social media as they are seen as belonging to two different worlds, work and education versus leisure and play [3]. However, there is an opportunity here. Lovejoy and Saxton [14] demonstrated Twitter's apt capacity for stakeholder engagement and showed it to be more effective than mass communication and information that is already available on websites. Ultimately little is also known to date about how prospective undergraduates are making use of online social resources, whether it is beneficial and critically with whom they are engaging. Prior work has demonstrated that these information 'hubs' [16] not only exist but are a critical component of online information behaviour and so we seek to investigate this.

3 Methodology

In order to effectively collect the interactions of prospective undergraduates on Twitter three data collection periods were identified which represent the *Period 1: before*, *Period 2: during* and *Period 3: after* stages that aspiring students pass through. A combination of basic linguistic analysis – based on searching on Twitter through some important keywords or tokens – and qualitative analysis based on manual checking of the retrieved tweets to find new themes or tokens, was used to identify the relevant tweets and categorise them. The three periods were:

Period 1 - Before. From the beginning of September until the UCAS deadline in mid-January. The deadline for most undergraduate courses occurs in the middle of January for a September enrolment later that year. During this stage prospective undergraduates must do two things; they must first decide that they want to apply to one or more (up to five universities) and then secondly they must navigate the practical application and process.

Period 2 - During. From the start to the middle of August. The second data collection period spans A level (the final school leaving examination) results day and also the beginning of the *clearing process* – a process that takes place immediately after the results of the A level examination is announced. In this process candidates who have been unsuccessful in securing their places at a preferred university, selected through their application in Period 1, because of their not meeting the condition in terms of exam grades, may check and seek admission to other universities if places are still available. Up to this point university offers are typically conditional, so the grades received at this stage will affect the options available. Depending on the outcome of their results the prospective undergraduates must then decide based on the offers available which they wish to pursue (if any).

Period 3 - After. From the beginning of September until the end of December. The last data collection stage covers enrolment at university, their first week (known as freshers' week in the UK) and their first semester.

We located and captured relevant posts on Twitter in the following manner:

1. We started with the specific term "UCAS", which is uniquely specific to those in the UK (all university applications go through UCAS's online system). Stemmed variants of this were then also captured (e.g. #UCAS).
2. Queries were expanded to capture terms such as *application* or *applying* and *university* that might suggest someone was considering or talking about university applications.
3. Query results were sampled and checked in order to locate other words, hashtags (terms proceeded by hash signs indicate the subject of a tweet and therefore can be a useful tool for identifying relevant content) or phrases that might also be relevant.

It was found to be prudent to conduct manual checks of the results and alter or remove queries which were obviously not relevant. For example, terms such as *university*, which is used in many countries required a geographic filter. Similar care had to be taken with abbreviations such as *uni* as this is also a type of sushi.

In total the number of tweets retrieved across all three periods of progression totaled 494,180. The figures, broken down by period, are shown in Table 1.

Table 1. Total number of tweets collected.

Data collection period	Number of tweets
1. Before (UCAS applications)	155,100
2. During (Summer – Exam results/clearing)	180,473
3. After (Autumn – Enrolment and first semester)	158,607
Total	494,180

4 Classification of Stakeholders

Stakeholders were understood to potentially be any individuals, parties, public or private organisations, charities, trusts or collectives. In order to identify stakeholder terms and tokens (a group of words describing the same subject/individual) in the first instance two key approaches were employed:

1. Terms that have been identified in a review of relevant literature (e.g. Ofsted [15]). Specific terms were taken and then very basic stemmed variants (i.e. plurals) were used to create basic tokens.

2. The evidence itself was used to identify stakeholder terms. Term frequency was used to identify agents. The cut-off point for identifying terms has been set at 1,000 references per data collection period, past which point the stakeholder in question is being referred to less than 1% of the tweets during that time.

Whilst naturally some overlap occurred by employing both of the methods detailed above, the approach proved to be prudent. As the evidence goes on to demonstrate, some key stakeholders (e.g. the National Careers Council) were not present or referenced at all; however this absence is in itself interesting and might otherwise have been missed if we had only relied solely on term frequency to locate and identify agents.

4.1   Patterns of Behaviour and Context

The volume of communication does not stay at a consistent, fixed level during any of the points of transition. Indeed the volume of chatter behaves differently and varies depending on the context. For example, if we consider the overall volume of captured tweets during the application process there is a distinct pattern. As Fig. 1 illustrates, communications peak on weekdays and falls during the weekends. For many prospective undergraduates this will represent days when they are in college and/or sixth form. There is then a lull during the Christmas holidays before a short peak that occurs just before the deadline in January. If we then compare this to the volumes of communication being exchanged during the release of exam results the pattern is distinctly different. This takes place during school holidays and demonstrates a single spike where there is a lot of sudden communication when decisions need to be made very quickly.

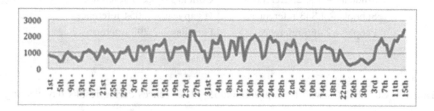

Fig. 1. Volume of tweets during the application process

As a final point of comparison if we consider the volume of communication during the first semester at university it is again distinctly different. Here there is an initial rise during freshers' week when the students first arrive, enroll, and settle in, etc. which slowly falls to a low level. Here conversations in Higher Education don't follow a Monday to Friday pattern as they did previously during the application process. Just as the patterns in the volume of communications differ during the three different periods of progression so do the different actors talking, being talked about, and/or being talked to. The following tables show the key stakeholders (those with the highest number of references) during each stage of aspiring undergraduates' progression.

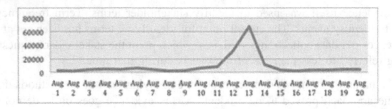

Fig. 2. Volume of tweets during results day/clearing

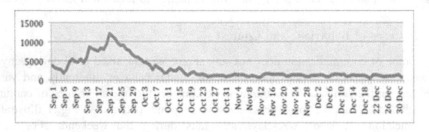

Fig. 3. Volume of tweets during students' first semester

Table 2. Stakeholders with the highest number of references during the application process

Stakeholders	
Universities – 11,745 references	UCAS – 9,897 references
@ucas – 9,462 references	#ucas – 6,336 references
Students – 4,932 references	Colleges – 4,257 references
Schools – 4,843 references	@gapyear – 3,054 references
People – 2,466 references	Families – 2,298 references

Table 3. Stakeholders with the highest number of references during results day/clearing

Stakeholders	
Universities – 19,109 references	Students – 16,073 references
Freshers – 1,773 references	Everyone – 9,997 references
UCAS – 9,972 references	@ucas – 9,986 references
Colleges – 7,479 references	Schools – 7,768 references
#university – 5,479 references	People – 4,176 references

Table 4. Stakeholders with the highest number of references during students' first semester

Stakeholders	
Universities – 19,609 references	Students – 17,471 references
Freshers – 14,101 references	#freshers – 9,983 references
Instagram – 7,251 references	@freshers – 6,964 references
freshershome – 6,613 references	Colleges – 6,412 references
dlvr – 5,722 references	neuvoo – 5,973 references

We have initially considered only the ten most prominent actors in each period in this case here as the total number of stakeholders recorded in each period is considered separately below (Fig. 4).

The stakeholders identified here (Tables 2, 3 and 4) reflect the environments and provide insight into the key online actors present on Twitter during each data collection period. Stakeholder terms (e.g. UCAS) have been kept verbatim and not grouped together as stakeholder tokens here as the differences (e.g. UCAS and @ucas) can differentiate, for example, whether actors are being talked about, or, to. The spelling here (e.g. singular versus plural) is also indicative of the nature of the references, for example 'universities' rather than 'university' reflects a more casual referral to Higher Education institutions as a group than specific references to a particular organisation. There are subtle shifts between the most prominent stakeholders at each stage, for example four of the top ten terms during student's first semester are referring to peers/other students. This reflects a shift to a more social, peer orientated information environment, where references to family and institutions such as UCAS and schools have all but disappeared.

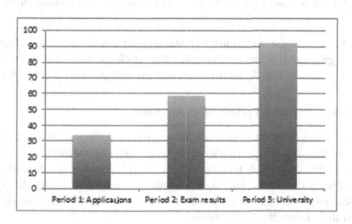

Fig. 4. Total number of different stakeholder tokens during each data collection

The total number of different stakeholder tokens increased notably between each period as Fig. 4 illustrates. There were a total of 34 stakeholders identified during the application process compared with 59 during the exam results/start of clearing, which rose to 92 during the students' first semester at university. This is interesting as it demonstrates that the range of stakeholders involved in communicating online during undergraduates' first semester is exponentially more diverse than during their initial application period.

4.2   Similarities Between Periods of Progression

In considering what the three periods might have in common only a very small number of core stakeholders were found to be present (more than 1%) during all three stages of progression.

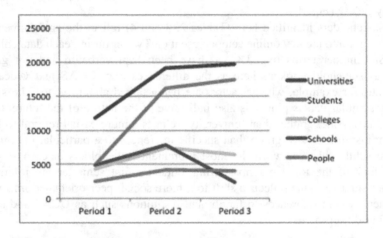

Fig. 5. Stakeholders present (shown by number of Tweets; y axis)) during all three stages

As Fig. 5 shows there were only five stakeholder tokens present during all three periods of progression, of these *universities* and *students* increased in frequency (as shown in the Y axis in Fig. 5) whilst references to *colleges* and *schools* decreased.

4.3   Differences Between Periods of Progression

The majority of stakeholders tended not to be present during all three stages of progression. Other than the prospective student themselves stakeholders only tended to be present during stages in which they potentially had an interest, or, an active role. For example, as Fig. 6 illustrates, UCAS references are prevalent during the application and results/clearing process but drop off to a negligible level once individuals have moved on to their respective universities.

Figure 6 shows some examples of the shifts that occur with stakeholders that are present across at least two of the data collection periods. Whilst UCAS references remain relatively consistent until the point at which students no longer need them, particular social references to friends and other social media networks (e.g. Facebook) increase.

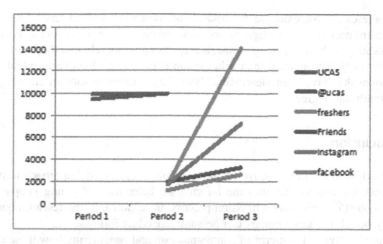

Fig. 6. Shift in stakeholder trends between data collection periods

There were no overlaps (for exceptions see Figs. 5 and 6), which given the number of stakeholders identified shows just how much from beginning to end the online social environment had changed. Given the limited overlap it is worth highlighting the stakeholders, or patterns of stakeholders, that are only present in conversations during certain stages of a student's progression. In particular:

- References to *families* only occur to any significance (more than 1%) during the application phase.
- The nature of commercial individual users that were prevalent during each stage changed and were specific to the decisions being made at that point. For example, in order, relative to each data collection period; @gapyear, @alevelresults, and @jobsplane.

4.4 Stakeholder Gaps

What is also worthy of note are the gaps present in the data. Rightly, or wrongly, there are some key stakeholders, which are largely absent from conversations taking place on Twitter (see Table 5).

Table 5. Example of stakeholders during the application process with few or no references

Tokens with the fewest references	
National Careers Council – 0 references	Jobcenter – 0 references
Children's Trusts – references	Ofsted – 1 reference
Local Authorities – 1 reference	National Careers Service – 5 references
Department of Education – 6 references	Careers Advisers – 80 references

In some cases, for example for tokens for 'brothers' and 'sisters' (189 and 89 references respectively) low figures are unsurprising. Even if an actor is actively communicating with their sibling online, it is potentially unlikely that they will actively use a term to clearly identify their relationship every time. However, several official organisations that have been identified as being key sources of support are not present to any significant degree.

5   Conclusion

The research reported here is novel in that it employs an atypical approach to provide new knowledge and insight into the information behaviour of young people in the specific context of university admission process. In response to the research questions originally posed, the key findings can be summarised as follows.

In regard to 'typical' patterns of communication and considering how these change, we can see that contextual factors such as time factor considerably in patterns in the volume of communication during each period of progression for aspiring/new undergraduates. As such each period of progression is unique and accurately reflects patterns and events as they happen. When the aspiring undergraduates, the study population, are at school, the highest level of communication takes place during the week (Fig. 1). However, this pattern does not show up in period 3 when the subjects are at the university, and moreover the volume of communications surges within the first few weeks and then it drops (Fig. 3). Of course the volume of communication is very high during the clearing week (Fig. 2). These findings show a clear relationship between people's lifestyle and the nature of their communications on Twitter in reference to a particular subject, in this case university admission.

If we consider the second research question, which seeks to identify the importance and roles of stakeholders we can see that the data suggests distinctly different online environments during each stage of progression. For the first time, this study identifies the key stakeholders identified in Twitter communications by aspiring undergraduates (Tables 2, 3 and 4). Indeed, we can see that as prospective students progress more actors join the conversation and the environment becomes increasingly diverse. Comparatively very few stakeholders are actively present during all three stages of progression. Most stakeholders are active for only one, possibly two periods of the progression.

Despite students' known reluctance to engage with educational institutions online [3], three of the five stakeholder tokens that were continually being referenced during all three datasets were universities, schools and colleges. Of course there is nothing to suggest here that users were talking to these institutions, merely that they were being referenced. It would therefore make an interesting line of investigation going forward to consider a deeper form of discourse analysis that might address why Twitter is such a suitable medium for users to talk *about* institutions rather than directly to them. As a reflection of this and as a wider consideration UCAS would appear to have some success breaking this convention and stands in stark contrast to other central agencies that were referenced little, if at all.

There are wider lessons to be learnt here; not least as the methodology could be easily adapted and employed in other contexts, but would also facilitate additional qualitative lines of investigation (e.g. sampling). These findings may prove insightful for wider audiences given that they not only identify positive exchanges of communication (e.g. UCAS), but also can identify information black holes, where there are notable absences from key information providers.

References

1. Wakefield, R., Wakefield, K.: Social media network behavior: a study of user passion and affect. J. Strateg. Inf. Syst. **25**(2), 140–156 (2016)
2. Department for Education: Youth Matters (2005). http://webarchive.nationalarchives.gov.uk/20130401151715/, https://www.education.gov.uk/publications/standard/publicationDetail/Page1/Cm6629#downloadableparts. Accessed 15 June 2015
3. Jones, M., Harvey, M.: Library 2.0: the effectiveness of social media as a marketing tool for libraries in educational institutions. J. Librarianship Inf. Sci. (JOLIS) (2016). doi:10.1177/0961000616668959. Sage
4. Gil de Zúñiga, H., Jung, N., Valenzuela, S.: Social media use for news and individuals' social capital, civic engagement and political participation. J. Comput. Mediated Commun. **17**(3), 319–336 (2012)
5. Macskassy, S.A.: On the study of social interactions in twitter. In: ICWSM (2012)
6. UCAS: Four per cent rise in UK and EU students starting university and college courses (2014). http://www.ucas.com/news-events/news/2014/four-cent-rise-uk-and-eu-students-starting-university-and-college-courses. Accessed 21 Oct 2014
7. Hurlock, J., Wilson, M.L.: Searching Twitter: separating the tweet from the chaff. In: ICWSM, pp. 161–168 (2011)
8. Papacharissi, Z. (ed.): A Networked Self: Identity, Community, and Culture on Social Network Sites. Routledge, London (2010)
9. Elsweiler, D., Harvey, M.: Engaging and maintaining a sense of being informed: understanding the tasks motivating twitter search. J. Assoc. Inf. Sci. Technol. **66**(2), 264–281 (2015)
10. Castillo, C., Mendoza, M., Poblete, B.: Information credibility on twitter. In: Proceedings of the 20th International Conference on World Wide Web, pp. 675–684. ACM, March 2011
11. Lewandowsky, S., et al.: Misinformation and its correction, continued influence and successful debiasing. Psychol. Sci. Public Interest **13**(3), 106–131 (2012)
12. Flanagin, A.J., Metzger, M.J.: Perceptions of internet information credibility. J. Mass Commun. Q. **77**(3), 515–540 (2000)
13. Smith, L.M., Zhu, L., Lerman, K., Kozareva, Z.: The role of social media in the discussion of controversial topics. In: 2013 International Conference on Social Computing (SocialCom), pp. 236–243. IEEE (2013)
14. Lovejoy, K., Saxton, G.D.: Information, community, and action: how nonprofit organizations use social media. J. Comput. Mediated Commun. **17**(3), 337–353 (2012)
15. Ofsted: Going in the right direction? Careers guidance in schools from September 2012 (2013). http://www.ofsted.gov.uk/resources/going-right-direction-careers-guidance-schools-september-2012. Accessed 9 Nov 2014
16. Khoo, C.: Issues in information behaviour on social media. Libres **24**(2), 75–96 (2014)

An Analysis of Rumor and Counter-Rumor Messages in Social Media

Dion Hoe-Lian Goh[1](✉), Alton Y.K. Chua[1], Hanyu Shi[1],
Wenju Wei[1], Haiyan Wang[1], and Ee Peng Lim[2]

[1] Wee Kim Wee School of Communication and Information,
Nanyang Technological University, Singapore, Singapore
{ashlgoh,altonchua,wl60006,we0001ju,
wangll74}@ntu.edu.sg
[2] School of Information Systems, Singapore Management University,
Singapore, Singapore
eplim@smu.edu.sg

Abstract. Social media platforms are one of the fastest ways to disseminate information but they have also been used as a means to spread rumors. If left unchecked, rumors have serious consequences. Counter-rumors, messages used to refute rumors, are an important means of rumor curtailment. The objective of this paper is to examine the types of rumor and counter-rumor messages generated in Twitter in response to the falsely reported death of a politician, Lee Kuan Yew, who was Singapore's first Prime Minister. Our content analysis of 4321Twitter tweets about Lee's death revealed six categories of rumor messages, four categories of counter-rumor messages and two categories belonging to neither type. Interestingly, there were more counter-rumor messages than rumor messages. Our results thus suggest that, at least in the context of our study, online users do make an attempt to stop the spread of false rumors through counter-rumors.

Keywords: Rumor correction · Counter rumor · Social media · Death hoax · Content analysis · Twitter

1 Introduction

Social media platforms such as Twitter are one of the fastest ways to disseminate information. Unfortunately, they have also been used as a means to spread rumors and other forms of misinformation. For example, following the June 2017 terrorist attacks in London, rumors began circulating online that London mayor Sadiq Khan defended September 11th terrorists. Such a claim was of course false, and originated from an unrelated video of the mayor. In Asia, rumors swirled in social media that the ill-fated Malaysia Airlines flight MH370 from Kuala Lumpur to Beijing actually made a safe emergency landing somewhere in China, bring false hope to families and loved ones.

Online rumors, if left unchecked, have serious consequences especially if they turn out to be false. They may negatively impact social media platforms in terms of disseminating accurate information. They may damage the reputations of individuals and

© Springer International Publishing AG 2017
S. Choemprayong et al. (Eds.): ICADL 2017, LNCS 10647, pp. 256–266, 2017.
https://doi.org/10.1007/978-3-319-70232-2_22

organizations. Finally, they may harm social cohesion. Rumor correction is hence of utmost importance to control the negative effects from the spread of misinformation. One way to do this is through counter-rumors. In this paper, counter-rumors refer to messages used to refute rumors and spread the truth. Prior work suggests that counter-rumors are effective in combating rumors on the Internet [1]. This is because exposure to such messages reduces people's belief in the rumor in question, hence lowering their propensity to share that rumor [2].

Traditionally, rumors have been tackled by governments, affected organizations and mainstream news media [3]. However, on social media, the community of users play this role as well, although results have been mixed. On the one hand, some work has suggested that online communities are capable of self-correction and self-policing when presented with dubious information [4, 5], and that counter-rumors may be effective [2]. On the other hand, some research suggests that counter-rumors could reinforce misperceptions [6, 7].

One gap that motivates the current research is the relative lack of attention paid to the content generated by the online community in response to a rumor. For example, what types of messages do the community spread in a rumor situation? Importantly, what types of counter-rumor messages do the community create in response? Such questions are not addressed in existing work. We argue that understanding the nature of such messages created by online communities would translate into useful insights that will not only advance research but also benefit individuals and organizations in rebutting rumors.

Hence, the objective of this study is to examine the types of rumor and counter rumor messages generated in Twitter in response to the falsely reported death of a politician, Lee Kuan Yew, who was Singapore's first Prime Minister. The rest of the paper is organized as follows. Literature on rumor and rumor correction is reviewed. Data collection and analysis methods are next described, and the types of messages created are then presented. Thereafter the findings are discussed, together with implications of the work.

2 Related Work

Rumor may be defined as "unverified and instrumentally relevant information statements in circulation that arise in contexts of ambiguity, danger or potential threat, and that function to help people make sense and manage risk" [8]. It may also be defined as "a collective and collaborative transaction in which community members offer, evaluate and interpret information to reach a common understanding of uncertain situations, to alleviate social tension and to solve collective crisis problems" [9]. Put differently, rumors may be seen as a form of collective sense-making to a community attempting to understand ambiguous or uncertain situations when official information is lacking [8]. Nevertheless, rumors may negatively impact individuals, groups of people and even entire nations, depending on the topic, its content and the will of those that disseminate it.

There are a number of methods to neutralize rumors, including ignoring, confirmation of the truth, and denial. Ignoring a rumor is considered the weakest method of all and is used only if the rumor is highly implausible. However, rumors tend to take a life of their own and may spread uncontrollably. Thus, deliberate correction mechanisms, also known as counter-rumors, may be required [10, 11]. Rumors often carry some truth and counter-rumors confirming that part of the rumor that is true may be sufficient to neutralize its impact. Denial is a popular counter-rumor used to refute rumors [12] but its effectiveness has been questioned [13]. Other rumor coping tactics include providing the information that is in demand and enhancing trust and credibility by engaging in public relations [14, 15].

The increased use of social media and other online platforms to share information means that as an unfortunate side-effect, people have also used them to spread rumors and other forms of misinformation. This phenomenon has correspondingly attracted research attention. One stream of work deals with identifying rumors in online messages. Here, [16] developed and compared classifiers to predict whether images on Twitter about Hurricane Sandy were real or doctored. In so doing, they demonstrated that machine learning techniques could be used to identify fake images that may fuel rumors. Likewise, [17] investigated factors in online social networks that influenced judgments of information credibility. Using these results, they developed an automated method to identify and rank credible information sources and users for any given topic.

Another stream of work concerns the effectiveness of counter-rumors to curtail the dissemination of rumors. For example, [18] examined the effect of exposure to counter-rumors on people's decision to spread rumors in social media. They found that when people were exposed to counter-rumors before rumors, they were more likely to stop the spread of rumors than when the converse was true. Next, [2] showed that appropriate message design could reduce the spread of health-related rumors on social media. This included the use of warnings that the content has appeared in rumor websites and presenting counter-rumors generated by other users and sources.

While such research advances knowledge, one gap present is the relative lack of work done in analyzing the actual content of rumor and counter-rumors. We argue that understanding the nature of such content would lead to a better ways of curtailing the spread of false information.

3   Methodology

3.1   Background: The Rumored Death of Lee Kuan Yew

The death of an important political leader can significantly impact a country's social fabric and its economy. Unsurprisingly, there have been may instances where false rumors of the deaths of leaders have spread quickly, including Barack Obama and Kim Jong-Un. If left uncorrected, such rumors may have negative effects.

In this paper, we study the rumored death of Singapore's first Prime Minister, Lee Kuan Yew. In February 2015, Lee was admitted to Singapore General Hospital for treatment for severe pneumonia. Rumors of his passing began circulating on social media as his conditioned worsened. Things came to a head on 18 March 2015, when a doctored screen capture of an official announcement of his death, purportedly issued from the Prime Minister's Office (PMO), went viral on social media. The fake announcement stated that Lee, aged 91, had passed away at the Singapore General

Hospital on 5.30 pm that day. As the screen capture resembled official press released from the PMO, it misled many, including the foreign news media, who prematurely reported Lee's passing. Soon after this incident, the PMO responded that the press release was fake. Subsequent police investigations revealed the culprit of the doctored screen capture to be a 16 year old student.

3.2 Data Collection

The dataset for this study was drawn from Twitter, the popular microblogging website for disseminating information and increasingly, for scholarly inquiry into communicative behaviour [19] such as rumor research. Tweets from 17 March 2015 to 20 March 2015 (inclusive) were harvested using customized software. Specifically, those with the hashtags #LeeKuanYew and #LKY were downloaded, leading to a sample of 4321 tweets distributed across the four days as depicted in Table 1.

Table 1. Distribution of tweets used in the study.

Date	Quantity	Percentage
17 March 2015	20	0.46
18 March 2015	3135	72.55
19 March 2015	829	19.19
20 March 2015	337	7.80

The rationale for selecting the four days are as follows: As news of Lee's worsening health condition was publicized in the news, people began sharing their concerns, well-wishes, and rumors on Twitter. This online expression reached its peak on 18 March 2015 [20]. On that same day, the fake announcement of Lee's death was released at 2000 h, which led to further spikes in tweets. Soon, a local news channel (ChannelNewsAsia) announced that it had verified that the image was fake and debunked the rumor. Other correction tweets sent out by the local newspaper (The Straits Times) were retweeted widely too. The rumor messages eventually began subsiding around 2300 h on the same day, and eventually tailed off a few days after. We hence selected 18 March to collect the tweets, as well as 17 March and 19–20 March, which were the days before and after the main rumor event respectively.

3.3 Coding and Analysis

All tweets were analyzed and coded via an iterative procedure common in content analysis [21]. The unit of analysis was a tweet. First, each comment was classified based on categories derived from earlier rumor studies including [22, 23]. Second, for those not classifiable into these categories, we inductively constructed new categories by identifying similarities across entries and coding them into logical groupings [24]. This addition of new categories required that entries that were previously categorized be reviewed to check if they needed to be reclassified. This process was repeated till all comments could be consistently categorized. Categories and their definitions were recorded in a codebook where they were fully explained to coders. The final set of categories and their definitions are presented in Table 2.

In the present study, three coders were independently involved in the content analysis procedure, and the final intercoder reliability using Cohen's kappa was found to be 0.96. This value is above the recommended average [21].

Table 2. Categories of tweets (n = 4321).

Category	Description	Frequency (%)
Rumor oriented statements		
Belief	Expressing one's belief in the rumor	868 (20.1)
Providing Information	Including information relevant to the rumor	219 (5.9)
Personal Involvement	Describing one's experiences in the context of the rumor	208 (4.8)
Apprehensive	Expressions of fear, anxiety, dread or apprehension	53 (1.2)
Prudent	Cautionary statements used to qualify "hearsay"	21 (0.5)
Counter-rumor oriented statements		
Refutation	Providing evidence to refute the rumor	1009 (23.3)
Disbelief	Expressing one's disbelief in the rumor	612 (14.2)
Guide	Suggesting a course of action to refute rumor	267 (6.2)
Sarcastic	Ridiculing others' beliefs or comments that support the rumor	140 (3.2)
Interrogatory	Asking questions about the rumor	9 (0.2)
Others		
Uncodable	Content that is not related to the rumor or spam	454 (10.5)
Appreciation	Giving appreciation	427 (9.9)

4 Results

Table 2 divides the categories uncovered into three groups: those that fuelled the rumor, those that attempted to counter the rumor, and those that did not belong to the former two. In addition, Table 3 shows the distribution of categories within the rumor group while Table 4 shows the distribution for the counter-rumor group. A description of these categories is presented in the following paragraphs, together with excerpts from relevant tweets.

Within the categories that were rumor oriented statements, it was unsurprising that the largest number of tweets belonged to the Belief category. This comprised 20.1% of all tweets in our analyzed dataset as well as 63% among all rumor tweets. Essentially, these tweets indicated the person's belief that the rumor was true, that indeed, Lee Kuan Yew had passed away. It would appear therefore that those who generated such tweets believed that the doctored image was from the PMO. These tweets contained prayers, well-wishes or hope for Lee. Examples of tweets include "*Wishes from [name*

Table 3. Distribution of rumor tweets (n = 1369).

Category	Description	Frequency (%)
Belief	Expressing one's belief in the rumor	868 (63.4)
Providing Information	Including information relevant to the rumor	219 (15.9)
Personal Involvement	Describing one's experiences in the context of the rumor	208 (15.2)
Apprehensive	Expressions of fear, anxiety, dread or apprehension	53 (3.9)
Prudent	Cautionary statements used to qualify "hearsay"	21 (1.5)

Table 4. Distribution of counter-rumor tweets (n = 2037).

Category	Description	Frequency (%)
Refutation	Providing evidence to refute the rumor	1009 (49.5)
Disbelief	Expressing one's disbelief in the rumor	612 (30.0)
Guide	Suggesting a course of action to refute rumor	267 (13.1)
Sarcastic	Ridiculing others' beliefs or comments that support the rumor	140 (6.9)
Interrogatory	Asking questions about the rumor	9 (0.4)

removed] (-; #LeeKuanYew", "praying really hard for #LeeKuanYew am really worried. hear that his condition has worsened", "Our thoughts go out to #LeeKuanYew and his family. #LKY. #GetWellSoonMrLee", and "May you RIP, and you will be missed. #LeeKuanYew").

The next two largest categories in this group were Providing Information (5.9% of all tweets; 15.2% of rumor tweets) and Personal Involvement (4.8%; 15.2%). The former refers to tweets that include information relevant or in support of the rumor. Here, the majority of tweets quoted from various sources including traditional media outlets and non-traditional ones such as blogs and other online platforms. In particular, to support the notion that Lee had passed away, the tweets focused on verified information that he had been ill preceding the death announcement. Examples include a retweet from another user "MM Lee's condition has deteriorated further" and a retweet from a new source "Former prime minister #LeeKuanYew is critically ill, condition has deteriorated". The Personal Involvement category refers to tweets that describe the person's involvement with the rumor. Unlike Providing Information, this category contained information from an individual's perspective, leading to a more personal touch. For example, a user tweeted a photo of people keeping vigil at the hospital (Singapore General Hospital - SGH) where Lee was, "The surreal scene at SGH tonight. Eating. Drinking. Waiting. Repeat. #LeeKuanYew [link removed]".

The remaining categories in this group of rumor oriented statements were small in number, with each comprising about 1% or less of the entire analyzed dataset:

- Apprehensive tweets (1.2%; 3.9%) expressed a range of negative emotions such as fear, dread and anxiety over the death of Lee. In particular, concerns were about the future of Singapore, as Lee had been instrumental in building the country (*"without him, I'm scared for our future"*).

- Prudent tweets (0.5%; 1.5%) were those that expressed caution while providing information related to the rumor. This sense of hesitancy was probably appropriate given the momentous event in the country's history. For example, a user claimed that there was an announcement from the PMO's office about Lee's death, but was unsure about its existence *"There is a photo being circulated on the PMO website about #LKY. Until I see it up on the site, I'm unable to verify if photo is real"*.

In terms of counter-rumor oriented statements, the largest category belonged to Refutation tweets and it was also the largest among all our uncovered categories at 23.3% of the dataset as well as 49.5% of all counter-rumor tweets. Essentially, these tweets attempted to debunk the rumor of Lee's death by providing various forms of evidence, such as retweeting content from various traditional and new media sources. Examples include *"RT @STcom: PMO lodging police report about fake website announcing death of Mr Lee Kuan Yew [link removed] #LeeKuanYew"* and *"#Lee-KuanYew is dead according to this #PMO website screengrab sent to Redwire. Hoax? Yes says the PMO. Cops notified. [link removed]"*. Closely related to Refutation was the Disbelief category which comprised tweets expressing skepticism about the rumor. This was the second largest counter-rumor category at 14.2% of the entire dataset and 30% of counter-rumors. However, unlike the former category, the tweets here did not provide evidence from other sources but were more personal in terms of expression. One example would be: *"1. LKY is not dead yet. 2. Stop saying he is dead. 3. If you have nothing better to say about him, don't say. #LeeKuanYew"*.

Next, the Guide category (6.2%; 13.1%) referred to tweets which provided instructions or advice to others about refuting the rumor of Lee's death. Put differently, such tweets went beyond providing evidence of the false rumor and included a call to action for stopping its dissemination. An example of this category is a plea from a user *"Kindly do not spread rumours about Mr #LeeKuanYew. The image that is spreading is edited from that of Mrs #LKY. [link removed]"* while another tweeted *"He's a person. The media does not pronounce him dead, a doctor does. Until then, stop jumping the gun. #LKY"*.

The Sarcastic category (3.2%; 6.9%) contained tweets that ridiculed other users and tweets that supported the rumor of Lee's death. Perhaps users were frustrated or concerned about the spread of the false rumor and poured scorn on those that believed it. Examples include *"Fail. @[name removed] falls for a hoax. #LeeKuanYew"* and *"This is how rumors get around. Blind leading the blind. Ugh."*. Finally, Interrogatory tweets (0.2%; 0.4%) were questions seeking more information about the rumor. A typical example included "Serious, did #LeeKuanYew die?" Given the uncertainty surrounding Lee's death, the number of questions asked was surprisingly small.

There were also two categories that did not belong to either the rumor or counter-rumor category that were uncovered during our analysis. First, the Appreciation category comprised tweets that were thankful of Lee's sacrifices and contributions towards nation-building such as *"Thankful for Mr #LeeKuanYew. Some people devote a specific period to doing something, this man devoted his life"* and even a simple hash tag *"#ThankYouLKY"*. It should be noted that these tweets neither supported that Lee had passed away or not, but that this rumor reminded them of his work for the country. Second, the Uncodable category (10.5%) consisted of tweets that were spam, not meaningful, or not related to the rumor. Examples include a context-less "*#LKY*", punctuation/special characters or links to irrelevant websites.

5 Discussion

The primary objective of the present study was to uncover the types content generated by the online community arising from a rumor. We used the rumored death of a Singapore politician, Lee Kuan Yew, as the context of our work and analyzed 4321 tweets harvested from Twitter. Our results yielded the following insights.

First, our analysis showed that there were more counter-rumor messages than rumor messages. The former comprised 47.14% of the dataset while the latter totaled 31.7%. This corroborates with prior work that online communities have the potential to correct misinformation [5] through counter-rumors. Our dataset indicates that as rumor oriented messages started circulating on Twitter in response to the fake announcement of Lee's death, other users began posting tweets to stop the rumor. These counter-rumor messages were predominantly of the Refutation category where evidence from local news reports were quoted to dissuade those who wrongly believed in Lee's death. At the same time, users also posted tweets belonging to the Guide category, telling others that the rumor was false and that they should not circulate such content further (e.g. "*What's this fake news being circulated about Mr #LeeKuanYew passing away? Pls DONT post anything unless you're V V sure.*"). There were also other users who were frustrated with the rumor-mongering despite the evidence and resorted to posting tweets in the Sarcastic category to insult those who perpetuated the rumor (e.g. "So many dumb people that believe he's dead. #LeeKuanYew"). In sum, the fact that there Twitter users who actively posted various types of messages to debunk and stop the false rumor of Lee's death bodes well for the use of social media to disseminate counter-rumors.

Next and on a related note, our study highlights the importance of source credibility in the use of counter-rumors [25]. In particular, Twitter users who posted messages to debunk Lee's rumored death extensively retweeted from local news outlets such as the Straits Times (newspaper) and ChannelNewsAsia (TV news channel), which are considered authoritative and credible in the Singapore context. It would seem that by doing so, the hope was that people's perceptions could be shaped to achieve corrective behavior, that is, the curtailment of the rumor. Ironically, it was the foreign news outlets that wrongly believed in the fake announcement and prematurely reported Lee's demise. Unsurprisingly, a number of tweets belonging to the Sarcastic category were directed at them (e.g. "*Can't believe [news outlet name removed] is so dumb not to verify the source #Singapore #LKY*"). This finding also suggests that online users are able to distinguish between real and fake information even if the sources appear credible.

Lastly, our analysis reveals an interesting observation that counter-rumor messages were largely evidence-based while rumor messages were mostly personal opinions. This is seen in Table 2 where Refutation was the biggest counter-rumor category, while

Belief was the biggest rumor category. As mentioned previously, Refutation messages provided evidence (e.g. *"RT @[name removed]: China's CCTV official weibo apologises for unverified news update on #LeeKuanYew. [link removed]"*) from credible sources while Belief messages contained expressions that indicated that the rumor was true without any evidence (e.g. *"RIP…. You will be dearly missed. #LeeKuanYew"*). Put differently, counter-rumor messages were factually driven while rumor messages were emotionally driven. This finding lends support to prior work [26, 27] that emotions such as anxiety fuel rumor transmission, but also extends such work that counter-rumor transmission is primarily evidence-based.

6 Conclusion

We contribute to the understanding of how online communities respond to a rumor by analyzing the content created on Twitter. In particular, we uncovered the various categories of rumor and counter-rumor messages that were posted, and show that online users do attempt to correct falsehoods with appropriate evidence from credible and authoritative sources. Stated differently, counter-rumor messages were primarily factual in nature, in contrast to rumor messages which were driven by personal opinions, hearsay and emotions.

One practical implication of our work is that social media platforms such as Twitter are viable outlets to disseminate counter-rumor messages. If organizations and individuals involved in such activities make a concerted effort in releasing these messages on social media, other interested users will eventually retransmit them to their social networks. In so doing, the rumor may eventually be quelled. Further, our results also suggest that it would be helpful to identify social media users who are active contributors, and who are inclined to assist debunking rumors. By tapping on their social networks, counter-rumor messages can be more easily disseminated. In addition, it would appear that those users who are likely to aid in discrediting rumors are discerning in terms of the content they read. Therefore, it would be appropriate that counter-rumor messages are factual and informative in nature, rather than emotionally charged.

There are some shortcomings that could limit the generalizability of our findings. First, only one microblogging site, Twitter, was examined. Users of other microblogs might have different usage patterns requiring separate investigations. On a related note, only one death hoax (albeit a significant one) was studied – that of Lee Kuan Yew. Other individuals or rumor events may yield different types of content generated. Further, our results are constrained by data (tweets) that is openly available on Twitter and without any clarifications with the tweet creators. For future research, our study could be extended by examining other events such as natural disasters, health crises, organizational crises, and draw comparisons of rumors and counter-rumors across each type. Further, extending this study to other types of social media platforms such as Facebook would be helpful. Next, it would be worthwhile to investigate how the rumor and counter-rumor messages actually spread across individuals' social networks. Finally, while we studied rumor and counter-rumor messages from the perspective of the content creators, it would also be useful to study the perspective of the content consumers, and understand the impact of such messages on opinion and behavior.

Acknowledgement. This work was supported by the Ministry of Education Research Grant AcRF Tier 2 (MOE2014-T2-2-020).

References

1. Bordia, P., DiFonzo, N., Haines, R., Chaseling, E.: Rumors denials as persuasive messages: effects of personal relevance, source, and message characteristics. J. Appl. Soc. Psychol. **35**, 1301–1331 (2005)
2. Ozturk, P., Li, H., Sakamoto, Y.: Combating rumor spread on social media: the effectiveness of refutation and warning. In: Proceedings of the Hawaii International Conference on System Sciences, pp. 2406–2414. IEEE Press (2015)
3. Donovan, P.: How idle is idle talk? One hundred years of rumor research. Diogenes **54**, 59–82 (2007)
4. Shklovski, I., Palen, L., Sutton, J.: Finding community through information and communication technology in disaster response. In: Proceedings of the 2008 ACM Conference on Computer Supported Cooperative Work, pp. 127–136. ACM Press (2008)
5. Starbird, K., Maddock, J., Orand, M., Achterman, P., Mason, R.M.: Rumors, false flags, and digital vigilantes: misinformation on Twitter after the 2013 Boston Marathon Bombing. In: Proceedings of iConference 2014 (2014)
6. Nyhan, B., Reifler, J.: When corrections fail: the persistence of political misperceptions. Polit. Behav. **32**, 303–330 (2010)
7. Schwarz, N., Sanna, L.J., Skurnik, I., Yoon, C.: Metacognitive experiences and the intricacies of setting people straight: implications for debiasing and public information campaigns. Adv. Exp. Soc. Psychol. **39**, 127–161 (2007)
8. DiFonzo, N., Bordia, P.: Rumor Psychology: Social and Organizational Approaches. American Psychological Association, Washington, DC (2007)
9. Oh, O., Agrawal, M., Rao, H.R.: Community intelligence and social media services: a rumor theoretic analysis of tweets during social crises. MIS Q. **37**, 407–426 (2013)
10. Bernard, S., Bouza, G., Piétrus, A.: An optimal control approach for E-rumor. Revista Investigacion Operacional **36**, 108–114 (2014)
11. Tripathy, R.M., Bagchi, A., Mehta, S.: A study of rumor control strategies on social networks. In: Proceedings of the 19th ACM International Conference on Information and Knowledge Management. ACM Press (2010)
12. Rosnow, R.L.: Communications as cultural science. J. Commun. **24**, 26–38 (1974)
13. DiFonzo, N., Bordia, P., Rosnow, R.L.: Reining in rumors. Org. Dyn. **23**, 47–62 (1994)
14. Kimmel, A.J.: Rumors and Rumor Control. Lawrence Erlbaum Associates, Mahwah (2004)
15. Kimmel, A.J., Audrain-Pontevia, A.: Analysis of commercial rumors from the perspective of marketing managers: rumor prevalence, effects, and control tactics. J. Mark. Commun. **16**, 239–253 (2010)
16. Gupta, A., Lamba, H., Kumaraguru, P., Joshi, A.: Faking sandy: characterizing and identifying fake images on Twitter during hurricane sandy. In: Proceedings of the 22nd International Conference on World Wide Web, pp. 729–736. ACM Press (2013)
17. Canini, K.R., Suh, B., Pirolli, P.L.: Finding credible information sources in social networks based on content and social structure. In: 2011 IEEE Third International Conference on Social Computing, pp. 1–8. IEEE Press (2011)
18. Tanaka, Y., Sakamoto, Y., Matsuka, T.: Toward a social-technological system that inactivates false rumors through the critical thinking of crowds. In: Proceedings of the 46th Hawaii International Conference on System Sciences, pp. 649–658. IEEE Press (2013)

19. Kwak, H., Lee, C., Park, H., Moon, S.: What is Twitter, a social network or a news media? In: Proceedings of the 19th International Conference on World Wide Web. ACM Press (2010)
20. Lin, Z., Pazos, R., Benites, Y.: 1923–2015 Lee Kuan Yew: How the Twittersphere reacted to the news (2015). http://leekuanyew.straitstimes.com/ST/recap/index.html. Accessed 5 Aug 2015
21. Neuendorf, K.A.: The Content Analysis Guidebook. Sage Publications, Thousand Oaks (2002)
22. Bordia, P., DiFonzo, N.: Problem solving in social interactions on the internet: rumor as social cognition. Soc. Psychol. Q. **67**, 33–49 (2004)
23. Pendleton, S.C.: Rumor research revisited and expanded. Lang. Commun. **18**, 69–86 (1998)
24. Heit, E.: Properties of inductive reasoning. Psychon. Bull. Rev. **7**, 569–592 (2000)
25. Oh, O., Kwon, K.H., Rao, H.R.: An exploration of social media in extreme events: rumour theory and Twitter during the Haiti earthquake 2010. In: Proceedings of the International Conference in Information Systems (2010)
26. Allport, F., Lepkin, M.: Wartime rumors of waste and special privilege: why some people believe them. J. Abnorm. Soc. Psychol. **40**, 3–36 (1945)
27. Liu, F., Burton-Jones, A., Xu, D.: Rumors on social media in disasters: extending transmission to retransmission. In: Proceedings of the 18th Pacific Asia Conference on Information Systems (2014)

Automatic Discovery of Abusive Thai Language Usages in Social Networks

Suppawong Tuarob$^{(\boxtimes)}$ and Jarernsri L. Mitrpanont

Faculty of Information and Communication Technology,
Mahidol University, Salaya, Thailand
suppawong.tua@mahidol.edu, jarernsri.mit@mahidol.ac.th

Abstract. Social networks have become a standard means of communication that allows a massive amount of users to interact and consume information anywhere and anytime. In Thailand, millions of users have access to social networks, a majority of which include young children. The colloquial nature of social media inherently encourages certain expressions of language that do not conform to the standard, some of which may be considered abusive and offensive. Such ill-mannered language fashion has become increasingly used by a large number of Thai social media users. If these abusive languages are exposed to adolescents without proper guidance, they could compulsorily develop a familiar attitude towards such language styles. To address the issue, we present a set of algorithms based on machine learning, that automatically detect abusive Thai language in social networks. Our best results yield 86% f-measure (88.73% precision and 83.53% recall).

Keywords: Abusive language detection · Thai natural language processing · Large scale social networks

1 Introduction

Social networks such as Twitter, Facebook, and Google+ have become a norm for colloquial communication when face-to-face interaction is unavailable. A wide variety of social media services are currently and publicly available with diverse purposes and target users. In 2017, 20.4 millions Facebook users in Thailand are reported active[1]. This number is expected to grow to 21.6 millions by 2018. With colloquial settings in nature, social networks house various dimensions of communication, ranging from organizations' official channels to groups of cyberbullies. Oftentimes, language usages in social networks not only deviate from the standard language usages (e.g. emoticons, undefined terms, broken grammars, incomplete sentences, etc.), but also are not well-mannered and inappropriate. We call such dialect *abusive languages*.

In Thailand, existence of abusive languages in social networks is considered normal. Messages like "กูขับรถจะชนแล้วเนี่ย" (equivalent to ''Shit! I'm about

---

[1] https://www.statista.com/statistics/490467/number-of-thailand-facebook-users/.

© Springer International Publishing AG 2017
S. Choemprayong et al. (Eds.): ICADL 2017, LNCS 10647, pp. 267–278, 2017.
https://doi.org/10.1007/978-3-319-70232-2_23

to hit that fucking car.'') and "นักเรียนโรงเรียนนี้สันดานเสียกันทุกคนเลยว่ะ"
(equivalent to ''Every single kid in this school is retarded!'') are
ubiquitous and frequently used to communicate among certain groups of users,
especially teenagers. If such abusive language is exposed to adolescents without
proper advice, they will generally have familiar attitude towards such language
fashions, and eventually treat abusive usages of language a standard of practice.
In Thailand, this problem has become aggravate, mainly due to the following
problems:

1. **Lack of effective automated abusive language screening tools.** Unlike
   English, natural language processing techniques for Thai are still experimental and under research investigation [15]. Most of the available Thai NLP
   tools deal with primitive computational linguistic tasks such as chunking [3]
   and tokenization [12]. For abusive language screening, existing methods have
   used keyword look-up techniques to detect impolite words in a given message. These techniques, however, only work if a message explicitly contains
   an impolite word defined in the dictionary–they are unable to detect messages containing distorted versions of rude words, and those whose meaning
   are offensive.
2. **Lack of empathy and sense of appropriateness.** Harsh and offensive
   language is ubiquitous in social networks in Thailand, compared to other
   developed countries. A potential cause may be the lack of empathy and sense
   of responsibility. Offensive and hate speeches are often used among certain
   groups of social media users.
3. **Lack of parental guidance.** While many social media services impose
   restrictions on users' ages, such rules are hard to reinforce in Thailand. It
   is normal to see young children on Facebook, without parental guidance. As
   a result, young children are often prematurely exposed to inapposite content
   in social media, that potentially shape their understanding of appropriateness
   of language usage in the public domain.

The problem of automatic Thai abusive language detection is framed as a
text classification problem, where a message is classified whether it contains
abusive content or not. Existing methods check each message for existence of
inappropriate keywords, defined in the dictionary. However, such methods are
only applicable for messages composed with explicit, inappropriate words. While
social media users are creative at distorting original forms of words, directly
detecting inappropriate words that are defined in the dictionary may fail to
capture a wide variety of word alteration. Furthermore, Thai natural language
technology still falls short when it comes to semantic processing; hence, methods
that detect offensive messages (in terms of meaning) remain yet to exist. Here,
we propose to address this problem using machine learning based techniques
where a machine learner is trained with term features. Different term weighting
schemes are explored including binary, term frequency (TF), inverse document
frequency (IDF), and TF-IDF. The best results are achieved by the Discriminative Multinomial Naive Bayes classification algorithm trained with inverse
document frequency features.

In summary, this paper has the following key contributions:

1. We study real-world examples of and present a classification scheme for inappropriate usages of Thai language in social networks.
2. We present a set of text classification algorithms for automatic discovery of messages composed with inappropriate Thai language.
3. We empirically validate and compare the efficacy of the classification algorithms using standard information retrieval experimental protocols.
4. We make the labelled dataset available for others to use for research purposes.

2 Background and Related Works

With rapid growth of social media availability and user base, concerns have arisen that involve the control policy of inappropriate contents, especially when they are a few clicks away from being exposed to children. In this section, we review existing works related to ours.

2.1 Automatic Abusive Language Detection

Methods for detecting abusive language usages have evolved rapidly in the past decade. However, most of the methods are developed specially for English language and/or require specific information that not all social media services can provide. Razavi et al. framed the abusive language detection problem into a classification problem where each social media message is first translated into a word vector [18]. Two feature selection layers are applied. The first layer employs the NaiveBayes classifier to assign a discriminative weight to each feature, then roughly 1,700 features, ranked by the weights, are selected. The second feature selection layer first adds probability-based auxiliary feature sets, and employs the Multinomial Updatable NaiveBayes classifier to select top important features. Then, a rule-based classifier [11] is trained to predict whether a message is *Okay* or *Flame*. While the proposed method sounds promising, the choice of feature extraction and selection algorithms are quite arbitrary without supporting and empirical reasoning. Further, their method was evaluated on a dataset of merely 1,525 messages with only 32% positive samples. Such a small dataset may not well capture wide variety of language styles in social media, whose noise and colloquialism are norm.

To remedy the sparseness of social media data, works have attempted to use contextual information to improve the classification performance. Dadvar et al. showed that context information of social media users such as comment history and user characteristics can improve detection of cyber-bullying content, compared to using the information from the message content alone [9]. Since we assume that a social media message contains only the textual content without any user information, their method would not be applicable to our problem. Burfoot and Baldwin experimented with multiple feature scaling methods, such as binary feature weight and bi-normal separation feature scaling [10], to train a

SVM classifier to classify a newswire article whether it is satirical or not [6]. The features extracted from an article include those from the headline and verbal quotes, which are assumed to be available in all articles. Their method is specifically crafted for newswire articles whose lengths and features are not compatible with social media messages (social media messages do not have headlines and verbal quotes), hence would not be applicable to our problem.

Another dimension of approaches to detect abuse in language usages would be to employ the knowledge from linguistic features. Chen et al. proposed the Lexical Syntactic Feature (LSF) architecture to detect offensive content and identify potential offensive users in social networks [7]. Warner and Hirschberg used a SVM classifier to learn the characteristics of hate speeches from their sentence structures [23]. Nobata et al. also presented a machine learning strategy that detects hate speeches, derogatory, and profanity in online user-generated content [16]. Besides n-grams features, they introduced English based linguistic and syntactic features to the feature space. Recently, Xu and Zhu proposed a method that analyzes each sentence in a textual document using English based parse trees, to identify sentences that are offensive [16]. While showing promising results, these methods were designed for English text only, and hence would not be applicable to our problem, where candidate messages are composed in Thai.

3   Methodology

The abusive Thai language detection in social media is transformed into a classification problem where a social media message is classified as positive if its content is offensive, and negative otherwise. A message is represented with a vector of feature values, each of which represents the weight of the corresponding term. All the distinct terms are collected from all the messages and stored in the dictionary. In this work, we experiment on multiple term weighting schemes, namely binary, term frequency (TF), inverse document frequency (IDF), and term frequency-inverse document frequency (TF-IDF). Featurized training data is then used to train machine learning based classifiers, drawn from diverse families of classification algorithms.

3.1   Term Weighting Schemes

Different term weighting schemes are considered. Since literature on Thai social media text is very limited, making it difficult to inherit any findings on efficient term weighting schemes that work best for the Thai social media setting. This section describes different term weighting schemes we explore. Let $\mathbb{S}$ be the set of training messages, $V = \langle v_1, ..., v_M \rangle$ be the vocabulary extracted from $\mathbb{S}$, t be the test message, and $F(t) = \langle f_1, ..., f_M \rangle$ be the feature vector of the test message t. We define the weighting schemes as follows:

Binary Weight. The binary weighting scheme is the simplest representation of term vectors. The feature value is 1, if the corresponding term appears in the message, and 0 otherwise. Regardless of its simplicity, the binary term weighting scheme may disregard the length of the document when terms are duplicated. For example, the message ``Well, well, well... There there. lol lol lol'' will produce the same binary term vector as the message ``Well, there. lol''. Mathematically,

$$f_i^{bin} = \begin{cases} 1 \ if \ v_i \in t \ and \ v_i \in V \\ 0 \qquad otherwise \end{cases}$$

Where f_i^{bin} is the binary value of the term v_i.

Term Frequency (TF). The term frequency weighting scheme counts the occurrences of each term in the message, hence taking the length of the message into account even when terms are duplicated. Mathematically,

$$f_i^{freq} = TF(v_i, t)$$

Where f_i^{freq} is the TF value of the term v_i, and $TF(v_i, t)$ is the number of occurrences of term v_i in message t.

Inverse Document Frequency (IDF). The IDF term weighting scheme is similar to the binary scheme, except that the value of each term is determined by its *meaningfulness* with respect to the corpus. The meaningfulness of a term has an inverse relationship with the number of documents it appears in. Formally, the IDF term weighting scheme is defined as:

$$f_i^{idf} = \begin{cases} log \frac{|S|}{1+|s \in S: v_i \in s|} \ if \ v_i \in t \\ \qquad 0 \qquad otherwise \end{cases}$$

Where f_i^{idf} is the IDF value of the term v_i.

Term Frequency-Inverse Document Frequency (TF-IDF). While the TF scheme takes frequencies of terms into account, the IDF scheme is able to identify meaningful terms, which are likely to be discriminative features. In order to combine these two schemes, we use the TF-IDF term weighting scheme, defined as:

$$f_i^{tfidf} = \begin{cases} \frac{TF(v_i, t)}{Max(TF(w,t):w \in t)} \cdot log \frac{|S|}{1+|s \in S: v_i \in s|} \ if \ v_i \in t \\ \qquad\qquad 0 \qquad\qquad otherwise \end{cases}$$

Where f_i^{tfidf} is the TF-IDF value of the term v_i. Note that, the term frequency part is normalized by the maximum number of distinct terms so that this portion would range from $[0, 1]$, and would be consistent when combining with the IDF portion.

3.2   Classification Algorithms

Nine classification algorithms are considered, that are drawn from different families of supervised learning algorithms, including *Bernoulli NaiveBayes (NB)* [13], *Discriminative Multinomial Naive Bayes (DMNB)* [19], *Maximum Entropy (MaxEnt)* [14], *Support Vector Machine (SVM)* [4], *k-Nearest Neighbor (kNN)* [1], *Decision Table/Naive Bayes Hybrid (DTNB)* [11], *Random Forest (RF)* [5], *Repeated Incremental Pruning to Produce Error Reduction (RIPPER)* [8], and *C4.5 Decision Tree* [17]. We use LibSVM[2] implementation for SVM, and Weka[3] implementation for the other classifiers.

4   Empirical Study

A empirical study of real-world Facebook[4] comments composed in Thai are used to validate the efficacy of the proposed models. Facebook data is particularly investigated due to its popularity among children and teenagers in Thailand. The next subsections will describe the statistics of the dataset along with the experiments and results.

4.1   Dataset

We use the Facebook Graph API[5] to crawl recent comments from selected Facebook pages, some of which house communities that use abusive languages on regular basis, such as อีเจี๊ยบ เลียบด่วน[6], น้องง[7], สัตว์โลกอมตีน[8], etc. Such pages often expose contents that ignite mass colloquial debates, hence creating an atmosphere that facilitates inappropriate usages of Thai languages.

Each collected social media message is retrieved in a JSON format with additional metadata such as user ID of the poster, message content, message ID, timestamp, and *Like* information. However, since we make a minimal assumption about information that comes with a message, only message content (as in Thai text) is scraped and stored. Each message is tokenized by Classifier-based Thai Word Tokenizer (CTWT)[9] which reported the F-measure of 93% when evaluated on BEST2010 corpus[10], and is the best practical open-source Thai text tokenizer we have tested on social media text in addition to LexTo[11] and BreakIterator[12].

---

[2] http://www.csie.ntu.edu.tw/cjlin/libsvm/.
[3] http://www.cs.waikato.ac.nz/ml/weka/.
[4] https://www.facebook.com/.
[5] https://developers.facebook.com/docs/graph-api.
[6] https://www.facebook.com/ejeab/.
[7] https://www.facebook.com/nongngneverdie/.
[8] https://www.facebook.com/sudlokomteen/.
[9] https://github.com/wittawatj/ctwt.
[10] http://thailang.nectec.or.th/best/?q=node/21.
[11] http://www.sansarn.com/lexto/.
[12] https://docs.oracle.com/javase/7/docs/api/java/text/BreakIterator.html.

Each message is hand-tagged with five labels by five undergraduate students who have solid background in information retrieval. Note that one message may be tagged with multiple labels. Different labels and examples are listed as follows:

Rude: A rude message contains one or more rude words. A rude word is a word that is deemed ill-mannered by itself. Examples of rude words include มึง, กู, เสือก, ตอแหล, ห่า, and their distorted variants. Examples of rude messages include "น้องไปเสือกเฟสคนนี้ด้วย" and " ทำได้แบบกุแล้วค่อยบอกว่ารวยนะคะซิส/ทำปากกู้ เอามือชี้บัตร". Note that a rude message does not necessarily infer hostile intention. Often, rude words are simply used to express informality.

Figurative: A figurative message is a message that uses words or expressions with a meaning that is different from the literal interpretation. Often, such messages contain non-abusive terms that must be interpreted as slang, such as ควาย, ดอก, สัตว์, เตี้ย, แรด, and their distorted variants, to correctly infer the original intention of the message poster. Examples of figurative messages include " มันจะให้เหลือเพจของพวกมันเองสัตว์" and "อีดอก ไหนๆมติก็ผ่านละ เริ่มใช้เลยละกันเนาะ อ๊าา อ๊าอ๊าา #ไทยแลนด์เหนือ".

Offensive: An offensive message may not contain any rude or slang words, but its intention is to offend, threaten, or irritate a person or a group of people. Such messages are often composed with sarcastic and harsh languages. Examples of offensive messages include "ดารารุ่นหลังๆนี้ไร้สาระ ไม่ได้ทำตัวตัวอย่าง แบบอย่างแก่สังคมเอาเสียเลย", "ใครไปรุมทำร้ายมันให้ปากบวมทีเหอะ".

Dirty: A dirty message explicitly invokes sexual interpretation, and normally is embedded with explicit sexual words. Example of such messages include "ชันนัดเปิดกับผู้ชายในเพจเกือบ30คนแล้ว ทายมต่องกัวเขารู้ตัวจริง", "ที่นอนดึกนี่เลี่ยนใช้ไหม". (Note that, the sexually explicit words in the examples are distorted from the original messages for appropriateness.)

Non-Abusive: A non-abusive message is a message that does not fall into the above four abusive categories. Labellers are instructed to tag a message as non-abusive only if the message is safe to be viewed by young children. Example of non-abusive messages include "อยู่กำแพงแสนเหมือนกันเย็น ฉ่าไปเลย", "ดูรูปแล้วได้กลิ่นกระดังงาลอยมาเลยค่ะ".

In this work, we treat rude, figurative, offensive, and dirty messages as *abusive*, so that we can frame the abusive Thai language detection into a binary classification problem (i.e. abusive vs. non-abusive). Table 1 illustrates the statistics of the dataset, categorized by different labels. Among abusive categories, the rude category has the majority of messages. This is intuitive since using rude words in colloquial context has become a common practice for Thai language users. An interesting point to note is that the average length of an abusive message (18.37 words) is longer than that of a non-abusive message (12.78 words) by 44%. We conjecture that abusive language users tend to post comments filled with strong emotions, hence resulting in a longer emotionally descriptive language.

Table 1. Each message is tagged with relevant labels. *Avg. Words* is the average number of words in a message. *SD Words* is the standard deviation of the message lengths. *Note: the total number of *abusive* messages is not the sum of the numbers of messages tagged with abusive labels, since a message can fall into multiple abusive categories.

Label		# of Messages	Avg. Words	SD Words
Abusive	Rude	1,128	20.05	18.83
	Figurative	566	19.23	18.20
	Offensive	226	24.44	20.71
	Dirty	407	18.77	19.55
	Total (Abusive)	*1,997 (57.11%)	18.37	16.81
Non-Abusive		1,500 (42.89%)	12.78	8.84
Total		3,497	15.97	14.23

4.2 Experiment Setup

We prepare four sets of featurized data, each of which uses a different term weighting technique. Standard classification evaluation metrics are used, including precision, recall, and F-measure, that focus on the positive (abusive) class. 10-fold cross validation is used to comprehensively validate the efficacy of each pair of a feature set and a classification model. For each fold, a 10% of the training data (hold-out) is set aside for tuning the classification probability threshold to maximize the F-measure.

4.3 Results and Discussion

To see which term weighting technique would best represent the dataset, all the four feature sets derived from different term weighting techniques (i.e. Binary, TF, IDF, and TFIDF) are tested on each classifier.

Table 2. Comparisons of the classification performance of each classification model trained with different feature sets, in terms of f-measure. *Avg* is the average f-measure of all the classifiers trained with the corresponding feature set.

Term Weighting	NB	DMNB	SVM	MaxEnt	kNN	DTNB	C4.5	RIPPER	RF	Avg
Binary	0.7612	0.8601	0.8359	0.7225	0.4188	0.7103	0.6857	0.7058	0.8524	0.7281
TF	0.7612	0.8601	0.8359	0.7302	0.4188	0.7103	0.6857	0.7023	0.8586	0.7292
IDF	0.7612	0.8601	0.8359	0.7200	0.4188	0.7103	0.6857	0.7219	0.8561	**0.7300**
TFIDF	0.7612	0.8601	0.8359	0.7251	0.4188	0.7103	0.6857	0.7095	0.8524	0.7288

Table 2 enumerates the f-measure rates of different classification models trained with different feature sets. An interesting point to note is that some of the classifiers, namely NB, DMNB, SVM, kNN, DTNB, and C4.5 are not affected

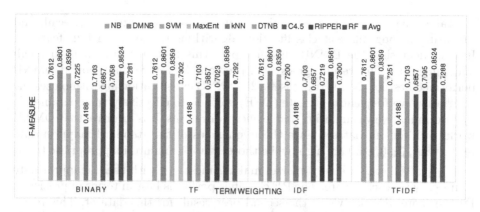

Fig. 1. Bar chart illustration of the classification performance, in terms of f-measure, grouped by term weighting techniques.

by the different term weighting schemes. For NB, DMNB, and DTNB classifiers, the underlying algorithm is Bernoulli Naive Bayes, which is only applicable for binary attributes (and hence would convert non-zero attribute value to 1, resulting in the same feature values as those of binary weighting scheme). For kNN and C4.5 classifiers, since each social media is quite short (16 words on average), it is likely that a message only contains one occurrence of each word that appears in the message. If such an assumption holds, the binary word vector of such a message would be exactly the same as its TF word vector, and would not affect the location of the neighbors (kNN) or the splitting criteria (C4.5) much. Figure 1 illustrates the information in Table 2, and clearly shows that the average f-measure of the IDF features is highest. Hence, we will use the IDF features for further analysis.

Table 3. Comparison of the classification performance of different classification models, trained with IDF features, in terms of precision, recall, f-measure, training time, and testing time. *Note that kNN does not require training process, hence its training time is not considered. *Bold/italic* figures represent the best performance in each metric.

Classifier	Precision	Recall	F-Measure	Training Time (s)	Test Time (ms)
NB	0.7380	0.7867	0.7612	1.94	675.00
DMNB	0.8873	*0.8353*	*0.8601*	*0.00300*	*1.56*
SVM	0.8370	*0.8353*	0.8359	8.44	15.63
MaxEnt	0.6772	0.7693	0.7200	180.22	32.81
kNN	0.6576	0.3080	0.4188	*0	631.25
DTNB	0.8667	0.6327	0.7103	55.96	10.94
C4.5	0.8847	0.5767	0.6857	10.71	1.70
RIPPER	0.8000	0.7113	0.7219	12.27	1.60
RF	*0.8888*	0.8267	0.8561	23.91	279.69

Table 3 compares the classification results in terms of precision, recall, and f-measure among different classification algorithms trained with IDF features. It is evident that the DMNB classifier performs best in terms of both recall and f-measure. This result agrees with previous literature that showed DMNB performed best for their text datasets [2]. DMNB classification algorithm uses the discriminative frequency estimate (DFE) method to effectively tune parameters by discriminatively computing frequencies from terms. It is intuitive that DMNB works well for our dataset since the frequencies of the standard inappropriate terms (e.g., มึง, กู, etc.) are high, while those of non-standard inappropriate terms (e.g., มรึง, กรู, etc.) are very sparse, making messages with these inappropriate terms easy to discriminate. The RF classifier performs best in terms of precision. Furthermore, RF also yields the second best result for this dataset. This result agrees with the previous findings that RF classification algorithm has a built-in automatic feature selection and randomness mechanisms, making it resilient to high-dimensional, sparse data [20–22].

5   Conclusions

Abusive language usages have been a major problem in Thailand. This problem has become exponential with the growth of social media services, that allow a massive pool of users to have access to the online content and interact with each other. Our work presented in this paper is an attempt to automatically discover abusive language usages in large scale social networks. We proposed a machine learning based methodology that automatically classifies a social media message whether it contains abusive content (i.e. rude, figurative, offensive, and dirty) or not. The classifier that implements the Discriminative Multinomial Naive Bayes algorithm, trained with inverse document frequency term features, performs the best with the f-measure of 86%, using a dataset of 3,497 Thai Facebook social media messages. To the best of our knowledge, we are the first to investigate the problem of abusive language detection in Thai language domain, whose natural language processing technology is still in its infancy. As future works, we could test our algorithms on different datasets collected from different social media services. We could also explore the use of the grammatical structure of Thai language to improve the efficacy of the classification.

Acknowledgment. This research project was partially supported by Faculty of Information and Communication Technology, Mahidol University.

References

1. Aha, D.W., Kibler, D., Albert, M.K.: Instance-based learning algorithms. Mach. Learn. **6**(1), 37–66 (1991)
2. Aref, A., Tran, T.: Using ensemble of Bayesian classifying algorithms for medical systematic reviews. In: Sokolova, M., van Beek, P. (eds.) AI 2014. LNCS (LNAI), vol. 8436, pp. 263–268. Springer, Cham (2014). doi:10.1007/978-3-319-06483-3_23

3. Atsawintarangkun, P., Theeramunkong, T., Haruechaiyasak, C.: A statistical and rule-based method for chunking verbal units in thai texts. Thammasat Int. J. Sci. Technol. **17**(2), 70–86 (2012)
4. Bishop, C.M.: Pattern Recognition and Machine Learning. Information Science and Statistics. Springer-Verlag New York, Inc., Secaucus (2006)
5. Breiman, L.: Random forests. Mach. Learn. **45**(1), 5–32 (2001)
6. Burfoot, C., Baldwin, T.: Automatic satire detection: are you having a laugh? In: Proceedings of the ACL-IJCNLP 2009 Conference Short Papers, pp. 161–164. Association for Computational Linguistics (2009)
7. Chen, Y., Zhou, Y., Zhu, S., Xu, H.: Detecting offensive language in social media to protect adolescent online safety. In: 2012 International Conference on Privacy, Security, Risk and Trust (PASSAT) and 2012 International Conference on Social Computing (SocialCom), pp. 71–80. IEEE (2012)
8. Cohen, W.W.: Fast effective rule induction. In: Twelfth International Conference on Machine Learning, pp. 115–123. Morgan Kaufmann (1995)
9. Dadvar, M., Trieschnigg, D., Ordelman, R., de Jong, F.: Improving cyberbullying detection with user context. In: Serdyukov, P., Braslavski, P., Kuznetsov, S.O., Kamps, J., Rüger, S., Agichtein, E., Segalovich, I., Yilmaz, E. (eds.) ECIR 2013. LNCS, vol. 7814, pp. 693–696. Springer, Heidelberg (2013). doi:10.1007/978-3-642-36973-5_62
10. Forman, G.: BNS feature scaling: an improved representation over TF-IDF for SVM text classification. In: Proceedings of the 17th ACM Conference on Information and Knowledge Management, pp. 263–270. ACM (2008)
11. Hall, M.A., Frank, E.: Combining Naive Bayes and decision tables. In: FLAIRS Conference, vol. 2118, pp. 318–319 (2008)
12. Haruechaiyasak, C., Kongthon, A.: Lextoplus: a Thai lexeme tokenization and normalization tool. In: WSSANLP-2013, p. 9 (2013)
13. John, G.H., Langley, P.: Estimating continuous distributions in Bayesian classifiers. In: Eleventh Conference on Uncertainty in Artificial Intelligence, pp. 338–345. Morgan Kaufmann, San Mateo (1995)
14. Le Cessie, S., Van Houwelingen, J.C.: Ridge estimators in logistic regression. Appl. Stat. **41**, 191–201 (1992)
15. Mitrpanont, J., Chongcharoen, P.: Th_wsd: Thai word sense disambiguation using cross-language knowledge sources approach. Int. J. Comput. Theory Eng. **7**(6), 428 (2015)
16. Nobata, C., Tetreault, J., Thomas, A., Mehdad, Y., Chang, Y.: Abusive language detection in online user content. In: Proceedings of the 25th International Conference on World Wide Web, pp. 145–153. International World Wide Web Conferences Steering Committee (2016)
17. Quinlan, J.R.: C4.5: Programs for Machine Learning. Elsevier, San Francisco (2014)
18. Razavi, A.H., Inkpen, D., Uritsky, S., Matwin, S.: Offensive language detection using multi-level classification. In: Farzindar, A., Kešelj, V. (eds.) AI 2010. LNCS (LNAI), vol. 6085, pp. 16–27. Springer, Heidelberg (2010). doi:10.1007/978-3-642-13059-5_5
19. Su, J., Zhang, H., Ling, C.X., Matwin, S.: Discriminative parameter learning for Bayesian networks. In: Proceedings of the 25th International Conference on Machine Learning, pp. 1016–1023. ACM (2008)
20. Tuarob, S., Bhatia, S., Mitra, P., Giles, C.L.: Algorithmseer: a system for extracting and searching for algorithms in scholarly big data. IEEE Trans. Big Data **2**(1), 3–17 (2016)

21. Tuarob, S., Mitra, P., Giles, C.L.: A hybrid approach to discover semantic hierarchical sections in scholarly documents. In: 2015 13th International Conference on Document Analysis and Recognition (ICDAR), pp. 1081–1085. IEEE (2015)
22. Tuarob, S., Tucker, C.S., Kumara, S., Giles, C.L., Pincus, A.L., Conroy, D.E., Ram, N.: How are you feeling? A personalized methodology for predicting mental states from temporally observable physical and behavioral information. J. Biomed. Inform. **68**, 1–19 (2017)
23. Warner, W., Hirschberg, J.: Detecting hate speech on the world wide web. In: Proceedings of the Second Workshop on Language in Social Media, pp. 19–26. Association for Computational Linguistics (2012)

User Behaviors

Effects of Search Tactic on Affective Transition While Using Google: A Quasi-Experimental Study of Undergraduate Students

Songphan Choemprayong[1](✉)(iD) and Thanaphorn Atikij[2](iD)

[1] Behavioral Research Informatics Research Unit, Department of Library Science, Faculty of Arts, Chulalongkorn University, Bangkok, Thailand
songphan.c@chula.ac.th
[2] Department of Psychology, Library Science, and Geography, Faculty of Liberal Arts, Thammasat University, Bangkok, Thailand
th.atikij@gmail.com

Abstract. As emotion plays an essential role during the search process, this study explores the effect of search tactics on emotional transition. Thirty-eight Thai undergraduate students from two large public universities in Bangkok were asked to perform three search tasks using Google. Participants were asked to think aloud while performing the tasks. Semi-structure interviews and direct observation were applied to observe participants' search tactics, based on Smith's Internet Search Tactics model. Using a multilevel hierarchical logistic regression, the results show that Evaluation tactics are positively associated with emotional transition, while File Structure tactics, search success, and task difficulty are negatively associated with emotional transition during search.

Keywords: Emotional state · Search tactic · Affective search · Search engine · Google · Information retrieval

1 Introduction

Emotion is a part of human cognition and behavior. It has helped humans survive and express personalities. For instance, someone who is curious feels satisfaction when he or she discovers the answer to a critical question, perhaps leading to sustain quest for knowledge and a thirst to understand his/her surroundings. Anger may contribute to a drive to overcome obstacles and reach a certain goal, while fear may be associated with cautiousness and thoroughness. Emotions play essential roles in social interactions [33].

Emotion also plays an important role in interaction with information and related tools. Numerous studies found that human interactions with information, from various aspects and viewpoints, are affected by and associated with emotions (e.g., [3,5,15,38]). An increasing number of studies are exploring the roles of emotion in human-information interaction, particularly in the context of

© Springer International Publishing AG 2017
S. Choemprayong et al. (Eds.): ICADL 2017, LNCS 10647, pp. 281–294, 2017.
https://doi.org/10.1007/978-3-319-70232-2_24

searching and retrieving information [10]. The understanding of human affective systems in context can lead to the development of affective computing which enhances the ability of a computer system to recognize and react to human emotions in a more appropriate and natural way. It is expected that affective computing would contribute to more attractive and more satisfying user experiences [20, 24].

Searching is one of the most popular information activities in exploring affective elements. Searching is a critical action to help users finding relevant information and solving information overload condition. The importance of searching has been increasingly essential in an environment where information available online is now ubiquitous and overwhelming. Bates [2] distinguishes between search behavior, search strategy, and search tactics in order to differentiate how these concepts are operationalized. Affective states have been connected to search behavior in multiple perspectives, for example, search stage (e.g., [15]) and search action (e.g., [19]). Lopatovska and Arapakis [20] reviewed relevant literature regarding how various search constructs influence the dynamic of emotion/feelings. These constructs include, for instance, personalized interface features, messages from a computer, computer mouse reaction, usability elements (i.e., ease of use, availability of assistance, navigation, and document style), search task completion and performance, search task difficulty, and prior knowledge and personal interest in the search task. While these search constructs complement the understanding of the relationship between search and emotion, the relationship between affective state and search tactic are less known.

Search tactic is a facilitating and operationalizable construct covering searching cognition, behavior, and action in a more granular level. Search tactic concerns how an individual decides to approach the search within a short time-frame. Bates [2] outlined 29 search tactics grouped into 4 main categories. An example of Bates' search tactic is CORRECT tactic which refers to how a user "watch for and correct spelling and factual errors in one's search topic". The etiological characteristics of these tactics have also been discussed [3]. Smith [35] later revised Bates' classification into 34 tactics. Apparently, applying these search tactics could possibly stimulate emotional response during search session.

Since search tactic concerns a movement in a short period of time and it is assumed that emotion state changes constantly during search session, it would be more appropriate to focus on the transition of emotional state, rather certain emotional state, at this exploratory stage. Therefore, this study particularly aims to investigate the effect of search tactic on the transition of emotional state. As the most popular search engine, this study uses Google search as a context since the participants would have experiences using the system. The findings from this study would help provide recommendations for designers to improve search system as well as for educators to improve training activities and materials.

2   Literature Review

To understand the relationship between affective state and search tactic, this literature review covers the discussion in three areas including: (1) emotional state and its classification, (2) search tactic, and (3) the relationship between emotion and search behavior.

2.1 Emotion and Its Measurement

Emotion has been given various definitions. For example, the Oxford Advanced American Dictionary [26] defines emotion as "a strong feeling" and explains that a decision is dependent on emotion, rather than rational thought (pp. 486–487). Random House Webster's College Dictionary [30] identifies emotion as an affective state of an awareness (p. 403). Emotion can be considered to be experience emerged from self-awareness. It includes feeling and outburst generated from experience.

Emotion can be categorized into multiple states and levels. The classification can be viewed from multiple perspectives. Lopatovska [19] distinguishes between emotion, mood, and feeling and argues that the literature regarding affective information behavior uses various definitions of emotion. Perhaps this may be because these three constructs are complex and, therefore, it is difficult to operationalize them.

In a more concrete approach, Mehrabian [22] identifies two forms of emotion: emotional temperament and emotional state (p. 262). An emotional state can change quickly depending upon different situations. An emotional temperament is a static personality trait that is exhibited over a longer period. It is a fundamental state of a human being that is responding to different situations in his/her life.

Instead of attempting to cover static emotions, this study focuses on emotions as fleeting emotional states. Operationally these are defined as a mental state and physical reaction sensitive to external stimulation in a particular moment. It can be considered as an outcome of human experience expressing through behaviors or actions, whether or not the individual is aware.

To identify an exact expression of emotion is a difficult task [8]. Shiota and Kalat [34] compare the classification of emotion to the classification of color where the mixture of emotion can occur in diverse ways. So far, the measurement of emotions can be achieved via either discrete or dimensional approach [20].

The most primitive classification of emotion divides emotion into positive and negative groups. Positive and Negative Affect Scale (PANAS), one of the most popular emotion measures, is a measure developed corresponding to this approach [37]. There are other classification systems manifesting emotion in a more multidimensional perspective.

For instance, Plutchik [28] categorizes emotion into eight primary categories, including surprise, sadness, disgust, anger, anticipation, joy and trust (p. 56). In this classification scheme, Plutchik also considers emotional intensity, similarity, and polarity in the scheme. Ekman [7] divides emotion into 6 primary categories: fear, anger, disgust, happiness, sadness and surprise. Ekman recognizes other emotions as sub-level categories. In addition, Russell [31] explains emotion as a mixture of emotional constructs within a complex circle of three polarities:

pleasure vs. displeasure (P), arousal vs. non-arousal (A), and dominance vs. submissiveness (D).

One of the most popular classification system of emotion is the Inventory of Emotion by Parrott [27]. Derived from the results of cluster analysis, Parrott's inventory uses emotion terms to divide emotion expressions into 3 hierarchical levels (i.e., primary, secondary, and tertiary emotion). The inventory comprises of 135 terms representing emotional expressions. The primary emotion expressions include: (1) love (including affection, lust/sexual desire, and longing as secondary expressions); (2) joy (including cheerfulness, zest; contentment; pride, optimism, enthrallment, and relief as secondary expressions); (3) surprise (including only surprise as a secondary expression); (4) anger (including irritation, exasperation, rage, disgust, envy, and torment as secondary expressions); (5) sadness (including suffering, sadness, disappointment, shame, neglect, and sympathy as secondary expressions) and; (6) fear (including horror, and nervousness as secondary expressions). The rest of the terms are classified in the tertiary level under secondary expressions. It is apparent that the hierarchical tree-structure of Parrott's inventory can facilitate the operationalization of emotion classification where self-report technique is utilized. Therefore, this study applies Parrott's inventory to classify expressions of emotional state.

2.2   Search Tactic

Search tactic refers to a short-term search action or a temporary finding for a specific item, focusing on a decision to proceed a search action at a certain time. While search tactic and search strategy share a similar goal, to gain access to a desired object or item [11], search tactic is practically different from search strategy. A search tactic can be simply defined as "a move to further the search," while a search strategy is "a plan for the whole search" [2]. In another word, search strategy is a combination of multiple search tactics.

Bates [2] developed Information Search Tactics model. The model covers 29 search tactics, grouped into four categories, including both manual and online search tactics. The four categories include Term tactics, Query Reformulation tactics, Information Structure tactics, and Monitoring tactics.

Smith [35] revised Bates' model to cover emerging search techniques, technologies, and interactions in an online environment. Smith's model comprises of 34 search tactics (eighteen of them are derived from Bates' model) organized into five main search tactics including: (1) Monitoring tactics concerns how a searcher "keep any search on track" using provided tools; (2) File Structure tactics follow provided structure (e.g., URL, directory, and domain name) to look for alternatives; (3) Search Formulation tactics covers different ways in which terms are entered into a search system in the first place; (4) Term tactics refer to how a searcher broaden or narrow search terms using various tools such as directory, thesaurus, or related pages to navigate information; and (5) Evaluation tactics covers various ways for a searcher to judge the quality of search results. Since Smith's model is more relevant to the current context of online searching, this study employed Smith's model in classifying participants' search tactics.

2.3   Emotion and Search Behavior

While none has specifically considered a relationship between emotional transition and search tactics, there are several research studies outlining the relationship between emotion and search behavior in general. The following discussion highlights certain theoretical frameworks and evidences supporting such a relationship.

In her classic Information Search Process model, Kuhlthau [15] found that the duration of search process is associated with searcher's emotion. In addition, emotions or feelings occur throughout all six stages in search process from the beginning till the end, i.e., "uncertainty" in the Initiation process, "optimism" in the Selection process, "confusion," "frustration," or "doubt" in the Exploration process, "clarified" in the Formulation process, "confidence" in the Collection process, and "relief," "satisfaction," or "disappointment" in the Presentation or Completion process.

Emotion has also been discussed throughout Wilson's model of information behavior [38]. The feeling of satisfaction is found to be one of the determinants for an information user to choose a particular channel to seek information (p. 251). In his General Model of Information-Seeking Behavior, Wilson also pointed out that, when one is searching for information, emotion plays an essential role in one's thought and psychological state throughout the search.

In Dervin's Sense-Making [5], emotion is a key element in many aspects in the metaphor. For instance, the feeling of doubt is regarded as one of the initiators for information users to recognize their needs (i.e., "gap"). Additionally, emotion also helps a user decide and it is a component to fulfill the "bridge," [9] in addition to cognition, thought, belief and knowledge.

In Berry-picking model, Bates [3] explains how individuals create their own query for information search. She indicates that the urge of information need is unstable and can always be changed. Individual's searching behavior is viewed as a resembling of gathering berries. Emotional constructs highlighted in this model include, for example, satisfaction with search results, and the feeling of sufficiency of information acquired [11].

On the other hand, emotions are found to be affected by search experience as well as certain properties of information retrieved. Lopatovska and Mokros [21] explored emotions of searchers after reading personal blogs and found that emotional responses, either positive or negative ones, are primarily rooted from document's stylistic properties (e.g. readability), personal interest toward a document. Mooney et al. [23] found, through the detection of physical response, that emotional states can be triggered by utilizing search tools or interacting with an information object such as movie films. Nahl and Tenopir [25] studied novice users' emotions and thoughts on search behavior. They discovered that hesitation, desire to confirm, fear, surprise, and other emotions affect online system search process.

Lopatovska [19] found that certain actions during interaction with a search system may exhibit particular affective states. For example, scroll-up a web page may be negatively associated with fear, while left mouse double-click may be associated with disgust and sadness in a positive direction.

As discussed above, while the causal-effect relationships between emotion in general and search behavior have been widely observed, a micro perspective of such association has yet to be well recognized and may need to be explored to extend the understanding between emotional transition and search behavior in a more specific detail which can be useful for practical and theoretical development.

While a number of search constructs have been observed regarding their influences on emotion, other related factors have found to interact with the relationship between online search and emotion. These factors include perceptions toward search task (i.e., difficulty, familiarity, interest, relevant, and uncertainty) (e.g., [1, 13, 14, 21]), and search task completion and performance (e.g., [4, 36]). In addition, Internet self-efficacy also influence search success and searcher's emotion during completing search tasks [25].

3   Methods

This study applies a quasi-experimental approach which was approved by Chulalongkorn University's Research Ethics Review Committee. The data was collected from January to February 2017. Participants of this study include 38 currently enrolled undergraduate students from two large public universities in Bangkok metropolitan area. Applying a convenient sampling technique, the recruitment ads were posted in numerous spots throughout both campuses. Prior to the beginning of the data collection the participants were asked to provide informed consent.

The participants were asked to perform three search tasks, one at a time. A pre-test evaluation of their emotional state was administered prior to the beginning of the first search task to provide a benchmark. During each search tactic performed, the participants were asked to think aloud their thoughts and emotions. Even though the participants were informed about the Parrott's Inventory of Emotion [27] at the beginning of the study, they were allowed to express emotions in their own terms. The researcher mapped each participant's expression to the Parrott's Inventory of Emotion. The emotion mapping was done by one of the researchers simultaneously as the think aloud protocol was performed. The researcher matched the participant's expression to a closest term in the Inventory, regardless of the emotion hierarchies. For example, emotions such as liking and fondness are considered as the tertiary emotion of love, while satisfaction, delight, and happiness are the tertiary emotions of joy. These tertiary emotions were eventually recoded to their primary emotions. To validate the mapping process, the researcher probed the participant to confirm each chosen emotional state before continuing to the next search action.

In addition to emotions listed in Parrott's Inventory, neutral state was added to an instrument. The result from a pilot study shows that neutral is among one of the most common emotional expressions occurred during search.

For each task, participants were given no more than 20 min to complete their search. The search history was reset after the answers from each task were submitted. There were short breaks in between the three tasks to minimize the possibility of carry-over effect. This study also used Screenpresso for Windows Version 1.5.6, a screen capture program, to monitor activities made on the screen, and Sound Recorder program on Windows to record the subjects' verbal responses.

Since search task is a controlled variable in this study, we developed three search tasks based on Kim's classification of search tasks [12] in conjunction with Ramdeen and Heminger's tasks [29]. The tasks were tested and adjusted to improve face validity during a pilot study. Each search task asks participants to use Google to find appropriate answers. For factual search, the participants were asked to provide one correct answer for a closed question (i.e., provide an author's name). For analytical search, the participants needed to analyze by evaluating and selecting appropriate answers (i.e., select the best weight control technique for oneself). For exploratory search, the participants were provided with an open-ended question (i.e., explore recipes to cook and prepare for a party with a specific theme). Critical evaluation is not required for exploratory search, while it is necessary for analytical search.

The study also collected other search task variables including participants' perceptions toward search task (i.e., task difficulty, complexity, interest, relevance, and uncertainty) collected at the completion of each of the three tasks, search success (in LaPlace ratio, indicating how likely the next search action will succeed) (see [16, 17]), time used for each task, and number of search tactics performed. Participants' variables, including gender, field of study, and level of Internet self-efficacy (ISE), were categorized using a translated Eastin and LaRose's Internet Self-Efficacy Scale [6] (consisting of 8 items on a 7-level Likert scale collected prior to the first task).

In addition, we also observed at what stage a search tactic was performed in reference to the whole search task (i.e., indicating whether a search tactic was performed near the beginning or the end of each search task). These variables were reported as associated factors of either search tactic or emotional state elsewhere (e.g., [1, 12, 18, 32]). All measurement scales for latent variables (e.g., search tactics, Internet self-efficacy, emotional scale) were tested for reliability using Cronbach's Alpha yielding acceptable results ($\alpha > 0.7$).

Since the emotional transition in this study considers only the change of emotional expressions in a primary level, emotion expressions were recoded by comparing expression of emotions on a primary level before and after performing a search tactic, yielding only two values for emotional transition (i.e., changed and unchanged). The emotional transition becomes a dependent variable in this study.

Data were analyzed by using SPSS for Windows Version 24 and Microsoft Excel 2010. Descriptive statistics, such as metrics of frequency, percentage, means, and the measure of association (i.e., Chi-square) were applied. Since the analysis in this study has two units of analysis (participant and search task), a multilevel hierarchical logistic regression (mixed effect) was applied to assess the effect of search tactics on emotional transition controlling for other independent variables. Pearson correlation analysis was performed among all independent variables. The results indicate no strong relationship among all independent variables.

4   Results

4.1   Participants' Characteristics

Consisting of 6 men and 32 women, thirty-eight undergraduate students were recruited to the study. They all completed the three tasks given. Twelve were studying in the sciences, thirteen were studying social science, and another 13 were in humanities disciplines. The median of self-reporting on the Internet Self-Efficacy scale for all participants was 4.81 on an 8-point scale, demonstrating a moderate level of comfort with the Internet.

4.2   Search Tactics

In total, participants performed 1,295 search actions over the course of the three tasks. Since multiple search tactics can occur in one search action, the total number of search tactics counted was 1,744. It was found that Monitoring tactics were performed the most in all three tasks (approximately 47 times per 100 search actions on all search tasks), followed by File Structure tactics (about 31 times per 100 search actions on all search tasks) as shown in Table 1.

Table 1. Distribution of search tactics by search tasks

Tactics	Factual search		Analytical search		Exploratory search		Total (N = 38)	
	f	Ratio[a]	f	Ratio[a]	f	Ratio[a]	f	Ratio[a]
Monitoring	201	48	188	50	226	45	615	47
File Structure	116	28	118	31	167	33	401	31
Search Formulation	101	24	41	11	85	17	227	18
Term	71	17	69	18	100	20	240	19
Evaluation	61	15	110	29	90	18	261	20

[a]This table reports a ratio per 100 search actions since multiple search tactics can be found in a search action.

4.3   Emotional Transition

For emotional transition, we found that the ratios of primary emotional transition per 100 search actions are not much different between changed and unchanged emotional expressions (Table 2). There are about 607 search actions (approximately 53%) that result in changes of emotional states, while 688 search actions (about 47%) yield unchanged emotional states. The analytical search yielded more changed than unchanged emotional states, while the distributions are in the opposite direction for the other two search tasks. However, an ad-hoc Chi-square analysis found no significant relationship between search tasks and emotional transition.

Table 2. Distribution of emotional transition by search tasks

Emotional transition	Factual search		Analytical search		Exploratory search		Total (N = 38)	
	f	%	f	%	f	%	f	%
Unchanged	227	55	181	48	280	56	688	53
Changed	189	45	196	52	222	44	607	47

4.4   The Effect of Search Tactics on Emotional Transition

The result from multilevel hierarchical logistical regression as shown in Table 3 indicates that four factors are associated with emotional transition (1 – emotional

Table 3. Effects of search tactics on emotional transition

Independent variables	Coefficient	p-value
Constant	0.546	0.525
Monitoring tactics	−0.061	0.722
File Structure tactics	−0.380	0.038*
Search Formulation tactics	−0.000	1.000
Term tactics	0.058	0.767
Evaluation tactics	0.555	0.000**
Science major	0.074	0.720
Male	−0.001	0.997
Internet self-efficacy	−0.079	0.452
Task success	−0.530	0.012*
Search time	−0.029	0.248
Task difficulty	−0.144	0.044*
Task complexity	0.001	0.992
Task interest	0.054	0.433
Task relevance	−0.022	0.730
Task uncertainty	0.052	0.579
No. of search actions	0.013	0.414
Stage of search tactics performed	0.018	0.931

*p-value $<.05$
**p-value $<.01$

state is changed; 0 – unchanged) including File Structure tactics ($\beta = -0.380$; $p < .05$), Evaluation tactics ($\beta = 0.555$; $p < .01$), task success ($\beta = -0.530$; $p < .05$), and task difficulty ($\beta = -0.144$; $p < .05$).

From these outcomes we observe that emotional transition is positively influenced when Evaluation tactics are employed and negatively influenced when File Structure tactics are utilized and the search task succeeds and the task is perceived as difficult. In other words, a change of emotional state is likely to emerge when Evaluation tactics are used. On the opposite direction, when File Structures tactics are used, it is likely that emotional state would remain unchanged, particularly when a search task was successful, and the task was perceived as difficult.

Considering the two tactics that significantly influence emotional transition, Table 4 displays the top 10 pairs of pre/post emotional states that occurred when applying File Structure and Evaluation tactics. The pre-emotional state refers to the emotional state before a tactic is deployed, and the post-emotional state refers to the emotional state after a tactic is utilized. The arrow indicates the direction from a pre-emotional state to a post-emotional state.

Table 4. Top 10 pre/post emotional states for File Structure and Evaluation tactics

Pre/post emotional states	File Structure tactics (times)	Pre/post emotional states	Evaluation tactics (times)
Joy→Joy	192	Joy→Joy	87
Sadness→Joy	36	Joy→Sadness	34
Neutral→Neutral	28	Sadness→Joy	16
Fear→Joy	26	Joy→Love	13
Neutral→Joy	16	Joy→Fear	13
Joy→Love	12	Neutral→Joy	10
Anger→Joy	10	Joy→Anger	10
Fear→Fear	6	Neutral→Neutral	9
Surprise→Joy	6	Love→Joy	8

For File Structure tactics, Joy→Joy is by far the most common emotional transition that emerged. It is apparent that other unchanged emotional states are well presented, including Neutral→Neutral and Fear→Fear. Additionally, it is interesting to note that all the rest of pre/post emotional states in the Top 10 are the changes from negative (e.g., Sadness, Fear, Anger) to positive expressions (i.e., Joy and Love).

For Evaluation tactics, unlike File Structure tactics, the number of changed emotional states are more strongly represented in the table. We found only two unchanged emotional states in the Top 10 (i.e., Joy→Joy and Neutral→Neutral). The changed emotional states in the Top 10 include Joy→Sadness, Sadness→Joy, Joy→Love, Joy→Fear, Neutral→Joy, Joy→Anger, and Love→Joy.

5   Conclusion and Discussion

The objective of this study is to explore whether search tactics could influence emotional transition. In this quasi-experimental study, thirty-eight undergraduate students were voluntarily recruited to perform three different search tasks on Google. Controlling for various associated factors, we found that Evaluation tactics are more likely to influence changes of emotional states. On the other hand, File Structure tactics are more likely to influence in the opposite direction (i.e., unchanged emotional state).

To obtain an insight of Evaluation tactics, the following are categorized as Evaluation tactics: (1) CONTEXT (e.g., checking other pages on the site and developing the comprehension of the site as well as judging the authority of site); (2) CROSSCHECK (using other sources to validate information); (3) CACHET (using search tools, such as directories, to look for evidence of pre-evaluation or certification); and (4) AUDITION (using appearance such as graphics, images, writing styles as an indicator of creditability). These tactics may require the user's judgment to decide whether or not s/he found appropriate results. The result of making a judgment could either be favorable or unfavorable to depending on the user's expectations. Therefore, Evaluation tactics are more likely to cause emotional transition. Since there has been no prior empirical observation discussing the relationship between these search tactics and emotion, further research studies should explore how emotions/feelings emerge and change while these particular search tactics are employed.

For File Structure tactics, the tactics in this category include BIBBLE, PROVIDER, URL, HUBSPOKE, FIND, BACKLINK, VALUEADD, SOCIAL-MEDIATE, and TIMETRAVEL. These tactics use various Internet structures such as URL, domain name, links to access further information. They are tactics that, perhaps, are stepping stone to other tactics (e.g., Evaluation tactics). When applying File Structure tactics, users may not set an expectation on the outcomes as they are uncertain about the outcomes. If the result does not meet their expectations, they may just keep looking and do not feel any burden. Therefore, the emotional state while using File Structure tactics tend to be unchanged. However, when they find what they are looking for unexpectedly (i.e., information encountering), this would yield a positive emotional state, as shown in Table 4.

The results in this study would lead to practical recommendations for both system designer as well as information literacy instructors on when and where Evaluation tactics are allowed or helpful. Evaluation tactics do not happen only at the end of each search task, but are distributed throughout search sessions. Search system designers paid attention to how a system communicates with users when Evaluation tactic is employed. For example, positive responding messages should be encouraged and various alternatives and solutions should be provided at the point of Evaluation tactics are used. On the other hand, allowing users to apply File Structure tactics would likely to limit a system to receive affective feedback to the search system. In this case, a search system may exert less effort to collect or analyze transaction data on File Structure tactics to increase the efficiency of system performance.

Based on this study, there are numerous opportunities for future studies to extend understanding of affective elements in information search and retrieval. For instance, since this study relies heavily on a self-report technique for observing emotional states, different observation techniques (e.g., facial expression, voice expression, or electrocardiogram) could help validate the results. Other classification systems of emotion may be applied in order to facilitate categorizing the fluid nature of human emotion. In addition, the pool of participants could also be extended to include the general population.

Most importantly, understanding the stimulus of emotional transition is quite complex since various unobserved factors may influence user's emotional state, such as, room temperature and content displayed on screen. It is very hard to control these external variables even in an experimental setting.

Acknowledgement. This study is supported by the M.L. Joy Nunthiwatcharin grant and the 90th Anniversary of Chulalongkorn University fund (Ratchadaphiseksomphot Endowment fund). The authors would like to thank Pimrumpai Premsmit, Somsak Sriborisutsakul, and Manika Wissessathorn for their valuable comments and suggestions. In addition, we would like to express our gratitude to Nuttirudee Charoenruk for her guidance on statistical analysis and Jennifer Goodman for editorial assistance.

References

1. Arapakis, I., Jose, J., Gray, P.: Affective feedback: an investigation into the role of emotions in the information seeking process. In: Proceedings of the 31st Annual International ACM SIGIR Conference on Research and Development in Information Retrieval, pp. 395–402. ACM (2008). doi:10.1145/1390334.1390403
2. Bates, M.: Information search tactics. J. Am. Soc. Inform. Sci. **30**(4), 205–214 (1979). doi:10.1002/asi.4630300406
3. Bates, M.: The design of browsing and berrypicking techniques for the online search interface. Online Rev. **13**(5), 407–424 (1989). doi:10.1108/eb024320
4. Bilal, D., Kirby, J.: Differences and similarities in information seeking: children and adults as web users. Inf. Process Manag. **38**(5), 649–670 (2002). doi:10.1016/S0306-4573(01)00057-7
5. Dervin, B.: An overview of sense-making: concepts, methods, and results to date. In: ICA Annual Meeting, Dallas, Texas (1983). http://communication.sbs.ohio-state.edu/sense-making/art/artdervin83.html
6. Eastin, M., LaRose, R.: Internet self-efficacy and the psychology of the digital divide. J. Comput. Mediated Commun. **6**(1) (2000). doi:10.1111/j.1083-6101.2000.tb00110.x
7. Ekman, P.: Expression and the nature of emotion. In: Scherer, K., Ekman, P. (eds.) Approaches to Emotion, Chap. 3, pp. 319–344. Psychology Press, New York (1984)
8. Ellis, D., Tucker, I.: Social Psychology of Emotion. Sage, Los Angeles (2015)
9. Fidel, R.: Theoretical constructs and models in information-seeking behavior. In: Human Information Interaction: An Ecological Approach to Information Behavior, pp. 49–82. MIT Press, Cambridge (2012), doi:10.7551/mitpress/9780262017008.001.0001

10. Fourie, I., Heidi, J.: Ending the dance: a research agenda for affect and emotion in studies of information behaviour. In: Proceedings of ISIC: The Information Behaviour Conference. Leeds, 2–5 September 2014. http://www.informationr.net/ir/19-4/isic/isic09.html

11. Hearst, M.: Search User Interfaces. Cambridge University Press, Cambridge (2009). http://searchuserinterfaces.com/

12. Kim, K.S.: Effects of emotion control and task on web searching behavior. Inf. Process. Manag. 44(1), 373–385 (2008). doi:10.1016/j.ipm.2006.11.008

13. Kracker, J.: Research anxiety and students' perceptions of research: an experiment. Part I. Effect of teaching Kuhlthau's ISP model. J. Am. Soc. Inf. Sci. Technol. 53(4), 282–294 (2002). doi:10.1002/asi.10040

14. Kracker, J., Wang, P.: Research anxiety and students' perceptions of research: an experiment. Part II. Content analysis of their writings on two experiences. J. Am. Soc. Inf. Sci. Technol. 53(4), 295–307 (2002). doi:10.1002/asi.10041

15. Kuhlthau, C.: Inside the search process: information seeking from the user's perspective. J. Am. Soc. Inform. Sci. 42(5), 361–371 (1991). https://doi.org/10.1002/(SICI)1097-4571(199106)42:5<361::AID-ASI6>3.0.CO;2-#

16. Laplace, P.S.: Théorie Analytique des Probabilités. Courcier, Paris (1820)

17. Lewis, J.R., Sauro, J.: When 100% really isn't 100%: improving the accuracy of small-sample estimates of completion rates. J. Usab. Stud. 1(3), 136–150 (2006)

18. Liu, J., Kim, C.: Information seeking tasks: why do searchers feel them difficult? In: Proceedings of HCIR 2012, Cambridge MA, 4–5 October 2012. doi:10.1002/meet.14505001125

19. Lopatovska, I.: Toward a model of emotions and mood in the online information search process. J. Am. Soc. Inf. Sci. Technol. 65(9), 1775–1793 (2014). doi:10.1002/asi.23078

20. Lopatovska, I., Arapakis, I.: Theories, methods and current research on emotions in library and information science, information retrieval and human-computer interaction. Inf. Process. Manag. 47(4), 575–592 (2011). doi:10.1016/j.ipm.2010.09.001

21. Lopatovska, I., Mokros, H.: Willingness to pay and experienced utility as measures of affective value of information objects: users' accounts. Inf. Process. Manag. 44(1), 92–104 (2008). doi:10.1016/j.ipm.2007.01.020

22. Mehrabian, A.: Pleasure-arousal-dominance: a general framework for describing and measuring individual differences in temperament. Curr. Psychol. 14(4), 261–292 (1996). doi:10.1007/BF02686918

23. Mooney, C., Scully, M., Jones, G.J.F., Smeaton, A.F.: Investigating biometric response for information retrieval applications. In: Lalmas, M., MacFarlane, A., Rüger, S., Tombros, A., Tsikrika, T., Yavlinsky, A. (eds.) ECIR 2006. LNCS, vol. 3936, pp. 570–574. Springer, Heidelberg (2006). doi:10.1007/11735106_67

24. Nahl, D.: Learning the internet and the structure of information behavior. J. Am. Soc. Inform. Sci. 49(11), 1017–1023 (1998). doi:10.1002/(SICI)1097-4571(1998)49:11<1017::AID-ASI8>3.0.CO;2-Z

25. Nahl, D., Tenopir, C.: Affective and cognitive searching behavior of novice end-users of a full-text database. J. Am. Soc. Inform. Sci. 47(4), 276–286 (1996). doi:10.1002/(SICI)1097-4571(199604)47:4<276::AID-ASI3>3.0.CO;2-U

26. Oxford Advanced American Dictionary for Learners of English. Oxford University Press, New York (2011)

27. Parrott, W.: Emotions in Social Psychology: Essential Readings. Psychology Press, Philadelphia (2001)

28. Plutchik, R.: A general psycho evolutionary theory of emotion. In: Plutchik, R., Kellerman, H. (eds.) Theories of Emotion, vol. 1, pp. 3–33. Academic Press, New York (1980)
29. Ramdeen, S., Hemminger, B.: A tale of two interfaces: how facets affect the library catalog search. J. Am. Soc. Inf. Sci. Technol. **63**(4), 702–715 (2012). doi:10.1002/asi.21689
30. House, R.: Random House Webster's College Dictionary. Random House Reference, New York (2005)
31. Russell, J.: Is there universal recognition of emotion from facial expression? A review of the cross-cultural studies. Psychol. Bull. **115**(1), 102–141 (1994). doi:10.1037/0033-2909.115.1.102
32. Savolainen, R.: Information seeking and searching strategies as plans and patterns of action: a conceptual analysis. J. Doc. **72**(6), 1154–1180 (2016). doi:10.1108/JD-03-2016-0033
33. Scherer, K.: What are emotions? And how can they be measured? Soc. Sci. Inform. **44**(4), 693–727 (2005). doi:10.1177/0539018405058216
34. Shiota, M., Kalat, J.: Emotion. Wadsworth Cengage Learning, Belmont (2012)
35. Smith, A.: Internet search tactics. Online Inform. Rev. **36**(1), 7–20 (2012). doi:10.1108/14684521211219481
36. Wang, P., Hawk, W., Tenopir, C.: Users' interaction with world wide web resources: an exploratory study using a holistic approach. Inf. Process. Manag. **36**(2), 229–251 (2000). doi:10.1016/S0306-4573(99)00059-X
37. Watson, D., Clark, L.: The PANAS-X: manual for the positive and negative affect schedule-expanded form (1994). http://ir.uiowa.edu/psychology_pubs/11/
38. Wilson, T.: Models in information behaviour research. J. Doc. **55**(3), 249–270 (1999). doi:10.1108/EUM0000000007145

Exploring Personal Music Collection Behavior

Sally Jo Cunningham[1](✉) [iD], David Bainbridge[1] [iD],
and Annette Bainbridge[2]

[1] Waikato University, Hamilton, New Zealand
{sallyjo,davidb}@waikato.ac.nz
[2] Independent Scholar, Hamilton, New Zealand

Abstract. In this paper we describe the results of an ethnographic exploration of personal music collection behavior, focusing on music media and formats, collection organization schemes, and approaches to music acquisition and use. The question of when a song becomes 'mine'—that is, part of a personal collection—is surprisingly difficult to answer given the advent of music streaming services, the adoption of distributed collection schemes, and the ephemeral nature of other common music sources.

Keywords: Music behavior · Ethnography · Collection organization

1 Introduction

In this paper we explore how users develop, organize and access their personal music collections. We do so through an ethnographic study. More specifically, we present here our findings from collating and analyzing over 150 pages of auto-ethnographies, resulting from a user study with 28 participants designed to solicit information on their personal use of music. A key theme that emerged from this process was a user's notion of ownership of music, which we frame in the paper as 'what makes a song mine?' This in turn builds on the forms of storage and modes of access to music a user engages with—additional aspects that rose to prominence through the analysis of the study. We detail these aspects in the paper and discuss their implications.

In Sect. 2 we review related work, before describing our methodology (Sect. 3) which includes details about how the data was collected, and a summary of the demographics of the users that participated in the study. Section 4 presents the results of our analysis, which is broken down into four parts: collection storage; collection organization; patterns of sharing (or not); and ownership. We conclude with a summary of our findings and a discussion on practical ways this can be utilized by users.

2 Related Work

Reviews of the Music Information Retrieval literature have noted that there are relatively few empirical studies of human music behavior, and that the existing studies are mainly usability analysis of research prototypes or lab-based experiments [4, 5, 10, 12]. Studies outside MIR tend to focus on summarizing behavior over large populations

© Springer International Publishing AG 2017
S. Choemprayong et al. (Eds.): ICADL 2017, LNCS 10647, pp. 295–306, 2017.
https://doi.org/10.1007/978-3-319-70232-2_25

rather than examining the variation in individual activities (for example, the economic effects of music piracy [7, 13]). The few naturalistic studies of authentic information behavior 'in the wild'—exploring music acquisition and collection organization [2, 3, 5, 9] and use (e.g., playlist and mix construction [1])—have dated. The set of readily available, commercial music services and the potential music activities that they support have changed rapidly over the past few years. This present paper is one attempt to capture the music information behaviors of real users as they navigate this current (as of 2016) music environment.

3   Methodology

This study is based on analysis of a set of 28 auto-ethnographies describing the participant's music collecting behavior. Here we describe the data collection (Sect. 3.1) and its analysis (Sect. 3.2).

3.1   Data Collection

Participants for this study were students enrolled in a third year Human-Computer Interaction course in New Zealand in 2016. The semester-long project for this course was 'to design a systems to help people manage their personal music collections', and to that end the students first documented their own music behavior through self-interviews, self-observations, and a three day diary study.

Prior to conducting this self-investigation, the students were provided with a series of lectures totaling seven hours on ethnography, interview and observation techniques, and ethical considerations. They also participated in three small-group workshops that included exercises focused on interviewing and observations. Students were provided with a set of sample self-interview questions and were encouraged to extend that as necessary to cover their personal music behavior. For the diary study, the students were given a diary template in which to document music collection management activities (e.g., adding to or deleting music from the collection) over three days (not necessarily consecutive). The students then summarized their diary activities in the context of their self-interviews.

The results of their investigations were submitted for assessment as one component of the course project. While completion of the investigation was compulsory for the course, students could opt out of having their work later analyzed for research purposes.

3.2   Data, Participant Demographics, and Analysis

The self-interviews and diary study summaries for 28 students were retained for analysis after the completion of the course. 15 of the participants were male and 13 female; 21 were aged between 20 and 26, while 7 were aged between 28 and 40. All students whose work is included in this study are either citizens or permanent residents of New Zealand. The students are hereafter referred to as P1, P2, ... P28. Their self-described personal interest in music runs across the spectrum: from passionate engagement ("*Unless I'm talking to people, I am nearly always listening to music*" [P10]) to transactional (P29 creates only "*tasked based*" playlists such as his "'*Good Morning' playlist, which contains slightly upbeat and happier music, ... solely designed for use in the morning when I have a shower*") to the nearly a-musical ("*I am just not a musically inclined person*" [P9]).

The self-investigation reports for these 28 participants totalled approximately 154 pages. These were analyzed using grounded theory methods [8]; analysis proceeded through iterative reading, code development, and coding as the categories emerged inductively from the auto-ethnographies.

Qualitative, opportunistic studies cannot elicit a comprehensive, statistically valid model of music behavior. Instead, they are intended to build a 'rich picture' of the music collection activities manifested by these students, from their own perspective [11]. This descriptive, inductive approach highlights the motivations behind the behavior and its affective elements—aspects difficult to uncover with quantitative, large scale study designs.

4 Results

4.1 Collection Storage Devices/Services

It is increasingly difficult to answer the question of where an individual's music collection is stored: the students used strikingly diverse devices, media, applications, and techniques to store and access their music collections (Table 1). Physical storage of digital files is spread across a range of mobile/on-the-go devices (phones, MP3 players, tablet) and larger devices (laptops, desktops, PlayStation). Very large collections may be held on external storage devices (external hard drives, external mobile storage cards) that allow the entire collection be made more portable (for example, to be used in a friend's house); these are used to back up some or all of the collection as well.

Eight of the 28 students still included traditional music media (vinyl albums, cassette tapes, music CDs, sheet music) in their active collection, though these were mainly remnants of pre-MP3 era collections. Vinyl albums were appreciated by two participants for their superior sound quality—though one could not at the time play them ("*I am keeping them in storage and hope to one day purchase a record player that is compatible with my stereo system so that I can play them on special occasions*" [P3]). Cassette tapes and CDs were mainly used when travelling in elderly cars, and as a whole were legacy media. In all cases where the CDs were retained, the songs were copied to actively used devices. Only three participants reported continuing to purchase the occasional CD of a favorite artists or as a gift—primarily because the possession of a tangible artifact was valued in these cases ("*... because it's nice to have something real*" [P15]). These physical media purchases were, however, limited to music that the participants had strong ties to ("*... I have to really love a song/album or artist for me to be willing to purchase it, otherwise I just download it for free ...*" [P20]). Sheet music is the opposite case: it is now primarily purchased online but is printed out for use.

The bulk of each individual's collection was, then, in digital form: stored on the individual's devices (laptop, desktop, mobiles), and/or held online (in personally

Table 1. No. of students utilizing each storage/access device, application, or technique.

Physical devices		Streaming, networked, 'music locker' services, file management		Physical media	
Laptop/desktop	21	Spotify	14	Vinyl albums	2
Mobile phone	19	Pandora	1	Music CDs	1
MP3 player	7	MyMusicCloud	1	Cassette tapes	8
iPad	1	Google Play Music	1	Sheet music	1
External drive	7	Google Drive	2		
External memory	2	iTunes	9	**Other**	
Home network drive	1	Windows Media Player	5	Youtube (subscriptions, favorites)	4
Playstation	1	WinAmp	1	Browser bookmarks	2
		foobar2000	1	Personal memory	2
		Plex	1	Online stores	1

administered storage such as Google Drive or managed through services such as iTunes), and/or streamed. The majority (23 of the 28 participants) had collections distributed over a variety of devices and services. At opposite ends of the spectrum in terms of collection storage, two participants had collections that were entirely streamed (with no personally held files) and three administered their collections only as files under their direct control (stored on personal devices and online storage facilities); the remaining 23 were mixed in their usage of collection storage options.

File management poses problems for a music collection: not only does the user struggle with the usual problem of handling backups (and indeed, two students reported suffering catastrophic collection losses in the past due to hardware failure), but they must also move files between the listening devices. External hard drives or online 'music lockers' (cloud music services such as Google Play Music) can solve both problems (allowing very large collections to be accessed in their entirety), but can be inconvenient (e.g., carrying an external drive with its cable) or expensive (e.g., requiring continuous internet access across all devices). A partial solution is to use local storage in the listening device (laptop, desktop, phone, MP3 player) to store the currently favored songs or to store those songs appropriate for listening in that device/location (e.g., songs for walking to university held on iPod [P1]). But once a set of files is distributed then it is difficult to keep the sub-collections in sync and to maintain collection coherence.

This problem is exacerbated by the use of multiple devices in multiple locations, together with multiple music/file management software: "... *there is not a single service/software that fits my needs, meaning that I have to manage my collection across three or four services, and sometimes separately on each device that I have.*

This causes song overlaps in my music collection, as well as requiring me to add a single song to multiple services if I want to add it to my collection." [P17]

Additionally, students using file management systems are tasked with also maintaining the appropriate metadata for their songs, particularly if the music is downloaded from torrents and other 'dodgy online sources' [P23], gifted from friends, or transferred from elderly physical media. Moving to music management systems tied to online metadata sources (e.g., iTunes) brings access to quality metadata—but only for legally acquired music. At this point owners of a large locally managed music file collection are faced with a decision: abandon their pirated music (as three students did) or maintain separate sub-collections—which, as above, leads to so many difficulties that the legally questionable music gradually becomes less actively listened to.

Perceived advantages to using an online music management system go beyond support for synchronization across devices and protection against loss due to hardware failure. Students who take pride in the completeness or 'quality' of their collections value complete, high quality metadata to document their music—not only at the individual song level but also tying together songs into an album and albums to the artist. Accurate metadata also supports effective search and browsing of a collection—which is a significant consideration when a collection can contain thousands of songs. Album cover art in particular is a surprisingly important metadata element given the decline in possession of physical albums; it makes a collection 'well organized' [P7] and also is useful in searching and browsing (*"It's always nice to have the associated album cover kept with the song to help me recognise it more quickly"* [P22]).

Of the streaming services used by the participants, Spotify dominated, primarily because one of the local telecoms bundled a premium membership with internet service. Streaming services are attractive in that they provide legal access to vast music repositories (Spotify claims more than 30 million songs as of October 2016 [6]); the songs are of high sound quality and accurate metadata is easily accessible; and user-constructed playlists are available across all devices. A streaming service can unobtrusively monitor a user's interactions with music across devices, making it easier to find/re-find specific songs (*"I use Spotify's "Recently played" system often to replay a song I've recently discovered. I like it because it's a nice way to help me find albums, playlists, and artists that I've listened to recently, and I don't have to search using keywords to try find them again."* [P13]). This cross-platform search facility is so effective that it can make the possession (and subsequent management) of music files less attractive: *"Spotify [premium] can access local files and playlists can be created with both local and streamed music. However I usually search and stream music through Spotify even if the music is stored locally. I prefer not to have to remember what music is stored locally and what isn't. I now access the music from my iTunes collection from Spotify through streaming."* [P14].

So why, then, have only 2 of the 15 participants who use streaming services adopted streaming as their sole music platform? Several sticking points can be teased out of the auto-ethnographies: inability or unwillingness to pay for a subscription to the premium service (as the free service does not include crucial benefits such as ad-free service that would make the switch worthwhile); concern over continued access to playlists and favorite songs if the service ceases to exist or if the individual's subscription to the premium service lapses; a reluctance to abandon legacy digital collections that the user has purchased and/or put significant effort into organizing (even when, as in the quote from P14 above, that collection is less frequently accessed); and, surprisingly given the massive size of the streaming service archives, an inability to source all music of interest from a single service.

This last point results from a limitation in the large-scale licensing approach taken by music streaming companies. Students interested in music from *"lesser known groups"* [P13]—for example non-Western music, the work of local or regional artists, or newly released music from non-commercial labels—look to YouTube when streaming services fail them. YouTube also provides a video accompaniment that is sometimes preferred over the static cover art image available from streaming services (*"It's nice to watch the accompanied music video sometimes while listening. ... I like singing along to music I listen to. This is why lyric videos on YouTube are my preference.."* [P21]). This associated video can add to the personal music experience (though the individual does not necessarily always wish to view video when listening to a song; *"However, after viewing this a few times, I tend to just listen to the recording."* [P3]) or can serve to enhance social gatherings (P1 appreciates *"...a nice background video when listening to songs at a party or other setting"*). Participants report incorporating songs and video found on YouTube into their collection directly (by adding the downloaded file to their music management application) or indirectly (via channel subscriptions and favoriting inside YouTube).

4.2 Collection Organization

Physical media (CDs, vinyl, cassettes), if still actively used, were largely stored near their players (e.g., cassettes and CDs in cars, vinyl and CDs near their players in the home)—a practical and long-lived organization scheme [2]. If the CDs and vinyl albums themselves were not played, then their specific physical location was not recorded in the ethnographies (e.g., they were simply 'in the house' [P19]); by contrast, in an earlier study of collection management over primarily physical (CD) collections, participants took pride in the appearance and display of their collections [2].

Digital music that has been downloaded or copied from CDs is largely organized in the first instance (that is, in storage on physical devices and in the initial collection display of onscreen) according to the default schemes for underlying file structure for the music file management applications (e.g., iTunes, Windows Media Player): tracks are grouped into albums (sorted by track number), albums are grouped by artist (often sorted alphabetically by album title), and artists are generally displayed alphabetically. Genre may also be available if the music was sourced legally or if the individual has added this information manually. These basic sorting/filtering/browsing options are sufficient for some participants (e.g., *"Otherwise I don't organize my music but rather rely on something like the windows media player to display the songs in appropriate albums, artists or generics [sic: genre] when looking for songs to try or play."* [P4]).

User-constructed playlists offer the potential to create more sophisticated views of a file-based music collection and are the primary mechanism by which the participants interacted with (and identified) 'their' music in streaming services. The students' playlists included a wide variety of organizing principles: by activity or event that the songs would accompany (e.g., 'gaming playlist', 'party music' [P1]; 'getting ready for the day' [P17]; 'Christmas' [P21]); by genre ('anime, k-pop, etc' [P10]), country of origin ('Original Philippine Music' [P21]) or artist ('Bill Evans' [P24]); by the mood that the songs would reflect or influence ('sleepy music' [P15]; 'low mood playlist' [P1]); by current enjoyment of the individual songs (e.g., P10 maintains a *'favs'* playlist); and general playlists to fill in time (*"I have many playlist [sic] to organize some of the music that I wouldn't mind listening to if I just needed to listen to music in general."* [P26]).

The ordering of songs within a playlist is only significant for playlists organized by artist—in which case there is a preference for ordering the songs by album and then by track within the album. P24, for example, prefers *"to listen to songs as part of a collection of songs intended to be played together such as an album. ... [I prefer]a sense of harmony and unity during a music listening session. [I find] the change in style and tone from one artist to another jarring and distracting."* Otherwise, the participants are generally satisfied with accepting the service's default ordering or by listening to the songs on shuffle. Only P25 reported a personal strategy for playlist ordering, which cleverly took advantage of the system's record of her collection management activities and the shuffle facility:

> Spotify automatically puts the songs into a playlist from oldest to newest so any new songs are put at the end of a playlist, this means that whenever I go to listen to my playlist I always scroll to the bottom to begin playing from there. Although I always begin my playlist with one of the newer songs added I always listen to my music on shuffle... I believe I do this because I genuinely enjoy being surprised by which song is played, the anticipation you get from listening to the radio and not knowing if a recent hit or country throwback is going to be played is replicated by this system of listening to music.

The time needed to curate these specialized playlists can be significant: *"I am currently in the midst of redoing my playlists. This is a process where I will review each playlist, adding and deleting songs as I see fit for my current taste, for example, removing songs that I am growing tired of and adding ones I have recently found. ... I will go through my entire collection for each playlist to ensure my playlists are perfectly up to date. This process generally takes around 2 weeks as going through 6000 songs does take time."* [P1] This level of personal investment appears only with those most passionately engaged with music. The majority of students took a more relaxed attitude towards playlist construction; many playlists relied heavily on some combination of the music metadata to semi-automatically group songs into a playlist (e.g., by artist and genre), the system's tracking of their personal listening habits (e.g., to group recently listened to music), or a brief investment of the individual's time (e.g., P17 would *'sit down in the morning'* to create the day's playlist just prior to leaving her home).

Playlists are also used operationally in collection management. Three participants report maintaining a single large, unordered playlist, additional to their more specialized playlists, which includes the entirety of their Spotify holdings (e.g., *"my general playlist where I mostly save my songs"* [P21]). This served as an inventory of their collection and could, for example, be mined when creating thematic playlists, but this de facto catalog is also playable—a playlist of their full collection (*"...and when I listen to it, I listen to it on shuffle."* [P25]). P7 was concerned with having a well-organized collection, which to him means, *"Every song having an artist and album. All albums should have album artwork."* Ad hoc playlists can assist in identifying songs that do not meet these standards: for example, *"I use iTunes "Smart Playlists" feature to filter songs that are missing artwork for example so I can add artwork to these item..."* [P7]

P6 describes an elaborate, playlist-based screening process for adding songs to his collection on Spotify:

1. I will identify it using the shazam app, which is linked to my Spotify account and will automatically add it to a Spotify playlist. 2. I will then place it in a maybe playlist which contains songs that show potential for my music collection. 3. I will then listen to the maybe songs over a period of a week. 4. If I am no longer happy with the song, I will remove it. 5. If I like the song, but only would like to listen to it occasionally – it goes into my Sometimes playlist. 6. If I am still happy with the song, I will officially add it to my music collection.

This strategy is interesting as it illustrates the porous boundaries of many collections—here a song is only officially 'in' P6's collection after passing through this series of hurdles, yet all the while the song is 'in' P6's Spotify account. We return to this question of when a song is part of a collection—when it is 'mine'—in Sect. 4.3.

Users of Spotify also found value in its automatically generated playlists—particularly Spotify Discover, which once a week presents a user with a customized playlist based on their current collection and listening habits—and in the specially curate playlists prepared by other users, Spotify curators, and artists. A key benefit is that these playlists reduce the effort required identify new artists and genres of interest, making it easier to expand a collection by adopting their contents as a whole or in part: *"They ... are an excellent way to easily find new music, and enjoy all music based on a particular genre. I find it is the best option for expanding my listening tastes, with very little hassle or research. ... Spotify has changed the way I listen to music. When previously I would stick to the music I had always listened to due to the high level of work required to source new music that I like, I now enjoy large varieties of music and get bored quickly of the same music over and over."* [P2].

4.3   Sharing

Spotify has been used by most of the study participants for sharing music as well as creating their own collections. The students appreciated the fact that using Spotify for streaming music meant less time having to deal with other options of more dubious legality [P6] and felt that it took little effort to follow playlists *"that have been made by other people"* [P21]. One student had even created a joint playlist with a family member in which they both had the right to veto songs. This same student was also quite happy to use Spotify's social filter *"which broadcasts to other friends using Spotify what you are listening to"* [P2]. This resulted in a wide circle of friends having access to music options recommended from within their social group.

The other main method of music sharing noted by study participants was through YouTube and music blogs (P15, P13, P12). This can be through methods as simple as sending a popular YouTube music video link to a friend through social media [P12]. For some students, YouTube as a medium was preferred over Spotify because *"Spotify does not offer any way for me to view music videos"* [P13]. YouTube's *"suggested section"* was mentioned as a reliable way of finding *"lesser-known groups"* [P13]. However, for several study participants the sheer volume of devices and apps through which it is possible to share music collections is a hindrance rather than a help, as very few of them are synchronized. One student admitted that they do not share music for one reason only—*"lack of knowledge"* on how to share them. The list of devices used by this participant *"PC in bedroom, Mac Laptop, iPhone"* has meant a continual struggle *"to find the best way to access my collection on all devices"* [P27].

4.4 What Makes a Song 'Mine'?

One of the student participants recalled entering a family discussion based on his diaries which centred around the "drifting away of tangible music artifacts" [P29]. Personal connections with the music were linked by some students in the study with possession of *"physical copies"* [P29], particularly if they had *"the original physical cds stored at home"* [P8]. Several participants noted for instance that it was harder to discard tangible artifacts such as CDs because *"I actually bought them"* [P8], or because *"it is one of my favourite bands and it is important to support the artists"* [P15].

Conversely playlists were seen to have a more ephemeral nature with students regularly *"adding and deleting songs"* as they see fit [P1]. Quite commonly students would regularly review their collections and music would be discarded because they have listened *"to the music until I am sick of it (or bored of it)"* [P15]. Whilst music management systems such as Spotify were seen to introduce students to *"large varieties of music"* they also noticeably encouraged a tendency in users to *"get bored quickly of the same music over and over"* [P2].

Students noted that the accessibility of wide-ranging music and the sheer volume of choice could be overwhelming and also contributed to a lack of personal engagement with their playlists. Participants noted that it was all too easy to accumulate *"music, much of which is never listened to"* [P23] or to add a song to a playlist and then *"not remember adding a song, or even the song itself"* [P24]. One student concluded that Spotify *"does away with a user's emotional attachment to music"* [P1]. It also encourages the continual searching for novelty in music, with another student becoming frustrated that *"I have run out of music to look for...due to there not being songs released as fast as I can listen to or manage"* [P1].

Interestingly, the participants pointed to degrees of 'mineness' for songs. Certainly music on physical media (vinyl, CD, cassette) is owned but it might, or might not be part of an individual's collection, depending on whether the music is playable (that is, whether the individual owns a physical media player or it has been copied to physical/online storage). Participants whose collections were entirely or primarily in the form of music files (stored in physical devices and/or in personal online accounts) felt a sense of ownership of these songs/files (*"Once I have a copy on my hard drive it is defiantly* [sic] *mine"* [P4]). Even in this case, however, the act of adding metadata, organizing the files, or creating custom playlists added to the sense of 'mineness' (in calculating the value of his collection P7 considered both the monetary cost for acquiring the music as well as *"the amount of time I have spent organising and adding things. It would take a long time to recreate"*).

The act of streaming alone was not considered by participants to constitute ownership of a song, nor was moving it to playlist necessarily sufficient (see, for example, P6's tiers of temporary playlists in Sect. 4.2). Downloading a song from a streaming service to access offline (possible only for premium Spotify users) was seen as a solid commitment to the song (P7). A song appearing on auto-generated playlists such as Spotify's "Recently played" was seen as being in "*a bit of a grey area*", as it was "*in a stage where I haven't full [sic] committed to wanting it, but it's nice to have available as a song that grows on me.*" [P13] Continuous access—whether via streaming or offline—is seen as a primary requirement for 'mineness' by some ("*I would consider a song as 'mine' if I am able to repeatedly play it when I want.*" [P17]) and irrelevant by others ("*I classify music as mine if I have it in my collection and listen to it or if there is a song I really enjoy listening to but haven't got around to adding to my collection yet. Or, a song I have really enjoyed in the past and no longer have in my collection but still recognize it as mine or "My jam".*" [P19]).

Small wonder, then, that some participants moved to more personal definitions of 'their' music, based on their personal engagement with a song—where the decision that a song was 'mine' precedes its actual acquisition: "*... it's [mine] when I've heard a song a couple of times or enough times that I consciously think "I like this song/album/playlist and I will want to listen to this again", and only then will I save the music to my Spotify or my hard disk, thereby calling the music 'mine'.*" [P11]

Given the diversity of media, devices, and music services involved in a given collection, as well as these diverse and changing views what constitutes a collection, it is not surprising that the students often struggled to estimate the size of theirs. What in the past was a straightforward question—how many CDs do you have? How many albums?—is now difficult to find a metric for. For file based collections, students could more easily cite the number of gigabytes than the number of songs. For collections based in streaming services, what does one count? Where with albums one could confidently estimate the total number of songs in the collection, a playlist has no lower or upper limit—and songs can (and are frequently) repeated across playlists within a collection. Where physical media collections tended to grow monotonically ("*I don't throw away the physical CDs ... because I am a bit of a collector and because I bought them*" [P8]), digital file collections and playlists are frequently in a state of flux: songs are added and removed, playlists are created and discarded. And, of course, there is often overlap between the holdings across different physical media (five participants stored their collection across more than four devices) and the different collection management services (seven participants used more than one music management application).

5   Discussion and Conclusions

For users making increasing use of music streaming services and cloud storage, our ethnographic study leads us to recommend that (in terms of what is mine) it is a user's *list* of songs that is best to identify with as their own. This is what captures the intellectual thought processes they have gone through in forming their personal music collection (to date)—wherever/however it is stored, and independent of what the rights of the actual artefact (the song) is.

The benefits of this encapsulation of what is 'mine' is that it can be readily represented as a list is a set of controlled metadata fields. One might even classify such a representation of their intellectual activity as being the user's ultimate or 'uber' playlist—and it is extremely useful to treat this as the currency that dealings/manipulation with music content should be expressed in.

From [P24]: "*I use iTunes for music that I want to listen to anywhere, regardless of whether I have an internet connection or not. However, most of the music I have on iTunes is also saved on Spotify*". In this case, while [P24] does not explicitly make reference to our metadata-list representation of 'mine', it is their implicit knowledge of what their uber playlist is which lets them organize things in this way. The writings of [P24] suggest they view iTunes as being synonymous with what their personal music collection is. As a secondary aspect to the given quote, if [P24] was to take their approach just that bit further and have all the iTunes entries saved in Spotify, then they have essentially achieved a form of backup of their collection by working at the metadata level, without taking any steps that could result in failure because they do not have the necessary rights to the actual music file.

Mapping this idea back to users who operate local file system collections. It is really the metadata that is important, and if this (which is really imprinting what is 'mine' about the music they listen to) is what is saved/backed up carefully then it would not take much effort to restore this in the event of: a catastrophic failure; obsolesces creep; no longer playable; etc.

References

1. Cunningham, S.J., Bainbridge, D., Falconer, A.: More of an art than a science, supporting the creation of playlists and mixes. In: ISMIR, pp. 240–245 (2006)
2. Cunningham, S.J., Jones, M., Jones, S.: Organizing digital music for use: an examination of personal music collections. In: ISMIR (2004)
3. Cunningham, S.J., Masoodian, M.: Management and usage of large personal music and photo collections. In: Proceedings of IADIS, pp. 163–168 (2007)
4. Lee, J.H., Cunningham, S.J.: Toward an understanding of the history and impact of user studies in music information retrieval. J. Intell. Inf. Syst. **41**(3), 499–521 (2013)
5. Brinegar, J., Capra, R.: Understanding personal digital music collections. Proc. Am. Soc. Inf. Sci. Technol. **47**(1), 1–2 (2010)
6. CNET. https://www.cnet.com/how-to/best-music-streaming-service/. Accessed 28 Apr 2017
7. Glaser, B., Strauss, A.: The Discovery of Grounded Theory: Strategies for Qualitative Research. Weidenfeld and Nicholson, London (1967)
8. Kibby, M.: Collect yourself: negotiating personal music archives. Inf. Commun. Soc. **12**(3), 428–443 (2009)
9. Mörchen, F., Ultsch, A., Nöcker, M., Stamm, C.: Visual mining in music collections. In: From Data and Information Analysis to Knowledge Engineering, pp. 724–731 (2006)
10. Pampalk, E., Rauber, A., Merkl, D.: Content-based organization and visualization of music archives. In: Proceedings of the Tenth ACM International Conference on Multimedia, pp. 570–579. ACM, New York (2002)

11. Resch, A., Berk, J., Akers, L.: Recognizing and Conducting Opportunistic Experiments in Education: A Guide for Policymakers and Researchers. National Center for Education Evaluation and Regional Assistance, USA, REL 2014-037 (2014)
12. Weigl, D., Catherine, G.: User studies in the music information retrieval literature. In: ISMIR, pp. 335–340 (2011)
13. Rob, R., Waldfogel, J.: Piracy on the high C's: music downloading, sales displacement, and social welfare in a sample of college students. J. Law Econ. **49**(1), 29–62 (2006)

Doctor-Patient Communication of Health Information Found Online: Preliminary Results from South East Asia

Anushia Inthiran[✉]

Department of Accounting and Information Systems, University of Canterbury,
Christchurch, New Zealand
anushia.inthiran@canterbury.ac.nz

Abstract. Citizens in the South East Asia (SEA) region are active on the Internet. Some information on general online health information searching behaviour in the SEA region is known. However, not much is known about the doctor patient communication of health information found online. In this study, 50 participants who have performed an online health search were interviewed. Participants were asked to describe the doctor-patient communication process of having looked up information online. Preliminary results indicate participants who spoke to the doctor about information found online fell into the elementary or guarded category. Participants who did not talk about information found took an unreceptive approach. Results of this study provide theoretical information to advance the field of information science in the SEA region.

Keywords: Communication · Doctor · Online health · Patient · South East Asia

1 Introduction

An activity that is slowly gaining popularity within the SEA region is online health information searching [1–3]. The availability of free and publicly available online resources coupled with fast and affordable Internet access have encouraged citizens in this region use online means to obtain health information. Existing studies conducted in SEA provide information on general online search behaviour of health consumers. For example, results of a study conducted in Singapore indicate Singaporean youths search for information online pertaining to diseases such as diabetes, cancer, information on sexually transmitted diseases, pregnancy, birth control and HIV/AIDS [1]. In an urban city in Malaysia, health searchers dominantly use Google. However, sites like MedlinePlus, Medline, The Mayo Clinic, The National Institute of Health Website (NIH), The Johns Hopkins University Website and WebMD were also utilised [2]. When searching for health information for their child, parents in SEA performed a doctor and non-doctor type visit search [3]. On the other hand, undergraduate students in Thailand use online sources to obtain information on general health, disease, treatment, and nutrition [4].

© Springer International Publishing AG 2017
S. Choemprayong et al. (Eds.): ICADL 2017, LNCS 10647, pp. 307–313, 2017.
https://doi.org/10.1007/978-3-319-70232-2_26

Whilst there is information on the general practices of online health information searching within the SEA region what is unknown is if health searchers communicate or discuss information found online with the doctor. The focus is on online methods of obtaining information as health consumers in SEA indicate that this is the easiest and fastest method to obtain health information [3]. In developed countries, good communication and discussion between doctor and patient led to better overall health outcomes, fewer hospitalizations, lower healthcare expensenses and greater patient satisfaction [5, 6]. Aspects of clinical care in the SEA region is undergoing positive transformation with the likes of shared decision making [7], taking into account patient values and patient centred healthcare practices [8]. Good doctor-patient communication would further enable this transformation. Previous studies conducted in SEA indicate many barriers exist in enabling doctor-patient communication [9–12]. However, what remains unknown is what took place when a conversation was initiated? In this study, the intention is to describe the doctor –patient communication process within the SEA setting. The research questions set out for this study are: (i) how was the conversation initiated? and (ii) how was information exchanged during the conversation? This study is one of the first to provide a description on the doctor-patient communication process in SEA.

2 Related Work

In SEA, there is a large gap in communication between doctor and patient due to patients' unpreparedness for participatory consultation style and adherence to paternalistic communication styles [9]. Patients expect doctors to sort out their concerns, confusion and hesitance within the context of polite communication [9]. On the other hand, doctors predominantly use biomedical utterance and adhere to their own medical agenda. This method of communication conflicted with patients need for the use of social-emotional utterances [10]. In some cases, whilst doctors encouraged communication, patients were reluctant to ask for clarification and prefer that the doctor communicates in a manner that is easily understood by the patient [12].

Strong cultural hierarchy and social norms within SEA such as respect towards people of higher status (doctor) add to the burden of having to communicate. This cultural and social norm include the importance of maintaining harmony and not wanting to disagree with the doctor [12]. Thus, indicating patients would rather take on a passive role when communicating with the doctor. Doctor–patient communication also appears to be affected by other cultural characteristics such as social distance and closeness of relationships [10]. Patients felt that in order to preserve social distance and closeness of relationship, patients need to demonstrate 'respect' to the doctor by minimising conversation or by not appearing to be 'difficult'.

Whilst doctors and patients indicate they would prefer a partnership-oriented style of communication, the one-way communication method is mostly practiced [10]. The two main reasons for this is because of the setup of healthcare systems in SEA and time limitation during patient consultation [10]. Interestingly, results of a study conducted in Malaysia indicate patients were unsatisfied with time spent communicating during the consultation [11]. Thus, whilst patients wanted to communicate, barriers that existed within the communication setting prevented them from doing so.

Low health literacy rates in SEA also limited the possibility of communicating with the doctor [13]. Patients with low health literacy may feel uncomfortable with having a conversation with the doctor. Due to the lack of medical knowledge, patients may take on a passive role by merely agreeing with the doctor.

3 Methodology

A purposeful sampling technique was used. The criteria was that patients must have performed an online health search in the past. Participants were recruited via call for participation notices placed in universities and bulletin boards at community centres. A questionnaire and semi-structured interview was used to collect data. The questionnaire was designed to collect socio-demographic and health search experience details. The interview questions were mostly designed to be open ended and adapted from a previous study [3, 14]. Specifically in this study, participants were asked the following questions: (i) if they had spoken to the doctor about information found, (ii) why did they speak/did not speak to the doctor about information found, (iii) to describe their experience of having to initiate the conversation and (iv) to describe the conversation process. The English language was the medium used to conduct the interview. A pilot test was conducted prior to the main experiment with 5 participants. As a result of the pilot test, the interview questions were fine-tuned.

The interview was audio recorded and transcribed verbatim. This technique was selected to allow close links to be created between the data and the researcher [15]. Open coding was used and coding categories were derived inductively from the audio recording to fit the grounded theory approach [15]. Audio recording was transcribed verbatim. The conventional qualitative content analysis technique [16] was used. A master list of codes was first created based on induction. These codes were revisited after every third participant. These codes were then reduced to themes using the constant comparative method. Responses from participants were first categorised based on if they had spoken to the doctor about information found. Thereafter, responses from each category were coded into themes.

4 Results

We interviewed 50 participants of who are citizens of the SEA region. Participants' average age was 36 years (SD = 4.7). There were 30 female and 20 male participants. Participants education qualification ranged from a diploma (college degree) to a PhD. Occupations ranged from administrators, consultants and business owners. On average participants had a general search experience of 15.9 years (SD = 4.1). Participants average health search experience is 8 years (SD = 2.1). Participants comprised of the following nationalities: Malaysian (40%), Indonesian (24%), Thai (20%) and Cambodian (16%). On average the interview took 10 minutes Table 1 provides details on the doctor patient communication details and communication style.

Table 1. Doctor patient communication detail and communication style

Communicated with the doctor	Percentage (%)	Communication style
Yes	24	Elementary
	20	Guarded
Occasionally	18	External motivator
No	38	Unreceptive

From the 50 participants interviewed, 22 participants spoke to the doctor about information found. The remaining participants either did this occasionally or choose not to speak to the doctor about information found. Responses for participants who spoke to the doctor about information found were divided into two categories. The first category is named elementary conversation and the second is named guarded conversation. In the elementary conversation category, participants indicate minimal communication. A few sentences were exchanged about participants having found information online. In some cases, participants indicate that the doctor advised them to conduct more searches to find out more information. In other cases, the doctor cautioned them about believing everything they read.

- "I told the doctor I found some things such as…the doctor agreed with information I found and encouraged me to continue searching…"
- "I asked the doctor is this true? …then the doctor did the search and asked me, is this what you saw? I said yes…then the doctor said you can find anything on the Internet, some maybe correct some are not so you need to be careful…"
- "I told the doctor that I searched on the Internet before coming to the clinic. The doctor said 'that is a good start'-I then described what I found."

In the guarded category participants were cautions about approaching the subject of having found information online. In this category, conversation about information found went on for longer than just the exchange of several sentences. The aim of the conversation was to seek clarification and obtain opinion. Participants were confident about information they had found and did not cross check information found with the doctor (as demonstrated in the elementary category). Rather, participants wanted to know if the doctor considered other possible alternatives to medication, diagnosis, prognosis and treatment options. Participants also wanted to exert ownership and authority of the health situation. Initiating the conversation and broaching the subject of having searched for health information online took some effort. Participants indicate having to choose words carefully and not wanting to overstep the doctor-patient boundary.

- "If I found something I will talk to the doctor about it. In most cases it is okay. But you must be careful with how you say things… instead of saying I read this and that - I ask, could it be this or that? Will you check for this…and that…?"
- "Sharing information with the doctor? [laughs] I am careful that I choose my words carefully. I don't want to infringe on them or offend them. I say enough for them to know that I have done some homework…so they should know I have done some searching."

A total of 9 participants from 50 occasionally spoke to the doctor about health information found. There were two factors that encouraged discussion. The first was related to the health condition and the second is when the patient in question was a child. When a health condition was perceived by participants to be serious (high blood pressure, diabetics, heart condition, kidney condition) participants were more likely to talk to the doctor about information found online. If the patient in question is a child, then discussion always took place between the parent and the doctor. Thus, participants in this category are named external motivator as they relied on external factors to initiate the conversation.

- "If I think that my condition is serious, I would certainly ask the doctor many things based on what I have found... I do not hold back when asking..."
- "If it is related to my child, then I will surely ask many questions. In fact, I will tell the doctor quite openly that I have been searching on the Internet."

A total of 19 participants from 50 did not talk to the doctor about information found online. These participants took a laid-back approach. Participants felt that it was not their place to do so and preferred not to bring up any information they had found. Participants in this category are named unreceptive.

- "No I don't talk to the doctor about it. I don't want to say too much"
- "There is no need and I am fine if a conversation does not happen"
- "I do not think it makes a difference... so I don't bother"

5 Discussion

There were two ways in which participants who always spoke to the doctor initiated the conversation: elementary and guarded. In the elementary category, the conversation had little depth and the aim was to obtain the doctors confirmation about information read. Participants appear quite comfortable in initiating the conversation and there were no reservations. It is noted that the doctor had encouraged participants to search and yet cautioned them about believing information on the Internet. This behaviour is to be lauded as it empowers patients, keeps communication lines open and creates awareness on the authenticity of health information online. In the guarded category, participants indicate cautiously informing the doctor about information found and in some cases implied implicitly that a search had been conducted. The conversation had more depth and participants took ownership in considering alternatives. In this category, elements of patient centred healthcare and shared decision making were exhibited [9]. Participants in the guarded category could possibly be health literate and therefore were keen to know more of the doctors thought and decision making process. However, it is noted that participants ensured communication took place in a respectful manner, hence observing matters pertaining to cultural norms and hierarchy [9, 10].

Participants in the external motivator category added new information to the domain knowledge. Results of previous studies indicate communication style [10, 11, 13], cultural and social norms [11, 13], communication setting [11, 12] and health literacy levels [13] hindered doctor patient communication. Results of this study indicate seriousness of illness and patient category (child) were motivators in initiating a conversation with the doctor. Conversation took place openly without any reservation for communication style [10, 11, 13] or adherence to cultural and social norms [11, 13]. It is postulated that perhaps the seriousness of the illness and the patient in question superseded any inhibitions. Participants who did not speak to the doctor about health information were unreceptive. There could be several possible reasons for this. Participants may feel that the doctor knows best and therefore choose not to have a conversation. In the same vein, participants may feel that the doctor is not interested to hear from them. This aspect requires further investigation.

Practical contributions include the need for patient and doctor training and education programmes to encourage and foster continued communication and discourse. For example, doctors need to be taught on the need to communicate with patients to understand their health beliefs, as well as the need to encourage patients to communicate. It is pertinent that doctors take on a collaborative role rather than a consultative role during the communication process. Such an initiative was heralded in Indonesia successfully [17]. Community awareness campaigns should advise patients on acceptable methods in which communication should take place as well as the benefits of having a discussion with the doctor. Online health portals could provide suggested questions that patients should talk to the doctor about. This will help patients initiate a conversation confidently. In future work, phase two of the experiment will be conducted with a larger group of participants. It is also the intention to conduct a similar study from the perspective of the doctor. For example, do doctors encourage communication? It is acknowledged that results of this study are preliminary however it does provide rich information on doctor-patient communication initiation and details of the conversation from the viewpoint of the patient.

Acknowledgement. The author thanks participants of this study.

References

1. Rao, P., Theng, Y.L.: Assessing young adults' web searching for health information: an exploratory study in Singapore, Medicine 2.0. In: World Congress on Social Media, Mobile Apps, Internet, Web 2.0 (2014). http://www.medicine20congress.com/ocs/index.php/med/med2012/paper/view/1039?trendmd-shared=0. Accessed 16th Jan 2017
2. Inthiran, A., Alhashmi, S.M., Ahmed, P.K.: Online consumer health: a Malaysian perspective. In: International Federation Information Processing (IFIP) WG9.4 Newsletter (2013) - Information Technology in Developing Countries. http://www.iimahd.ernet.in/egov/ifip/jun2013/inthiran.htm
3. Inthiran, A., Soyiri, I.: Searching for health information online for my child: a perspective from South East Asia. In: International Conference on Asian Digital Libraries, pp. 76–81 (2015)
4. Kitikannakorn, N., Sitthiwioranan, C.: Searching for health information on the Internet by undergraduate students in Phitsanulok, Thailand, vol. 3, pp. 313–318 (2009)
5. Boston Children's Hospital: Communication breakdown: how can we get patients and doctors talking again. http://www.childrenshospital.org/clinician-resources/resources/getting-patients-and-doctors-talking. 15th June 2017

6. Travaline, J.M., Ruchinskas, R., D'Alonzo, G.E.: Patient-Physician communication: why and how. J. Am. Osteopath. Assoc. **105**(1), 13–18 (2005)
7. Ng, C.J., Lee, P.Y., Lee, Y.K., Chew, B.Y., Engkasan, J.P., Irmi, Z.I., Hanafi, N.K., Tong, S.F.:. An overview of patient involvement in healthcare decision-making: a situational analysis of the Malaysian context. BMC Health Serv. Res. (2014). http://www. biomedcentral.com/1472-6963/13/408. Accessed 15 Jan 2017
8. Lee, Y.K., Low, W.Y., Ng, C.J.:.Exploring patient values in medical decision making: a qualitative study. PLoS One (2013). http://www.ncbi.nlm.nih.gov/pubmed/24282518. Accessed 15 Jan 2017
9. Claramita, M., Utarini, A., Soebono, H., Van Dalen, J., Van der Vleuten, C.: Doctor-patient communication in a Southeast Asian setting: the conflict between ideal and reality. Adv. Health Sci. Educ. Theor. Pract. (2011). http://www.ncbi.nlm.nih.gov/pubmed/20658353. Accessed 13 Jan 2017
10. Carteret, M.: Cultural values of asian patients and families, dimensions of culture. Cross Cult. Commun. Health Care Prof. (2013). http://www.dimensionsofculture.com/2010/10/cultural-values-of-asian-patients-and-families/. Accessed 10th Jan 2017
11. Ganasegeran, K., Perianayagam, W., Manaf, R.A., Jadoo, S.A., Al-Dubai, S.A.R.: Patient satisfaction in Malaysia's busiest outpatient medical care. Sci. World J. **2015** (2015). Article ID 714754
12. Claramita, M., Susilo, A.P.: Improving communication skills in the Southeast Asian health care context. Perspect. Med. Educ. **3**(6), 474–479 (2014). doi:10.1007/s40037-014-0121-4
13. Chen, S.F., Tsai, T.S., Wang, M.H.: Health literacy and impact factors of the Southeast Asian immigrant women in Taiwan, Honor Society of Nursing. In: Sigma Theta Tau International 24th International Nursing Research Congress (2013). http://www. nursinglibrary.org/vhl/bitstream/10755/304306/1/Chen_HealthLiteracy.pdf. Accessed 29 Mar 2017
14. Inthiran, A.: Information Search and collaboration activities of health consumers in South East Asia. In: Proceedings of the 2017 Conference on Conference Human Information Interaction and Retrieval, pp. 245–248 (2017)
15. Strauss, A., Corbin, J.: Basics of Qualitative Research: Techniques and Procedures for Developing Grounded Theory, 2nd edn. Sage. Social, Thousand Oaks (1998)
16. Zhang, Y., Wildemuth, B.M.: Qualitative analysis of content. Analysis **1**(2), 1–12 (2005)
17. Claramita, M., Susilo, A.P., Kharismayekti, M., van Vleuten, D.J., Van der, C.: Introducing a partnership doctor-patient communication guide for teachers in the culturally hierarchical context of Indonesia. Educ. Health Change eLearning Pract. **26**(3), 147–155 (2013)

Video Seeking Behavior of Young Adults for Self Directed Learning

Cliff Loke(✉) ⓘ, Schubert Foo, and Shaheen Majid

Wee Kim Wee School of Communication and Information,
Nanyang Technological University, Singapore, Singapore
cloke002@e.ntu.edu.sg, {sfoo,asmajid}@ntu.edu.sg

Abstract. The proliferation of Internet has made information more accessible to many people, including self-directed learners to support their learning needs. With technology and the Internet's omnipresent, students today have grown up and immersed themselves in technologies for leisure and learning. These younger information seekers appear to be comfortable with finding information on the Internet. Videos have been used in numerous environment to support learning. Public online video repositories such as YouTube, Vimeo, and others serve as good resources for self-directed learning (SDL). This paper describes part of the research done on video seeking behavior of post-secondary students when performing an exploratory search to identify suitable videos for their learning. In video seeking, the participants in the study exhibited at least two levels of assessment to determine the video(s) that satisfy the search task. Both levels of assessment suggest that the video seekers looked for cues and video metadata that can acquaint them the video's content with minimal effort.

Keywords: Information seeking behavior · Self-directed learning · Post-secondary students · Young adults

1 Introduction

An information gap exists in every individual and information seeking to fill such gaps is an essential human information behavior. Information retrieval is the process of presenting this knowledge gap or information need [1] to an information system that will match this query against its collection of information, and present the results to the information seeker. Information seeking behavior (ISB) models are often used by researchers to study the dynamics of interaction between humans and systems.

Internet search engines, such as Google, have shaped the way people seek information on the Internet. Such changes and developments have led researchers to revisit information seeking models [2]. Different information seeking models have been used in different contexts to present alternative information seeking perspectives. Students today have grown up and immersed themselves on the Internet. There are no doubts that students have espoused the Internet to seek resources for entertainment as well as learning [3]. The technology integration into classrooms and proliferation of the Internet have brought changes to teaching approaches and practices [4, 5], influencing how learning might take place. Learning approaches such as ambient learning and

S. Choemprayong et al. (Eds.): ICADL 2017, LNCS 10647, pp. 314–324, 2017.
https://doi.org/10.1007/978-3-319-70232-2_27

cyberlearning [6] have been embraced by students. This suggested self-directed learning (SDL) activities adopted by the students. While seemingly technologically savvy, studies revealed that people growing up in the digital age may not have the information literacy to discern the quality of resources they find and used more experimental or trial and error strategies to attain their resources [7, 8]. Coupled with the advent of socially generated resources and the lack of gatekeepers on the quality of information found on the Internet, it is challenging to find quality learning resources effectively.

Post-secondary students in Singapore are represented by adolescents, between 16 to 22 years of age, who are continuing education beyond secondary school. In a report by the Ministry of Education, Singapore [9], a total of 109,439 students enrolled in the year 2015 by vocational institutes (such as Institute of Technical Education (ITE)), art schools (such as Nanyang Academy of Fine Arts), and Polytechnics (such as Singapore Polytechnic). Studies showed that secondary school students in Singapore have poor information literacy skills [10, 11], despite being relatively IT literate. The video presents itself as a resource to support learning for students, especially of vocational nature where there is an emphasis on practical learning. Videos can often satisfy a learner's information needs when textual information sources may not be adequate, such as demonstration of a technique or skill.

Adolescent learners are developing cognitively and often satisfice when finding information. The transit from formal classroom learning to self-directed learning, calls for independence in finding resources to support learning. Although many interface features have been developed to support better searches they are not widely used by these searchers. Many adolescent learners prefer to use convenient and easy to use features, such as the keyword search. This often results in poor search results, especially for complex tasks, such as exploratory search. There is a need to know what are the desired interface features by these adolescent learners and explore how these interface features help them in performing better video searches. An examination of their video seeking behavior can provide insights to how and what interface features they use to locate and select videos.

This paper presents part of the study to explore the desirable video retrieval interfaces and features when young learners find videos to support their learning in vocational learning. This study used the think-aloud protocol to understand how adolescents, in the age range of 18–22, locate and select videos to support their SDL. This can offer interface designers insights in the development of user-centered video retrieval interfaces and services that can better support the video seeking process.

2 Related Literature

Videos can be retrieved through content-based or semantic approach. In content-based approach, videos are retrieved by the matching of sample video clips [12], whereas semantic approach requires a description of the actual meaning of the content [13]. As words predominate human communications, it is natural for humans to put forth a query using the textual format, favoring the semantic approach [14]. However, videos are multi-dimensional and complex as it integrates moving images, text, and audio. Video content is also time-based and sequential, with each video frame comprising of pixels. These make the indexing of video semantics challenging. Metadata can express the semantic information of videos. Being multidimensional, richer forms of metadata are extracted from a video as compared to textual resources. This can afford a wide array of search features, suggesting that video searching can be rendered differently as compared to textual resources.

In establishing an interface design framework for a digital video library, Lee and Smeaton [15] analyzed several abstract information seeking behavior models. A user-centric approach was used to identify salient interface features and functionalities. The consideration of user interactions and search strategies is pertinent in defining such interface frameworks. Five stages of video seeking identified are *browsing/selecting video, querying within the video, browsing within the video, playing the video, and re-querying*. The framework proposed a mixed approach in supporting the different stages. Combining content-based (visual searching) and semantic (keyword searching) approaches [14], an interaction framework was presented to guide the development of video retrieval systems. The researchers posit that semantic approach produces the best results for querying while content-based information is suitable for browsing and selection. Hence, a combination of both approaches is required for the different stages in video searching. By understanding the video seeking behavior in a situated context, effective video interfaces are developed that best fits the seeking behavior.

In SDL, the process of finding and evaluating resources is integral as learners have autonomy over their learning [16]. Finding resources to aid their learning can involve two types of search tasks, lookup fact finding and exploratory search [17]. People can change their searching behavior as search tasks become more complex [18]. This is due to the increasing level of uncertainty [19]. The challenge to find the right resource for learning is compounded by topics that are new as the search task becomes complex. As a search task becomes more complex, finding appropriate resources can become more cognitively loaded. Research has shown that many learners faced difficulties in finding the appropriate resources when learning autonomously [20]. Hence, in the search for unstructured data on the Internet, exploratory searches present challenges for the self-directed learners. As self-directed learning requires quality information, the learners need to be able to search for information effectively and the younger self-directed learners may find such exploratory video searches even more challenging.

Following the premise that by understanding the video seeking behavior of post-secondary students, desirable and effective video retrieval interfaces can be developed to make video search for SDL more efficacious. The richness of the video retrieval interface features influences the amount of interaction with the retrieval system as well as having implications on the decision-making process [21]. In turn, this affects how interface designers develop effective interfaces. This paper describes part of a doctoral study that explores the video seeking behavior of post-secondary students.

3   Methodology

This study adopted an inductive research approach to explore the video seeking behavior and to uncover salient interface features and services used by young learners during video seeking for learning and to identify search techniques and strategies used.

The participants performed two exploratory search tasks. A combination of think aloud technique with video capture of the screen actions and interviews were used to collect data, providing data collection and data sources triangulation. A pilot run was conducted to validate the procedure the questions used in the interview sessions.

3.1 Participants

A total of 14 post-secondary school students (male: M1 to M10, female: F1 to F4) were recruited to perform two exploratory tasks each for the study. These students have completed their secondary school education and are currently enrolled post-secondary institutions such as polytechnics or ITE. The participants were recruited through advertisements placed in their institutions, word-of-mouth and lightning talks to students when given access to the lectures.

The participants are enrolled in a variety of courses, ranging from a foundational program that introduces various diploma pathways to specialized vocational certificates such as Aerospace Engineering and Chemical Process Engineering. These different courses that the participants are enrolled in provided more insights to the video seeking behavior as compared to having participants from a single institution and from only one type of course. The inclusion criteria of having experience in video searching in public video repositories were indicated in the advertisement as well as in the lightning talks conducted. This purposeful inclusion was to ensure that the participants would have sufficient experience that will exhibit their video seeking behavior when applied to their learning needs. Participation in the study was voluntary and the data were kept confidential. Upon completion of the search tasks and interviews, the participants were each given SGD10 as incentive for their participation.

3.2 Search Tasks

To ensure that the search tasks are realistic and relevant, as well as to provide motivation in conducting the search, the search tasks are topics that are related to the participant's course of study. The search tasks were designed in consultation with the lecturers teaching the students, ensuring that the tasks meet its aim to be relevant and realistic. Two search tasks were developed and each participant performed the tasks within a single session.

The first search task was related to the topics that will be taught in the near future. The search tasks would be within the domain of the course that the participants enrolled in but would be exploratory in nature as the topics are yet to be taught in their courses. As the participant did not have sufficient knowledge of the problem domain, these tasks were considered to be open-ended and investigative, involve uncertainty, and invoke learning [22]. An example of such task would be asking the participant to find a video that explains how microbes can cause diseases.

The second search task required the participant to extend what they have learnt to propose a project. In this task, learning and investigation were essential as the participant needed to organize and synthesize what they have learned in order to propose a project [23]. There were also no clear indications for when the search task for such information was completed. This search task elicited uncertainty and would require several search iterations for decision-making. An example of this task would be asking the participant to scope a capstone project related to optical lens and eye diseases. The participants were free to perform their video search using any public video repositories that they wanted and have encountered. This resulted in 28 search sessions from 14 participants.

3.3   Study Procedure

The researcher's laptop has been set up to video-capture the participant's video seeking process as well as installed with popular Internet browsers such as Internet Explorer, Google Chrome, and Mozilla Firefox. This allowed the participants to have their preferred choice of browsers for the search session. The researcher's mobile phone tethered the Internet access, giving a consistent Internet bandwidth for all the video seeking sessions.

The participants began the session by watching a 1-minute video demonstrating how a think-aloud session is conducted, allowing them to be acquainted with the protocol. The participants then proceeded with the first search task, verbalizing their actions, thoughts, and rationale for decision-making. Upon completion of the first search task, short interview segment clarified the doubts that had arisen from the search session. The participants continued with the second search task and ended the session with a post-task interview. The interview solicited feedback on the search session and sought the interface features that the participant would like to have. Hence, a combination of video capture of the screen activity, voice recording of the participant's verbalization and interviews served as the data collection methods and data sources. Each typical data collection session for one participant lasted approximately 30 min to 45 min.

A notable challenge faced by the participants of the think-aloud technique is the moments of silence while they continue to perform the actions or tasks [24]. To mitigate this, place cards were created to remind participants to verbalize what they were looking at, what they were thinking (reasons for decision made), what were their feelings, and the action performed. Despite such prompts, not all of the participants were able to articulate their thoughts while being entrenched into the video seeking process. For such instances, the researcher interrupted the search process and remind the participants in verbalizing their thoughts, actions, and feelings.

3.4   Data Analysis

To analyze the data collected, a two-cycle coding approach [25] was adopted in this study. A code is a short phrase or single word that captures the significant meaning in the data collected. Through the coding cycles, thematic categories emerged to provide insights to the research questions. Prior to coding, the researcher performed transcription. Seven principles for transcriptions [26] were used to guide the transcription for quality and reliability. The audio recordings comprised of verbal accounts generated from the think-aloud protocol as the participant performed the search tasks, and interview responses that occurred during the study session. Screen actions of the participants captured by the screen video software were embedded as part of the transcription and kept within parenthesis. The inclusion of actions into the transcripts was to provide a complete account of the video seeking behavior as well as to confirm the verbal accounts. An example of the inclusion of screen actions in the transcription is as follows:

"This video is too static. (Mouse over the progress bar of the video and view the thumbnails along the way. Stopped when participant spotted something that he is familiar with). At least they put more images rather than text." M2. Having the screen actions embedded in the transcripts allowed verification of verbalisations and offered additional point of analysis. Through the transcription process, the researcher started familiarizing with the data.

A codebook was developed inductively through repeated examination of the data. The codebook structure contained the code label, a brief description, a full description that explained the inclusion and exclusion criteria, and an example. The codebook provided consistency in operationalization of the codes.

The first cycle of coding used structural and emotion coding [25]. Structural coding provides a basic and focused filter of the raw data while emotion coding allows subjective video seeking experience of the participants to be explicitly identified. The transcriptions were examined in a sentence-by-sentence manner and labelled with a conceptual phrase that represents the sentence. This revealed the various interactions with the retrieval system as well as the salient interface features that the participants like, desire, or frustrate them. The first cycle coding produced 26 codes related to the video seeking behavior and the retrieval interfaces used by the young adolescent learners when performing exploratory search for learning videos. The second cycle of coding used thematic analysis. The thematic analysis identified themes that emerged from the data, capturing patterns in relation to the phenomena of interest. Initial thematic analysis revealed 10 candidate themes. The final thematic analysis produced five main themes that relate to the video seeking behavior of the participants and interface features. Candidate themes emerged from the initial examination of the first cycle codes and the final themes were produced through iterations of code examination. An independent coder was recruited and trained using the codebook to perform coding with two randomly selected transcripts. The Cohen's *kappa* score of 0.82 was reported.

4   Findings and Discussions

The complexity of a video and the advancement of retrieval technology have changed how people search for videos for different purposes. The participants turned to You-Tube as the de facto video repository. The data analysis yielded five themes related to video seeking behavior of the post-secondary students in a learning context. The five themes relating to video seeking behavior are: (1) the selection of video resources; (2) query formulation/reformulation; (3) selecting the video(s) for preview; (4) previewing the video, and (5) decision for search task. The last two themes are discussed in this paper.

In video seeking, the participants exhibited at least two levels of assessment to determine the video(s) that satisfy the search task. The first level of assessment was performed on the result list after the search query. This assessment shortlisted the video

(s) for preview. The cues were processed heuristically in this level of assessment. As the result list from the query could contain a large number of videos, it is possible that heuristic-based assessment can allow the shortlisting of video with minimal effort.

4.1 Previewing the Video

The participants previewed the video(s) to make an assessment on the video. The design of Internet browsers led many participants to open several browser tabs concurrently for each video that was selected for preview. As commented by participant M3, '*So I will select this video for viewing later by opening the link on a new tab. I will pause it as I want to continue to watch the original video. This way, I will remember that I have something more to cover.*' Switching between the results list and videos to be preview allowed the participants to keep track on which video(s) have been previewed. This revealed a need for a feature to keep track of the videos that have been previewed.

The video search in public video repository resulted in a large number of video resources. After the preliminary selection of the videos, the participants performed a preview of the video in order to make an evaluation of the video's suitability. As it is common for the duration of instructional learning videos to be long, the learners would turn to interface features that can help them learn about the content of the video in a quick manner.

Video skimming is one of the most common techniques used by the participants to preview the video. Video skimming was performed in several ways. Participants M2, M3, M6 and F1 used the thumbnails that appeared on the position of the mouse as it moves along the progress bar of the video to locate various segments within the video. Other participants clicked on the progress bar of the video or used the arrow keys to navigate around the video content. The purpose of video skimming is to reinforce the content of the video in a quick manner so that the video seeker can ascertain that the video is useful. This behavior might have happened due to the large number of video resources that were under consideration and the effort used to find resources to support their learning could be minimized. This manner in seeking relevance was supported in previous studies with young children where they perform a quick evaluation of the online content to determine if the resource is worthy of review [27]. As noted by the participants:

'*I will skim through the first 5 min, usually. To see if it looks correct. Or if it completely doesn't make sense to me, I might be on the wrong track.*' (M1)

'*I will fast forward a bit while looking at the thumbnail on the progress bar. (mouse over the progress bar). This allows me to give an idea what the video is about.*' (M2)

'*I feel as if browsing the video to get a sense of the video. And I do not think that I will be using this video as the way they presented this is like unusual to me. I am not used to this kind of style of presentation. Looking through just some of the content of this video, I feel that it is not going to be relevant to me.*' (M4)

Participants formed an impression on what the video may offer in the preview stage. Previewing also allowed the participants to affirm their initial assumptions formed on the video. Participant M3 and M4 performed video skimming through the content to find scenes that match what they had anticipated from prior assessment during the selection for preview. The video seekers used various techniques to skim the content and match it to the requirements that they have set implicitly. Automatic video-skim techniques that can communicate the essential content of the video with less time [28] could improve the understanding of the video's content.

The video content can be also be summarized by using video metadata such as descriptions. The implicit concern over 'click-baits' could undermine the confidence in video seeker's when referring to author-input metadata. The use of socially generated metadata could potentially be more neutral. However, participants appeared wanting to examine the content of the video rather than stopping their evaluation of the video on metadata. More interactive video exploration techniques like elastic skimming [29] may help these video seekers form a better impression on the video. Sometimes, the video seeking process may be deemed as completed when the video previewed strongly matches what the video seeker is expecting. In some other cases, the video seeker may seek more cues to affirm their selection.

4.2   Decision for Search Task

After the preview of the video(s), the video seeker will make a decision for the search task, whether to deem the search as completed or have a need to perform subsequent search iterations. When the video seeker had an inclination towards a particular video that was previewed, socially generated cues, such as the comments of the video, were explored to draw a conclusion on the quality and suitability of the video and affirms the selection. As mentioned by one of the participants, M4, '*I am looking at the comments for anything interesting and has the keywords from my search. ... The reason for doing this was to reinforce my judgment that this video would actually be useful to what I am doing.*' These socially generated cues are like collective opinions that can be seen as giving more neutral stand on the quality of the video.

Socially generated comments can potentially point out the strengths and flaws of the video. Hence, comments can have a strong influence in the final decision whether to accept or discard the video. This could be useful when seeking opinions on more subjective topics. However, socially generated cues are often not moderated and this could lead to a reduction of the quality of these cues. The user comments may contain information that is deemed as not constructive.

The examination of socially generated cues in consumer research show that it can influence decision making [30]. Several factors, such as number of comments and length of comments can affect the readability of these cues. The right balance of the number of comments for the video is important when using these socially generated comments. When the comments are too few to form any substantial opinion, the comments are usually not worthy of consideration as commented by participant M6, '*I look at the comments sometimes as it might point out some flaws or relevance. But this is not a very popular video so I don't really get a lot from this*'. However, when the comments are overwhelming in numbers, the video seekers may find it too time-consuming to read all the comments. This suggests a possibility of a word cloud or other suitable form of feature to summarize the salient comments on the video when the number of comments exceeds a threshold. This could reduce the cognitive load on the video seeker when such opinions are summarized using visual representations. For less popular videos, the number of comments might not be sufficient to give an indication on the quality of the video.

When the video resource is deemed to be positive, video seekers might be encouraged to leverage on that video resource to seek out other similar resources. The "Up-Next' feature found on YouTube is a common feature leveraged on by the video seekers when they wanted to continue the search for more related videos. As noted by participant, M1, '*So because I can't find any other videos from the search list, what I intend to do is to look at the right side of the video, where related videos are recommended.*' Video seekers use features that are conveniently located and easy to use. Features such as the "Up-Next" listing offers both ease of use and convenience. However, the labeling of the feature should be self-explanatory to avoid ambiguity and lead to false assumptions by video seekers.

5 Conclusions

Exploratory search tasks that often occur during SDL present fuzziness and ambiguity in the search process as the self-directed learners venture into a learning domain that is new and not fully conversant with them. Searching for information on the Internet to support learning is common. Videos are fundamentally used as support for learning, hence effort and cognitive load should be minimal in video seeking. In video seeking, the study revealed that two levels of assessment took place to determine the video(s) that satisfy the exploratory search task. The first assessment was performed using heuristic cues on the video results list to shortlist video(s) for preview. The next assessment was performed after the preview of the shortlisted video(s) to decide whether to accept the video or to continue searching or browsing for more videos. Both levels of assessment suggest that the video seekers looked for cues and video metadata that can acquaint them with the video's content with as little effort as possible. Techniques such as elastic skimming [29] may help in reducing the effort in previewing the video.

Video resources can offer more metadata so that the content of the video can be searched more explicitly. Socially generated cues are known to influence decision making, especially in more subjective context. This pooling of socially generated information has been consulted heuristically to make quick evaluation of resources online [31]. Such metadata can be developed into useful decision-making and evaluation features. More investigations are needed to understand the type of heuristic metadata, such as date of upload and socially generated cues, such as comments, and how they can be presented, help perform the shortlist and affirm the video selection better.

As part of future studies, the list of desirable video retrieval interface and features will be identified and used as a basis to build a mock-up that would be used to validate the interface and features. The number of self-directed learners using public video repositories to support their learning is increasing. Young self-directed learners, such as post-secondary students, will find video retrieval more effective with the implementation of these interface features. These interface features support interactions in video seeking behavior of these learners, and are desirable for them. This can ease the cognitive load while performing video seeking activities that support SDL.

References

1. Belkin, N.J., Oddy, R.N., Brooks, H.M.: ASK for information retrieval: part I. background and theory. J. Doc. **38**(2), 61–71 (1982). doi:10.1108/eb026722
2. Meho, L.I., Tibbo, H.R.: Modeling the information-seeking behavior of social scientists: Ellis's study revisited. J. Am. Soc. Inf. Sci. Technol. **54**(6), 570–587 (2003). doi:10.1002/asi.10244
3. Goerke, V., Oliver, B.: Australian undergraduates' use and ownership of emerging technologies: Implications and opportunities for creating engaging learning experiences for the net generation. Australas. J. Educ. Technol. **23**(2), 171–186 (2007). doi:10.14742/ajet.1263
4. Hicks, S.D.: Technology in today's classroom: are you a tech-savvy teacher? Clearing House J. Educ. Strat. Issues Ideas **84**(5), 188–191 (2011). doi:10.1080/00098655.2011.557406
5. Inan, F.A., Lowther, D.L.: Factors affecting technology integration in K-12 classrooms: a path model. Educ. Technol. Res. Dev. **58**(2), 137–154 (2010). doi:10.1007/s11423-009-9132-y
6. Arnone, M.P., Small, R.V., Chauncey, S.A., Mckenna, H.P.: Curiosity, interest and engagement in technology-pervasive learning environments: a new research agenda. Educ. Technol. Res. Dev. **59**(2), 181–198 (2011). doi:10.1007/s11423-011-9190-9
7. Geck, C.: The generation Z connection: teaching information literacy to the newest net generation. Teach. Libr. **33**(3), 19–23 (2006)
8. Ng, W.: Can we teach digital natives digital literacy? Comput. Educ. **59**(3), 1065–1078 (2012). doi:10.1016/j.compedu.2012.04.016
9. Education Statistics Digest. M.O. Education, Editor, Singapore (2016)
10. Foo, S., Majid, S., Mokhtar, A., Zhang, X., Chang, Y.K., Luyt, B., Theng, Y.L.: Information literacy skills of secondary school students in Singapore. Aslib J. Inf. Manag. **66**(1), 54–76 (2014). doi:10.1108/AJIM-08-2012-0066
11. Chang, Y.K., Zhang, X., Mokhtar, A., Foo, S., Majid, S., Luyt, B., Theng, Y.L.: Assessing students' information literacy skills in two secondary schools in Singapore. J. Inf. Lit. **6**(2), 19–34 (2012). doi:10.11645/6.2.1694
12. Little, J.J., Gu, Z.: Video retrieval by spatial and temporal structure of trajectories. In: Minerva, M.Y., Chung-Sheng, L., Rainer, W.L. (eds.) Proceedings of SPIE, vol. 4315, pp. 545–552
13. Snoek, C.G., Huurnink, B., Hollink, L., de Rijke, M., Schreiber, G., Worring, M.: Adding semantics to detectors for video retrieval. IEEE Trans. Multimedia **9**(5), 975–986 (2007). doi:10.1109/tmm.2007.900156
14. Amir, A., Srinivasan, S., Efrat, A.: Search the audio, browse the video—a generic paradigm for video collections. J. Adv. Sig. Process. **2**, 209–222 (2003). doi:10.1155/s111086570321012x
15. Lee, H., Smeaton, A.F.: Designing the user interface for the Físchlár digital video library. J. Dig. Inf. **2**(4), 251–262 (2006)
16. Butcher, K.R., Sumner, T.: Self-directed learning and the sensemaking paradox. Hum.-Comput. Interact. **26**(1), 123–159 (2011). doi:10.1080/07370024.2011.556552

17. Marchionini, G.: Exploratory search: from finding to understanding. Commun. ACM **49**(4), 41–46 (2006). doi:10.1145/1121949.1121979

18. Aula, A., Khan, R.M., Guan, Z.: How does search behavior change as search becomes more difficult? In: Proceedings of the 28th International Conference on Human Factors in Computing Systems, pp. 35–44. ACM, New York (2010). doi:10.1145/1753326.1753333

19. White, R.W., Roth, R.A.: Exploratory search: beyond the query-response paradigm. Synth. Lect. Inf. Concepts Retriev. Serv. **1**(1), 1–98 (2009). doi:10.2200/s00174ed1v01y200901icr003

20. Bouchard, P.: Pedagogy without a teacher: what are the limits? Int. J. Self-Directed Learn. **6**(2), 13–22 (2009)

21. Burgoon, J.K., Bonito, J.A., Bengtsson, B., Cederberg, C., Lundeberg, M., Allspach, L.: Interactivity in human–computer interaction: a study of credibility, understanding, and influence. Comput. Hum. Behav. **16**(6), 553–574 (2000). doi:10.1016/s0747-5632(00)00029-7

22. Wildemuth, B.M., Freund, L.: Assigning search tasks designed to elicit exploratory search behaviors. In: Proceedings of the Symposium on Human-Computer Interaction and Information Retrieval - HCIR 2012. ACM: Cambridge (2012). doi:10.1145/2391224.2391228

23. Kules, B., Capra, R.: Creating exploratory tasks for a faceted search interface. In: Second Workshop on Human-Computer Interaction, HCIR 2008 (2008)

24. Sharp, H., Rogers, Y., Preece, J.: Interaction Design: Beyond Human-Computer Interaction. Wiley, New Jersey (2007)

25. Saldaña, J.: The Coding Manual for Qualitative Researchers. Sage Publications, London (2009)

26. Mergenthaler, E., Stinson, C.: Psychotherapy transcription standards. Psychother. Res. **2**(2), 125–142 (1992). doi:10.1080/10503309212331332904

27. Hirsh, S.G.: Children's relevance criteria and information seeking on electronic resources. J. Assoc. Inf. Sci. Technol. **50**(14), 1265–1283 (1999). doi:10.1002/(sici)1097-4571(1999)50:14%3C1265:aid-asi2%3E3.3.co;2-5

28. Christel, M.G., Smith, M.A., Taylor, C.R., Winkler, D.B.: Evolving video skims into useful multimedia abstractions. In: Proceedings of the SIGCHI Conference on Human Factors in Computing Systems, pp. 171–178. ACM Press, New York (1998). doi:10.1145/274644.274670

29. Haesen, M., Meskens, J., Luyten, K., Coninx, K., Becker, J.H., Tuytelaars, T., Poulisse, G., Pham, P.T., Moens, M.: Finding a needle in a haystack: an interactive video archive explorer for professional video searchers. Multimedia Tools Appl. **63**(2), 331–356 (2011). doi:10.1007/s11042-011-0809-y

30. de Vries, L., Gensler, S., Leeflang, P.S.: Popularity of brand posts on brand fan pages: an investigation of the effects of social media marketing. J. Interact. Market. **26**(2), 83–91 (2012). doi:10.1016/j.intmar.2012.01.003

31. Metzger, M.J., Flanagin, A.J., Medders, R.B.: Social and heuristic approaches to credibility evaluation online. J. Commun. **60**(3), 413–439 (2010). doi:10.1111/j.1460-2466.2010.01488.x

Author Index

Printed in the United States
By Bookmasters